INTELLECTUAL PHILOSOPHY.

A SYSTEM

OF

INTELLECTUAL PHILOSOPHY.

BY REV. ASA MAHAN,

FIRST PRESIDENT OF CLEVELAND UNIVERSITY

"How charming is divine Philosophy!
Not harsh, and crabbed, as dull fools suppose,
But musical as is Apollo's lute,
And a perpetual feast of nectared sweets,
Where no rude surfeit reigns."

REVISED AND ENLARGED FROM THE SECOND EDITION.

NEW YORK:

A. S. BARNES & CO., 51 JOHN-STREET.

CINCINNATI:—H. W. DERBY.

1854.

WILLIAM H. SHAIN & CO.,
STEREOTYPERS, HUDSON, OHIO.

DEDICATORY PREFACE

TO THE FIRST EDITION.

THE following Treatise presents the sum of a course of Lectures, which, for six or eight years past, I have been in the habit of delivering to successive classes, on the subject of Intellectual Philosophy. One thing I may say in relation to this subject, without boasting. No class have yet passed through this course, without becoming deeply interested in the science of Mental Philosophy; and, in their judgment, receiving great benefit from the truths developed, as well as from the method of development which was adopted. Hence the desire has been very generally expressed by those who have attended the course of instruction, as well as by others who have become acquainted with the general features of the system taught, to have it presented to the public in a form adapted to popular reading. In conformity to such suggestions, as well as the permanent convictions of my own mind, the following Treatise has been prepared. In preparing it, it has been my aim to reject light from no source whatever from which it could be obtained, and at the same time to maintain the real prerogative of manly independence of thought. The individuals to whom I feel most indebted as a philosopher, are Coleridge, Cousin, and Kant — three luminaries of the first order in the sphere of philosophy. How far proper discriminations have been made in the study of their works, the reader will be able to judge. With these remarks, I would simply add, that

To THE BELOVED AND HONORED PUPILS, WHO HAVE HITHERTO PASSED FROM UNDER MY INSTRUCTION AS A TEACHER OF MENTAL SCIENCE, THE FOLLOWING TREATISE IS NOW AFFECTIONATELY DEDICATED, WITH THE EXPRESSION OF THE FOND HOPE, THAT IN ALL FUTURE CLASSES, WHICH IT MAY BE MY PRIVILEGE TO INSTRUCT, I MAY, IN THE LANGUAGE OF ANOTHER, "FIND THE SAME LOVE OF PHILOSOPHY, AND THE SAME INDULGENCE TO THE PROFESSOR."

PREFATORY NOTE

TO THE REVISED EDITION.

Since the publication of the first edition of this work, the author has had the benefit resulting from successive years in teaching the same, and of a careful reading of other works upon the same subject. In this manner, he has been enabled to perceive defects that needed correction in the work, as first presented. The work is now given to the public, as the result of his mature reflections upon this fundamental science. Some of the most important chapters have been so entirely rewritten and remodeled, as to render the present, in some important respects, a new work on Intellectual philosophy. I may notice, among others, the chapter on Sense, the examination of the true as distinguished from false systems of Philosophy, in the chapter on Miscellaneous Topics, and the development of the evidence of the being and perfections of God, in the last chapter. The author has always been fully persuaded of the correctness of his views in respect to external perception, but has felt a growing dissatisfaction with his manner of presenting the subject, in the chapter referred to. In the present edition, this subject, so fundamental to a right system of mental science, is so presented as to meet his ideas in most, if not all respects. One of the great wants of the age is a fundamental examination of false systems of Philosophy, as developed in

Materialism, and in the various forms of Idealism, as distinguished from the true system. This he has attempted, and, as it appears to him, accomplished, in the chapter on Miscellaneous Topics. The improvements made, in presenting the topic last named, will be appreciated, we think, by all who carefully read the chapter in which they appear. It has been the aim of the author to give to the public a work, on this great science, which should meet the fundamental philosophic wants of the age. As such an attempt, he commends his production to the careful study of all who would understand this science.

I close with a suggestion to teachers who may introduce this work to their pupils as a text-book. No system of questions is here proposed. Each topic has a heading, however, which gives the subject-matter therein developed. My own method of teaching has always been, to read to the class this heading, and then require the student to state, in his own words, the subject-matter contained in the topic referred to. Two benefits result to the pupil by this mode of teaching: 1. He is made to *understand* the subject much better than he can by any system of questions. 2. He acquires the important habit of first forming distinct conceptions of a subject before speaking, and then of clothing his thoughts in appropriate language. Much higher and more perfect forms of mental discipline are acquired by this mode of teaching, than by any other which we have ever tried.

Cleveland, Ohio, *August* 1854.

CONTENTS.

CHAPTER V.

CONSCIOUSNESS.

CHAPTER VI.

SENSE.

CHAPTER VII.

SECONDARY FACULTIES.

UNDERSTANDING.

CHAPTER VIII.

FACULTY OF JUDGMENT.

CHAPTER IX.

ASSOCIATION.

CHAPTER X.

MEMORY AND RECOLLECTION.

MISCELLANEOUS TOPICS.

CHAPTER XI.

IMAGINATION.

CHAPTER XII.

REASON.

CHAPTER XIII.

RECAPITULATION, WITH ADDITIONAL SUGGESTIONS.

CHAPTER XIV.

SPONTANEOUS AND REFLECTIVE DEVELOPMENTS OF THE INTELLIGENCE.

CHAPTER XV.

ORIGIN OF IDEAS.

CHAPTER XVI.

LAWS OF INVESTIGATION.

CHAPTER XVII.

REASONING.

CHAPTER XX.

MATTER AND SPIRIT.

CHAPTER XXI.

IMMORTALITY OF THE SOUL.

CHAPTER XXII.

THE IDEA OF GOD.

INTELLECTUAL PHILOSOPHY.

CHAPTER I.

INTRODUCTION.

CLASSIFICATION OF THE SCIENCES.

ALL substances may be classified under two general divisions, Matter and Mind. This arrangement presents a twofold division of the sciences, to wit, Material, and Mental.

OBJECT OF MENTAL PHILOSOPHY.

Mental Philosophy is the science of Mind, and of the human Mind in particular. Its *object* is a correct classification of the phenomena, for the purpose of a full and distinct development of the Powers, Susceptibilities, and Laws of the human Mind. This department of inquiry being completed, Mental Philosophy, as a science, then ascends to an investigation of the wide field of Moral Obligation, for the purpose of developing the *extent, limits,* and *grounds* of human responsibility.

WHAT IS TO BE EXPECTED FROM SUCH INVESTIGATIONS.

The field before us is of almost boundless extent. We are not, therefore, to expect, that any one treatise will present all that may be known of the human Mind. All that I hope to accomplish, is to introduce the inquirer to the science, and give to his inquiries, in respect to it, a right direction. His own investigations will then lead him to exhaustless treasures of wisdom and knowledge.

MENTAL PHILOSOPHY, AS A SCIENCE, POSSIBLE.

Every substance in existence is known, and can be known by us, through and only through its respective phenomena. This, with us, is the changeless condition of knowledge, in respect to all realities which lie around us in the universe. Every power or substance in existence is knowable to us, so far only as we can know its phenomena. The question, then, whether Mental Philosophy is possible to us, depends wholly upon this, whether the Mind, in the action of its varied powers and susceptibilities, is so revealed to itself, that it can know its own operations or phenomena? To this question, but one answer can be given. We are so constituted, that we have a knowledge of whatever passes in the interior of our minds. This power, or law of our Mental Faculties, explain the fact in whatever manner we please, is denominated Consciousness, which is a faithful witness of whatever passes within us. On the authority of Consciousness, all men do and must rely. Here Skepticism itself assumes the garb of positive faith: for in the language of Descartes, "let a man doubt everything else, he cannot doubt that he doubts;" and "he cannot doubt that he doubts" for this reason, that he cannot but rely, in some form or other, upon the testimony of his own Conciousness.

Not only are all things which pass within us given as phenomena of Consciousness, but we have also the power of retaining these phenomena under the eye of the mind, until we have fully resolved them into their original elements, and marked their characteristics. This power or exercise of the mind is denominated reflection, and is conditioned on the Will.

Mental Philosophy then becomes possible for the same reasons, and on the same conditions, that physical science, or Natural Philosophy is possible. Facts equally undeniable, and equally distinct and palpable, are given as the foundation of both sciences. All that is required in either instance, is, that our researches be conducted upon right principles — that we introduce into our investigations nothing but actual facts, — that these facts be correctly arranged and classified, — and that none but legitimate conclusions be drawn from them.

THE METHOD IN CONFORMITY TO WHICH PSYCHOLOGICAL RESEARCHES SHOULD BE CONDUCTED.

Having shown that Mental Philosophy, as a science, is possible, we will now contemplate the question in respect to the *Method* which should be adopted in conducting our investigations. Every philosopher commences his inquiries in conformity to a certain *ideal* of which he has conceived, and which he has assumed, as involving the most perfect method in conformity to which such investigations can be conducted. A remark of Cousin on this point demands special attention. "As is the method of a philosopher, so will be his system; and the adoption of a method, decides the destiny of a philosophy." It becomes us, therefore, at the threshold of our inquiries, to stop, and with great care, determine the Method in conformity to which we are to investigate the powers, susceptibilities, and laws of the mysterious substance before us. The following Principles I would propose as involving and announcing the true Method to be adopted:

1. We should present to our own minds, with great distinctness, the question, what are the *facts* which lie at the basis of all our conclusions in respect to this science; facts

upon which all legitimate conclusions do and must rest? They are, as all must admit, the facts which lie under the eye of Consciousness. But what are these facts? In other words, what are the sole and exclusive objects of Consciousness? Not, surely, as Cousin observes, the "external world, or its Creator — not the substance, nature, essence, or Faculties of the soul itself." They are the soul in its *manifestations* — in the exercise of its various Faculties. Upon these all our conclusions in regard to the nature of these Faculties, as well as upon the nature of the soul itself, and of all other objects are based. As the sole basis of physical science, we have the phenomena of perception. As the basis of Psychology, we have the phenomena of Consciousness, and these only. As we know the mind only through its phenomena, or manifestations, so all legitimate conclusions in respect to it must be revealed and affirmed by these manifestations. Hence I remark,

2. That in pursuing our investigations according to the true Psychological Method, we shall commence with no questions in respect to the *nature* or *essence* of mind, whether it is material or immaterial, or in respect to its various powers, or functions, nor in respect to the *origin* of mental phenomena. All such questions are to be adjourned, until we have *observed, characterized, and classified* the phenomena, or operations, which *now*, in our *present* state of mental development, lie under the eye of Consciousness. The question, in regard to the *origin* of mental phenomena, involves, as its foundation and starting point, a knowledge of such phenomena as they now exist. Otherwise we are inquiring after the *origin* of that of the *nature* of which we are profoundly ignorant. So also, if, before we have attained this knowledge, we study and attempt the resolution of questions pertaining to the *nature* or *essence* of the mind, or in respect to its Faculties, we violate

the fundamental law of all correct philosophizing, to wit: that substances are known and are to be studied only through their phenomena. The true Psychological Method does not neglect any legitimate questions in respect to ontology, or the origin of mental phenomena. It simply adjourns these, till another preliminary department of inquiry has been completed.

In pursuing our inquiries in respect to mental phenomena, and in respect to the characteristics of particular phenomena, two rules of fundamental importance present themselves,—to wit: Suppose or assume, as real, nothing which does not exist — and omit, or disregard, nothing which does exist.

3. The phenomena which lie under the eye of Consciousness clearly indicate a diversity of mental powers, or functions. In conformity to the true Psychological Method, a fundamental aim of the Mental Philosopher will be, to adopt those principles of classification by which these different powers or functions shall be distinctly revealed to the Mind. Two self-evident principles will guide him in determining the different powers or functions of the Mind. 1. Phenomena, in their fundamental characteristics alike, are to be attributed to one and the same Faculty. 2. Phenomena, in their fundamental characteristics unlike, suppose a diversity of powers or functions. Hence the vast importance of classification with exclusive reference to fundamental characteristics.

4. Amid the endlessly diversified phenomena of Consciousness, there are, in the depths of the Mind, particular phenomena, which reveal the *Laws* which govern the action of the different mental powers. One of the principal aims of the Mental Philosopher, in conformity to a correct Psychological Method, will be, to fix upon, and develope those facts, or phenomena, by which the *Laws* of thought, feeling, and action, are revealed. No department of inquiry in the

wide field of Mental Science is of greater importance than this.

5. Having, by careful reflection, and in conformity to correct principles, ascertained, classified, and arranged the phenomena of the Mind, as they now lie under the eye of Consciousness, a correct Psychological Method would then lead us to move the important questions pertaining to the *origin* of these phenomena, to Ontology, and to the nature, extent, limits, and grounds of Moral Obligation. This completes the circle of investigations in the wide domain of Mental Science. Much will be done for Philosophy, if this circle is completed according to the method above developed.

The above the only correct Psychological Method.

A moment's reflection will convince us, that this is the *philosophical*, and I may add, the only philosophical Method. The powers of nature, external and internal, are known to us only in their manifestations, or through their respective phenomena. These manifestations must, of course, be known, or we must remain in total ignorance of the powers themselves.

This is the *universal* Method, the Method which lies at the basis of all real science pertaining to Matter or Mind. In pursuing our investigations in strict conformity to the principles of this Method, we shall be conducted to no conjectural conclusions, but to certain knowledge; provided we have marked with correctness existing phenomena, and have proceeded logically from the facts thus given, to our conclusions. It puts us, to say the least, upon the right road to knowledge. If we "fall out by the way," the fault will be our own, and not that of the Method adopted.

If we arrive at correct conclusions, we shall, also, in the light of the Method pursued, understand and be able to assign the *reasons* for those conclusions, a most important attainment in the progress of mental development. If, on the other hand, we adopt any false conclusions, our Method itself presents the best means for their correction. No individual will long remain in the embrace of any important error, who has adopted a correct method of investigation, and who rigidly adheres to the principles of that method.

Utility of this Science.

But little need be said to impress the inquirer with a conviction of the importance of our present investigations.

Mental Philosophy is the science of self-reflection. It teaches us to know ourselves, in our relations to God, and to the universe around us.

The importance of this science may likewise be seen in the light of its relations to all other departments of human investigation. "Whatever be the object of inquiry," says Cousin, "God or the world, beings the most near or remote, you neither know nor can know them, but upon one condition, namely, that you have the faculty of knowledge in general; and you neither possess nor can attain a knowledge of them except in proportion to your general faculty of knowledge. Whatever you attain a knowledge of, the highest or the lowest thing, your knowledge in the last result rests, both in respect to its extent and its legitimacy, upon the reach and validity of that faculty, by whatever name you call it, Spirit, Reason, Mind, Intelligence, Understanding." One of the first and great inquiries of man, then, is the nature, extent and limits of this faculty. This is Intellectual Philosophy. This is Psychology, a science, which indeed is not the whole of Philosophy, but "must be allowed to be its foundation and starting point."

By developing the laws of human belief, and by habituating

the mind to contemplate and investigate CAUSES through their respective phenomena, this science also furnishes a light, to guide our investigations in every other science, and presents the strongest possible motives to lead us onward.

Nor is its connection with morality and religion less important and influential. Indeed, here lies its chief importance. The development of the laws of evidence, will place in a clear light, the ground of our assent to the Divine authority of Christianity, so far as external evidence is concerned. A development of the powers and susceptibilities of the mind itself, will lead us to a correct understanding of the bearing of the internal evidence of Christianity. A development of the grounds of moral obligation will lead us to perceive distinctly, and to feel deeply, our obligation to obey the moral precepts of Christianity. Every truth, every principle and precept of Christianity, supposes some one or more faculties or susceptibilities of the mind, to which they are addressed. A distinct knowledge of these faculties and susceptibilities, places those truths and principles in the clearest possible light before the mind.

One other consideration will show clearly the important bearing which our present inquiries have upon religion. The study of Mind, according to the Method above announced, implies, as its foundation and starting point, a careful investigation of mental phenomena. Among these phenomena, *ideas* occupy a very important place, and among the most fundamental and important of all our ideas, are the conceptions of the infinite and perfect, that is, of God, of eternity, of immortality, of moral obligation, and of retribution. In developing the characteristics, origin and grounds of these ideas, we are determining our convictions in regard to many of the most important and fundamental truths of religion. We are moulding and forming convictions which will, and must determine the meaning, which we shall attach to the most important portions of the Sacred Volume itself.

If we should appeal to facts, we should find the fullest verification of all that is said above. All the forms of corrupt Christianity which have appeared for the last eighteen centuries, all the false religions which have ever cursed the earth, all the forms of infidelity and skepticism, which the seathings of human depravity have, in any age, thrown upon the surface of society, have had their foundation in systems of false Philosophy. No maxim is more fully verified, by universal observation than this: as is a man's Philosophy, so is his Theology. The changeless laws of our being renders us, in all departments of research and action, philosophic beings. In religion, we can no more be exempt from the influence of Philosophy, than in all other departments of investigation. Suppose we professedly, as some have done, repudiate all Philosophy, and approach the Sacred Volume, to be taught of God, irrespective of any philosophic speculations. What is this but the enunciation of a peculiar system of Philosophy — a system which, after all, will determine, in many essential respects, the meaning which we shall attach to the most important responses of the Sacred Oracles? God hath joined Philosophy and Religion together. We do violence to the nature which he has given us, when we attempt to put them asunder. False Philosophy is the mother of false religions. A correct Philosophy is the handmaid of true Religion.

In short, in every condition and relation of life, next to the wisdom, which, by direct inspiration, "cometh from above," is a correct and comprehensive knowledge of Mental Philosophy, important to man. To the citizen, this science is useful by giving him the reasons of the duties devolved upon him in all the relations of life. To the theologian, it will be of great use, by enabling him not only to understand correctly the truths and principles of Christianity, but also to present them in such a manner that he will "commend himself to every man's conscience in the sight of God." How true also is the sentiment advanced by the great philosopher of England, to wit, that no man is qualified to fill the sphere of an enlightened statesman, who has not thought much and profoundly upon the infinite, the just, the right, the true, and the good.

State of Mind requisite to a successful prosecution of this Science.

It remains to speak upon one topic more, the *spirit* requisite to a successful prosecution of this science.

The first requisite that I mention is this, a deep conviction of the *importance* of the science. We pursue nothing with energy which, to our minds, does not possess an importance demanding the exertion of our entire powers. If I could impress the inquirer with a due conviction of the importance of our present investigations, and could excite in him a purpose of corresponding inflexibility to master the science, I should not have any unpleasant apprehensions in respect to the result.

I mention, in connection with the above, another requisite, to wit, *a love of the science* for its own sake; that is, for what presents itself to the mind, as intrinsic in the science itself, as well as an account of its relative value. That which strongly appeals, not only to our convictions of what is valuable, but to the *sensibilities* of our nature, we readily pursue with the most untiring energy and perseverance. But two things are requisite to excite in any mind this *love* for the science under consideration — a proper conviction of the *importance* of the science, and familiarity with its great truths and principles. We are naturally such philosophic beings, that almost nothing else delights us so much as philosophic truths and principles, when we once become acquainted with them.

Another essential requisite is the habit or spirit of *self-reflection.* All legitimate conclusions pertaining to this science rest upon the facts which lie under the eye of Consciousness. To know these facts, that eye must be fixed with long and intense gaze upon them, till their fundamental characteristics are distinctly revealed. Without the spirit of self-reflection the inquirer will make but poor progress in Mental Philosophy. With it, he will "go from strength to strength."

The inquirer who would make progress in this science, must also be deeply imbued with a *teachable spirit.* This is the true and only true philosophic spirit. Under its influence the mind "cries after knowledge, and lifts up its voice for understanding." "It seeks for her as silver, and searches for her as for hid treasures." "Wisdom enters into the heart, and knowledge is pleasant to the soul." The love of truth, for her own sake, takes full possession of the mind. To "sit under her banners," and "dwell in the light of her countenance," all opinions, all systems and prepossessions, contrary to her teachings, are readily sacrificed. Facts are weighed with the utmost care for the exclusive purpose of knowing their characteristics; and all conclusions, however contrary to all performed theories, are readily admitted, which sustains to such facts the relation of logical antecedents or consequents. In this state of mind, the student will not fail to "understand righteousness, and judgment, and equity; yea, and every good path."

I mention as another indispensable requisite, *untiring industry and perseverance.* "There is no royal road to knowledge" of any kind; much less to a knowledge of ourselves. Before we attain that high eminence from which the goodly mountains, waving forests, verdant hills, luxuriant valleys, and majestic rivers of this "land of promise," this "land flowing with milk and honey," shall lie out with distinctness beneath the enraptured vision; we shall find many a tiresome wilderness to pass, many a rugged steep to climb, and sometimes, perhaps, almost "through the palpable obscure," will we be compelled to "find out our uncouth way." But when that eminence has been attained, no one feels that he has "labored in vain, and spent his strength for nought." Every individual, who is not fully prepared for the toil of *hard and tireless thinking*, had better abandon this study before he commences it. Otherwise, in addition to all the wretchedness of ignorance, he will be subject to the more depressing influence of conscious unworthiness of the possession of this treasure of knowledge.

I will allude to but one requisite more — a *deeply serious state of mind*. In no other state are we prepared for deep communion with the mysteries, and for profound contemplations of the sublime and majestic creations of truth. To walk among her "cloud-capped towers, gorgeous palaces and solemn temples," and to worship at her shrine, here is no place for triflers here. A trifler neither knows himself nor respects himself. He is, therefore, wholly unprepared to inquire for, or appreciate when found, the most momentous of all the revelations of truth, those respecting the nature, character and relations of himself.

The individual who commences, and continues to prosecute, his inquiries pertaining to this science, in the spirit above described, will find in the end a full reward of his labors. The object of the author is not to think for the inquirer, but to enable him to think for himself.

CHAPTER II.

CLASSIFICATION OF MENTAL PHENOMENA AND POWERS.

"All the facts," says Cousin, "which fall under the Consciousness of man, and consequently under the reflection of the philosopher, resolve themselves into three fundamental facts, which contain all others. These facts which, beyond doubt, are never in reality, solitary, and separate from each other, but which are essentially not the less distinct, and which a careful analysis ought to distinguish without dividing, in the complex phenomena of intellectual life; these three facts are expressed in the words TO FEEL, TO THINK, TO ACT." Is this a full and correct classification of the phenomena of the human mind? Are these distinctions real? Are all mental phenomena included in these fundamental facts? These questions I answer in the affirmative, for the following reasons:

1. No mental phenomena can be conceived of, which do not fall under one or the other of these facts. What mental operation can we conceive of, which is not a thought, feeling, or choice, purpose, or determination?

2. These classes of phenomena differ from one another, not in *degree* but in *kind*. How entirely distinct, for example, is thought, in every degree and modification, from feeling, on the one hand, and mental determination, on the other. Feelings, also, of every kind and modification, stand at an equal remove from thoughts and mental acts or determinations. So of the class last mentioned. Choice in every degree or form

makes, in its fundamental characteristics, no approach whatever to thoughts or feelings.

3. All men recognize the states of mind designated by the above expressions, as actually existing in human Consciousness, and as clearly distinguishable from each other. When I affirm to the peasant, or to the philosopher, at one time, that I think so and so; at another that I have particular feelings; and at another still, that I have resolved, or determined upon a particular course of conduct; both alike readily apprehend my meaning, and understand me as referring to states of mind perfectly distinct.

4. In all known languages there are terms employed to designate these three classes of phenomena; terms, each of which is applied to one class exclusively, and never to either of the others. Thus, the term *thought* is never applied to any mental phenomena but those designated by the words *to think*. We never use it to designate feelings, or mental determinations of any kind. The terms *sensation* or *emotion* are never applied to any but the phenomena of *feeling*. In a similar manner, we never apply the terms *purpose*, *willing*, *determining*, &c., to the phenomena of thought or feeling, but exclusively to those designated by the words *to act*. The existence of such terms undeniably evince, that the different classes of phenomena, under consideration, are recognized by universal Consciousness, not only as existing, but as entirely distinct from one another.

5. As a final reason I would adduce an argument presented in the work, recently published, on the Will. "The clearness and particularity with which the universal Intelligence has marked the distinction under consideration, is strikingly indicated by the fact, that there are *qualifying* terms in common use, which are applied to each of these classes of phenomena, and never to either of the others. It is true that there are

such terms which are promiscuously applied to all classes of phenomena. There are terms, however, which are never applied but to one class. Thus we speak of *clear thoughts*, but never of clear feelings or determinations. We speak of *irrepressible feelings and desires*, but never of irrepressible thoughts or resolutions. We also speak of *inflexible determinations*, but never of inflexible feelings or conceptions. With what perfect distinctness, then, must the universal Consciousness have marked thoughts, feelings, and determinations, as phenomena entirely distinct from one another — phenomena differing not in *degree*, but in *kind*."

Mental Faculties indicated by the phenomena above classified.

The threefold classification of mental phenomena, above established and elucidated, clearly indicate a tri-unity of mental faculties and susceptibilities equally distinct from one another. These faculties and susceptibilities we designate by the terms Intellect or Intelligence, Sensibility or Sensitivity, and Will. To the Intellect we refer all the phenomena of *thought*, of every kind, degree, and modification. To the Sensibility we refer all *feelings*, such as sensations, emotions, desires, and affections. To the Will we refer all mental *determinations*, such as volitions, choices, purposes, &c.

OBJECT OF MENTAL PHILOSOPHY.

The object of Mental Philosophy is a full development of the phenomena, characteristics, laws, and mutual relationships and dependencies of these different faculties.

MEANING OF THE WORDS MENTAL FACULTIES

When I speak of a diversity of Mental Faculties, I would by no means be understood as teaching the strange dogma, that the mind is made up of parts which may be separated from one another. Mind is not composed of a diversity of substances. It is one substance, incapable of division. Yet this simple substance, remaining, as it does, always one and identical, is capable of a diversity of functions, or operations, entirely distinct from one another. This diversity of capabilities of this one substance, we designate by the words Mental Faculties. As the functions of thought, feeling, and willing, are entirely distinct from each other, so we speak of the powers of thought, feeling, and willing, to wit, the Intelligence, Sensibility, and Will, as distinct faculties of the Mind.

The remarks made above respecting the Mind itself will, at once, appear equally applicable to each of the Mental Faculties which have been enumerated. As we speak of the Intelligence, for example, as a Faculty of the Mind entirely distinct from those of the Sensibility and Will, without supposing that the Mind is not strictly one substance, so we may speak of the different Powers, or Faculties of the Intelligence itself, without implying that *that* Faculty is composed of a diversity of parts. The term Faculty, whether applied to the whole Mind, or to any of the departments of the Mind, implies a diversity of *functions* of the same power, or substance, and not a diversity of substances, or parts.

CHAPTER III.

PHENOMENA OF THE INTELLIGENCE.

We are now prepared to enter directly upon the great inquiry to be pursued in this Treatise, — *the Phenomena, Faculties, and Laws of the human Intelligence.* As all that we know, or can know, of this, as well as of every other department of the Mind, is revealed to us through the phenomena which lie under the eye of Consciousness, the first inquiries which now present themselves are, What are the phenomena of thought thus revealed? What are their fundamental characteristics? In conformity to what principles shall they be classified and arranged?

PRINCIPLE OF CLASSIFICATION.

There is one principle, in conformity to which all intellectual phenomena may be properly classified, and in the light of which, the fundamental characteristics of such phenomena may be very distinctly presented. I refer to the *modes* in which all *objects* of thought are conceived of by the Intelligence. Of these modes, there are two entirely distinct and separate, the one from the other. Every object of thought is conceived of as existing either *contingently* or of *necessity*, that is, that object is conceived of as existing, with the possibility of conceiving of its non-existence, or it is conceived of as existing, with the impossibility of conceiving of its non-existence. If we have any conceptions of an object at all, we

2*

must conceive of it as falling under one or the other of these relations. The principle of classification, therefore, is fundamental, and of universal application.

CONTINGENT AND NECESSARY PHENOMENA OF THOUGHT DEFINED.

Every thought, conception, cognition, or idea, then, by whatever term we may choose to designate it, all the phenomena of the Intelligence, may be classed, as *contingent*, or *necessary*. A conception is *contingent*, when *its object may be conceived of as existing with the possibility of conceiving of its non-existence.*

An idea is *necessary* when *its object is conceived of as existing with the impossibility of conceiving of its non-existence.*

All the phenomena of the Intelligence must, as shown above, fall under one or the other of these relations. It remains now, to illustrate the principle of classification here adopted, by a reference to an adequate number of particular phenomena, as the basis of important distinctions pertaining to the different functions or powers of the Intelligence. In the notice which we shall take of particular phenomena, other important characteristics, aside from those under consideration, will be developed, while these will be kept prominently in mind, as the grounds of classification.

IDEAS OF BODY AND SPACE.

Two prominent ideas, those of *body* and *space*, will first claim our attention. They are to be analyzed as they now lie in the Intelligence, in its present state of development. That these ideas exist in all minds, which have attained to any considerable degree of development, none can doubt, and none will deny. The question to be resolved is, what are their fundamental characteristics?

Idea of body contingent. That of Space necessary.

We will begin with the idea of body. A careful analysis of this idea will undeniably evince the fact, that it has the characteristic of *contingency;* in other words, that its *object* may always be conceived of, as existing, with the possibility of conceiving of its non-existence. Take any body we please, the book, for example, that lies before us, our own physical organization, the habitation in which we dwell, the earth itself, or the entire physical universe together, and we shall find, on careful reflection, that we may conceive of them as existing, or as not existing. We believe, that things equal to the same things are equal to one another, because we cannot even conceive the opposite to be true. We believe, on the other hand, that body exists, not because we cannot *conceive* that it does not exist, but on the testimony of our senses. We believe, on such testimony, in the reality of body, as a fact, the non-reality of which is conceivable. We believe in the above axiom, on principle, as a truth, the opposite of which is inconceivable. Many have, as a matter of fact, denied the reality of an external, material universe; but none ever denied the truth of the above principle, and others of a kindred character. The reason is obvious. The idea of body is contingent, the conception of the existence or non-existence of the object of that idea being equally possible to the mind. The axiom or principle under consideration, on the other hand, is a necessary truth, its non-truth being in itself inconceivable, and naturally impossible.

We now turn to a consideration of the idea of space. We can, as shown above, readily conceive of the non-existence of all bodies, of the external material universe itself. When we have done this, however, can we even conceive of the non-reality of space, in which the universe does or may exist? We cannot. We conceive of space as a reality. Can we conceive of it, as not being? We cannot. No intelligent being can by any possibility form such a conception. Of this every one cannot, on reflection, but be distinctly and absolutely conscious. When we have conceived of the non-existence of any one particular body, or of all others, even of the universe itself, let us attempt to conceive of the non-reality of space, in which we necessarily conceive of these objects as existing, and we shall find the formation of such a conception, an absolute impossibility. The idea of space, then, is necessary. We conceive of the *object* of that idea, as existing, with the impossibility of conceiving of its non-existence.

OTHER CHARACTERISTICS OF THESE TWO IDEAS.

It now remains to mark other characteristics of these important ideas. The following may be presented, as the most fundamental:

The idea of body is conditioned and relative. That of space is unconditioned and absolute.

An idea is conditioned and relative, when its *object* can be conceived of, as existing, but upon the condition of conceiving of the reality of the object of some other idea, the reality of the latter object, being necessarily supposed, as the condition of that of the former. An idea is unconditioned and absolute, when the reality of its object does not, of necessity, suppose that of the object of any other idea, and when the Intelligence cannot but conceive, that the former object must exist, whether any other object does, or does not exist.

Now when we conceive of body, as existing, we necessarily, as the condition of its existence, suppose the reality of another object, to wit, space in which body does, and must exist, and without which the latter cannot exist. If body is, as the condition of its existence, space must be. The principle, body supposes space, is just as necessary as any other axiom, the principle above referred to, for example, that things equal te the same things are equal to one another. The idea of body, then, is conditioned and relative, the reality of the object of that idea necessarily supposing, as the condition of its existence, that of the object of some other idea, that of space.

When, on the other hand, we conceive of space, we conceive, as the condition of its existence, of no other reality. Space must be, whether anything else exists or not. The idea of space, then, is unconditioned and absolute, the reality of its *object* supposing, as the condition of its existence, the reality of the object of no other idea.

The idea of body implies that of limitation. The idea of space implies that of the absence of all limitation.

We always, and of necessity, conceive of body as limited. Under this condition we not only conceive of all particular bodies, but of the universe itself. The idea of body, then, implies that of limitation. In other words, body is finite.

Space, on the other hand, we necessarily conceive of, as without limits. Its idea implies that of the absence of all limitation. In other words, space is infinite.

The idea of body, a sensible representation. That of space, a pure rational conception.

When we form a conception of any particular body, we can readily conceive of something else with which the former may be compared, and by which it may be represented. The human countenance, for example, can be represented upon canvas. The idea of body, then, is a *sensible representation.*

When, on the other hand, we have formed an idea of space, we find that we know, and can conceive, of no existence with which the former can be compared. It bears no resemblance whatever to any other object which we know, or of which we can form a conception. The idea itself is wholly unlike any other idea which exists, or ever has existed in the mind. The idea of space is a pure rational conception.

The remark just made will be found, on reflection, to be applicable to each necessary idea existing in the Intelligence. Each one exists entirely alone, and in total separation from all others of every kind, as far as *resemblance* is concerned. The idea of time, for example, substance, cause, right and wrong, obligation, &c., each bears no resemblance to either of the others, or to any other actual or conceivable existing in the mind.

The following then may be stated, as the most important characteristics of these two ideas:

1. The idea of body is contingent. That of space is necessary.

2. The idea of body is conditioned and relative. That of space is unconditioned and absolute.

3. The idea of body implies that of limitation. Or, body is finite. The idea of space implies the absence of all limitation. In other words, space is infinite.

4. The idea of body is a sensible representation. That of space is a pure rational conception.

IDEAS OF SUCCESSION, AND TIME, OR DURATION.

These ideas are in all intelligent minds. No individual, whose Intelligence has been developed at all, will fail to understand you, when you speak of one event, as having happened; of another, as having succeeded it, and of the fact that that succession took place in some definite period of time. We will now mark the characteristic of these ideas.

Idea of Succession contingent. That of Time necessary.

You can conceive of some one event as having happened, and of another as having succeeded it. In other words, you have the idea of succession. Can you not conceive, that neither of these events occurred? Every individual can readily form such a conception. The same holds true of all events, of all succession of every kind, and in all time. The idea of succession, like that of body, is contingent.

But when we have conceived of the total cessation of succession, we find it absolutely impossible to conceive that there is no time, or duration, in which succession may take place. We can no more conceive of the non-existence of time, than we can of that of space. The idea of time, then, like that of space, is necessary.

Other Characteristics of these Ideas.

When we conceive of succession, we necessarily affirm, as the condition of its existence, the reality of something else, that is, of time, in which succession takes place. The idea of succession, like that of body, is *conditioned* and *relative.*

On the other hand, when we affirm the reality of time, we suppose, as the condition of its existence, the existence of nothing else. Time is, and must be, whether anything else exists or not. The idea of time, then, is unconditioned and absolute.

Once more; whenever we can conceive of succession, we necessarily conceive of time before, and after it. The idea of succession, therefore, implies that of limitation, or succession is limited, finite.

The idea of time, however, implies the absence of all limitation. Duration never began; nor will it ever cease to be. In other words, time is infinite. The following are the most important and fundamental characteristics of these two ideas:

1. The idea of succession is contingent. That of time is necessary.

2. The idea of succession is conditioned, and relative. That of time is unconditioned and absolute.

3. The idea of succession always implies that of limitation. Or succession is finite. The idea of time, on the other hand, implies that of the absence of all limitation. In other words, duration is infinite.

IDEAS OF THE FINITE AND OF THE INFINITE.

Body and space, succession and duration, are given to us, as we have seen, with the following characteristics: Body and succession are limitable; time and space are illimitable. In other words, the former are finite, the latter infinite. "Now the ideas of the finite and the infinite," as remarked by Cousin, "may be detached from the ideas of body and succession, time and space, provided we keep in mind the subjects from which they are abstracted."

These ideas then are in the mind. They are also distinct, the one from the other. Consequently the one cannot be derived from the other. The multiplication of the finite cannot give the infinite. Nor by dividing the infinite do we find the finite. Being correlative ideas, the one necessarily supposes and suggests the other. The one cannot possibly exist in the mind without the other. Yet, as above remarked, the one is perfectly distinct from the other.

Nor is one of these ideas less distinct than the other. When I speak of the infinite, every one as readily and distinctly apprehends my meaning, as when I speak of the finite. The following propositions, for example — body is limitable; space is illimitable — are equally intelligible to all minds, the one as the other.

There are other forms in which these ideas appear in the

Mind, in all of which they sustain, to each other, the same relations, and possess the same characteristics. When the Mind conceives of power, wisdom or goodness, as imperfect, or limitable, or finite, it necessarily conceives of similar attributes which are perfect, illimitable, and infinite. When it conceives of anything which is and began to be, it, of necessity, conceives of something else, which not only is, but always has been.

If any individual still affirms that he has, in reality, no idea of the infinite, we have only to ask him, whether he understands the import of the words he employs, when he makes such an affirmation? whether he is not conscious of speaking of something, which, in thought, he himself clearly distinguishes from all that is limitable, or limited? These questions he will readily answer in the affirmative. In this answer he clearly contradicts the affirmation under consideration. For, if he really, as he affirms, has no idea of the infinite, he would not know the meaning of the terms he uses, nor could he, in thought, clearly distinguish the infinite from all that is limitable, or finite.

If also we have no real or positive idea of the infinite, we can have none of time and space, for they are positive ideas, and their objects are given in the Intelligence, as positively or absolutely infinite.

REMARKS OF LOCKE.

Four remarks of Locke, pertaining to the idea of the Infinite, demand a passing notice.

His first remark is, that it is an "endlessly growing idea." On the other hand, the idea of the Infinite is always fixed. Being a simple idea, it must, when once generated in the mind, remain there, at all times, one and identical. It may become more and more vivid. In the respect under consideration, however, this idea undergoes no modification whatever. Who has ever found, since the ideas of infinite space and duration were developed in his Mind, that these have undergone the least modification, as far as growth is concerned?

Again: Locke maintains that the idea of the Infinite is *obscure*. Still it exists, and as a phenomenon of Consciousness, falls, most legitimately, under the cognizance of the philosopher. But in what sense is this idea obscure? To those faculties of the Intelligence which pertain to the finite, it must for ever remain obscure. To that faculty, however, which apprehends truths necessary and absolute, it is as plain as any other idea whatever.

According to Locke, also, the idea of the infinite is merely a *negative* idea. "We have," he says, "no positive idea of Infinity." This is directly contradicted by the testimony of universal Consciousness. Who is not conscious that his ideas of God, of space, and time, all of which are given in the Intelligence as infinite, are just as positive as any of our conceptions whatever? We might also, with the same propriety, maintain that our conceptions of the finite are negative, as that our ideas of the infinite are. Being correlative ideas, if one is assumed as positive, the other will be relatively negative of course. In themselves, however, both are alike positive and equally so.

Once more: "Number," says Locke, "affords the clearest idea of the infinite." This is to reduce the infinite to the finite; for number, however large, is always limited — that is, finite. The multiplication of the finite may call into exercise the faculty which apprehends the infinite, and thus render our idea of the latter more distinct and vivid (as all acts of attention do) than it otherwise would be. In no other sense, however, can such repetitions give us the Infinite.

CHARACTERISTICS OF THESE IDEAS.

Having established the fact, that the idea of the infinite, as well as that of the finite, is in the mind, it now remains to mark their respective characteristics.

Idea of the Finite contingent and relative; that of the Infinite necessary and absolute.

Whatever substance we conceive of as finite, we cannot but regard as existing contingently. We cannot regard it, as in its own nature, a necessary existence. Hence, for all that we conceive of as finite, we naturally and necessarily inquire after a cause. We do not ask the question, had it a cause? but *what* caused it? The idea of the finite, therefore, is contingent, and consequently relative.

On the other hand, whatever we regard as infinite, we necessarily apprehend as uncaused—that is, as existing by necessity. When we trace back any chain of causes and effects, for the purpose of finding a first cause, at each successive link we always inquire for its antecedent, till we arrive at the Infinite. Here we pause; here our inquiries cease; here we recognize ourselves at once, as in the presence of an existence which is not contingent, but necessary and absolute. The idea of the Infinite, therefore, is necessary and absolute.

IDEAS OF MENTAL PHENOMENA, AND OF PERSONAL IDENTITY.

Every individual believes, that he is now the same being that he was yesterday, and will be to-morrow. Numberless and ever-varying phenomena are constantly passing under the eye of Consciousness. Many are recalled of which we were formerly conscious; yet they are all referred to the same individual subject. Every phenomenon of thought, feeling, and willing, of which we are now conscious, which we recall as having, in some former period, been conscious of, or which we expect to put forth in some future time, is given in the Intelligence in this exclusive form — I think, I feel, I will; I did think, I did feel, I did will, so and so. The same holds equally true of all similar phenomena which we contemplate, as about to occur in future time. Whatever the phenomena may be, the same identical I is given as its subject. This is what is meant by personal identity. It is the unity of our being, of the I, or self, as opposed to the plurality and ever-changing phenomena of Consciousness. Having shown that the idea of mental phenomena and of personal identity are in the Mind, we will consider their characteristics.

Idea of Mental Phenomena contingent and relative.

You have a Consciousness of some thought, feeling, or act of Will. You remember similar phenomena of which you were formerly conscious. You conceive of them as now being, or as having been actual realities. Can you not conceive of them as not being, or as never having taken place? You can. Can you conceive of such phenomena as existing or having existed, without referring them to some subject? In other words, can you conceive of some thought, feeling, or volition as now existing, or as having existed, in former times, without referring it to some subject, some being which thinks, feels, or wills? You cannot. All the phenomena of Consciousness are contingent and relative.

Idea of Personal Identity necessary.

How is it with the idea of personal identity? You are now conscious of some thought, or feeling, or act of Will. You recall others, of a similar nature, of which you have been formerly conscious. This you refer to one and the same subject, the I of Consciousness, as it is sometimes called. This reference you and all mankind alike must make. This reference mankind universally make in all the transactions of life. Under its influence we hold ourselves and others bound to fulfill contracts made years ago. Under its influence, the virtuous are commended and rewarded, and the vicious blamed and punished for actions long since performed. Under its influence we anticipate the retributions of eternal justice, in a future state, for the deeds done in the body. Is it possible to avoid making this reference? It is not. You cannot possibly conceive of a thought, for example, without referring it to some subject which thinks. You cannot be conscious of any mental phenomenon, or recall any others of which you were formerly conscious, without referring them to one and the same subject, yourself. The idea of personal identity, then, is necessary.

NECESSARY IDEAS DISTINGUISHED AS CONDITIONAL AND UNCONDITIONAL.

Here an important distinction between necessary ideas demands special attention. When we contemplate the ideas of space and duration, for example, we find that the objects of these ideas must exist, whether anything else exists or not. Those ideas, therefore, are not only necessary, but unconditioned and absolute. On the other hand, the ideas of personal identity, and of substance and cause, which we shall hereafter consider, are not, in this sense, necessary. They are only *conditionally* necessary. Phenomena being given, substance *must* be. An event being given, the supposition of a cause is necessary. Phenomena and events not being given, we do not affirm the existence of substances or causes. The phenomena of Consciousness not being given, we do not affirm the reality or identity of the self, the subject of these phenomena. Such ideas are *conditionally* necessary, and not like those of space and time, not only necessary, but unconditioned and absolute.

IDEAS OF PHENOMENA AND SUBSTANCE.

Idea of substance explained.

If the observations which have been made upon the idea of personal identity, have been distinctly understood, the characteristics of the idea of substance will be readily apprehended. All the phenomena of Consciousness and Memory are, as we have seen, by a necessary law of our being, referred to one and the same subject. The phenomena are accidents, perpetually changing. The subject, however, remains the same. Now, in the language of Cousin, "Being, one and identical, opposed to variable accidents, to transitory phenomena, is substance." But thus far we have only personal substance. The same principle, however, applies equally to all external substances. Through the medium of our senses, such objects are given to us as being possessed of a great variety of qualities, and as existing in a great variety of states. The qualities and states, which are perpetually varying, we necessarily refer to one and the same subject, a subject which remains one and identical, amid the endlessly diversified phenomena which it exhibits. This is substance.

Idea of Phenomena contingent and relative — that of Substance necessary.

Now as it is with our ideas of the phenomena of Consciousness and personal identity, so it is with our ideas of external phenomena and external substance. The former is contingent and relative; the latter is necessary. When any phenomenon appears, we can readily conceive that it had not appeared. Its appearance also we can admit, only on the supposition of something else, to wit, substance, to which this appearance is necessarily referred. Our ideas of phenomena, therefore, are contingent and relative.

On the other hand, the idea of substance, relatively to phenomena, is necessary. Phenomena being given, substance must be. It is impossible for us to conceive of the former without the latter.

Our ideas of Substance not obscure, but clear and distinct.

According to Locke, "we have no clear idea of substance in general." This idea also, he represents, as "of little use in philosophy." In reply, it may be said, that our idea of substance is just as clear and important, as those of time, space, and personal identity. Of this every one is conscious. The same function of the Intelligence which apprehends one of these ideas, apprehends them all. Take away the power to apprehend one, and the power to apprehend every other of these ideas is annihilated. Philosophy itself also becomes an impossibility. How could we reason philosophically about ourselves, in the absence of the idea of personal identity? Equally impossible would it be, to reason about objects external to us, in the absence of the idea of substance. This and kindred ideas, instead of being "of little use in philosophy," are, in reality, the foundation of all our explanations of phenomena, external and internal.

We often hear individuals, in expatiating upon the great ignorance of man, affirming, that all we "know of realities within and around us, is their phenomena. Of the *substances* themselves, we know nothing." In reply to such rhapsodies, it may be said, that our knowledge of every substance of every kind, is just as clear, distinct, and extensive, as our knowledge of its phenomena. In phenomena, substances stand revealed, the substance being *as* its phenomena. In the phenomena of thought, for example, we know *ourselves*, as thinking beings or substances, our powers being as the thoughts which they generate. Our knowledge of the *power* of thought, is just as distinct as that of thought itself. The same holds true, in respect to all substances, material, and mental.

IDEAS OF EVENTS AND CAUSE.

The universe within and around us, presents the constant spectacle of endlessly diversified and ever-changing phenomena. Some of these are constantly conjoined, in the relation of "immediate and invariable antecedence and consequence" The connection between others is only occasional. In reference to events of the former class, the mind judges, that the relation between them is not only that of antecedence and consequence, but of *cause and effect.* In reference to every event, however, whether its antecedent is perceived or not, we judge that it had a cause. This judgment is *universal,* extending to all events, actual and conceivable. It is absolutely impossible for us to conceive of an event without a cause. Let any one make the effort to form such a conception, and he will find that he has attempted an impossibility.

Here it should be noticed, that we do not affirm that every *effect* has a cause. That would be mere tautology. It would be equivalent to the affirmation, that whatever is produced by a cause, is produced by a cause. All this might be true, and the proposition, every event has a cause, be false, notwithstanding.

The idea of Events contingent and relative; that of Cause necessary.

The relation between the idea of an event, and that of a cause, may be readily pointed out. Whenever the mind witnesses, or is conscious of, the occurrence of an event, it apprehends that event as contingent and relative. It might or might not have happened. There is no impossibility in making these different suppositions. The occurrence of an event also necessarily supposes something else, to wit, a cause. On the other hand, no event uncaused can possibly be conceived to have taken place. The idea of an event, then, is contingent and relative. The idea of cause is necessary, conditionally so, as shown above.

THEORY OF DR. BROWN, AND OTHERS.

The speculations of certain philosophers respecting the subject under consideration, here demand our attention. The relation of cause and effect, according to Dr. Brown and others, is nothing more than that of "immediate and invariable antecedence and consequence." "A cause," says Dr. B., "is nothing else than an immediate and invariable antecedent." According to this philosopher, in no instance whatever is there any reason, in the nature of any particular cause, why it should produce one event rather than another. Succession, mere antecedence and consequence immediate and invariable, without any reason in the nature of the antecedent and consequent why this order of succession should arise, rather than another, is all that exists in any instance. In regard to this theory, it is enough to say that no man does or can believe it. Let any man, for example, behold a piece of wood and a metallic substance put together into a heated furnace. The wood is immediately consumed, and the metal changed from a solid to a fluid state. Can he avoid the conviction, that there is, in the nature of these two substances, a reason, why, that when acted upon by the same cause, one is consumed, and the other changed from a solid to a fluid state? When the Almighty said, "Let there be light, and there was light," who dares believe that there was not, in the nature of that fiat, a reason, why, as its consequent, light, rather than any other substance, should appear? When two pounds weight are placed on one side of a balance, and five on the other, who does not believe, that aside from the particular sequence which follows here, there is, in the circumstances supposed, a reason why one particular sequence should follow, rather than any other? In the succession of day and night, also, we have an order of sequence immediate and invariable. Is this equivalent to the declaration, that day causes night, or night causes the day? It would be so, if the theory under consideration was true. For all the conditions of that theory are here fulfilled. We have an order of sequence immediate and invariable.

As a further illustration, let us, for a moment, consider the theory of "pre-established harmony" between the action of the Soul and Body, proclaimed by Leibnitz. According to this author, Matter and Mind do, and can exert no influence upon each other, whatever. I will, for example, a motion of my arm, or of any other part of the body, and the motion follows. Still my volitions have no influence in causing or controlling that motion. So in all other instances. God, foreseeing the states of our minds, has so constituted our bodies, that the action of the latter shall always be in perfect harmony with that of the former, though wholly uninfluenced by it. In this theory, the relation of cause and effect, as announced by the theory of Dr. Brown, is perfectly fulfilled. Between the states of our minds, and the corresponding action of our bodies, we have an order of sequence immediate and invariable. But who does not regard the Liebnitzian theory as announcing a relation totally distinct and opposite to what is universally believed to exist between our minds and bodies? When we say, that the motion of the body is in immediate and perfect harmony with that of the mind, we say one thing. When we say, that the action of the mind *causes* that of the body, we introduce, in the judgment of all men, an entirely different idea. Sequence immediate and invariable is all that we *perceive* to exist between any antecedent and consequent; but it is, by no means, all that we *believe*, yea *know* to exist.

OBSERVATIONS OF MR. DUGALD STEWART.

The following remarks of Mr. Stewart also demand a passing observation:

"It seems now to be pretty generally agreed among philosophers, that there is no instance in which we are able to perceive a necessary connection between two successive events, or to comprehend in what manner the one proceeds from the other, as its cause. From experience, indeed, we learn, that there are many events, which are constantly conjoined, so that the one invariably follows the other: but it is possible, for anything we know to the contrary, that this connection, though a constant one, as far as our observation has reached, may not be a necessary connection; nay, it is possible, that there may be no necessary connections among any of the phenomena we see; and if there are any such connections existing, we may rest assured that we shall never be able to discover them."

Again:

"When it is said, that every change in nature indicates the operation of a cause, the word *cause* expresses something which is supposed to be necessarily connected with the change, and without which it could not have happened. This may be called the *metaphysical* meaning of the word; and such causes may be called *metaphysical* or *efficient causes.* In natural philosophy, however, when we speak of one thing being the cause of another, all that we mean is, that the two are constantly conjoined, so that when we see the one, we may expect the other. These conjunctions we learn from experience alone;

and, without an acquaintance with them, we could not accommodate our conduct to the established course of nature."

These remarks certainly cannot hold in regard to the primary qualities of matter, as, for example, solidity considered as the antecedent, and resistance as the consequent. Is it possible to conceive of the existence of an object which is extended and solid, which is at the same time destitute of the power of resistance?

Here I would drop the suggestion, whether it is possible to conceive of any substance as existing, which is destitute of power; and whether our ideas of substance and of power are not, in fact, identical? For my own part, I find it impossible to conceive of *substances* which are not real *powers*.

IDEA OF POWER.

The idea of Power, is that of causation in its quiescent state, or as the permanent attribute of a subject irrespective of its action, at any particular moment. When particular effects are attributed to particular causes, while the nature of the substances containing such causes remains unchanged, the mind considers the power to repeat such effects under the same circumstances, as the permanent attributes of those substances. This is the idea of power, as it exists in all minds. All substances, in their active state, are Causes — in their quiescent state, are Powers. Powers are of two kinds, active and passive. The latter are commonly called susceptibilities. As the existence of powers and causes is indicated by their respective phenomena, so the nature of such powers and causes is indicated by the characteristics of their respective phenomena.

The idea of Power, sustaining, as it does, the same relation to phenomena, that that of cause and substance do, is, of course, like those ideas, universal and necessary.

CONCLUSION OF THE PRESENT ANALYSIS.

Here our analysis of intellectual phenomena will close, for the present. It might have been extended to almost any length. Enough has been said, however, to indicate the *principle* of classification adopted, and to show its universal applicability, as well as to lay the foundation for the important distinctions, &c., in respect to the intellectual powers, an elucidation of which will be commenced in the next Chapter.

CHAPTER IV.

APPLICATION OF THE PRECEDING ANALYSIS.

LOGICAL AND CHRONOLOGICAL ORDER OF IDEAS.

In applying the results of the preceding analysis, one of the first questions which arises, respects the *relations* of intellectual phenomena, contingent and necessary to each other. With regard to this question, I would remark, that there are two, and only two important relations which such phenomena sustain to each other — the relation of *logical* and *chronological* antecedence and consequence. The latter relates to the order of acquisition, or to the question, Which, in the order of time, is first developed, in the Intelligence. The former relates to their order in a logical point of view, that is, to the question, Which sustains to the other, in the process of ratiocination, the relation of logical antecedent.

Logical order.

In regard to the order last mentioned, I would remark, that one idea is the *logical* antecedent of another, when the latter necessarily *supposes* the former, that is, when the reality of the *object* of the latter can be admitted, only on the admission of that of the *object* of the former. The ideas of events and cause being given in the Intelligence, for example, we find that we can admit the reality of an event on one supposition only, to wit, that of a cause which produced the event. We say, therefore, that the idea of cause is the *logical* antecedent of that of events.

Now, if we contemplate ideas in this view, it will be perceived at once, that necessary ideas are, in all instances, the logical antecedents of contingent ones. What was shown above to be true of the ideas of event and cause, is self-evidently true of the ideas of body and space, succession and time, the finite and the infinite, and phenomena external and internal, and substance and personal identity. Every contingent idea is *relative*, necessarily supposing, as its logical antecedent, some necessary idea.

Chronological order.

Contingent ideas, on the other hand, are the *chronological* antecedents of necessary ideas, that is, in the order of actual development in the Intelligence, the former precedes the latter. Two considerations will render this proposition demonstrably evident.

1. Necessary ideas are given in the Intelligence, only as the logical antecedents of contingent ones. Space, for example, is known to us, only as that in which bodies or substances exist. In no other light can we possibly know or conceive of it. Now that which is and can be known to us, only as the *place* of some other thing, cannot have been known to us prior to that thing; otherwise, the former might be known and conceived of, irrespective of the latter. The same holds true of the ideas of succession and time, phenomena and substance, events and causes. The latter class of ideas can be conceived of, only as the logical antecedents of the former. The former therefore must have been originated in the Intelligence, prior to the latter.

2. While necessary ideas can be defined, only as the logical antecedents of contingent ones, the latter can be defined without any reference to the former — a fact which could not be true, if the latter were not the chronological antecedents

of the former. Cause, for example, can be defined, only as that which produces events. An event, as any one can perceive, by consulting his dictionary, can be, and is defined, without any reference to the idea of cause. Contingent ideas therefore are the chronological antecedents of necessary ones.

PRIMARY INTELLECTUAL FACULTIES PRE-SUPPOSED BY THE PRECEDING ANALYSIS.

The preceding analysis has fully prepared us to proceed legitimately and safely to another very important inquiry — the Primary Intellectual Faculties pre-supposed by that analysis. As stated in the Introduction, the being and characteristics of every power or substance in existence, are indicated to us by its respective phenomena. The *perception* of such phenomena, being itself a phenomenon of the mind which perceives, supposes, in the mind, corresponding powers of perception. When the Intelligence apprehends a fact, or truth of any kind, such act implies, in the Intelligence, corresponding powers of apprehension. Now truths, perceived by the Intelligence are, as we have seen, of two kinds, contingent and necessary. The perception of such truths indicates a corresponding distinction of intellectual functions, or powers. The faculty or faculties which perceive, and affirm the reality of contingent phenomena, are clearly distinguishable from that which affirms the reality of truths necessary and universal.

But contingent phenomena perceived by the Intelligence, are distinguishable, with equal clearness, as *objective* and *subjective*, that is, part pertain to the Mind itself, and part to external material substances. These facts most obviously demand a twofold division of the Intellectual faculties which pertain to contingent phenomena, as objective and subjective. The analysis completed in the last Chapter, presents to our contemplation three distinct faculties of the Intelligence:

1. That which perceives the phenomena of the mind itself, the faculty which gives us *subjective* phenomena. This function of the Intelligence is denominated Consciousness.

2. The faculty which perceives the phenomena of external material substances, or which gives us *objective* phenomena. This function of the Intelligence is denominated Sense.*

3. The faculty which apprehends truths necessary and universal. This intellectual function, or faculty, is denominated Reason.

These Functions why called Primary.

Consciousness, Sense, and Reason, are called the *primary* faculties of the Intelligence, for two considerations:

1. Because, that with them, all our knowledge commences.

2. All our complex cognitions are composed of elements given by these faculties. All the phenomena of the intelligence are either simple or complex. All simple ideas are found to be the direct intuitions of one or of the other of these faculties. All complex ideas are found, on a careful analysis, to be composed of elements previously given by these faculties. The truth of this last remark will be fully confirmed in the progress of our subsequent investigations.

Also called Intuitive Faculties.

The faculties above named are also sometimes denominated Intuitive Faculties. The reason is, that each alike, pertains to its objects, by direct *intuition*. Consciousness, for example,

* The term Sense will be used throughout this treatise, in strict accordance with this definition. This is the first meaning assigned to it by Webster, and is the meaning generally attached to it when employed, as it is in this treatise, to designate a special function of the Intelligence. A great diversity of meanings attach to it when employed for other purposes.

by direct intuition, and not through any medium, apprehends the phenomena of the mind. The same is true of the faculty of Sense in respect to the phenomena of external material substances. The action of Reason is conditioned on the prior action of Sense and Consciousness. It is not through any medium, but by direct intuition, however, that Reason affirms truths universal, necessary, and absolute. Like the former, therefore, it may, with equal propriety, be denominated a faculty of intuition. These faculties, as we shall see hereafter, give us the elements of all our knowledge.

RELATION OF PRIMITIVE INTUITIVE FACULTIES TO EACH OTHER.

We are now prepared also for another very important inquiry — the *appropriate spheres* of the primary faculties relatively to each other. This inquiry can now be met in very few words. Sense, and Consciousness, give us *phenomena* external and internal. Reason gives us the *logical antecedents* of phenomena thus perceived and affirmed. This is its appropriate and exclusive sphere relatively to the other faculties. It cannot enter the domain of either Sense or Consciousness, and judge of the validity of its affirmations. The same holds true of each of these last-mentioned faculties, relatively to the domain of the other, and that of Reason too. Each faculty has its own exclusive sphere in which it is wholly independent of either or both of the others, and independent in this sense, that the validity of its affirmations cannot be tested at the bar of either of the others. Its response, when questioned, in respect to what it has affirmed is, "What I have written, I have written." When Sense, for example, has made an affirmation pertaining to the phenomena of an external material substance, all that Consciousness can do, pertaining to the subject, is, to give that affirmation as it is, together with its characteristics.

Of the *validity* of the affirmation, it can say nothing. Reason can give the logical antecedent of that affirmation, and that is all. With its validity it has no more to do, than Consciousness has. The same will hereafter be shown to be true of Reason, in respect to every other function of the Intelligence.

IMPORTANCE OF THE TRUTHS ABOVE ELUCIDATED.

If the truth of the conclusions above stated be admitted, they will be found to be of fundamental importance in philosophy. They will put an end at once to the wild speculations of many philosophers of the Super-sensual school, both in this country and in Europe. Here lies, for example, the great error of Kant, the father of modern Transcendentalism. He first gives us a most profound, and correct analysis of intellectual phenomena, together with a statement equally correct, of the faculties pre-supposed by those phenomena. He then arraigns all the other faculties at the bar of Reason, there to test the validity of their affirmations. It is no matter of surprise at all, that the result of the trial should be thus announced by the philosopher himself who instituted it, a trial, the entire results of which, as we shall hereafter see, and a moment's reflection must convince us, must and can rest upon nothing else than groundless assumptions, and not at all upon the real affirmations of the Intelligence. "We have therefore intended to say," says Kant, in giving the results of his philosophy, "that all our intuition is nothing but the representation of phenomenon — that the things which we invisage [form conceptions and judgments of] are not that in themselves for which we take them; neither are their relationships in themselves so constituted as they appear to us; and that if we do away with our subject, or even only the subjective quality of the senses in general, every quality, all relationships of objects in space and time, nay, even space and time themselves would disappear, and cannot exist as phenomena in themselves, but only in us. It remains utterly unknown to us what may be the nature of the objects in themselves, separate from all the receptivity of our sensibility. We know nothing but our manner of perceiving them, which is peculiar to us and which need not belong to every being, although to every man. With this we have only to do." The above extract contains the following strange paralogisms, contradictions and absurdities:

1. That our Intelligence *takes*, that is, affirms things not to be, what the same Intelligence takes, that is, affirms them to be. Kant first employs the Intelligence to find out what things are. He then employs the same Intelligence to demonstrate, that these very things are not what the Intelligence had previously affirmed them to be. As if a merchant should profess, that by his yard-stick, he had demonstrated, that he had a thousand yards of cloth, and then, that, by the same yard-stick, he had as fully demonstrated the fact, that he had no real cloth at all, and that neither the yard-stick nor the cloth were, in themselves, what the yard-stick had shown them to be.

2. That, while our Intelligence represents nothing whatever as it is in itself, this same Intelligence does correctly represent "our manner of perceiving objects" — a most palpable contradiction, surely. For if our Intelligence does not represent things as they are, it surely will not represent our "manner of perceiving" as it is.

3. Kant affirms, that all that we have to do with objects, is "according to our manner of perceiving them," that is, as they are given, in our Intelligence. He then teaches us, that these objects are not as our Intelligence affirms them to be. This, certainly, is doing with objects far otherwise than "according to our manner of perceiving them."

Now all these absurdities and contradictions which Kant gives as the results of his philosophy, and which constitute its distinguishing peculiarities, would have been prevented, together with the tide of skepticism, which, through that philosophy, has desolated so large a portion of Europe, had that great philosopher, after demonstrating the reality of Reason, as a faculty of the Intelligence, raised, and correctly answered, the inquiry pertaining to the true sphere of that faculty relatively to other functions of the Intelligence. Philosophers of the Super-sensual school have run wild with Reason, just as those of the Sensual school did with Sensation and Reflection.

The possession of Reason is the great distinguishing characteristic of humanity, that characteristic which separates man at an infinite remove from the lower orders of creation around him, and places him among the great Intelligences of the universe. The full demonstration of Reason, as a function of the Intelligence, has placed the philosopher whom Coleridge not unappropriately denominates the "venerable sage of Koningsburg," among the brightest intellectual luminaries of earth. When the appropriate sphere of this divine faculty in man, relatively to the action of the other functions of the Intelligence shall be fully settled, then philosophy, instead of being the sport of wild and blind assumptions, will stand unmoved upon the rock of eternal truth. This subject will be resumed again in a subsequent part of our investigations.

CLASSIFICATION OF INTELLECTUAL PHENOMENA GIVEN BY KANT.

It was stated above, that Kant has given a most profound and correct analysis of intellectual phenomena, together with a development equally correct of the intellectual faculties presupposed by those phenomena. I will close this chapter by giving a concise statement of the results of his analysis.

Intellectual phenomena, according to this philosopher, are divided into two classes — those derived from *experience*, and those not derived from experience — the empirical and rational.

The operations of our own minds, for example, together with the qualities of external material substances, are given us by the direct intuitions of Sense and Consciousness. Such intuitions, therefore, are exclusively empirical, being derived solely from experience.

On the other hand, space is an object neither of Sense nor Consciousness. Its reality we know, and know absolutely; but not as an object of experience. The same is true of the ideas of Time, the Infinite, Substance, Cause and Effect, &c.

Rational intuitions are by Kant denominated "intuitions *à priori*." *Events*, for example, are objects of experience; as such we know them. But the proposition, every event has a cause, we know *à priori*, and not by experience.

Intuitions *à priori*, have these characteristics, and by these they are distinguished from empirical intuitions, viz.: *universality and necessity*. Though we might know by experience, that such and such events have a particular cause, we cannot know from experience, *that every event has a cause;* much less, that every event *must have a cause.* Experience, if it could give us what *is*, could not give us the fact that *what is, must be.*

The above classification, it will readily be perceived, is, in reality, identical with that elucidated in the preceding Chapter, and leads to precisely the same division of the Intellectual faculties, a division which Kant, in fact, presents, as the result of his investigations. The "à priori" phenomena of Kant are those there given as necessary, while his empirical intuitions are the contingent phenomena of Sense and Consciousness.

CHAPTER V.

CONSCIOUSNESS.

CONSCIOUSNESS DEFINED.

Of this function of the Intelligence various definitions have been given by different philosophers. The following is the definition given by Dr. Webster. "The knowledge of sensations and mental operations, or of what passes in our own mind; the act of the mind which makes known an internal object." Cousin represents it as that function of the Intelligence which "gives us information of everything which takes place in the interior of our minds." "Perhaps the most correct description of the mind *in* Consciousness, *i. e.*, of the conscious states of the mind," says the translator of Cousin's Psychology, "is the being aware of the phenomena of the mind — of that which is present to the mind; and if self-consciousness be distinguished, not *in genera*, but as a special determination of Consciousness, it is the being aware of ourselves, as of the *me*, in opposition to the *not me*, or as the permanent *subject*, distinct from the phenomena of the mind, and from all outward causes of them." In simple Consciousness, according to this author, we have a knowledge, in conformity to the statement of Cousin, of whatever passes in the interior of our own minds, that is, of all our mental exercises. In *self-Consciousness*, which is only a special form or determination of the former, we know ourselves in those phenomena, and thus distinguish ourselves from all external causes of them. This, certainly, is a very distinct and correct exposition of the subject.

The definition of Professor Tappan, given in his work on the Will, though somewhat lengthy, demands special attention, on account of the distinctness and correctness with which the subject is there presented.

"Consciousness," he says, "is the necessary knowledge which the mind has of its own operations. In knowing, it knows that it knows. In experiencing emotions and passions, it knows it experiences them. In willing, or exercising acts of causality, it knows that it wills or exercises such acts. This is common, universal, and spontaneous Consciousness.

"This definition may appear to some an identical proposition — the mind knows its knowledges, the mind knows its emotions, the mind knows its acts of causality, may seem to be implied, if not affirmed, when we say, the mind knows, feels, and wills. Therefore, we would say further:

"By Consciousness more nicely and accurately defined, we mean the power and act of self-recognition: not, if you please, the mind knowing its knowledges, emotions, and volitions; but the mind knowing itself in these."

In the above definitions the subject is presented with such distinctness, and correctness, that I shall attempt no particular definition of my own. In the exercise of Consciousness, we are not only aware of some mental state, or exercise, but we know ourselves, in that state, as the subjects of it. In every exercise of thought, feeling, and willing, we not only know what these states are, but know ourselves in them, as exercising them, and as the subjects of them. Hence all mental phenomena, as given in Consciousness, are expressed in propositions like the following: — I think, I feel, I will; — the mental phenomena being given, together with the self, the I, as the subject of them.

A remark, which I deem of special importance to make here, is this: In Consciousness, we not only know mental phenomena as they are, but what is in reality implied in such knowledge; we know also the *fundamental and distinguishing characteristics* of such phenomena. If we could merely know, by Consciousness, mental-phenomena, and not also their distinguishing characteristics, we could never classify and arrange such phenomena as the basis of important conclusions in the science of Mind. Whatever intelligent affirmations we can make respecting ourselves, as beings capable of thinking, feeling, and willing, we must affirm, on the exclusive authority of the characteristics of such phenomena, characteristics perceived and affirmed by Consciousness.

SELF-CONSCIOUSNESS CONDITIONED ON REASON, BUT NOT A FUNCTION OF REASON.

The exercise of *Self-Consciousness*, contemplated as a particular form or determination of Simple Consciousness, is conditioned on the prior exercise of the Reason. It is by Reason, as we have already seen, that we know that phenomenon supposes substance, or a subject, and that each particular phenomenon supposes a particular subject. But for Reason, therefore, whatever mental phenomena might be given in Consciousness, we could not know, that, for such phenomena, any subject whatever is supposed. Simple Consciousness gives us mental phenomena. Self-Consciousness, a particular form, or determination of the former, connects such phenomena with the subject, the reality of which Reason has affirmed, and connects them in the propositions, I think, I feel, I will, &c. While, therefore, Self-Consciousness is conditioned on the Reason, the former, as a function of the Intelligence, is clearly distinguishable from the latter. This is further evident from a single consideration. Reason is the organ of *à priori*, that is, universal and necessary truths. This is its exclusive sphere. All the affirmations of Consciousness, even in the form called

Self-Consciousness, bear the characteristic of contingency. A sound philosophy, therefore, will not fail, as philosophers sometimes have done, to distinguish these different functions of the Intelligence from each other.

NATURAL, OR SPONTANEOUS, AND PHILOSOPHICAL, OR REFLECTIVE CONSCIOUSNESS.

Consciousness, in its simple spontaneous form, is common to all mankind, in the natural development of their Intelligence. In the language of Cousin, it is, "in all men a natural process." Every individual is accustomed to use the propositions, I think, I feel, I will, &c. All persons are accustomed, also, to speak of themselves, as conscious of particular states, or exercises of mind. This shows, that they not only are conscious of their mental exercises, but also are aware of the function of the Intelligence exercised under such circumstances. All men, also, in the spontaneous developments of Consciousness, clearly distinguish themselves as subjects of mental phenomena, from all external causes, or objects of the same. They may not be able technically to express this distinction with the clearness and definiteness that a philosopher would. They may not be able to understand at first, the meaning of the terms he would employ to express that distinction. Still it is, to them, a no less palpable reality, than to him.

Now Consciousness, which is thus seen to be, "in all men, a natural process, some," in the language of the philosopher above named, "elevate this natural process to the degree of an art, a method, by reflection, which is a sort of second Consciousness — a free re-production of the first; and as Consciousness gives all men an idea of what is passing in them, so reflection gives the philosopher a certain knowledge of everything which falls under the eye of Consciousness." Reflection, or philosophic Consciousness, is simple or natural Consciousness directed by the Will, in the act of careful attention to the phenomena of our own minds. As natural Consciousness is one of the characteristics which distinguishes man from the brute, so philosophic Consciousness is the characteristic which distinguishes the mental philosopher from the rest of mankind.

The above remarks may be illustrated by a reference to two common forms of observation in respect to external material substances. The phenomena of such substances all mankind alike notice, and to some degree reason about. It is the natural philosopher, however, who attentively observes these phenomena, for the purpose of marking their fundamental characteristics, as the basis of philosophic classification, generalization, &c. The same holds true in respect to the two forms of Consciousness under consideration. Mental phenomena all men are conscious of, and all men, to a greater or less degree, are accustomed to reason about. The philosopher, however, by laborious efforts of self reflection, most critically attends to these phenomena, for the purpose of marking their characteristics, classifying and arranging them according to philosophic principles, and thus determining the powers and laws of mental operations. In simple Consciousness, we have a knowledge of whatever passes in our minds. In reflection, we have the same phenomena classified and generalized, according to fundamental characteristics thus perceived and affirmed.

PROCESS OF CLASSIFICATION AND GENERALIZATION IN REFLECTION, ILLUSTRATED.

I will now present a short illustration of this process, for the purpose of elucidating the *proper method* of questioning Consciousness, although in so doing I shall allude to a mental process of a secondary character, hereafter to be explained. The mind perceives, we will suppose, some object, an external material substance, denominated body. With this perception there arises the conception of the object as existing somewhere, — in space. The proposition, this body exists somewhere, or in space, falls under the eye of Consciousness. It is taken up by reflection, and by the process of abstraction, hereafter to be described, the two elements constituting the proposition are separated from each other. Thus the mind obtains two distinct ideas, that of body and space. These two ideas are now separately considered and marked with their respective characteristics of contingency and necessity. Again, some event is perceived. With this perception arises the conviction that it had a cause. The proposition, this event had a cause, falls under the eye of Consciousness. It also is taken up by reflection, and by the process above described, two new ideas, that of event and causation, marked by their respective characteristics of contingency and necessity, are obtained. These two ideas now being in the mind, by the laws of association, the other two, above referred to, are suggested and ranged with them in two distinct classes, as contingent and necessary ideas. Here we have the process of classification. Now on a further examination of the particular ideas comprehended under either of the above classes, some new characteristic common to them all, may be discovered; as, for example, all contingent ideas may be found also to have the characteristic of relative. This becomes a general fact, and we have it in the process of generalization. The Intelligence now takes up these phemomena, originally given by Consciousness, and then analyzed, arranged, and generalized by reflection, and gives us the powers and susceptibilities of the Mind, as indicated by these phenomena, &c.

FUNCTIONS OF CONSCIOUSNESS.

Such are the nature and functions of Consciousness, together with the knowledge derived through it.

1. In its original spontaneity, it gives us all the phenomena of the mind.

2. In connection with the Reason, it gives us ourselves as the subjects of these phenomena, and as distinguished from all existences around us, perceived or apprehended.

3. In reflection it gives the same phenomena, analyzed, arranged, and generalized.

4. From these data, the Intelligence gives us the nature, faculties, susceptibilities, and laws of mental operation, indicated by these phenomena.

NECESSITY OF RELYING IMPLICITLY UPON THE TESTIMONY OF CONSCIOUSNESS.

In the Introduction, a proof of the possibility of mental philosophy, as a science, was attempted. On this point I shall add nothing more here. I will make a few remarks upon the necessity of relying with implicit confidence upon the testimony of Consciousness, as the basis of all conclusions pertaining to the science of Mind. The great reason, as I suppose, why many individuals are prejudiced against mental philosophy, as a peculiarly difficult, obscure, and uncertain science, is a secret distrust of the validity of the facts which lie at the basis of the science; in other words, in the credibility of the witness through whom the facts are obtained. In respect to physical science, no such distrust is felt. Mankind generally rest with implicit confidence in the validity of Sense, with regard to external, material substances. With equal assurance do they, consequently, rest on any conclusions legitimately drawn from such phenomena respecting the nature and laws of the substances revealed in those phenomena. Now, why should we not repose the same faith in the validity of the testimony of Consciousness, in respect to those phenomena which constitute the basis of an infinitely more important science, the knowledge of Mind, than we do in our senses in respect to external, material phenomena? Of these two sciences, that which is by far of the highest concernment to us, we should not suppose would rest upon the most uncertain basis. If we look also at the real facts of the case, can any one tell us, or even conceive of the reason why we should rest with less assurance in the truth of that of which we are conscious, than in that which is perceived and affirmed by the external senses?

The visionary speculations, and dreamy theories of many of the most distinguished mental philosophers of ancient and modern times, has no doubt contributed (and rightly, too, if mad speculations are the legitimate results of the principles of the science), to the impression on the minds of many, that the Scotchman's definition of Metaphysics must be the true one, to wit: "Metaphysics is, when he that is listening dinna ken what he that is speaking means, and he that is speaking dinna ken what he means himself." It should be borne in mind, however, that up to the time of Bacon, a remark precisely similar would have been equally applicable to the speculations of natural philosophers; and that while the principles of physical science have, since that period, been settled upon the right foundation, the true method in mental science is of comparatively recent development. I will here drop the suggestion, whether posterity will not regard itself as almost as much indebted to Victor Cousin for the annunciation of the true method in mental Science, as to Bacon for announcing the same in respect to physical? Mental philosophy, just emerging from the darkness of ages, seems now to have gained the high road to truth, with its laws of investigation correctly settled. If we would make sure and rapid progress, two things are indispensable — that we enter upon our investigations with implicit confidence in the validity of the facts of Consciousness, as the basis of the science of mind — and that we adhere with equally assured confidence to all conclusions to which those facts legitimately conduct us.

CONSCIOUSNESS, A DISTINCT FUNCTION OR FACULTY OF THE INTELLECT.

We are now prepared to answer the question, whether Consciousness is a distinct function, or faculty of the Intelligence? All philosophers, when speaking of it without reference to any pre-formed theory, agree in speaking of it as a function as distinct and real as any other, Sense and Reason, for example. Yet, by some, the fact that it is such a faculty has been denied. Consciousness, says the translator of Cousin's Psychology, "is not to be confounded either with the Sensibility (external nor internal) nor with the Understanding, nor with the Will; neither is it a distinct and special faculty of the Mind; nor is it the principle of any of the faculties; nor is it, on the other hand, the product of them." It would be somewhat difficult, after so many negations, to put anything very positive into a definition of the subject. Yet the learned author has himself given to this something a "local habitation and a name." "Consciousness," he says, "is a *witness* of our thoughts and volitions." Now as this witness has a special function distinct from every other function of the Intelligence, ought we not to conclude that it is a special function of that Intelligence?

The *act* of knowing also implies the *power* of knowledge. A knowledge unlike all other knowledges, implies a special function of knowledge, a function distinct from every other. Is not the knowledge obtained by Consciousness, thus distinct from all other knowledges? Does it not, therefore, imply a special function distinct from every other function of the Intelligence?

Consciousness also, must be a special function, or it must be a peculiar function of some other faculty, or of the whole together. From Sense and Reason, it is as clearly distinguishable, as either of those is from the other. No one will pretend, that it is a special function of any of the secondary faculties hereafter to be named, nor of all the Intellectual faculties together. What shall we regard it then but a special function of the Intelligence?

One other consideration which I present, is, as it appears to me, quite decisive of the question under consideration. The exercise of Consciousness is dependent on the Will, in the same sense, that that of the other special functions of the Intelligence is. When, for example, an external object makes an impression upon one or more of the organs of Sense through this function, there is an instant and spontaneous apprehension of the *cause* of that impression. Before that cause is *distinctly* perceived, however, the perceptive faculty must, by a voluntary act of attention, be directed particularly to the object. The specific control which the Will thus exercises over this faculty, clearly indicates it, as a special function of the Intelligence. Now a relation precisely similar, as shown above, in respect to its spontaneous, and reflective determinations, does the Will exercise over Consciousness. We have the same evidence that it is a special function of the Intelligence, that we have that Sense is.

THEORY OF DR. BROWN.

I will close my remarks upon the subject of Consciousness, by a reference to the theory of Dr. Brown in respect to it. Consciousness, according to this philosopher, is simply a general term expressive of all the phenomena or states of the mind. "Sensation," he says, for example, "is not an object of Consciousness differing from itself, but a particular sensation is the consciousness of the moment, as a particular hope, or fear, or grief, or resentment, or simple remembrance, may be the actual consciousness of the next moment."

A single example will fully demonstrate the incorrectness of this theory. I affirm (what is actually true), to myself, or some other individual, that I am in pain. This affirmation implies three things — the existence of the feeling as a state of the Sensibility — an apprehension of pain in general, together with that of the particular feeling referred to — and a reference of that feeling to myself as the subject, this apprehension and reference being exclusively states of the Intelligence. Now this knowledge of the feeling under consideration, with its reference to myself as the subject, is an act of Consciousness; an exercise of the Intelligence which accompanies all mental states, and which differs as much from sensation, or any other state of the Sensibility, as thought differs from such states. Sensation then is an object of Consciousness differing from itself. The same holds true in respect to all mental exercises. The state itself is one thing. The knowledge of that state, and reference of it to ourselves is quite another. This last exercise of the Intelligence is Consciousness, an exercise as distinct from the state of which it takes cognizance, as that state is from the object which causes it.

MEANING OF THE TERM CONSCIOUSNESS, AS EMPLOYED BY SIR WILLIAM HAMILTON.

There is an apparent, though not real, discrepancy, if not contradiction, in the analysis of the Intellectual faculties, as given by Sir William Hamilton, and that developed in this Treatise, as far as the function of Consciousness is concerned. This discrepancy, on careful examination, however, will be found to consist, not in the analysis itself, but simply and exclusively in the use of terms, which each philosopher is permitted to employ according to his own definition. For the term Consciousness, as defined and employed in this Treatise, he substitutes that of Self-Consciousness, which, as the following paragraph will show, he uses in strict conformity to the definition above referred to. In the same paragraph also, he defines "External Perception or Perception simply," in perfect accordance with that given of the term Sense, as employed in this Treatise.

"*External Perception* or *Perception* simply, is the faculty *presentative* or *intuitive* of the *Non-Ego* or Matter, if there be any *intuitive* apprehension allowed of the *Non-Ego* at all. *Internal Perception*, as Self-Consciousness, is the faculty *presentative* or *intuitive* of the phenomena of the *Ego* or mind."

In a subsequent paragraph, he defines Consciousness itself, as the *general* faculty of *Intuition*. As thus defined, it would include Sense, Consciousness, and Reason, as these terms are defined and employed in this Treatise, and would differ from each of these functions of the Intelligence, only as the whole differs from each of its parts. "Consciousness," he says, "is a knowledge *solely of what is now here present* to the mind. It is therefore only intuitive, and its objects exclusively presentative. Again, Consciousness is a knowledge of *all that is now here present* to the mind: every immediate object of cognition is thus an object of Consciousness, and every intuitive cognition itself, simply a special form of Consciousness."

When, therefore, our author affirms that we are *immediately* conscious of the existence of the "*Non-Ego* or Matter," that is, of its primary qualities, he means, not that such qualities are the immediate objects of Self-Consciousness, as he has defined the term, that is, of Consciousness as defined in this Treatise, but that they are the immediate, that is, the "presentative or intuitive" objects of the faculty of "External Perception, or Perception simply," that is, of Sense, as this function of the Intelligence is defined in this Treatise. No difference of opinion obtains, therefore, between us and our author, so far as the analysis of the primary faculties themselves of the Intelligence is concerned. The only difference, which does obtain, is in the use of terms, in respect to which even, we would not willingly depart from such authority as Sir William Hamilton, but for the fact, that a single term is needed in a Treatise like this, to express each special function of the Intelligence, that the nomenclature which we have adopted has this special advantage over that adopted by our author, and that, with all, it is equally definite, and is now very generally obtaining in mental philosophy.

CHAPTER VI.

SENSE.

SENSE has already been defined, as that Faculty or Function of the Intelligence, by which we apprehend the phenomena, or qualities [primary qualities, as we shall hereafter see] of external material substances.

As thus defined, the exercise of this faculty should be carefully distinguished from those states of the Sensibility denominated *sensations*, states which always accompany external perception, but which are, notwithstanding, none the less, for that reason, distinct from it. Sensation is *that state of the Sensibility which immediately succeeds any impression made by any cause upon the physical organization.* Sensation is exclusively a state of the Sensibility. Sense is no less exclusively a function of the Intelligence. Of these distinctions we should never lose sight, when reasoning upon this department of mental science.

SPONTANEOUS AND VOLUNTARY DETERMINATION OF SENSE.

Sense, like Consciousness, is, in its primitive developments, a simple spontaniety of the Intelligence. Its action, in this state, is, in no degree, conditioned on that of the Will. Perception, in its *distinct* form, is conditioned on attention, which is nothing but the perceptive faculty directed by the Will, and hence, for the want of a better term, or phrase, called the voluntary determination of the faculty. Attention in the direction of Consciousness, that is, when directed to mental phenomena — is called *reflection.* When in the direction of the faculty of external perception — that is, towards the phenomena of material substances — it is called *observation.*

The necessity of observation, that is, of attention, in the voluntary direction of the perceptive faculty towards phenomena obscurely given in the spontaneous developments of that faculty, may be readily illustrated. A portion of a congregation, for example, who have been listening to a certain speaker, have fallen into a state of slumber. The speaker suddenly stops, and immediately are all aroused. Now, if the audience had not, in some form, heard the voice which broke upon their ears, why were they roused? Yet, if inquired of, in respect to what had been spoken to them, they would, for the obvious and exclusive reason, that they had not attended to it, be wholly unable to answer. How often do we hear the remark, I gained no distinct conception of that part of a discourse. My attention happened, at the time, to be directed to something else.

The attention may, in some instances, be so fixed upon some object in one direction, that the Sensibility and Intelligence both may be almost, if not quite, totally isolated from what would otherwise deeply affect us in another direction. A gentleman, for example, who was employed about the machinery in a factory, had one of his fingers entirely cut off, by the sudden and unexpected starting of a portion of that machinery which carried, with great velocity, a circular saw. So intensely did his attention instantly become occupied with the prevention of the destruction of the whole machinery, that he was not aware of the injury done to his own person, nor was he sensible of the least pain from it, till the accident was pointed out to him by another who stood by. As soon, however, as the injury was discovered, the pain from it became intense.

The *basis* of attention is the spontaneous action of the Sensibility and Intelligence — action which always occurs, when the proper conditions are fulfilled, and when the mind is not isolated from objects in other directions, by its intense action upon some object (as in the case above cited), in some specific direction.

MENTAL PROCESS IN PERCEPTION.

The process of the mind, in the perception of external objects, is doubtless originally something like this: An impression is made upon the Sensibility, or a sensation is produced, by the action of some external material object upon the physical organization. In connection with the sensation, there is a direct and immediate spontaneous apprehension (perception), of the presence and quality (primary quality, as we shall hereafter see), of the object which caused the sensation. To this quality the attention, by an act of volition, is then directed. Thus the apprehension or perception becomes clear and distinct. Sensation always, as a matter of fact, accompanies Sense-perception. Sensation, also, is the *occasion* of the perception, but not its cause, that cause being always found in the correlation between the nature of the Intelligence, as a *faculty*, and that of the Non-Ego or Matter, as an *object* of knowledge.*

* The distinction between a *condition*, and a *cause* of a given event is obvious, and may be readily elucidated. The removal of an obstruction may be the occasion of the descent of a heavy body towards the earth; but it is, in no proper sense, the cause of such an occurrence, the principle of attraction being itself the real cause. So, in the language of Sir William Hamilton, "Sensation proper is the *condition*

OBJECTS OF PERCEPTION.

The *objects* of Sense-perceptions, which, as we shall hereafter show, always pertain directly and immediately to said objects, are the *qualities* (primary or secundo-primary qualities, terms hereafter to be defined) of external material substances, qualities, such, for example, as extension, form, solidity, &c. The secondary qualities, such as those of taste, smell, sound, &c., are apprehended *indirectly* and *mediately*, through, and in the consciousness of sensations. Such qualities are to us the index, and the only index we have, of the nature of their respective subjects. In the consciousness of thought, feeling, and acts of will, we know ourselves, as thinking, feeling, and acting beings. So in the consciousness of Sense-perceptions, and sensations, produced in us by external material substances, we know such substances as the *subjects* of the qualities thus perceived and apprehended.

COMMON AND PHILOSOPHIC DOUBTS IN RESPECT TO THE COMPARATIVE VALIDITY OF THE AFFIRMATIONS OF SENSE AND CONSCIOUSNESS.

While the mass of mankind appear to exercise more confidence, theoretically, in the testimony of Sense than in that of Consciousness, the case seems, in many instances, to be reversed in respect to philosophers. The testimony of Consciousness the latter appear to regard as valid in respect to *subjective*, while that of Sense is not, in their estimation, equally so in respect to *objective* phenomena. Now the reason of the presence of these phiiosophic doubts, as Coleridge would call them, in the latter instance, and of their absence in the

sine qua non of a perception proper of the primary qualities." The cause proper of the perception, on the other hand, is found, as said above, in the correlation between the nature of the Intelligence, as a *faculty* and of the Non-Ego or Matter as an *object* of perception.

former, arises, as I suppose, from the fact that philosophers have attempted to explain the *quo modo* of external perception, and not that of internal. This is the very reason for the doubts under consideration, assigned by Coleridge himself. "As this," he says [to wit, the belief *that there exist things without us*], "on the one hand, originates neither in grounds nor arguments, and yet, on the other hand, remains proof against all attempts to move it by grounds or arguments (*natura furca expellas tamen usque redebit*); on the one hand, lays claim to IMMEDIATE certainty as a position at once indemonstrable and irresistible; and yet, on the other hand, inasmuch as it refers to something essentially different from ourselves, nay, even in opposition to ourselves, leaves it inconceivable how it could possibly become a part of our immediate Consciousness (in other words, how that which is *ex hypothesi* continues intrinsic and alien to our being); the philosopher, therefore, compels himself to treat this faith as nothing more than a prejudice, innate indeed and connatural, but still a prejudice." Now why does this philosopher compel himself to treat as a groundless prejudice and an untruth that which himself acknowledges to be an innate, connatural belief, an irresistible affirmation of his own and of the universal Intelligence? Simply because he cannot explain the *quo modo* of external perception — cannot see *how* an object not ourselves, and wholly unlike ourselves, as matter is universally conceived to be, should be to us an object of knowledge. If that is a reason why we should compel ourselves to treat as false what we know to be true, it should certainly induce us to treat his theory as equally false. For how can we explain the *manner* in which that which is intrinsic and a part of ourselves, should be presented to us, by our Intelligence, as wholly extrinsic and foreign, and even opposed to ourselves — how it can present that which is exclusively *subjective*, as wholly *ob-*

jective—that which is purely spiritual, as wholly material—that, in short, which is "without form and void," as possessed of a definite form? The *quò modo* of knowledge, according to this last theory, would be found quite as difficult of explanation as in conformity to any other whatever.

Let us now suppose that philosophers should undertake to explain the *quo modo* of knowledge by Consciousness. How, for example, can I perceive and attend to an object external to myself, and yet have, at the same time, a consciousness equally distinct of the act of perception itself? Suppose they should attempt to explain such mysterious acts of the Intelligence as these, and at the same time compel themselves to treat as a prejudice all mental affirmations, the mode of origination of which they cannot explain. Would not their philosophic doubts be quite as strong in respect to the validity of Consciousness, as with regard to that of any other function of the Intelligence?

THE PROVINCE OF PHILOSOPHY.

Philosophy, it should be borne in mind, has to do with facts as they are, with the nature of the powers revealed in those facts, and with the laws in conformity to which those powers act. With the mode of their action, further than this, it has nothing to do. In the fall of heavy bodies to the earth, for example, we learn that attraction is a property of all material substances. We then set ourselves to determine the law which controls the action of this property. Here we are within the legitimate domain of philosophy. But suppose we attempt to explain the *mode* in which the attractive power acts. "Such knowledge is too wonderful for us. It is high, we cannot attain unto it." Philosophy, well satisfied with her own legitimate and wide domain, resigns such things to the Eternal One, who created all the powers of the universe, and consequently understands the mode of their action. All that philosophy can say in regard to the mode of action of any power is, that such is its nature.

COMPARATIVE VALIDITY OF THE AFFIRMATIONS OF SENSE AND CONSCIOUSNESS.

We are now prepared to contemplate the comparative validity of the affirmations of these two functions of the Intelligence, Sense and Consciousness. I will suppose that I have a perception of some external object, as possessed of the qualities of extension, form, and color. In Consciousness I recognize the existence of this perception as a phenomenon of my own mind. Which of these affirmations are, in reality, the most valid, and which would a wise and sound philosophy impel me to esteem and treat as such — the affirmation of Sense, in respect to the qualities of the external object, or of Consciousness, in regard to the existence and character of the affirmation of the former faculty, as a phenomenon of the Mind itself? Neither, surely. Each faculty pertains alike to its object, by direct and immediate intuition. The affirmation of each is alike positive and absolute in respect to its object. The action of one is, in reality, no more a mystery than that of the other. The *quo modo* of the action of each is alike inexplicable, and no more inexplicable than the mode of action of every other power in existence. It is a sage remark of Dr. Brown, when speaking of the mode in which causes produce their respective effects, that "*everything* is mysterious, or nothing is." When philosophy leads us to doubt the real affirmations of any faculty of the Intelligence, then philosophy itself becomes impossible, and the attempt to realize it, the perfection of absurdity.

TRUE THEORY OF EXTERNAL PERCEPTION.

The way is now prepared for an enunciation of the theory

of external perception, taught in this Treatise. Knowledge implies two things, an *object* to be known, and a *subject* capable of knowing. Between the nature of the subject and object there must be such a mutual correlation, that, when certain conditions are fulfilled, knowledge arises, as a necessary result of this correlation. Between matter and mind this correlation exists. The latter knows the former, because the one is a *faculty*, and the other an *object* of knowledge. Mind perceives the qualities of matter, because the former has the *power* of perception, and the latter is an *object* of perception.

Mind also exists in a tri-unity, consisting, as we have seen, of the Intelligence, Sensibility, and Will. To each of these departments of our nature, the external world is correlated. Certain conditions being fulfilled, particular qualities of material substances become to the Intelligence, direct objects of knowledge. Other conditions being fulfilled, they affect our Sensibility, producing in us certain sensations, either pleasurable, painful, or indifferent. Our Will then acts upon these substances, controlling their movements, and modifying their states, while they, in turn, react upon the Will, modifying and limiting its control. In the first instance, knowledge is direct and immediate. In the second, through a consciousness of sensations, we learn the correlation between those objects and our sensibility. In the last, through a consciousness of the nisuses of our Will, and an experience of their results, we learn the correlation between these substances and our voluntary powers. In respect to the *manner* in which, when certain conditions are fulfilled, we know these objects, the only answer that philosophy gives or demands, is this: Such is the correlation between the nature of the knowing faculty and that of the objects of knowledge.

Theory Verified.

It is a sufficient verification of the theory above announced, that it is a statement of the case, as it presents itself to the universal Intelligence — that it is encumbered with no difficulties which are not involved in every theory of a different kind which has hitherto been presented, and is entirely free from those difficulties which are perfectly fatal to those theories. Every individual believes, that he knows the external world as correlated to the threefold departments of our nature under consideration, and in accordance with the principles above stated. Every theory also must rest, in the last analysis, in respect to the *mode* of knowledge, upon this one principle, *The mind knows, because it is a faculty of knowledge.* The difficulties which all theories, contradictory to that above announced, involve, are these: either they do not present the facts or conditions of knowledge, or the manner of knowing, as they are given in the universal Intelligence.

THE ABOVE THEORY VERIFIED AS A TRUTH OF SCIENCE.

As this Theory, however, is regarded, by the author of this Treatise, not only as true, but also as of fundamental importance in philosophy, a more extended and logical verification of it is deemed requisite, than that above given.

QUALITIES OF MATTER.

In accomplishing the object which I have in view, I would, in the first place, direct special attention to a consideration of the *qualities* of matter, as given in the universal Intelligence. According to Sir William Hamilton, such qualities may, and according to a strictly scientific arrangement, should be classed as, Primary-proper, Secundo-primary, and Secondary.

Primary qualities.

The first class, Primary-proper, include all those properties which belong to Matter, as such, and which cannot, in thought even, be separated from it as Matter. The necessary constituents of our idea of Matter, as such, are two, that it *occupies* space, and is *contained in* space. Hence, in the language of the author referred to, "we have thus eight proximate attributes: 1. Extension; 2. Divisibility; 3. Size; 4. Density or Rarity; 5. Figure; 6. Incompressibility absolute; 7. Mobility; 8. Situation." That which occupies space, and is contained in it, must have extension; else it would fulfill neither of these conditions. An extended substance occupying space and, at the same time, contained it, must also, be divisible, on the one hand, and possess size, on the other, Size which refers to the *quantity of space* which the substance occupies. When, on the other hand, we refer to the quantity of *matter* occupying space, we attain to the conception of the quality of Density or Rarity. That also which has Extension and Size must have Form or Figure. That too which occupies space, and is contained in it, must be susceptible of motion from one point of space to another, and must, at each successive moment, have a given situation in space. Hence we have the idea of the qualities of Mobility and Situation. These then must be reckoned as the qualities Primary-proper of Matter. They distinguish no one kind of material substance from another, but Matter itself from every other substance, and cannot, even in thought, be separated from it, as Matter.

Secundo-primary qualities.

The Secundo-primary qualities are those which pertain, not to Matter, as such, but which distinguish different *classes* of material substances from one another, and which pertain, as essential qualities, to such classes. Thus bodies are classed, in reference to their Gravity and Cohesion, also as Heavy and Light, as Hard and Soft, Solid and Fluid, Viscid and Friable, Tough and Brittle, Rigid and Flexible, Fissile and Infissile, Ductile and Inductile, Elastic and Inelastic, Rough and Smooth, Slippery and Tenacious, Compressible and Incompressible, Resilient and Irresilient, Movable and Immovable. I name the qualities, as given by the author above referred to. The classification is undeniably correct, and complete.

Secondary qualities.

The Secondary qualities are, properly speaking, subjective affections in ourselves, and not properties of Matter at all. They pertain to Matter, only as the causes, unperceived in themselves, of these affections or sensations. Such, for example, are the qualities represented by the terms Sound, Flavor, Savor, Tactual sensation, &c.

Whatever may be thought of the propriety of the phraseology adopted, no one can doubt the reality of the distinctions above made, or the consequent propriety of the corresponding classification of the qualities of Matter. My own opinion is, that it would be as well to retain, for the sake of convenience, the old classification of Primary and Secondary, making a subdivision of the first class, as Primary-proper and Secundo-primary.

What these qualities are in general.

As no form of statement can excel that given by our author of the *general characteristics* of these three classes of qualities, I will venture to take from his writings the following extract, in which we have a specific statement of such characteristics:

"1. The primary are less properly denominated Qualities (Suchnesses), and deserve the name only as we conceive them to distinguish body from not body — corporeal from incoporeal substance. They are thus merely the attributes of *body as body* — *corporis ut corpus.*

"The Secundo-primary and Secondary, on the contrary, are in strict propriety denominated Qualities, for they discriminate body from body. They are the attributes of *body, as this or that kind of body* — *corporis ut tale corpus.*

"2. The Primary rise from the universal relations of body to itself; the Secundo-primary from the general relations of this body to that; the Secondary from the special relations of this kind of body to this kind of animated or sentient organism.

"3. The Primary determine the possibility of matter absolutely; the Secundo-primary the possibility of the material universe as actually constituted; the Secondary the possibility of our relations as sentient existences to that universe.

"4. Under the Primary we apprehend modes of the *Non-ego;* under the Secundo-primary we apprehend modes both of the *Ego* and of the *Non-Ego;* under the Secondary we apprehend modes of the *Ego,* and infer modes of the *Non-Ego.*

"5. The Primary are apprehended as they are in bodies; the Secondary as they are in us; the Secundo-primary as they are in bodies, and as they are in us.

"6. The term *quality* in general, and the names of the qualities in particular, are — in the case of the Primary, unuivocal, one designation unambiguously marking out one quality — in the case of the Secundo-primary and Secondary equivocal, a single term being ambiguously applied to denote two qualities, distinct though correlative — that, to wit, which is the mode of existence in bodies, and which is a mode of affection in one organism.

"7. The Primary and also the Secundo-primary qualities are definite in number and exhaustive, for all conceivable relations of body to itself, or of body to body merely, are few, and all these found actually existent. The Secondary, on the contrary, are in number indefinite; and they actually hold no proportion to the possible. For we can suppose in animal organism, any number of unknown capacities of being variously affected, and, in matter, any number of unknown powers of thus affecting it, and this though we are unable to imagine to ourselves what these actually may be."

As our author subsequently shows, the "Primary are conceived as necessary and perceived as actual; the Secundo-primary are perceived and conceived as actual; the Secondary are inferred and conceived as possible." "The Primary are perceived as conceived. The Secundo-primary are conceived as perceived. The Secondary are neither perceived as conceived, nor conceived as perceived; for to perception they are occult, and are conceived only as latent causes to account for manifest effects." The Primary are given in Consciousness, as "modes of a not-self;" the Secondary as "modes of self;" and the Secundo-primary as "modes of self and of a not-self at once." — "In the apppehension of the Primary qualities the mind is primarily and principally active; it feels only as it knows. In that of the Secondary, the mind is primarily and principally passive; it knows only as it feels. In the Secundo-primary the mind is equally and at once active and passive; in one respect it feels as it knows, in another, it knows as it feels." Hence, as our author might have shown, our knowledge of the Primary qualities is given in our minds, as valid for all Intelligents. Our knowledge of the Secundo-primary is given, as, in one form, valid for all Intelligents, and in another, as valid only for ourselves in the present constitution of our sensitive nature. Our knowledge of the Secondary qualities is given, as valid for ourselves exclusively, and that in the sense last named.

REPRESENTATIVE AND PRESENTATIVE KNOWLEDGE.

Every one is accustomed to distinguish between that kind of knowledge which is *direct* and *immediate,* and that which is obtained, *mediately,* that is, through something differing numerically from the *object* of knowledge. The former kind of knowledge, Sir William Hamilton denominates *Presentative,* and the latter, *Representative* knowledge. "An immediate cognition," he says, "inasmuch as the thing known is *itself presented* to observation, may be called presentative, and inasmuch as the thing presented is, as it were, *viewed by the mind face to face,* may be called intuitive. A mediate cognition, inasmuch as the thing known is held up or mirrored to the mind in a vicarious representation, may be called a representative cognition." No remarks are necessary to show the reality of the above distinction, or the propriety of the phraseology employed to represent it.

TRUE THEORY OF PERCEPTION STATED AND VERIFIED.

I now lay down the following propositions pertaining to our knowledge of the qualities of matter, propositions which I will then proceed to verify: 1. Our knowledge of qualities Primary-proper of matter is exclusively *Presentative,* that is, is not *mediate,* but *direct* and *immediate* or *intuitive.* 2. Our knowledge of the Secundo-primary qualities is *partly Presentative,* and *partly Representative.* 3. Our knowledge of the Secondary qualities, is wholly and exclusively *Representative,* such qualities being revealed to us, only as the unknown causes of known sensations, and revealed also, as exclusively through such sensations.

That our knowledge of the Secondary qualities is wholly, and of the Secundo-primary, partly, to say the least, Representative, no one will deny. The only question that can arise, pertains to the *matter of fact*, whether our knowledge of the Primary qualities, and of the Secundo-primary is, in *any form*, Presentative, and not like that of the Secondary, wholly and exclusively Representative. That we have a direct and immediate, that is, Presentative knowledge of the two classes of qualities first named, to wit, the Primary, and Secundo-primary, I argue from the following considerations:

1. The fact of such knowledge cannot be shown, *à priori*, to be, in itself, impossible. If an individual should affirm, that things equal to the same things are not equal to one another, we should have no occasion to appeal to experience to determine the question, whether such a proposition is, or is not, true. Prior to such an appeal, or *à priori*, we know absolutely, from the nature of the case, that such a proposition is not, and cannot be true. Can we thus know, that a presentative knowledge of the qualities referred to, is in itself, an impossibility? Certainly not, and who will affirm the truth of the contrary proposition? Neither the *existence*, nor the *extent* or *limits*, of the Faculty of Knowledge, can be known, *à priori*. The existence of the *power* of knowledge is revealed wholly and exclusively, through the *fact* of knowledge. The extent and limits of the possible reach that power, can be determined, as exclusively, only by what the mind actually does know, and by what is logically implied in such knowledge. We can know, *à priori*, that knowledge cannot extend beyond the compass of realities. But how far such realities are, to the intelligence, *real* or *possible*, objects of knowledge, or what realities do, in fact exist as objects of knowledge, cannot be known at all, *à priori*, but, as said above, wholly and exclusively, by a reference to what the mind does, in fact, know, and to what is necessarily implied in such knowledge. Suppose, that extended substances actually occupy space, and exist

in it, and the Intelligence cannot affirm the reality of such existences, to be a natural impossibility, who will pretend to say, that a faculty of knowledge may not be given, to which the essential qualities of such substances, as Matter, and as particular classes of Matter, shall be objects of direct, and immediate or Presentative knowledge? Who will pretend, then, to know, *à priori*, that the human Intelligence, in the very condition of its present existence, is not, in fact, just such a faculty; that such qualities do not, in fact, exist, sustaining to it the relation of *objects*, while it sustains to them the relation of a *power* of real Presentative knowledge? The reality of such qualities as objects, and of the Intelligence, as a power of such knowledge, cannot be intelligently affirmed to be, in itself, impossible. Hence, no evidence does, or can exist, *à priori*, against the truth of the propositions under consideration.

2. It cannot be shown, *à posteriori*, that is, by an appeal to facts, that such knowledge does not, in fact, exist in the human Intelligence. We are absolutely conscious, that our knowledge of the Secondary qualities of Matter is not Presentative, but wholly and exclusively Representative. Have we, in fact, a similar consciousness, in reference to our knowledge of the Primary and Secundo-primary qualities of the same substance? The Secondary qualities are consciously given, in the Intelligence, wholly inferrentially as the unknown causes of known sensations. Is the quality of extension, in Matter, for example, given in the same Intelligence, consciously in the same manner, and as a precisely similar cause of a similar feeling? On the other hand, while the Secondary quality is given, in Consciousness, as the *unknown cause* of a *known state* of the *Sensibility;* is not the primary quality given, as a *known object* of a *known state* of the *Intelligence?* We are

conscious, that a state of the Sensibility lies between the Intelligence, and the unknown cause of that state, the Secondary quality, and that the reality of that cause is not directly perceived, but inferred. Are we also conscious, that a known sensation, or state of the Sensibility, lies between the known act of the Intelligence above referred to, and its known object, the Primary quality, that the sensation is, and the quality is not, the immediate object of perception, and that, consequently, the quality is consciously not perceived, but its reality, *mediately* inferred? If our knowledge of the Primary qualities of matter is not Presentative, but wholly and exclusively Representative, no one will pretend that we have a consciousness of the fact; nor will any one attempt to prove the fact, *à posteriori*, by an appeal to the facts of Consciousness.

Nor can the same fact be established by an appeal to any known facts connected with the condition of the mind, as connected with its *physical organization*. What shall be the extent, limits, or modes of its knowledges, in connection with such an organization, or whether it knows all or any of the facts referred to mediately or immediately, cannot be determined, *à priori*. All such questions can be intelligently answered, but by an appeal to Consciousness. Now we are not conscious, at all, that all our knowledge of the facts referred to, the Primary qualities of our own physical organism, for example, is, in no form, Presentative, but wholly and exclusively Representative.

Nor do any other known facts anywhere exist, in the universe of Matter or Mind, from which we can draw the inference that our knowledge of these qualities is not Presentative. The proposition that this knowledge is Representative, then, is neither a necessary intuitive truth, nor is it capable of being established, *à posteriori*, that is, by an appeal to facts.

3. Hence, I remark, in the next place, that the theory, that all our knowledge of Matter, is exclusively Representative, that is, through the consciousness of Sensations, rests upon absolutely nothing but a baseless assumption, an assumption wholly unsustained by any form or degree of evidence, *à priori*, or *à posteriori*, that is, an assumption neither self-evidently true, nor sustained by any known facts of Matter or of Mind. The only merit that can be claimed for it is, that like all false theories in mental science, it rests upon a partial induction of the facts of Consciousness. That all our knowledge of the Secondary qualities of Matter is exclusively Representative, and derived wholly through a known medium, Sensation, is an absolute fact of Consciousness. Upon this simple fact, the assumption, on which Philosophy, in all ages, has run off the track of truth, has been based, to wit, that *all* our knowledge of *all* the qualities of the same substance, is, and must be, of the same character, and derived exclusively through the same medium. No assumption conceivable is, or can be, more unreasonable in itself, or more unphilosophically induced. How unreasonable the assumption, that because qualities of a given character, and universally recognized as not fundamental, are known in a given manner, that therefore qualities of a totally different and opposite character, and universally recognized as fundamental, must be known in the same manner, and through the same uncertain medium.

4. The *origin* of this assumption should not be overlooked, in this connection, as having a not unimportant bearing upon our present inquiries. This assumption had its origin in an attempt to determine, *à priori*, the *nature*, *extent*, *limits* and *mode* of human knowledge, facts none of which can, by any possibility, be determined only *à posteriori*, or by an appeal to Consciousness. These are all, it should be borne in mind, as

facts, contingent and not necessary truths. They cannot, therefore, be determined, *à priori*, but must be resolved wholly *à posteriori*. This assumption, therefore, is the exclusive result of a most unscientific procedure in philosophy, a procedure in which mere guessing has ever been substituted for certain knowledge, when the latter was in the immediate presence of the philosopher, and when no higher merit was attained, than very poor guessing at that.

5. I now adduce, in favor of the truth of the three propositions under consideration, to wit, that our knowledge of the Primary qualities of Matter is wholly Presentative, that that of the Secundary-primary is partly Presentative and partly Representative, and finally, that that of the Secondary is wholly Representative, the direct, immediate, and absolute testimony of universal Consciousness. No one will deny, that in the universal Consciousness, the Primary quality is recognized as the known *object* of a known act of the Intelligence (Sense-perception), and that the Secondary quality is also recognized as the unknown *cause* of a known state of the Sensibility (Sensation). Nor does any one doubt that our knowledge of the Sensation itself is Presentative, wholly so. Now, in all proper Sense-perceptions, we have, undeniably, just as distinct and absolute a consciousness of a direct and immediate or Presentative aspect or knowledge of the Primary quality, extension for example, as we have of the Sensation itself, when produced by the unknown cause referred to, the Secondary quality. It would be a denial of the facts of Consciousness no more palpable, to affirm, that our knowledge of Sensation itself is wholly Representative, than it would be, to affirm, that our knowledge of the Primary qualities is not Presentative. No honest interpreter of the facts of Consciousness will deny the truth of these statements. The truth of the propositions under consideration can be denied, but upon one assumption,

that the same faculty affirms, with the same absoluteness, what is true in regard to Sensation, and what is not true in regard to Sense-perception. The true and only true interpretation of the facts of Consciousness, on the subject, is this: The Primary qualities are given in Consciousness, exclusively as the known presentative objects of known acts of the Intelligence, Sense-perceptions. The same holds true of the Secundo-primary, so far as they are given as qualities of Matter. So far forth as they are given as causes of Sensations, they are given as the otherwise unknown causes of known states of the Sensibility. The Secondary, on the other hand, are given exclusively as such causes of such states, and in no other form as objects of knowledge. In reference to the Secondary qualities, and of the Secundo-primary, so far forth as they are given as causes of sensations, we are conscious of the presence of a *medium* between us and the object of knowledge, and that it is wholly *through* such medium that the object is known. In reference to the Primary qualities, and the Secundo-primary, so far as the latter are regarded as essential qualities of their respective subjects, we are conscious of no medium between us and the object of knowledge, and still less of the fact, that it is wholly through such medium that the object is known. We can therefore, by no possibility, have a consciousness, that any form of knowledge whatever is Presentative, if we have not that such is the character of our knowledge of the qualities last named.

6. I remark, in the next place, that our knowledge of the Primary qualities has all the essential *characteristics* of Presentative, and none of those of Representative knowledge; while that of the Secondary has all of the characteristics of Representative, and none of those of Presentative knowledge. Our knowledge of the Secundo-primary, on the other hand, so far forth as they are given, as objects of Sense-perceptions, has

all, and exclusively, the characteristics Presentative, and so far forth, as they are given as causes of sensations, has all, and exclusively, the characteristics of Representative knowledge. In Representative knowledge, the object is never given, as *perceived*, but its reality exclusively, as *inferred*; precisely the opposite obtains, in all respects, in Presentative knowledge. In this case, the object is given, as known in itself, that is, its reality is given, not as *inferred*, but as *perceived*. These are the fundamental distinctions between Presentative and Representative knowledge.

Now the Secondary qualities of matter are given, in our Intelligence, as not known in themselves. Their reality is given exclusively, as inferred, as known only relatively. The Primary qualities are given exclusively, as known in themselves, and their reality as perceived, and not as inferred. The Secundo-primary are given partly, as perceived, and partly, as inferred, and that just so far forth as they rank with the Primary, on the one hand, and with the Secondary, on the other. We experience a sensation pleasurable or painful. We affirm, that it had a cause, and that in the cause, there is a quality adapted to affect our Sensibility, in the manner referred to, while that Sensibility remains constituted as it now is. The reality of the cause and the quality is given, as not perceived, but inferred, and the nature of the quality, not as known as it is in itself, but only relatively to our Sensibility. The Primary quality, on the other hand, that of extension for example, is given as known in itself, and its reality is affirmed as perceived, and not as inferred as the unknown cause of a known sensation, as is true of the Secondary qualities. The same holds true of all the Primary qualities, and of the Secundo-primary, so far as the latter take rank with the former. We can, by no possibility, make a distinction between Presentative and Representative knowledge, if we have not these two kinds of knowledge before us, if our knowledge of the Primary qualities of Matter is not exclusively of the former kind, and of the Secondary of the latter, and if that of the Secundo-primary does not, in the sense explained, partake partly of both.

7. There are also undeniable *facts* of Consciousness which can be explained but upon the admission of the truth of the propositions which I am now endeavoring to establish. It will not be denied either, that our knowledge of the Primary, and, in the sense explained, of the Secundo-primary qualities of Matter, is Presentative, or that *all* our knowledge of Matter is equally and in the same sense Representative, and derived entirely through the same medium, Sensation. On the latter supposition, all qualities alike should be given, in precisely the same form, as exclusively the unknown causes of known sensations, and all alike given, not as known in themselves, but only relatively. Their reality also should be given, as not perceived, but inferred. Now how can one class of qualities, all of which are alike exclusively objects of Representative knowledge, and known as exclusively through the same identical medium, be given in Consciousness, as the objects exclusively of Presentative and the other as exclusively of Representative knowledge; the one class as known in themselves, and the other as known only relatively; the one class, as exclusively the known objects of known perceptions, and the other with equal exclusiveness, as the unknown causes of known sensations; the one class as directly perceived, and the other as merely inferred qualities? On this theory, the theater of Consciousness is one exclusive scene of palpable contradictions more irreconcilable than the discords of Chaos and Old Night. If, on the other hand, we suppose that our knowledge of the Primary qualities is really and truly Presentative, and that of the Secondary as really and truly Representative, and finally,

that that of the Secundo-primary blends, in the sense explained, both forms of knowledge, then all the facts of Consciousness bearing upon the subject, are susceptible of a ready and perfectly consistent explanation, and they can be explained upon no other supposition.

8. I remark, finally, that the *existence* of the *conceptions* of these qualities, just as they lie in the Consciousness, can, by no possibility, be accounted for, on the supposition, that all our knowledge of Matter is derived exclusively through Sensation, and can be accounted for but upon the assumption of the truth of the propositions which I am endeavoring to establish. We will take, as an example, one quality, that of *extension*. The conception of this quality must have had its origin primarily in the mind, in consequence of the quality itself having been originally the object of immediate perception, that is, of Presentative knowledge; or it must have been derived mediately, as the logical antecedent or consequent of sensation. The direct and immediate perception of the quality will account for the idea of said quality in the mind. Suppose we reject this supposition, and attempt to account for the existence of the idea mediately, as the logical antecedent or consequent of Sensation. If the idea be assumed as the logical antecedent of the consciousness of Sensation, then the reality of the quality must be supposed to account for the existence of the sensation itself. If, on the other hand, the idea be assumed as the logical consequent of the consciousness of the Sensation, then the quality must be held as an effect of the Sensation, and Sensation as the cause of said quality. No one will take the latter position. Let us, for a few moments, look at the former. As the cause of the sensation, the quality would be known not as it is in itself, but only as the unknown cause of a known sensitive state. It would be the object, not of

absolute but of *relative* knowledge. Further, nothing is necessarily supposed, in the cause, which is not as absolutely revealed in the effect. Now the sensation has, in itself, the phenomena, neither of length, breadth, nor thickness. How can the consciousness of such a phenomenon suggest even the idea of the quality of extension, as the cause of such a phenomenon? Nothing conceivable can be more unphilosophical than the supposition of such an origination of this idea. Its existence in the Intelligence can be scientifically accounted for, but upon one supposition, that the quality of extension was itself originally given as the object of Presentative knowledge. So of all the other Primary qualities of Matter, and of the Secundo-primary, so far as they take rank with the Primary.

The truth, then, of the propositions under consideration, may be assumed as a truth of science, and, as such, employed in the elucidation of the various functions of the Intelligence.

FALSE THEORIES OF EXTERNAL PERCEPTION.

Theories of Sense-perception differing from that above elucidated, Theories formed by philosophers to explain the manner in which the mind perceives external material objects, divide themselves into two classes — those which affirm, that our knowledge of such objects is real — and those which affirm that it is not real, and that all that we can know of such objects is our manner of conceiving of them.

Of the former Theories, there are two subdivisions, both agreeing in this, that our knowledge of Matter is, in no form, Presentative. The first affirms, that we know external material objects through the medium of certain *Images* existing between such objects and the faculty of knowledge. The second affirms, that all our knowledge of such objects is exclusively representative, and derived wholly through the medium of *Sensation*. The former I will venture to denominate the Scholastic Theory. The latter has, by Sir William Hamilton, been very properly denominated the Cosmothetic Theory. The Theories which affirm that our knowledge of matter is, in no sense, real or valid for the reality or true character of its object, we will denominate the Idealistic Theories. As thus designated, we will notice them, in the order named above.

THE SCHOLASTIC THEORY.

To all of the forms in which this Theory has been developed, says Mr. Dugal Stewart, "I apprehend the two following remarks will be found applicable: First, that in the formation of them, their authors have been influenced by some general maxims of philosophizing borrowed from physics; and, secondly, that they have been influenced by an indistinct, but deep-rooted conviction of the immateriality of the soul; which, although not precise enough to point out to them the absurdity of attempting to illustrate its operations by the analogy of matter, was yet sufficiently strong to induce them to keep the absurdity of their theories as far as possible out of view, by allusions to those physical facts, in which the distinctive properties are the least grossly and palpably exposed to our observation. To the former of these circumstances is to be ascribed the general principle upon which all the known theories of perception are produced, to the latter, the various metaphorical expressions of *ideas, species, forms, shadows, phantasms, images;* which, while they amused the fancy with some remote analogies to the object of our senses, did not directly revolt our reason." Very little in addition to the observations above cited, need be said upon these theories. They all agree in leaving totally unexplained the very difficulties which they profess to explain, to wit, How can the mind perceive an object out of itself, and at a distance from itself?

The image between the mind and the object, is as really distinct from the mind, and as really removed from it, though at a less distance, as the object itself. Perception of the intermediate image is just as difficult of explanation, and as truly needs another intermediate image, as perception of the object.

THE COSMOTHETICAL THEORY.

According to the Cosmothetic Theory, we have no Presentative knowledge whatever of the material universe. All such knowledge, on the other hand, is, as we have said above, altogether Representative, and derived exclusively, through the medium of Sensation. If the material universe had no existence, and we had the same sensations that we now have, sensations produced by any cause whatever, the immediate interposition of Deity, for example, we should have, from the laws of our Intelligence, precisely the same Sense-perceptions, apprehensions, and knowledge that we now have, and the external universe would be just as real to us, as it now is, and in all respects just what it is. God has so constituted our Intelligence, that, on occasion of these Sensations, our perceptions, &c., became what they are. We are so constituted also, that we instinctively *believe* the universe to be what we have conceived it, or rather *perhaps* imagined it, to be. In constituting us with such an instinctive belief, the divine veracity stands pledged, that what we thus believe in must be real: for God would not constitute us thus to believe in what is unreal. Thus we are required to believe in an external material universe, not because we have, in fact, in our experience, any actual knowledge or perception of its reality, any real evidence of the fact. Our belief, on the other hand, really rests upon such grounds as the following: 1. Such is the constitution of our intelligence, that on occasion of sensations induced in us, we conceive of an external material universe, as their cause. 2. From the laws of the same constitution also, we instinctively believe in the reality of that of which we have formed a conception. 3. In this constitution, we have a direct revelation from the author of nature, that what we thus apprehend and instinctively believe in as real, is real. 4. On the ground, therefore, not of our own perceptions and knowledges, but of the veracity of the author of nature, we believe in the reality of the material universe. This is the ground on which Christian Theists, holding the Sensational Theory, do, in fact, believe in the reality of the material universe, and is the only ground on which they can, by any possibility, believe in it. On this Theory we need only make the following remarks:

1. It has already been proved to be false.

2. It is in itself, most palpably self-destructive, and self-contradictory. According to it, God has so constituted our Consciousness, that, in it, the material universe is given, as, in very fundamental respects, the object of real Presentative, while it is, in fact, the exclusive object of Representative knowledge, and also that certain qualities of Matter are given, as the known objects of known states of the Intelligence, while they are, in fact, nothing but the unknown causes of known states of the Sensibility. Now if the author of nature has deceived us in the constitution of our Consciousness, why should we suppose, that He has not done the same thing, in reference to our instinctive beliefs? If the voice of the author of nature is to be heeded, in our Instinctive beliefs, why not, in the revelations of Consciousness? We should then be required to contradict this Theory, and hold, that certain qualities of matter are, in reality, what they are given, in our Consciousness, as being, to wit, the real objects of Presentative knowledge.

3. This Theory also involves a most vicious reasoning in a circle. We first reason from this very universe to the reality

of the Divine existence and attributes, and then backward from the reality of the Divine existence and attribues to that of the universe from which we started. We must first know the universe, at least as real, before we can reason at all, legitimately, from it, to its author or any of his attributes. If the universe, as this Theory affirms, is in reality in itself unknown to us, we can only find, through it, an unknown God, a God, from whose attributes, we cannot legitimately reason to anything. Nothing further need be added to prove that such a Theory cannot be true.

THE IDEALISTIC THEORIES.

Of the Theories which affirm, that our knowledge of the material universe is, in no sense real, some affirm, that there are no objects whatever external to the mind, that what we have postulated, as the qualities of objects external to us, are, in fact, nothing but our own mental states seen by the eye of Consciousness. This is the Theory of Coleridge, and of modern Transcendentalists generally. Others maintain the reality of something called mind, on the one hand, and of a something not mind, on the other. They deny, however, that the latter can be to the former, in any sense, an object of real knowledge, or that either is, in itself, what we take it to be. When this unknown something, having in itself neither extension nor form, and existing nowhere and in no time (inasmuch as neither time nor space are realities in themselves, but only modes in us of conceiving of things as external to us), when I say, this unknown and nameless something, in some unknown and nameless manner, affects the unknown something called mind — the latter, by virtue of laws innate in itself, postulates to itself its own sensations as the qualities of substances distinct from itself. Thus the great universe, in which we contemplate ourselves as existing, together with time and space, in which we contemplate ourselves and the universe as having being, is nothing in itself but a fiction of our own Intelligence. This is the theory of Kant, stated without caricature. Both the kinds of theories under consideration agree in this, that what our Intelligence postulates as the qualities of external substances, are, in reality, nothing but mental states seen by the eye of Consciousness. External perception is nothing but the eye of Consciousness directed to an affection wholly subjective, which the Intelligence postulates as the quality of something objective and external to the mind. In Consciousness, mental affections of different kinds are given as subjective and objective: that is, some are given as phenomena of the mind itself, and others as those of objects external to the mind. Hence, according to philosophers maintaining these theories, Consciousness has two distinct functions, the external and the internal. When taking cognizance of some affection which the Intelligence has postulated as a subjective phenomenon, this is Consciousness in the exercise of its *interior* function. When taking cognizance of some affection which the Intelligence postulates as a phenomenon of an object external to the mind, this is Consciousness in the exercise of its *exterior* function. Sense, according to these theories, is not a faculty of knowledge at all; but only a receptivity of affections or impressions, postulated by the Intelligence as the qualities of objects external to the mind. Thus that which we have been accustomed to regard as a real world external to the mind, and altogether unlike ourselves, has no existence out of ourselves. Neither the universe, nor its author have any existence in itself. They are mere ideals of our own creating; ideals grand and perfect, and which we are therefore bound to regard and revere, not as realities in themselves, but as grand conceptions — sublime creations of our own Intelligences, creations which are true, as Coleridge remarks simply and exclusively, "because we have conceived them."

Reasons for these Theories.

Among the reasons given for these theories, the most important, and all that I now need to notice, are the following:

1. They explain the *possibility* of knowledge. Of all things real to us, as objects of knowledge, we have a direct and immediate Consciousness. All objects of knowledge, therefore, are brought within the sphere of direct mental vision. The possibility of perception is thus fully demonstrated.

2. These theories render the *reality* and *certainty* of knowledge self-evident. If nothing exists in the object, but what our Intelligence has put there, our knowledge of the object must be real, certain, and absolute. If, for example, nothing exists in a contribution box but what I have put there, and I know what I have put into it, then my knowledge of what the box contains is real and absolute. So when I contemplate an object which my Intelligence has postulated as external to myself, if that object is in reality nothing but a pure creation of my Intelligence, and contains nothing but what the same Intelligence has put into it, how demonstrably manifest it is, that my knowledge of the object is real and absolute.

Objections to these Theories.

But while these theories apparently, at first thought, commend themselves to our minds, as explaining things which would otherwise be wholly inexplicable to us, they are at once, in our Intelligence, met with difficulties perfectly insurmountable.

1. They leave totally unexplained the same mystery hanging over the subject which they profess to explain, that hung over it before, to wit, the *possibility* of knowledge. The distance

between the subject and object of knowledge is, to be sure, greatly abridged; inasmuch as all things are brought under the immediate vision of Consciousness itself. A theory, however, which is valid as an explication of the *possibility* of knowledge, must explain the possibility, not of one, but of all kinds of knowledge. Now the theories under consideration, explain, in a certain form, the possibility of what is called external perception. But they leave wholly unexplained the possibility of knowledge of another kind, the possibility of which needs to be explained, just as much as that of the former, to wit, *the possibility of knowledge by Consciousness.* Suppose an explication of the possibility of a knowledge of our own mental states be demanded, what answer can be given, but that which is rejected as valid, in regard to the possibility of external perception — to wit, that Consciousness, relatively to mental states, is a *faculty*, and the states themselves are *objects* of perception, or knowledge. Now this explication, the only one possible, in the case under consideration, and indeed in any case whatever, is equally valid, as an explanation of the possibility of external perception. We have only to postulate the Intelligence as a *faculty*, and external substances as *objects* of perception, and the possibility of such knowledge is just as manifest as knowledge by Consciousness, or through any other function of the Intelligence.

2. These theories leave another mystery, still more inexplicable, hanging over the question in respect to the possibility of knowledge, to wit, how can the Intelligence postulate a purely mental affection as exclusively the quality of an external object? In other words, how can the Intelligence give a phenomenon as pertaining, an object wholly distinct from and independent of the precipient subject, which, after all, is nothing but a phenomenon of that subject? Above all, how can the Intelligence first give an affection purely subjective, as a

quality exclusively objective, and afterwards give the same quality as exclusively subjective, and that without the possibility, as Coleridge acknowledges, of considering it, as anything but objective? All these contradictions take place in the interior of our intelligence, in respect to external perception, according to the theories under consideration — contradictions perfectly equivalent to the declaration, that the same thing, at the same time, is, and is not. Should it be said, that this process is possible to the Intelligence, because, that such is its nature, the same explanation renders equally explicable, the possibility of external perception as maintained in this Treatise, a fact denied exclusively on the ground of its inexplicability.

3. The explication which these theories give of the fact of perception is, in reality, the destruction of the fact, and not its explication at all. In the Intelligence, there appears a perception of an external object. Philosophy is called upon for an explanation of the fact. The fact to be explained is that of the perception of such objects. As such exclusively, it is to be explained, and not as something different from a real perception of something external. This is what philosophy is bound to do, if she speaks at all. Now what is the explication given by the theories under consideration? The perception of an object external to the mind, is explained by a profound demonstration, that no such object, nor perception of such object, exists in the Intelligence, and that such perception is an inexplicable impossibility. Now this is not the explanation of a fact, but its destruction, the most unphilosophical procedure — a procedure very much like the Frenchman's definition of the flea, to wit, an animal upon which, if you put your finger, he is not under it.

4. These theories involve an explication equally sophistical and unphilosophical of the question, in respect to the *certainty*

and *reality* of knowledge. An apprehension of an object exists in the Intelligence. Philosophy is called upon to answer the question, whether this apprehension is valid, in respect to the object? If it is so, our knowledge is real, certain. What answer do these theories give to this question? This: Our knowledge is certain and absolute, for the obvious reason, that the object has no existence at all; that the perception itself is the only thing real, and as it contains nothing but what the Intelligence has put into it, therefore our knowledge is real and absolute. What a strange answer this to the question, the only question submitted to philosophy, to wit, the validity of the perception relatively to its object.

5. These theories annihilate wholly all distinctions between truth and error, all criteria of truth whatever. The reality, the certainty of knowledge, according to these theories, consists in this — that as our conceptions are the only realities existing, and as these contain nothing but what the Intelligence puts into them, therefore our knowledge is real, is absolute. Now, this condition of certainty holds, in respect to one conception, just as well as another; and if this is the condition of certainty, the wildest vagaries of the maniac are just as true as the sublimest demonstrations of Newton.

6. Finally, all such theories give a totally false explication of the real procedure of the Intelligence in respect to knowledge of every kind. Let any one attempt to apply such theories, as elucidating the process of his own mind in its perceptions and knowledges, and the effect cannot be better expressed, than in the following extract of a letter written to Coleridge by a friend, explaining to the philosopher the effect of a careful study of his theory of the Imagination:

"As to myself, and stating, in the first place, the effect on my *understanding*, your opinions and method of argument were not only so *new* to me, but so directly the reverse of all I had ever been accustomed to consider as truth, that, even if I had comprehended your premises sufficiently to have admitted them, and had seen the necessity of your conclusions, I should still have been in that state of mind, which, in your note, p. 251, you have so ingeniously evolved, as the antithesis to that in which a man is when he makes a *bull.* In your own words, I should have felt as if I had been standing on my head.

"The effect on my *feelings,* on the other hand, I cannot better represent, than by supposing myself to have known only our light, airy, modern chapels of ease, and then, for the first time, to have been placed, and left alone, in one of our largest Gothic cathedrals, in a gusty moonlight night of autumn. 'Now in glimmer, now in gloom;' often in palpable darkness, not without a chilling sensation of terror; then suddenly emerging into broad, yet visionary light, with colored shadows of fantastic shapes, yet all decked with holy insignia and holy symbols; and ever and anon, coming out full upon pictures, and stone-work images, and great men, with whose *names* I was familiar, but which looked upon me with countenances, and an expression, the most dissimilar to all I had been in the habit of connecting with those names. Those whom I had been taught to venerate as almost superhuman in magnitude of intellect, I found perched in little fret-work niches, as grotesque dwarfs; while the grotesques, in my hitherto belief, stood guarding the high altar with all the characters of apotheosis. In short, what I had supposed substances, were thinned away into shadows, while, everywhere, shadows were deepened into substances:

> 'If substances may be call'd what shadows seem'd,
> For each seemed either!' "

Now, a theory which gives such an explanation of the process of the human Intelligence as this, does not give a true exposition of that process. There is surely no presumption in such an affirmation as this.

In the remarks above made upon the theories under consideration, I have anticipated some things which properly belong to a later department of mental science; no more, however, than was necessary to a distinct presentation of our present subject of investigation.

THE HYPOTHESIS THAT ALL OUR KNOWLEDGE OF MATTER IS DERIVED THROUGH SENSATION EXCLUSIVELY, THE MAIN SOURCE OF ERROR, IN PHILOSOPHY.

Before leaving this department of our inquiries, a few remarks are deemed requisite upon the main source of error, in Philosophy. All systems of false Philosophy, almost without exception, have one common basis, and start from one common assumption, to wit, that all our knowledge of Matter is Representative, and derived exclusively, through one medium, Sensation. If this hypothesis is true, as we have already seen, all our perceptions, apprehensions, and knowledge, pertaining to Matter, would be, in all respects, just what they are, provided we had all our present sensations, as they are, whatever may be the cause of such states, and whether any external material universe exists or not. As these causes also are, and must be, to us, according to this hypothesis, wholly unknown as they are in themselves, being given in the Intelligence exclusively, as the unknown causes of known states of the Sensibility, we can, by no possibility, determine whether our present impressions, in respect to them, be true or false, whether they are, in reality, extended or unextended substances, whether they are material or immaterial, finite or infinite, and whether they are objective or subjective, whether they exist out of, and separate from, the mind, as real *Non-Egoes*, or whether they are inherent principles of our own nature.

We have, therefore, and cannot but have, according to this hypothesis, just as many theories of perception, and of nature too, as we have *conceivable* causes of our sensations. All these theories have perfectly equal claims, and each of them has absolutely no claims whatever to be regarded as true. If also, our knowledge of what is given in Consciousness, as the *Non-Ego*, or Matter, is thus uncertain, it must be equally so in respect to the *Ego* or Mind itself. The same Intelligence which has thus deceived us, in the one case, cannot but have done the same in the other. Of nature, subjective and objective, we can have no certain knowledge. If we attempt to pass "through nature up to nature's God," every step of our progress must be in absolute midnight. We are advancing through the absolute unknown, to find the unknown. God, accordingly, can be nothing to us, but an unknown and unknowable something, sustaining unknown and unknowable relations to an unknown and unknowable something called the Universe. The only proper altar of worship that can be raised to such a being, will have upon it the inscription, "To the Unknown God." Absolute skepticism, in regard to the possibility of all knowledge, objective or subjective, and pertaining to the Finite or the Infinite, is the only true Philosophy. All systems of Realism resting as most of them do, upon the Sensational hypothesis, are moving on the track of truth, only by a happy, but palpable violation of their own foundation principle. David Hume was a universal skeptic, and the evangelical philosophers of his own age, who held with him this hypothesis, were believers in the truth, simply and exclusively because he reasoned logically, and they most illogicaly from the fundamental principle which they held in common. All the consequences above alluded to, arise from the hypothesis under consideration, and can, by no possibility, be separated from it.

In regard to this hypothesis, I need only remark, in this

connection, that we have already demonstrated, as we judge, the fact, that it cannot be true. In showing that our knowledge of *some* of the qualities of matter is, in fact, Presentative, we have shown that *all* our knowledge of Matter is not, and cannot be, what this hypothesis affirms it to be, exclusively Representative. In showing, as we have done, that some of these qualities are the known Presentative objects of known acts of the Intelligence, we have shown, that they are not, as they must be exclusively, according to this hypothesis, the unknown causes of known states of the Sensibility. Universal Consciousness is itself a lie, if this hypothesis is true.

There is one fundamental fact alluded to above, but which was not brought to bear in the preceding argument, that I will adduce in this connection. Our knowledge of the Secondary qualities of Matter, and of the Secundo-primary, so far as they take rank with the Secondary, is given in Consciousness, as valid, only to ourselves, and to ourselves only as our sensitive nature is now constituted. Our knowledge of the Primary qualities, and of the Secundo-primary, so far as they take rank with the former, is given in the same Consciousness, as valid for all Intelligents, whatever the constitution of their sensitive nature may be. Now, if all our knowledge of all the qualities of matter alike, was derived through Sensation, it would be given in its entireness in Consciousness, as only valid for ourselves, and for ourselves only in the present constitution of our sensitive nature. It is not thus given, and therefore the Sensational hypothesis is demonstrably false.

I remark, also, that fundamental facts pertaining to Sense-perception, are totally inexplicable on the Sensational hypothesis. In such perceptions, the object, whatever it may be in itself, the object actually perceived by the mind is given in Consciousness; 1st, as an object of direct and immediate perception; 2nd, as the known quality of a *Non-Ego*, or Matter;

3rd, as a *Non-Ego*, as possessed of definite extension and form. No one will question the truth of any of these statements. Now, according to the Sensational hypothesis, the reality truly perceived is nothing but a Sensation, and consequently, in no sense, an object-object, but wholly and exclusively a subject-object, that is, the real object of perception is not, in fact, a quality of the *Non-Ego* or Matter at all, but exclusively a phenomenon of the *Ego* or Mind. That also which is given in Consciousness, as having actual extension and form, the sensation itself, the sole object perceived according to this hypothesis, has, in reality, neither of these characteristics, nor any others of a kindred nature. Now by what known, or intelligently conceivable law of mind can that, which as an object of immediate perception, is given in Consciousness, as exclusively an object-object, be, in reality, nothing but a subject-object; and that also which, in itself, has absolutely no extension or form, be given in the same Consciousness, as having both these characteristics? The Sensational hypothesis is not an explanation of the facts of Consciousness pertaining to Sense-perception, but their total perversion, or destruction rather.

I remark, finally, what has already been shown, that this hypothesis rests, like all other false hypotheses, on a partial induction of facts, and that, in the presence of other facts equally palpable, of a contradictory nature. That we have sensations, and through them a certain form of knowledge, knowledge mediate and relative, of Matter, we know absolutely. That we have Sense-perceptions, and through these, a Presentative knowledge of other and more fundamental qualities of the same substance, we know with the same absoluteness. We are as absolutely conscious of the existence of such perceptions as we are of that of Sensations. It would be no more a denial of the palpable facts of Consciousness, to deny the reality of the one class of phenomena, than it would to deny that of the other. It would therefore be no more a denial of the palpable facts of Consciousness to affirm, that all our knowledge of Matter is through Sense-perceptions exclusively, and therefore, as exclusively, Presentative, than it would to affirm, as this hypothesis does, that all knowledge of this substance is through Sensation, and therefore exclusively Representative. On such a partial, and therefore false induction of the real facts of Consciousness, does this hypothesis rest, an hypothesis more fruitful of frightful error than almost any other that was ever introduced into the domain of philosophy. I need not, however, any further repeat arguments by which the total groundlessness of this hypothesis has been already demonstrated.

EXPLANATION GIVEN BY KANT AND THE TRANSCENDENTAL SCHOOL GENERALLY OF THE FACT OF SENSE-PERCEPTION.

According to Kant, all Sense-perception is exclusively through Sensation. The object really perceived, in such perception, is nothing but the Sensation itself. Yet this *subject-object* having, in itself, neither extension nor form, is given, in Consciousness, as an *object-object*, having both extension and form. In this, all forms of the Transcendental School, from Kant, through Fichte, and Scheling to Hegel, perfectly agree. Now what is that which, according to these Schools in Philosophy, renders to Consciousness this purely subject-object, having, in itself, neither extension nor form, an exclusively object-object, possessed of both the forenamed qualities? The Sensation itself, it is replied, gives the *content* of the perception, while the ideas of Time and Space existing, *à priori*, in the mind, gives it its *form*, and makes it appear as an object-object. "Space and Time," says Kant, "are the pure forms of them" [Sense-perceptions], "Sensation in general the matter." The thing really perceived, in such perceptions, or the content of the perception, is the Sensation. That which makes this immaterial, and consequently unextended and formless subject-object, appear wholly as a material object-object, having definite extension and form, is the ideas of Time and Space. I will venture the affirmation, that a greater absurdity never danced in the brain of Philosophy than that which is involved in this Transcendental exposition. Space and Time are given, in the Intelligence, as absolutely infinite quantities, the latter in two, and the former in all directions. Now how can ideas which pertain to their objects exclusively, as *infinitely* extended, make objects which really have no extension whatever *appear* as having this quality in a *finite* degree? How can ideas which pertain to their objects as having no form whatever, impart to that which is also itself without form, the appearance of having a definite form? If these ideas should impart the appearance of extension at all, they must, it would seem, impart to them that of infinite instead of finite extension. Further, if they should impart to sensations the appearance of extension at all, it would seem that they must impart to them all alike that of the same extension. So of form. How can ideas which pertain to their objects, as infinite, and consequently without form, impart to these different sensations, all of which are alike without extension or form, and in this respect, sustaining the same identical relations to precisely the same ideas, the appearance even of possessing different degrees of extension, and a diversity of forms? How can these ideas make sensations which are exclusively subjective phenomena appear whollo as qualities of objects exclusively external to the mind, having an existence out of, and independent of the mind? How can these ideas impart to one class of sensations the appearance of being wholly independent qualities of a *Non-Ego* or Matter, and to another, that of being as exclusively phenomena of the *Ego* or Mind itself, when all of them alike are exclusively phenomena of the *Ego*, and sustain precisely the same relations to the ideas themselves? We may just as reasonably suppose, that pure Time and absolutely empty Space contain, in themselves, infinite Intelligence and Almighty creative Power, as to suppose their ideas contain the qualities attributed to them in the Transcendental Schools of Philosophy.

Besides, this exposition of Sense-perception is based wholly upon a very gross psychological error. In this exposition, the ideas of Time and Space are given as chronological antecedents and determining causes or principles of Sense-perception; whereas they are, in fact, *chronological consequents* of such perceptions. These ideas, as we have seen in a former chapter, are the *logical* antecedents of those of body and succession, while the latter ideas are the *chronological* antecedents of the former. We must first perceive succession and extension before we can, in any degree, conceive of Time and Space, the former of which is given in the Intelligence, as the place of events, and the latter originally exclusively as that of extended substances. These ideas, then, instead of giving us the perception of extension and form, cannot exist, as ideas in the mind at all, that of Space especially, till after these qualities are actually perceived. The entire Transcendental exposition of Sense-perception is based wholly upon a singular reversal of the relations between an antecedent and its consequent; and with that exposition all the forms of this Philosophy must fall to the ground. Not one of these Theories can be true, if this exposition is false, as it has now, we think, been fully proved to be.*

* In a subsequent chapter it will be shown, that the ideas of Time and Space, instead of being laws of Sense-perception, as affirmed by Idealism, are in fact categories of understanding conceptions, that is, they are laws not of the Primary, as Kant affirms, but of the Secondary faculties.

IS COLOR A PRIMARY OR A SECONDARY QUALITY OF MATTER?

In all schools of Philosophy with which I am acquainted, color is assumed as exclusively a Secondary quality of Matter. Into this error, Sir William Hamilton has fallen, although he has himself given, with absolute correctness, the distinguishing characteristic which separates the Primary from the Secondary quality, and then, in express words, and as correctly given this identical characteristic to this one quality. The primary quality of matter, as he has defined it, is that quality which necessarily pertains to this one substance, as Matter, and which consequently cannot, in thought, be separated from it. Such qualities are Extension and Form, for example. We cannot even conceive of matter, as void of these qualities. They pertain to it as Matter. In the presence of this definite and distinguishing characteristic of the Primary quality, our author uses the following language, in a note under a paragraph in which he ranks color as a Secondary quality: "But as Aristotle has observed, we cannot imagine body without *all* color, though we can imagine it without *any one*." The same precisely he might have said of extension and form. We cannot imagine body without all extension and form, though we can imagine it without any one. That which cannot, even in thought, be separated from body, without annihilating it as body, must be ranked as a Primary quality of body, or it has no such qualities. Color, then, is such a quality of Matter, or by the showing of Aristotle and Sir William Hamilton both, it has no Primary qualities. Such also is this quality as given in the universal Intelligence. Such we cannot but regard it, even when attempting to demonstrate its rank among Secondary qualities, and when we suppose we have accomplished our object. "We know well," says Dr. Brown (a strange assertion, that we know well, what he goes on to show we cannot believe,

9*

even while attempting to prove it), "when we open our eyes, that whatever affects our eyes is within the small compass of their orbit; and yet we cannot look for a single moment, without spreading what we thus visually feel over whole miles of landscape. Still, I must repeat, not the slightest doubt is *philosophically* entertained by those, who, when they open their eyes, yield like the vulgar to the temporary illusion — that the colors, thus supposed to be spread over the external objects, or rather the rays of light that come from them, are merely the unknown causes of certain sensations in ourselves. When questioned on the subject of vision, we state this opinion with confidence; and even with astonishment, that our opinion on the subject, in the present age of philosophy, should be doubted by him who has taken the superfluous trouble of putting such a question. At the very moment, probably, at which we give our answer, we have our eyes fixed on him to whom we address it. His complexion, his dress, are regarded by us as external colors, and we are practically, at the very moment, therefore, belying the very opinion which we profess, and in speculation truly profess, to hold."

For myself, my opinions must undergo an essential modification before I shall hold a dogma philosophically, which I cannot intellectually but disbelieve, even in the act of attempting to demonstrate its truth.

There is a very singular mistake into which Sir William Hamilton appears to have fallen, in the subsequent part of the note above alluded to. "In like manner," he says, "where the qualities are mutual contradictories, we cannot positively represent to ourselves an object without a determination by one or other of these opposites. Thus we cannot conceive a body which is not either vapid or tasteless, either sonorous or noiseless, and so forth. This observation applies likewise to the first class." The cases cited are, in no form, parallels.

The terms "vapid and tasteless," "sonorous and noiseless," are contradictories, while "any color" sustains to "all color," the relation of a subaltern proposition merely. I can conceive of a body as vapid or tasteless, because we have here a secondary quality, which body consequently may or may not possess. I cannot, on the other hand, conceive of body as possessed of color, or as void of all color, for the reason, that we have here a Primary quality which body, as an extended visible substance, cannot but possess.

Hence I do not agree, in the absolute truth of the statements of this author, that "the primary are perceived as *in our organism*," and that the "primary qualities of things external to our organism we do not perceive, *i. e.*, immediately know." On the other hand, I hold, that vision is direct and immediate, when the proper conditions are fulfilled, and that consequently color "is an object not of sensation proper, but of perception proper, in other words, we perceive color not as an affection of our minds, but as a quality of external things." I believe that color is given, in Consciousness, as a direct and immediate known object of a known state of the Intelligence, and consequently its knowledge is Presentative, just as much and for the same reasons, that extension is. Every characteristic which our author has given by which we can distinguish Presentative from Representative knowledge, marks color as belonging to the former class It is not given, in Consciousness, as an unknown cause of a known sensation, but as a known object of a known Sense-perception.

VALIDITY OF OUR KNOWLEDGE OF THE NON-EGO OR MATTER.

If all our knowledge of Matter is through Sensation, then we can know it only in its relation to our Sensibility as now constituted, and consequently as an unkown and unknowable cause of such sensitive states. What this cause is, in itself, or whether it does or does not accord with our mediate apprehensions in regard to it, we can have no certain knowledge whatever. We must regard ourselves as mere dreamers inhabiting a dream-land, and whether our sleeping or waking dreams best accord with the objects to which we refer them, or whether both are alike deceptive, we have no means of knowing, both forms of perception and apprehension being alike and equally necessary results of the sensations produced in us at the time, and those sensations in neither instance proceeding from known or knowable causes. We must regard ourselves, not in the possession of real knowledge, but as the hopeless victims of baseless conjectures, conjectures the more torturing the more we philosophize upon them.

If, on the other hand, we not only know realities around us, as causes of certain sensitive states, but in all their fundamental qualities, as objects of immediate or Presentative knowledge, that is, as they are in themselves, then we are not inhabitants of a mere "dream land," but of a universe of knowable and known realities. In speaking of these realities, "we speak that we do know, and testify to that which we have seen," and the time is not distant when even philosophy, so long bewildered by false hypotheses, will receive our testimony. Every theory of knowledge but that which postulates the Intelligence relatively to realities within and around it, as a *power*, and such realities relatively to it, as *objects* of real knowledge, and every theory of nature material and mental but that of absolute Realism, will not only be condemned, as contrary to the Common Sense of the race, but equally to all the teachings of sound and valid Philosophy. In regard to the question of reality of the material universe, and of the validity of our knowledge in regard to it, I need but allude, in this connection, to the following considerations bearing upon such questions:

1. By no possibility can the reality of the one, or the validity of the other be disproved, and the one must be held as real and the other as valid, till the opposite in both particulars, is proved. The burden of proof lies upon the skeptic exclusively. There are but two ways in which the skeptic can, by any possibility, accomplish his object — by showing that the *conception* of such a reality is self-contradictory, like the proposition, that it is possible, for the same thing, at the same time, to be and not to be — or that such conception is contrary to some known and absolute truth, or truths, or to some of their logical consequents. Now such an end never has been accomplished in either of the forms named, and we may rest assured, that it never will nor can be. This we shall attempt specifically to show in a subsequent chapter.

2. The reality of the material universe is an object of *direct, immediate*, and, therefore, of *absolute* knowledge. We have the same absolute perception of it, that we have of any of our own mental states. The latter is no more given in Consciousness, as the objects of direct Presentative knowledge, than the former. We have the same grounds to hold our knowledge as valid, in the one case, that we have in the other. The following remarks of Sir William Hamilton on this topic, are deemed worthy of very special attention in this connection:

"In perception, Consciousness gives, as an ultimate fact, *a belief of the knowledge of the existence of something different from self.* As ultimate, this belief cannot be reduced to a higher principle; neither can it be truly analyzed into a double element. We only believe that this something *exists*, because we believe that we *know* (are conscious of) this something as existing; the *belief of the existence* is necessarily involved in the *belief of the knowledge of the existence.* Both are original, or neither. Does Consciousness deceive us in the latter, it necessarily deludes us in the former; and if the former, *though* a fact of

Consciousness, be false; the latter, *because* a fact of Consciousness, is not true. The beliefs contained in the two propositions:

"1*st. I believe that a material world exists;*

"2*d. I believe that I immediately know a material world existing,* (in other words), *I believe that the external reality itself is the object of which I am conscious in perception*): though distinguished by philosophers, are thus virtually identical."

In another place, he adds, "In our perceptive Consciousness there is revealed as an ultimate fact, a *self*, and a *not-self*, each given as independent—each known only in antithesis to the other. No belief is more *intuitive, universal, immediate,* or *irresistible,* than that this antithesis is real and known to be real; no belief is therefore more true. If the antithesis be illusive, *self* and *not-self, subject* and *object, I* and *Thou* are distinctions without a difference; and Consciousness, so far from being 'the internal voice of our Creator' is shown to be, like Satan, 'a liar from the beginning.'"

3. Neither the reality of the material universe, nor the validity of our knowledge in respect to it, can be denied, without, to be logically consistent, an universal impeachment of the Intelligence itself, as in respect to any subject external or internal, a faculty of real knowledge. If Consciousness has deceived us, in regard to the character of our knowledge of the *Non-Ego*, it should not be held as worthy of confidence in regard to any other mental states. Sound Philosophy requires, that we hold the universe of Matter as real, or nothing as real, our knowledge, in respect to it as valid, or as valid in respect to no subject whatever. *All* forms of real Presentative knowledge must be held to be valid for the reality and character of their respective objects; or to be logically or philosophically consistent, no form whatever must be thus held. Each form

must be held *à priori*, as just as possible in itself as any other, and each pertains, with the same directness and absoluteness to its respective objects. We must deny the reality of all our own mental states, and the validity of our knowledge, in respect to them, or to be logically consistent, we must admit the reality of the external material universe, and the validity of our knowledge in respect to it.

CONCLUSION OF THE PRESENT EXPOSITION.

The conclusion to which we are conducted, as the result of our investigations in this chapter, is this: Sense, like Consciousness, and Reason, is a source of real, valid knowledge. The basis for the procedures of the Secondary Faculties which are next to claim our attention, is not shadows, but eternal rock, the rock of truth. Through a real and known universe, we are advancing towards a real, and not "unknown God."

CHAPTER VII.

SECONDARY FACULTIES.

UNDERSTANDING.

THROUGH the faculty of Sense, and a consciousness of sensations, we have, as we have seen, intuitions of the qualities of external material substances; phenomena, such as are expressed by the terms extension, form, resistance, color, taste, smell and sound. By Consciousness, we have similar intuitions of the operations of our own minds, such as thinking, feeling, and willing. Through Reason, on condition of the perceptions of Sense and Consciousness, we have the intuitions of time, space, personal identity, substance, and cause. These intuitions being given, another and secondary intellectual process occurs, a process, in which these intuitions, necessary and contingent, are united into *notions* of particular things. Thus, our notion of body, for example, is complex, and when analyzed into its distinct elements, is found to be constituted exclusively of intuitions given by the faculties above referred to. We conceive of it as a substance, in which the qualities above named, inhere, a substance existing in time and space, and sustaining certain relations to other substances, of which we have notions similarly compounded. The same holds true of our notions of all substances whatever. They are all complex, and constituted exclusively of intuitions given by the primary faculties.

A notion, then, is a complex intellectual phenomenon, composed of intuitions. The faculties, or functions of the Intelligence, which give us the latter, we have already considered. What shall we call that which gives us the former? In other words what shall we call the *notion-forming* power of the mind? In conformity to a usage which has, since the time of Coleridge, extensively obtained, we denominate this faculty of the Intelligence, the Understanding. In strict conformity to this specific application, will the term Understanding, when special notice to the contrary is not given, be employed throughout this Treatise. It will be employed, not as Locke uses it, as designating the general intelligence, but to designate a special function of that Intelligence, a function in which intuitions contingent and necessary, given by the primary faculties, are combined into *notions or conceptions of particular objects, or classes of objects.*

NOTIONS PARTICULAR AND GENERAL.

Notions are of two kinds — particular and general. Particular notions are such as we form of individuals, and designate by terms which are applicable to such individuals only — such as John, Samuel. General notions appertain to classes of individuals, and are designated by terms of corresponding application, such as man, mountain. The *formation* of the notions last mentioned, will be considered in a subsequent chapter.

ELEMENTS OF WHICH NOTIONS ARE CONSTITUTED.

The elements of which all notions are constituted, are, as we have seen, of two kinds — contingent and necessary. A proper philosophical analysis of notions would lead us to contemplate them in the light of these two distinct classes of elements.

Contingent Elements.

The contingent elements entering into every notion are all expressed by the general term phenomenon. Now, phenomena present themselves under the following entirely distinct relations:

1. That of *inherence*, or those particular qualities which inhere in particular substances, and by which the substances in which they thus inhere, are distinguished from other substances. That all substances shall have qualities of some kind or other, is a necessary element of our idea of substance. The particular qualities which, in fact, inhere in particular substances, however, are contingent elements of our notions of such substances. Thus, whiteness should be reckoned as a contingent element of our idea of snow, sweetness of that of sugar, form of that of body, and thought, feeling, and will, of that of Mind. Those phenomena, then, which we contemplate as inhering in particular substances, as distinguishing clear characteristics of the same, we denominate Quality. One great object of observation and scientific research, is to determine what are the specific qualities which inhere in particular substances.

2. There is still another point of light in which substances are contemplated. One substance, we well know, is affected, or determined, in its state or states, by other substances. This property of being thus affected, we denominate *Susceptibility.* Thus gold is susceptible of fusion by heat, and water of existing in a solid, fluid, or vaporous state, from the different degrees in which it is penetrated by the same substance. Body is divisible, and Mind is susceptible of being pleasurably or painfully affected from an endless diversity of causes. The particular effects which particular subjects are capable of receiving, enter as contingent elements of our notions of such

substances, effects which, as intimated above, we designate by the term susceptibility.

3. Substances have what may be called *external relations* to each other, relations which we designate by the term *Coherence.* Thus individuals sustain to each other the relations of employer and agent, physician and patient, teacher and pupil, &c. Accordingly, when we think of one individual, we think of him as the child of some other particular person, and this last as the parent of that particular child. We think of particular objects, a farm for example, as the particular property of some particular individual, and such individual as the particular owner of said property. All such facts enter as contingent elements into our specific notions of particular objects as individuals, and such facts, I repeat, we designate by the general term Coherence. When we would complete our notions of such objects or individuals, one specific inquiry which we make is, What are the particular mutual relations existing between them and other objects or individuals?

4. The next class of contingent phenomena which constitute corresponding elements of our notions or conceptions, may be denominated *accidental.* The fact that any individual now existing was born *somewhere,* constitutes an essential element of our conception of him as a man. The fact that he was born in London, Paris, England, America, or any one particular place instead of some other, does not enter as such an element into our conception of him as a man, but constitutes a contingent element of our conception of him as such a being. That every living individual is either poor or rich, wise or ignorant, learned or unlearned, or that he occupies some intermediate position between these extremes, we know very well, from the nature of the case, cannot but be true of him. The particular position which he does occupy, or has occupied, however, enters as a contingent element into our conception

of him. Every object is conceived by us not only in respect to its inherent qualities and susceptibilities, and to the mutual relations existing by which it stands, in special coherence with other objects, but in reference to facts which accidentally pertain to it.

5. The relation of phenomena pertaining to *place*, next claim our attention. Thus, when any phenomenon appears, we ask, where is it? If one individual, for example, who is ignorant of the facts, should hear others speaking of the Astor House, he would at once ask after its location. The particular place where the house is located, is a contingent element of our conception of it. The same holds true of all other substances.

6. Phenomena present themselves under one other relation still, that of *antecedence*, and *succession*. When any event is announced to us, as having occurred, we ask the question, *when* did it occur? The answer to this question, that is, the *particular time* of the event, enters as a contingent element into our conceptions of it.

As far as my present investigations extend, the above present a complete enumeration of the contingent elements of all our notions. Whenever we contemplate an object, we always think of it in relation to what is intrinsic in the object, irrespective of other objects — to what we have witnessed in regard to the effects resulting from the action of other powers upon it, or from its action upon them — to its external relations to other objects — to accidental circumstances connected with it — to the place where it is located, or its phenomena have appeared, — and the *time* of such occurrences. I have hesitated considerably in respect to the question whether the last two classes should not be ranged under the fourth, and classed as accidents. To me, however, they appear sufficiently distinct to justify the arrangement above made.

NECESSARY ELEMENTS.

Of the necessary elements which enter into, and determine the characteristics of all our notions, a complete enumeration, in the present state of mental science, is hardly to be expected. We may hope, however, to make an approach somewhat near to that result.

Substance and Cause the fundamental elements of all Notions.

One fact, pertaining to this department of our inquiries, is quite evident. It is this: The fundamental elements which enter into all our notions, and which, as laws of thought, determine the character of such phenomena, are two: *substance and cause.* If we make inquiries respecting any object, for the purpose of perfecting our notions or conceptions of it, it is as substance or cause, that such object is contemplated. All our inquiries are but different forms in which these two ideas evolve themselves in the Intelligence.

Evolution of these Laws not Arbitrary.

A careful analysis will also convince us, that the forms in which these two laws of thought evolve themselves, are by no means arbitrary. On the other hand, their principles of evolution are perfectly fixed. Whenever we would make inquiries respecting substances or causes, for the purpose of perfecting our notions of them, we, on reflection, find that certain specific inquiries we do and must put, and that none others we can make. In the light of the answers obtained to such inquiries, are all our notions of substance and cause determined. An elucidation of these laws of thought, and as a consequence, an evolution of the direction of the Understanding in all legitimate inquiries after right notions of substances, constitutes one of the great problems in philosophy. A development of these laws, in other words, of the *Categories* of the Understanding, will now be attempted. Whether that development shall be complete or incomplete, the result will determine.

I. — TIME AND SPACE.

I begin with the categories of *time and space.* These are entirely distinct from each other. As the same remarks, however, are equally applicable to each, I shall consider them together.

Whenever any substances or phenomena are thought of, two inquiries arise in respect to them, *When and where* do, or did they exist or occur? When we think of the world, for example, we naturally raise the inquiries, *When* was it created? how *long* has it stood? what *place* does it occupy in the universe? So also when we think of any occurrence in, or on the earth, we raise inquiries precisely similar, to wit, When and where did they occur? The same holds true in respect to all objects of the Understanding. All substances, all causes, all phenomena are *thought of* in relation to time and space. The ideas of time and space, as laws of thought, enter into all our notions, or Understanding-conceptions.

ERRORS OF KANT.

1. *In respect to the relation of Phenomena and Noumena to Time and Space.*

Kant makes a distinction obviously correct, between the *impressions* which objects make upon us, and the *causes* of these impressions, or the objects themselves. The former he denominates phenomena. The latter, that is, what he regards as the unknown objects which produce impressions in us, he calls noumena. Now phenomena, he says, we necessarily conceive of, as in time and space. Noumena, on the other hand, have no such relation, indeed, no relation whatever, to either time or space. Here a great mistake of this profound analyzer of the human mind presents itself. Reason affirms absolutely, that noumena have as real a relation to time and space as phenomena do. Whatever is to us an object of thought, whether it be an object, as it exists in itself, or whether it be a phenomenon of such object, we do, and must, put the questions, When? — how long? — and where? — in respect to it. Noumena, as well as phenomena, do and must have their locations in time and space. In the language of Dr. Murdoch, we may triumphantly ask, "How can physical effects be limited to time and space, and not also the physical *causes* which produce them? Can a material thing operate or produce effects, where it is not present to produce them? Or can Reason any more conceive, *à priori*, of a necessity for phenomena to exist only in time and space, than for noumena to exist in the same manner? If, then, Reason decides *à priori*, or intuitively, that phenomena must so exist, does she not equally decide, *à priori*, or intuitively, that noumena must so exist?" The overlooking of this obvious and undeniable fact, led this great philosopher to accord to time and space a necessary reality, as laws of sensible intuition, that is, of external perception, and to deny all reality of them, as realities in themselves.

2. *Relation of the Ideas of Time and Space to Phenomena.*

Another error of this philosopher consists in representing the ideas of time and space as laws of sensible intuition, that is, of external perception, and not as categories of the Understanding. They are, Kant maintains, the "*forms* of the phenomena of external Sense, or the *aspects* in which those phenomena present themselves to our Senses." They not only determine the forms of phenomena, but alone render perception possible to us. Now a moment's reflection will convince us, that these ideas have no relation whatever to perception, external or internal, but exist in us exclusively as laws of the Understanding, or notion-forming power.

In the first place, these ideas, instead of existing in the mind prior to, and thus determining the *form* of phenomena, are chronologically, as we have seen, developed in the Intelligence subsequent to phenomena, external and internal. We must first *perceive* extension, for example, and thus form a notion of something extended, before we can *conceive* of space in which such objects exist. It is not, therefore, as this philosopher maintains, through the idea of space that objects present themselves to us, in perception, as extended. On the other hand, without the perception of extension, the idea of space, as the place of the object perceived, would not be developed at all. The same illustration holds equally in regard to time. This idea does not first exist in the mind, and then determine our perception of events, as simultaneous or successive. The prior perception of succession, on the other hand, develops the idea. Perception, in all forms and degrees, exists wholly independent of the ideas of time and space. The mistake of Kant, in this case, consists in putting the antecedent for the consequent.

Equally manifest is it, on the other hand, that these ideas do not give *form* to perception, but, as laws of thought, determine the characteristics of conceptions or notions. When we perceive or think of phenomena, and of substances also, then, as the ideas of time and space are developed, we put the inquiries, Where? when? how long? &c., in respect to them. We do not *perceive*, but *conceive* or think of objects, as in time and space. The ideas of time and space are, therefore, categories, not of Sense, but of the Understanding.

II. — IDENTITY AND DIVERSITY, RESEMBLANCE AND DIFFERENCE.

An essential element of our ideas of substance, is that of

identity and diversity. As the relation between substances and their phenomena is that of necessity, a necessary law of conceptions, or of notions, is that substances are as their phenomena. Hence the two great necessary laws which determine our notions of substances, to wit, similar phenomena, suppose similar substances; dissimilar phenomena suppose dissimilar substances. Under the categories of Identity and Diversity, Resemblance and Difference, all classification, as we shall see, in a subsequent chapter, proceeds. The conception of the likeness or unlikeness of an object to something else, enters, as an essential element, into all our notions of it. Perhaps some might be inclined to place the above ideas under a category hereafter to be considered — that of Relation. They are no less distinct from it, however, than either of those next to be mentioned.

III. — THE IDEA OF A WHOLE, AS INCLUDING ITS PARTS, OR PARTS IN REFERENCE TO THE WHOLE.

Every notion pertains to its object as a whole, including parts, or as a part relatively to a whole. This is a universal and necessary law of all Understanding-conceptions, or notions. Thus, when we conceive of the Mind, we necessarily conceive of it as a whole, including the Intelligence, Sensibility, and Will; or we think of some department of mental operation relatively to the whole Mind. If we would form a notion of any material substance, any body, the same holds true in a more specific and special sense. Body, as given in all Understanding-conceptions, or notions, is a whole, a compound, constituted of simple parts.

KANT'S ANTINOMY OF PURE REASON.

According to this philosopher, all transcendental ideas, that is, all the necessary elements of our notions of substances around us, involve palpable contradictions. Two distinct and opposite propositions are susceptible of equal and absolute demonstration from these ideas. For example, the two following propositions, which are perfectly contradictory to each other, are equally susceptible of demonstration:

1. "Every compound substance in the world consists of simple parts, and there exists everywhere nothing but the simple, or that which is compounded of it."

2. "No compound thing in the world consists of simple parts, and there exists not anywhere therein anything simple."

The amount of the proof of the first, which he denominates the Thesis, is this: If the compound is not made up of simple parts, then, if all composition were done away in thought, no compound part could remain; and as there is, in that case, none simple, nothing would remain, and, consequently, no compound would be given.

His proof of the second, denominated Anti-Thesis, is, that the simple, whatever it may be, must occupy space, and therefore be made up of parts existing externally to each other, and consequently compounded. The conception of the simple, which is not a compound of something which is itself compounded, is a contradiction, and of course an impossible conception. No simple, therefore, does or can exist. From the contradictions necessarily involved in the Thesis and Anti-Thesis above given, each of which, from the nature of Understanding-conceptions, he affirms, is susceptible of equal and absolute demonstration, he infers, as demonstrably evident, the non-reality of all material existences, such as we conceive of them; inasmuch as the supposition of their real existence involves contradictions perfectly synonymous with the affirmation that the same thing, at the same time, may be and not be. In reply, I remark,

1. That the proposition, that that which is compounded

must be made up of simple parts, is an intuition of Reason, and therefore incapable of demonstration, in the same sense that all other intuitions are. We may show, as in the Thesis above given, that the opposite proposition involves a contradiction, and that is all.

2. The conception of the simple is a pure idea of Reason, and not an Understanding-conception at all. The compound only is an object of perception, and consequently of Understanding-conceptions. All bodies, therefore, as the Understanding forms notions of them, must be compounded. Not so with the simple, as given by the Reason.

3. In his Anti-Thesis, Kant assumes the idea of the simple as an Understanding-conception, which, of course, involves the idea of composition, and hence his boasted demonstration is nothing but a singular paralogism. If we assume that the idea of the simple is a notion, that is, that it is complex and not simple, then we have the contradictions presented by Kant in his Thesis and Anti-Thesis. Take away this assumption, and the contradictions wholly disappear. I believe that it can be shown that all the antinomies of pure Reason, as given by this philosopher, involve paralogisms similar to the one under consideration.

IV. — THE CATEGORY OF QUANTITY.

Whenever we contemplate a notion which lies under any term whatever, we find that it always does and must refer to some *one* object, to a *number* or *multitude* of objects, or to a *total race* or *class* of objects. For example, the term man may be used to designate some one individual, or a plurality of men, or the total race of men. This is what is meant by the logical quantity of a notion or conception, and presents us with the category of Quantity — with its sub-categories, Unity, Plurality, and Totality. Under the first, we have the notion of an individual. Under the second, that of a number of individuals. Under the last, we have a multitude of individuals classed together as a total race, on the ground of common qualities. Whenever we inquire after the extent or logical quantity of any term, or of that of the notion which lies under that term, we ask in which of the senses above named is it to be taken?

The Category of Quantity distinct from that previously considered.

At first thought, the category of Quantity may be regarded as identical with that previously considered. The ideas of whole and of parts, however, are correlative ideas. It is not so with those of unity and totality. A class supposes individuals; but the individual does not necessarily suppose a class. Totality, as distinguished from individuality, is distinct from a whole as distinguished from parts.

V.—OF QUALITY.

To complete and perfect our notions of substances, a fundamental inquiry arises, to wit, what is this substance? When we would answer the question pertaining to the *nature* of the object, but one thing is considered—the *qualities* of the object. As it is a necessary intuition of Reason, that substance supposes quality, and that substances are as their qualities, hence arises the category of Quality.

In all distinct notions of an object, certain qualities are positively affirmed, others denied, and others affirmed in a limited degree, of the object. Thus, in our notions of an individual, for example, distinguished intellectual powers may be affirmed, prudence denied, and courage affirmed in a limited degree. This principle is observed when we would describe an object to others, for the purpose of conveying distinct conceptions of it to their minds. We designate the positive qualities which appear in it. We deny other qualities of it, which might appear, but do not. We then designate others which might appear in all its parts, or in a certain degree of perfection, but which appear only in a limited degree. Thus the category of Quality presents itself in three forms, or sub-categories, those of Affirmation, Negation, and Limitation. When an object has been placed in the light of all these, then our notions of its nature are full and distinct.

VI. — OF RELATION.

Another form in which objects are given to us in notions, or Understanding-conceptions, is their *relations* to other objects. According to Kant, the category of Relation also develops itself in three forms. When two objects are brought together for the purpose of comparing them with each other, we consider the question, what qualities *inhere* in one which do not in the other? Here we have the first sub-category of Relation, that of Inherence. Each substance is thus contemplated in its relations to its distinctive attributes or qualities.

Objects also are contemplated relatively to their powers of affecting other objects and determining their states, or their susceptibilities of being affected by such objects. The metals, for example, are conceived of, as susceptible of fusion from heat, and caloric as possessed of the power of producing such effects in metals. In the one case, we give our notions of the *powers* of substances, and in the other of their *susceptibilities.* Two substances also may be compared relatively to their powers and susceptibilities. Thus we have the relation, or sub-category of causality and dependence.

A third relation is that of reciprocity, denominated by Kant the sub-category of Community. When objects, for example, mutually attract or repel each other, this relationship differs entirely from that of cause and effect. All objects in the universe around are, in some form or other, thus correlated to each other. The relation of employer and agent falls under the principle under consideration.

Such is the category of Relation. When we have contemplated objects till we know them, in the light of their comparative qualities, or attributes — in reference to their powers of affecting other objects, or of being affected by them — and as they mutually and reciprocally affect each other, then our notions are complete, as far as the idea of relation is concerned.

VII. — OF MODALITY.

Every Understanding-conception respects its object, as a possible or impossible — a real or unreal existence — and as existing of necessity or contingently. These ideas enter, as necessary elements, into all our notions, and constitute what is denominated the *modality* of Understanding-conceptions. Suppose I convey the conception I have of some object, to any individual. He will naturally and necessarily inquire, Can such a thing be? Is it a reality? Does it exist of necessity, or contingently?

VIII. — THE IDEA OF LAW.

When we have formed our notions of objects, in the light of the preceding principles, another inquiry of great importance arises, to wit, according to what law, or laws, do those powers act? The forms in which the nomological idea, as it is denominated by Prof. Tappan, develops itself are various, according to the nature of the objects to which it pertains, and the point of view in which the object is contemplated. Still, as a necessary element, it enters into, and determines the character of all our notions of substances within and around us. When we come to speak of the Reason again, this idea, together with the conditions of its development, and the varied forms in which it appears will be the object of special remark. I deemed it important to simply refer it to here, on account of its omnipresent influence, in determining the character of all our Understanding-conceptions.

Such are the elements which enter into all our notions, or Understanding-conceptions. That the above analysis presents us with real elements of such phenomena there can be no doubt. But whether that analysis is complete, will be ascertained in the more perfect developments of mental science.

CONCEPTIONS AS DISTINGUISHED FROM NOTIONS.

Conception, as commonly defined by philosophers, is a past perception recalled in Memory or Recollection. It is rather, as it appears to me, the recalling of the *notion* formed of the object when perceived. Perceptions may be renewed but not recalled. The conceptions of individuals will vary, as the notions which they formed of objects when perceived. The terms notion and conception are often used as synonymous.

A FACT OFTEN ATTENDING PERCEPTION.

It is a fact with which all are familiar, that when we unexpectedly meet an object before unknown to us, but which, in certain particulars, resembles one well known, we seem for a time to see the latter with perfect distinctness. The reason of this phenomenon I suppose to be this: Under such circumstances, the *notion* we have of the known object is recalled with such vividness, that it almost exclusively occupies the attention of the mind.

MISTAKE OF MR. STEWART.

According to this philosopher, in all conceptions, the absent object is, in the first instance, always believed to be present, as an object of direct perception. Universal consciousness affirms the error of such a dogma. The mistake of Mr. S. arose, as I suppose, from his definition of conception, that is, that it is a past perception recalled. If this were true, I do not see but we must, not only at first, but at all times, regard the object of our conception, as directly present.

NOTIONS AND CONCEPTIONS CHARACTERIZED AS COMPLETE OR INCOMPLETE, TRUE OR FALSE.

In the former part of this Chapter, we have contemplated the elements, contingent and necessary, which enter into all Understanding-conceptions. It now remains to consider these phenomena *in their relation to their objects.* All Understanding-conceptions pertain to their objects, in two important relations, as *complete* or *incomplete,* or as *true* or *false.*

Such conception is complete, when it represents all the elements really existing in the object. It is incomplete, when it fails to do this. Absolute completeness characterizes probably none of our conceptions.

An Understanding-conception is true, when it represents completely or incompletely, the real attributes of its object, and nothing else. It is false, when it attributes to the object unreal attributes, or denies of it what is real.

Two facts are obviously true from the above definitions. 1. A conception may be incomplete, and yet true, it being true, when it attributes to the object nothing but what is real. Or a notion might be complete, and yet, in a certain sense, false; as it might attribute to the object all that is real, and something not real. 2. Conceptions may be wholly true, or wholly false; or partly true, and partly false. That is, they may attribute to their objects nothing but what is real, or nothing that is real; or they may attribute to them some things real, and some not real. Unmingled error seldom characterizes any of our conceptions.

MISTAKE OF COLERIDGE IN RESPECT TO THE UNDERSTANDING.

Coleridge defines the Understanding as the "faculty of judging according to Sense," a definition which he copied from Kant and other German philosophers. According to such philosophers, the Understanding pertains only to external material substances. It has nothing to do with the subjective, with Mind.

Now this is a great error in Philosophy. As a matter of fact, we form notions and conceptions of Mind as really as we do of anything not ourselves. Notions subjective as really exist, in Consciousness, as those which are objective. Nor can any reasons be assigned, why we should attribute the formation of the latter to one faculty of the Intelligence, and that of the former to another. The appropriate sphere of the Understanding is evidently limited only by the Finite. Reason alone pertains to the Infinite, the Absolute, and the Universal. All other realities fall within the range of the Understanding.

CHAPTER VIII.

FACULTY OF JUDGMENT.

ABSTRACTION.

ALL our notions, or Understanding-conceptions, are, as we have seen, complex, constituted of elements furnished by the primary faculties, Sense, Consciousness, and Reason. To make an abstraction of a notion is, in thought, on the ground of the ideas of resemblance and difference, to separate these elements from one another, giving special attention to some one, or more, or each of them in particular. Into our conceptions of body, for example, the elements of form, soldity, color, &c., enter. Now in the light of the ideas of resemblance and difference, the Intelligence perceives at once, that the element of solidity differs from that of form, and that of color from either of the others. In thought, therefore, either of these elements may be so separated from all the rest, that it shall be the object of special observation. Thus our conceptions of each element of the object, and consequently our notions of the entire object may become more or less distinct and complete.

ABSTRACT NOTIONS, WHAT, AND HOW FORMED.

When the Intelligence, in the sense above explained, makes abstraction of a particular element of an object or conception, it may, ever after, conceive and speak of that element without reference to the particular object from which it was abstracted. Then we have what is denominated an abstract notion, such as is designated by the terms redness, sweetness, hardness, &c.

GENERAL NOTIONS, HOW FORMED.

Originally all Understanding-conceptions are particular. From these, all notions, abstract and general, are formed. How is the general evolved from the particular? Let us suppose that, in conformity to the process above described, the Intellect has formed notions of two particular objects, mountains, for example. These two notions lie together under the eye of Consciousness. In the light of the idea of resemblance and difference, the mind at once perceives that there are certain elements, common to the two. Abstraction is made of these elements, and a third notion is formed, embracing them alone. Here is the first appearance of a general notion. When a third mountain is perceived, and a notion formed of that, the general notion undergoes a new modification, and now embraces those elements only common to the three. Thus the process of abstraction goes on, till the general notion pertains to those elements only common to all mountains. This same process takes place in all instances in which general notions are evolved from particular ones.

CLASSIFICATION.

The process of classification can now be readily explained. We will refer back to the case when two particular notions were in the mind, and the general was evolved from them. As soon as the notion last named appears, the two particulars are subsumed or classed under it. In the same manner every particular previously perceived is arranged under the general, in all the successive modifications which it subsequently undergoes.

Forms of Classification.

There are three distinct points of view from which objects are classified.

1. In view of general resemblances, they are classed, on the ground of common qualities, under general notions, such as man, animals, &c.

2. In view of some one quality without reference to resemblance in any other particular, they are classed under notions purely abstract, such as redness, whiteness, &c. We often class objects together, as white, hard, sweet, &c., without reference to their relations, in any other particulars.

3. Objects are classed together, in view of their correspondence to pure rational conceptions, such as a circle, square, right and wrong, &c.

Classification, in what sense arbitrary.

It will readily be seen that classification from one point of view, will run directly across and break up that which is formed from another. How distinct and opposite, for example, will classification be which is founded in view of some one abstract quality, such as redness, from that which is based upon general resemblance, and formed under a general conception. Equally distinct and unlike either of the others will be the arrangement of objects which are classed together under some pure rational conception.

For these reasons classification has, by many, been regarded as perfectly arbitrary. It is true, that we are at liberty to adopt either of the principles of classification above described we please. In this respect, the process is perfectly arbitrary. If we classify at all, however, we must adopt one or the other of the forms under consideration, no other forms being conceivable. When we have selected our principle also, the subsequent arrangement of objects in conformity to it is necessary. In very important respects, therefore, classification has its laws, which are by no means arbitrary.

GENERA AND SPECIES.

In the process of classification, objects are ranged together as genera and species. Thus we have the genus tree, and the different classes, or species of fruit-bearing and forest trees, ranged under it. A species also is often itself a genus relatively to particular and distinct classes belonging to that species. If fruit-bearing be assumed as the genus, then we have the apple, plum, peach, cherry trees, &c., ranged as species under this generic term. The illustration might be extended indefinitely, from the highest to the lowest forms of genus and species. Our present concern is with the *principle* on which objects are thus classed. It is that to which we have frequently referred in this Chapter, the idea of *resemblance and difference.* The genus is formed on the perception of remote resemblances. Species under the genus are formed on the perception of important differences; while objects are classed under the species, on the perception of resemblances more near and special. Thus the genus tree is formed on the perception of qualities common to all trees. The species fruit-bearing and forest trees, are separated from each other, on the perception of important differences, each species being formed on the ground of resemblances more near and particular than those designated by the general term tree.

In illustration of the process in which classes, as genus and species, are formed, we will take the case of the child. A certain object stands near the paternal mansion, which he has learned to designate by the term tree. By and by he sees another object resembling this in all important particulars. Here, he says, is another tree. In his mind they are distinguished as greater and less, and in respect of location. Here is the obscure development of the ideas of genus and species. At length, however, he perceives a tree differing in very important particulars from either of the others. He now asks the question, what *kind* of tree is this? The answer is, we will suppose, a maple tree. Then the inquiry arises, what tree is that which stands near the house? He is told that it is an elm tree. He has now the idea of the genus tree, formed on the perception of common qualities, and of two species, separated from each other on the perception of important differences. All trees subsequently perceived, presenting similar resemblances and differences, will be separated and arranged accordingly. As other trees, differing from either of these, are perceived, they will be separated and classed in a similar manner. Throughout the whole process, one idea guides the mind, that of resemblance and difference.

GENERALIZATION.

But few words are requisite in the explanation of the mental process called Generalization. A general fact is a quality common to every individual of a given class. It may be peculiar to that class; or, while it belongs to each individual of the class, it may appertain to individuals of other classes.

Rules in respect to Generalization.

1. No fact must be assumed as general, which does not belong to each individual of the class to which it is referred.

2. No general fact must be assumed as *peculiar* to one class, which, though strictly general in respect to that class, nevertheless appertains to individuals of other classes.

3. No fact must be assumed as general without a sufficient induction of particulars, to remove all doubt in respect to the question whether it is, or is not, a general fact.

The Term General sometimes used in a limited sense.

In common usage, a fact is called general, when it belongs to a majority of the individuals of a certain class. In such a case, its existence in connection with an individual of the class is only probable. Great injury is often done to individuals in the application of facts of this kind.

GENERAL TERMS.

In the progressive developments of mental science, the question has long been agitated among philosophers, whether when we use general terms, such as man, animal, there are ideas in the mind, and objects in the universe around us, corresponding to these terms, or whether they are mere terms, without corresponding ideas and objects. In respect to such terms, three distinct theories have been formed by as many different sects of philosophers.

Theory of the Realists.

The first was maintained by a particular class of the schoolmen, and deduced from certain principles, real or supposed, maintained by Aristotle. The theory was this: There exists in nature, not only individual substances, but certain *essences*, corresponding with the general ideas which exist in the mind. When, for example, we use the term man, it was maintained that there exists in the world around us a certain essence, which is found in no individual of the species, and which exists in connection with no individual, but which corresponds with the idea in the mind, which idea is designated by the above term. So of every other general term. The sect of philosophers maintaining this theory was called Realists. Their dogmas have been long since exploded.

Theory of the Nominalists.

Another theory directly opposed to the above, was maintained by a sect of philosophers which arose in the eleventh century. "According to those philosophers," says Mr. Stewart, "there are no existences in nature, corresponding to general terms; and the objects of our attention, in all speculations, are not ideas, but words." This sect was called the Nominalists. As there are no existences in nature, according to this sect, corresponding with general terms, all our speculations and reasonings, but for our knowledge of such terms, must be confined to individuals. The following from Mr. Stewart, who was an avowed Nominalist, will illustrate the meaning of the above remarks, as well as show their correctness: "It has been already shown, that without the use of signs, all our knowledge must be necessarily limited to individuals; and that we should be perfectly incapable, both of classification, and general reasoning." If the author means that without the use of signs, we should be unable to communicate our thoughts to each other, what he says is a mere truism, which is no less applicable to individuals. But if he means, as he evidently does, that without the use of signs, we could not reason upon general subjects, I reply,

1. That the existence of the names themselves implies the previous process of reasoning and classification, to which he supposes these terms give birth. A class must first be formed, and a judgment affirmed, before any particular term can be chosen to designate them. Now as the process of classification gives existence to general terms, which process must always be anterior to the terms themselves, the mind must possess the power of classification and general reasoning, in the absence of such terms. The mistake of the author consists in changing the order of sequence, putting the effect for the cause.

2. Individuals have been known who have lost entirely all recollection of general terms, and who have yet retained the power of classification and reasoning upon general subjects unimpaired.

3. If our reasonings upon general subjects respect not ideas, nor things, but words merely, then all general conclusions must be absolutely useless in all the concerns of real life. In such circumstances, we have to do with realities exclusively, and shall find no place for conclusions in respect to abstractions, or rather in respect to the *relations* of abstractions which have no existence in nature.

4. The fact, that general terms are always defined by a reference to individuals, shows clearly, that there are, in such individuals, realities corresponding to the terms employed.

Theory of the Conceptualists.

We come now to notice the doctrine of the sect denominated Conceptualists, or Notionalists. According to the doctrine of this sect, a general term, when considered *objectively*, denotes those qualities which exist alike in all individuals of a given class — when considered *subjectively*, it designates the *conception* of these qualities in the mind. Instead of there being no existences in nature, according to the doctrine of the Nominalists, corresponding to general terms, the Conceptualists maintain, that there is in every individual of a given class, that which corresponds with those terms. The doctrine of this sect, as will be seen, is equally removed from that of the Realists and Nominalists both. That the doctrine of this sect is correct, and the only correct view of the subject, is evinced, because:

1. When the mind affirms of any particular object, as soon as perceived, that it is a man, a horse, an animal, such affirmation supposes the existence in the mind of a certain notion, or

conception of a given class of objects, and the perception of the agreement of the given object, with that conception. It can be accounted for upon no other supposition.

2. Every person, when he appeals to his own Consciousness, knows, that when using general terms, he is designating conceptions really existing in his own mind, conceptions pertaining to real qualities of classes of objects existing around him.

3. General terms are always defined by a reference to the qualities existing in individuals of a given class, and no definition is allowed to be correct, which does not designate the qualities common to the whole class to which it is applied.

4. General conclusions, when correct, must be applicable to all the individuals of the particular class to which they are applied. This shows that such conclusions are based upon the conception of the common qualities of each individual of the class.

UNDERSTANDING AND JUDGMENT DISTINGUISHED.

Having explained the process of abstraction and classification, it now remains to compare this process with the action of the Understanding. A moment's reflection will convince us, that this process, and that of forming notions, are entirely distinct from each other, and must be referred to functions of the Intelligence equally distinct. To form a notion of A and B, and to affirm that they agree or disagree, are intellectual operations, entirely distinct from each other. The former process is called conception; the latter is called judgment. So also when the Understanding combines the elements given by the primary faculties into notions, particular and general, that is one thing. When the Intelligence classes an individual under a general notion, in the affirmation, this is a man, an animal, &c. — that is quite another thing, an intellectual process entirely distinct from the formation of notions. In this last process we conceive, that is, combine intuitions. In the former, we judge.

As the function of the Intelligence by which we form notions is called the Understanding, so that by which we judge, that is, abstract, classify, and generalize, is denominated the Judgment.

DISTINCTION BETWEEN THE UNDERSTANDING AND JUDGMENT VERIFIED.

A single additional consideration will fully verify the distinction above made between the Understanding and Judgment. We often meet with individuals in whom the Understanding is strongly developed, and embraces a wide range of objects. Yet the same individuals may be almost totally wanting in respect to the faculty of Judgment. They conceive distinctly and vividly of objects presented, yet make no important discriminations between them. They will read a book, for example, and give a full and distinct account of what it contains, and yet appear to be none the wiser for what they know. They, as is commonly said of them, appear to know everything, and yet can make little use of their knowledge. They form notions of objects just as they present themselves, without making important discriminations between them. This is owing to the fact that the Understanding, which simply knows objects as they appear, is exercised, while the Judgment, which separates things that differ, and ranges together those that agree, and then abstracts, classifies, and generalizes our conceptions, or rather the objects of thought, is wanting or inactive.

On the other hand we meet with individuals who, with a very limited acquaintance with particular objects, yet possess a great amount of what is called practical wisdom. Their information is limited, yet what they know is analyzed, classified, and generalized. In other words, in such individuals the faculty of Judgment is fully developed.

Such considerations clearly show that the function of the Intelligence denominated Understanding is one thing, while that of Judgment is quite another. With the *facts* upon which the distinction under consideration is based, all men are familiar. They recognize readily the distinction between information and knowledge, between conceiving of objects, and in this sense knowing them, and making important discriminations between them. In short, the basis for the distinction between the Understanding and Judgment is laid in facts recognized by all men.

OBSERVATIONS OF KANT.

The remarks of Kant upon the subject under consideration are so much to the point, that I will present one or two quotations from his Critick on the faculty of Judgment. "If the Understanding," he says, "in general be explained as the faculty of rules, the faculty of Judgment is that of *subsuming* under rules; that is to say, of distinguishing whether something does or does not stand under a given rule." Again: "The faculty of Judgment is a particular talent, which is not to be taught, but only exercised; and this, consequently, is the speciality of the so-called mother-wit, the want of which no schooling can supply; for although this may offer to, and, as it were, graft upon a limited Understanding, rules in abundance borrowed from another mind, still the faculty of availing himself correctly of these must belong to the hearer himself: and no rule which we could prescribe to him with this intention is, under the deficiency of such a natural gift, secure from misuse. A physician, therefore, a judge, or politician, may have many excellent pathological, judicial, or political rules in his head, to such a degree that he himself may become therein a profound teacher, and yet in the application of them will easily make a mistake, either because he is deficient in natural

Judgment (although not in Understanding), and certainly can see the general *in abstracto*, but cannot distinguish whether a case *in concreta*, fall under it, or from this cause, that he has not sufficiently been trained by examples and real business to this judgment."

Two characteristics, entirely distinct and opposite, of different individuals of distinguished minds, may very properly be alluded to here, as illustrating and confirming the distinction between the Understanding and Judgment above made. We often meet with individuals, public speakers, for example, distinguished for strong and vivid conceptions of whatever subject their minds are occupied with. Yet one of their discourses shadowing forth some bold and grand conception, will contain elements manifestly contradictory to those contained in a prior discourse of a similar character. Yet the speaker himself appears wholly insensible of such contradiction. He contradicts himself, without at all being sensible of the fact. A bold and strong conception with such a mind is, of course, true, together with all the elements embraced in it.

The productions of other minds are distinguished not only for logical and scientific arrangement, but for the consistency and harmony of the elements introduced into one discourse with those introduced into others. Such individuals seldom, to use a phrase commonly applied in such cases, cross their own tracks, and if they do this at any time, they will perceive it quite as soon as others.

How shall we account for such diversities? The answer is, that in the first instance, the Understanding, and frequently the imagination, are strongly developed, while there is a deficiency of Judgment. In the latter cases, there is a strong development of the faculty last named. Now, phenomena so diverse and opposite necessarily suppose faculties fundamentally distinct from each other.

RELATIONS OF THE UNDERSTANDING AND JUDGMENT.

Having shown the distinction between these faculties, it now remains, in the conclusion of the present Chapter, to show the *relations* between them. The Judgment pre-supposes the Understanding. The former can analyze, abstract, classify, and generalize only what is furnished by the latter. Understanding might exist without Judgment; but the latter cannot exist, or rather cannot act, without the former.

The Understanding also not only precedes, but succeeds the action of the Judgment. When the Judgment has abstracted, analyzed, classified, and generalized objects of the Understanding, the latter faculty then combines into its conceptions of such objects all the discriminations of the former faculty pertaining to them. When, for example, we have passed a judgment upon any individual, affirming that he belongs to a particular class, that judgment, ever after, enters as an essential element into our conception of him. This is universally true of all judgments and notions.

CHAPTER IX.

ASSOCIATION.

TERM DEFINED.

"THAT one thought is often suggested to the mind by another, and that the sight of one external object often recalls former occurrences, and revives former feelings, are facts," says Mr. Dugald Stewart, "which are perfectly familiar, even to those who are least disposed to speculate concerning the principles of our nature." This is what is meant by the term Association. It is that principle of our minds by which past thoughts and states are recalled, and revived, through the influence of present perceptions, thoughts and feelings. This law of the human mind was denominated by the old philosophers, "Association of ideas." By Dr. Brown it was denominated "Suggestion." By others, it is designated by the simple term, Association.

Term Association, why preferred.

I prefer the latter term to either of the former, because it alone expresses all the phenomena which require consideration, when treating of the subject before us. We find by experience, that not only thoughts and events are associated, but thoughts, events, and feelings also. The term Association of ideas, can be properly applied to ideas only. The same is true of Suggestion. An idea or event cannot properly be said to suggest feelings. Thoughts and events may be said to revive feelings; and feelings may be said to suggest thoughts and events. Association is the term, and the only term, which can properly be applied to all these different classes of phenomena.

THE ASSOCIATING PRINCIPLE NOT WITHOUT LAW.

Although the Mind is so constituted, that certain states follow certain other states, these phenomena, as philosophers have long since observed, not only do not follow each other at random, but are known to follow some one or more fixed law or laws. To ascertain and illustrate the operation of these laws, has been considered one of the great problems in Intellectual Philosophy; and has accordingly occupied a conspicuous place in almost every treatise upon the science. Mr. Hume, I believe, was the first philosopher who attempted to settle definitely the number of these laws. According to this philosopher, they are all reduced to three: Resemblance, Cause and Effect, and Contiguity in time and place. Others have since added that of Contrast.

LAW OF ASSOCIATION STATED AND DEFINED.

It is somewhat remarkable that while philosophers have observed, that the principle of Association acts, as a matter of fact, in accordance with the above so-called laws, they have not inquired after the ultimate *cause* of its action in these forms, and have not raised the inquiry, whether this cause is not always one and the same. Some bodies, vapor for example, rise from the earth, while others descend towards it. Some bodies float upon the surface of water, while others sink to the bottom. Philosophy has long since demonstrated the fact, that the cause of all these diverse effects is one and identical, in all instances. The same law which causes the stone to descend towards the earth, causes the vapor to rise above it. The same law which causes lead to sink to the bottom of a mass of water, causes other substances to float upon its surface. Does not a similar unity obtain, in the action of the associating principle? May not all the facts of Association be reduced to one common principle, and the laws of Association, as presented by philosophers generally, be shown to be but different forms in which this one principle develops itself? I think that this may be done, and that the principle referred to, may very readily be pointed out.

When the mind has once been in a given state, we are all aware that there is in it a strong tendency to return to that state again. Hence, if any one element of that state is reproduced from any cause whatever, a recurrence of that state to a greater or less degree, is very likely, from the known principle under consideration, to be occasioned. Every perception, every thought in the mind, induces a certain mental state. Now suppose, that by some new perception or thought, some element of this state is revived. By the law of mind under consideration, is not the state itself likely to be revived, in a greater or less degree, and with that state, is not the remembrance of the perception or thought referred to, likely to be recalled? Have we not here the universal law of Association? A train of thought passed through my mind on yesterday, for example. Another is now passing. As a consequence, the former train is recalled. What is the reason of this fact? It is this: Something in the present train has reproduced some element of the state of mind induced by the one which passed through the mind on yesterday. By means of this common state, and that exclusively, the latter train has been recalled. So in all other instances. The law of Association, then, may be thus stated: When present thoughts or trains of thought, recall former ones, it is always and exclusively because the present has induced the state of feeling, or some element of the state induced by the former. It is always, and exclusively by means of this common state, that such Associations arise in the mind. The truth of this proposition it will now be my object to establish.

THE PRESENT HYPOTHESIS, WHEN ESTABLISHED AS THE LAW OF ASSOCIATION.

To establish the hypothesis under consideration, as the law of Association, two conditions must be fulfilled:

It must be shown, in the first place, that all phenomena referred to the commonly admitted laws, can be accounted for on this hypothesis.

It must be shown with equal clearness, in the second place, that there are facts of Association which cannot be accounted for by these laws, but which admit of a ready explanation on this hypothesis, and upon none other conceivable by us. These positions being established, the Judgment affirms the hypothesis, as the exclusive and universal law of Association.

We are now prepared to take up the question, whether there are many, or but one law of Association, and whether the hypothesis under consideration gives us that law?

A PRIORI ARGUMENT.

It will be admitted on a moment's reflection, that there is a very strong *à priori* probability in favor of the supposition, that the facts of Association are controlled by one law, instead of many. The opposite position supposes a departure, in this single instance, from what we find true of all other classes of facts which lie within and around us in the universe. The phenomena of attraction in the material universe, for example, are many, and endlessly diversified. Yet they are all controlled by one law. Why should we suppose the phenomena of Association to be an exception? Should we not expect, in the ultimate analysis of facts, to find unity amidst diversity here, as well as everywhere else? This argument is adduced as of weight, simply in favor of the supposition of one instead of many laws, and not at all in favor of any one hypothesis, in distinction from another. Any one principle, which would lay claim to the prerogative of universal law, must fulfill the conditions above presented. We are now prepared for a direct investigation of the question, whether the hypothesis under consideration fulfills these conditions.

ALL THE PHENOMENA REFERRED TO THE COMMONLY RECEIVED LAWS, CAN BE EXPLAINED ON THIS HYPOTHESIS.

That many of the phenomena of Association can be accounted for, in consistency with the commonly admitted laws, will be denied by no person of reflection. That objects which resemble each other, that those which have been perceived at the same time or place, that sustain to each other the relation of contrast, or cause and effect, do mutually suggest each other, is undeniable. But do such phenomena necessarily suppose the existence of a plurality of laws? May they not all be referred to one, and that the one under consideration? Those of resemblance, obviously may. The same is true of those which sustain to each other the relations of contiguity of time and place, and of cause and effect. For they undeniably have co-existed with the same feelings or states of mind. The only phenomena which present the appearance of difficulty, are those of Contrast. That a giant and a dwarf resemble each other in but few particulars, and that they stand in striking contrast to each other, is readily admitted; but that, as objects of perception, or recollection, they may have co-existed with the same feelings, or states of mind, and as causes also of the same,

I as fully believe, as I do that the conception of a hero and a lion have co-existed in a similar manner. A giant and a dwarf are strongly contrasted, but each, as striking departures, though in different directions, from the common stature, may have co-existed with similar feelings of *wonder* or *surprise,* and as common causes of the same; and this may be the only reason why one suggests the other. In conversing upon this subject on a particular occasion, an individual present remarked, that he recollected having, at a particular time, seen a dwarf. A giant, which he had previously seen, was not suggested at all, but another dwarf whom he had before met with. I at once asked the speaker, if the giant referred to, was not a familiar acquaintance of his. He replied that he was. This fact readily accounted for the phenomenon of Association, presented by him. Familiarity had destroyed the feeling of strangeness, which had formerly co-existed with the perception or recollection of the giant. The same feeling, however, co-existing with the perception of the two dwarfs; the perception of one would of course suggest the other. In the same manner all the phenomena of Contrast may be reduced to the hypothesis before us.

PHENOMENA EXIST WHICH CAN BE ACCOUNTED FOR ON THIS, AND ON NO OTHER HYPOTHESIS.

1. *Those falling under the relation of Analogy.* — But how can we account for those associations which fall under the relation of analogy? A hero and a lion sustain no relation of external resemblance, by which one would suggest the other. Equally removed are they from the relations of contiguity, cause and effect, or contrast. But as causes of similar feelings, or states of mind, the conceptions of them have co-existed in the mind, in connection with such states; and this, I believe, is the only reason that can be assigned, why the contemplation of one suggests the other.

Milton's account of the fight of Abdiel and Satan, may present a striking illustration of the principle under consideration:

> "So saying, a noble stroke he lifted high,
> Which hung not, but so swift with tempest fell
> On the proud crest of Satan, that no sight,
> Nor motion of swift thought, less could his shield,
> Such ruin intercept. Ten paces huge
> He back recoiled; the tenth on bended knee
> His massy spear upstayed; as if on earth
> Winds under ground, or waters forcing way,
> Sidelong had pushed a mountain from his seat,
> Half sunk with all his pines."

Now, why did the conception of Satan, thus smitten down, suggest to the mind of Milton that of a mountain pushed from his seat? The only answer that can be given is, that the contemplation of each induces similar feelings or states of mind. So of all the phenomena of association falling under the relation of analogy. Suppose, further, that an individual relates to a number of men some incidents of a sublime, beautiful, heroic, horrid, or ludicrous character. How happens it that each hearer instantly recollects almost every incident of a similar character, which he has ever met with? These incidents resemble each other in one particular only, and sustain no other relation to each other than this: they have, as objects of perception or contemplation, existed in the mind as causes of similar feelings to those awakened by the incident under consideration. The hypothesis before us is the only one conceivable, which accounts for such phenomena.

2. *Phenomena of Dreaming.*—The phenomena of dreaming can readily be accounted for on this hypothesis, and, as I conceive, upon no other. In consequence of peculiar attitudes of the body, or states of the physical or mental system, certain

feelings are awakened in the mind. Those objects of thought or perception, which have formerly co-existed with similar feelings, are consequently suggested; and these are judged to be the causes of existing feelings. A sick man, for example, with a bottle of hot water at his feet, dreamed that he was walking upon the crater of Ætna, and that this was the cause of the burning sensation which he felt. He had formerly felt similar sensations when walking upon the crater of Vesuvius, and had just been reading of a traveler's walking upon the crater of Ætna. These facts fully account for his dream. In a similar manner, all the phenomena of dreaming may be accounted for. Can they be accounted for by the common laws of Association? I answer, no.

3. *Phenomena of Somnambulism.* — Some of the phenomena of somnambulism here deserve an attentive consideration. It is well known that somnambulists frequently pass from a state of wakefulness to that of sleep, and *vice versa*, very suddenly; and that in each change, there is an entire oblivion of what passed in the preceding state; while the train of thought, or the employment left, when passing from the present state, is, on returning to that state, instantly resumed, at the very point where it was left. Sentences left half finished, when passing out of one state, are completed as soon as the individual enters upon the same state again. How manifest, from such phenomena, is the fact, that the universal law of suggestion is based upon similarity of states or feelings.

4. *Facts connected with particular Diseases.* — There are many facts connected with particular diseases, which more fully confirm and illustrate the principle which I am endeavoring to establish. Take, as a specimen, the two following cases stated by Dr. Abercrombie, in his Intellectual Philosophy. I give them in the words of the author:

"Another very remarkable modification of this affection is referred to by Mr. Combe, as described by Major Elliot, professor of Mathematics in the United States' Military Academy at West Point. The patient was a young lady of cultivated mind, and the affection began with an attack of somnolency, which was protracted several hours beyond the usual time. When she came out of it, she was found to have lost every kind of acquired knowledge. She immediately began to apply herself to the first elements of education, and was making considerable progress, when, after several months, she was seized with a second fit of somnolency. She was now at once restored to all the knowledge which she possessed before the first attack, but without the least recollection of anything that had taken place during the interval. After another interval she had a third attack of somnolency, which left her in the same state as after the first. In this manner she suffered these alternate conditions for a period of four years, with the very remarkable circumstance that during the one state she retained all her original knowledge; but during the other, that only which she had acquired since the first attack. During the healthy interval, for example, she was remarkable for the beauty of her penmanship, but during the paroxysm wrote a poor, awkward hand. Persons introduced to her during the paroxysm she recognized only in a subsequent paroxysm, but not in the interval; and persons whom she had seen for the first time during the healthy interval, she did not recognize during the attack."

"Dr. Prichard mentions a lady who was liable to sudden attacks of delirium, which, after continuing for various periods, went off suddenly, leaving her at once perfectly rational. The attack was often so sudden that it commenced while she was engaged in interesting conversation, and on such occasions it happened, that on her recovery from the state of delirium she instantly recurred to the conversation she had been engaged in at the time of the attack, though she had never referred to it during the continuance of the affection. To such a degree was this carried, that she would even complete an unfinished sentence. During the subsequent paroxysm, again, she would pursue the train of ideas which had occupied her mind in the former. Mr. Combe also mentions a porter, who in a state of intoxication left a parcel at a wrong house, and when sober could not recollect what he had done with it. But the next time he got drunk, he recollected where he left it, and went and recovered it."

Here are manifest and striking facts of Association. On the commonly received laws of the associating principle, they cannot be explained at all. On the hypothesis under consideration, however, they admit of a most ready explanation. How can they be explained on any other hypothesis?

I will adduce another fact taken from the same author.

"A case has been related to me of a boy, who at the age of four received a fracture of the skull, for which he underwent the operation of trepan. He was at the time in a state of perfect stupor, and after his recovery retained no recollection either of the accident or the operation. At the age of fifteen, during the delirium of a fever, he gave his mother a correct description of the operation, and the persons who were present at it, with their dress, and other minute particulars. He had never been observed to allude to it before, and no means were known by which he could have acquired the circumstances which he mentioned."

But one explanation can be given of such a remarkable fact. During the interval between the surgical operation and the sickness referred to, the feelings existing in connection with the operation had never been revived, and from the peculiarity of the feelings could not have been. During this sickness, in consequence of the action of the fever upon the brain and skull, these feelings were revived. The consequence was, that the circumstances attending their existence were recalled. No other hypothesis can explain such facts.

5. *This Hypothesis established and illustrated, by reflecting upon the facts of Association.* — Every true explanation of the facts of Consciousness, will, as soon as it is understood, be confirmed in the conviction of every one who understands it, as he subsequently reflects on what passes in the interior of his own mind. This is, in a special manner true of the hypothesis under consideration. Every person who understands it, subsequently finds its truth confirmed and illustrated by his own reflections upon the facts of Association, as they fall under the eye of his Consciousness.

ARGUMENT SUMMARILY STATED.

The argument in support of the principle of Association under consideration may be summarily stated, in the following propositions:

1. It is known to exist as a law of Association, in certain cases — in all instances of Association founded on the relations of analogy. No other reason can be assigned why the conception of a hero, for example, suggests that of the lion, but the fact that they have each co-existed with similar feelings, and as causes of such feelings.

2. All the phenomena, explicable by the commonly received laws of Association, admit of an equally ready and consistent explanation, upon the hypothesis before us.

3. All other phenomena, which cannot be explained by the commonly received laws, admit also of a ready explanation, when referred to the above hypothesis.

4. No other hypothesis yet known, explains all the phenomena of Association.

We are at liberty then to assume, that the hypothesis with which we started, ceases to be an hypothesis. It may be regarded as *the law* of Association.

EXPLANATORY REMARKS.

To understand fully the operation of the associating principle, two circumstances pertaining to it demand special attention.

The first is the fact, that when a deep impression has been made upon the mind by any thought or perception, the feeling excited may not only be revived by some subsequent thought or perception, but those feelings may afterwards recur *spontaneously*, without any other apparent cause, than the well-known mental tendency to return to states in which our minds have previously existed. When we have listened to an enchanting musical performance, for example, who has not, months subsequent to the event, felt, in the depths of the inner being, the spontaneous movements of the cords of melody, which were so powerfully swept on the occasion referred to, and which, at once, bring the whole past scene into distinct remembrance? The law of Association is this: When any feeling which has co-existed with any past intellectual state is revived, whether that revival is spontaneous, or is occasioned by some present thought or perception, that state will recur again, as a consequence of the revival of this feeling.

The second remark is this: The feeling which has co-existed with any former intellectual state, need not be wholly, but only partially revived, in order to occasion the recurrence of that state. Let some present occurrence produce feelings of joy, wonder, surprise, or regret, for example. Should any subsequent event excite these feelings in only a very slight degree, the former occurrence would thereby be suggested. This is a universal characteristic of the action of the principle of Association.

REASONS WHY DIFFERENT OBJECTS EXCITE SIMILAR FEELINGS IN OUR MINDS.

The law of associations has been stated and illustrated. We are now prepared for another important inquiry, to wit, *On what principle is it that different objects, or rather thoughts and perceptions, excite similar feelings in our minds, and thus mutually suggest each other?* The following may be specified as the most important reasons why different objects excite such feelings:

1. In consequence of *natural resemblance between the objects themselves.* That objects naturally alike should excite similar feelings, is a necessary consequence of personal identity. Such objects do not suggest one another, because they are alike, but because, that being alike, they excite similar feelings. The principle of association in such instances, is the same as in all others.

2. Objects excite similar feelings, and thus mutually suggest each other, in consequence of *similarity of relations to the original principles of our nature.* Sweetness, beauty, and harmony, as mere objects of sense, are totally unlike. But they may and do sustain such a relation to the original principles of our nature, as to induce similar states of mind. Consequently, the perception of one may suggest that of the other. Thus the origin of figurative language, such as sweet or beautiful sounds, admits of a ready explanation. Also the sublime comparisons of poetry and oratory, founded upon the relations of analogy. An Indian orator, speaking of the American Revolution, said, "That it was like the whirlwind, which tears up the trees, and tosses to and fro the leaves, till

we cannot tell from whence they come, or whither they will fall. At length the Great Spirit spoke to the whirlwind, and it was still." Says another, whose age numbered more than one hundred years: "I am the aged hemlock. The winds of an hundred winters have whistled through my branches, and I am dead at the top." "And I heard," says the sacred writer, "as it were the voice of a great multitude, and as the voice of many waters, and as the voice of mighty thunderings, saying, Allelujah; for the Lord God omnipotent reigneth." Milton, speaking of the breaking up of the counsel of Pandemonium, says:

> "Their rising all at once, was as the sound
> Of thunder heard remote."

An aged soldier, in one of the tragedies, says of himself:

> "For I have fought when few alive remained,
> And none unscathed; when but few remained,
> Thus marred and mangled—as belike you've seen
> O' summer's night, around the evening lamp,
> Some scorched moths, wingless, and half consumed,
> Just feebly crawling o'er their heaps of dead."

How different, as mere objects of sense, are all the things compared together in the above quotations. But sustaining a common relation to the original laws of the mind, they induce similar feelings or states of mind. Consequently, the apprehension of one, suggests that of the other.

3. Objects co-exist with, and excite similar feelings, in consequence of a *perceived relation between the objects themselves;* such, for example, as the relations of cause and effect—parent and child, &c. Why it is that the feelings excited by one of these objects are transferred to the other as soon as the relation between them is perceived, we cannot tell. All that we can say is, that such is the constitution of our minds,

that when two objects are known to sustain such relations to each other, they will, in all ordinary circumstances, excite similar feelings, and the idea of one will, consequently, suggest that of the other.

4. Objects co-exist with similar feelings in consequence of mere *accidental association.* Whenever the mind has been brought from any cause whatever, into any particular state, the accidental perception of any object, or suggestion of any thought, however foreign to the cause of the present state, will so modify that state, that the new object will ever after sustain an entirely new relation to the Sensibility of our nature. To the present state of the mind, thus modified, it sustains the relation of a cause. Consequently, its subsequent presence as an object of perception, or of conception, will excite, in a greater or less degree, that state, and will of course recall the objects which formerly co-existed with the same state. Thus the same object may, at different periods of our lives, be associated with entirely different, and even opposite states of mind, and states of mind totally different from what they are naturally adapted to produce. Thus of course they may, and will recall entirely different objects to our remembrance. In many instances, we find it wholly impossible to account for the change which has taken place in the effect of particular objects upon our Sensibility, and consequently upon our trains of association; so gradual, and accidental, has been the transfer of the object from one state of feeling to another.

APPLICATION OF THE PRINCIPLES ABOVE ILLUSTRATED.

The law of Association which has been confirmed and illustrated, has many and very important applications. To a few of these special attention is invited, as we conclude the present Chapter.

Ground of the Mistake of Philosophers in respect to the Laws of Association.

We are now prepared to state distinctly the ground of the mistake of philosophers, pertaining to the laws of Association. Because objects sustaining certain relations to each other do mutually suggest one another, they have fastened upon these relations as the laws of Association. In this manner, they have overlooked the fact, that objects suggest each other, only on the ground of a common impression made by each upon the mind, and that the *relations* existing between them present the reason why they make a common impression, instead of revealing laws of the associating principle. Philosophers have noticed the fact, that some objects are associated on the exclusive ground of a common impression. Yet they have singularly overlooked the universal law of Association revealed in that fact. "Things," says Mr. Stewart, "which have no known relation to each other, are often associated, in consequence of their producing *similar effects* on the mind. Some of the finest poetical allusions are founded on this principle; and, accordingly, if the reader is not possessed of sensibility congenial to that of the poet, he will be apt to overlook their meaning or censure them as absurd." Now, had the question suggested itself to this philosopher, Is not this the condition and ground of all Association of every kind, and do not objects sustaining to each other the relations of resemblance, contiguity in time and place, contrast, cause and effect, and analogy, mutually suggest each other, because, that being thus related, they produce a common impression? he would have perceived, at once, that his mind had dropped down upon the universal law of Association.

Action of the associating Principle in different Individuals.

We are all familiar with the fact, that the action of the associating principle is very different in different individuals. This is evidently owing to two circumstances — natural temperament, and the diverse pursuits of individuals — one thereby being more deeply interested in, and consequently more deeply impressed with different objects, and with different elements of the same object, than another. Let any number of individuals of diverse temperaments, for example, contemplate the same painting, each will be more forcibly impressed with those features of it particularly correlated to his own peculiarities of natural temperament. Hence the corresponding diversity of the action of the associating principle, in such a case. So with a gentleman on a tour of observation, a merchant engaged in the purchase and sale of grain, and a farmer seeking a location for his family, in looking over the same plantation. Each will contemplate it in the light of the leading idea in his own mind. A corresponding diversity will of course exist in the impressions received, and in the consequent action of the associating principle.

Influence of Habit.

That actions and trains of thought, to which we have been long familiar, are performed and carried on by us with a degree of ease and exactness perfectly unaccountable to a new beginner, is obvious to every one. In respect to the ease and exactness with which trains of physical actions to which we have become habituated are repeated, two reasons may be assigned.

The first is, a certain conformation of the physical organization, so that, as soon as the train is commenced, the action of the muscles in obedience to the will is spontaneous and necessary in a given order of action.

The second is, the fact that all the actions under consideration have become indissolubly associated with the same state of mind. Of course, as soon as that state is reproduced, those actions are spontaneously suggested in their proper order.

The same remarks are equally applicable to trains of thought to which we have become habituated. When the mind has often existed in a certain state, there is, as shown above, a strong tendency, spontaneously, or on the slightest impression, to recur to that state again. The train of thought having become associated with this state is, of course, pursued with precision and facility.

Standards of Taste and Fashion.

"A mode of dress," says Dugald Stewart, "which at first appears awkward, acquires in a few weeks or months, the appearance of elegance. By being accustomed to see it worn by others whom we consider as models of taste, it becomes associated with the agreeable impressions which we receive from the ease, and grace, and refinement of their manners." Thus the pronunciation common to the higher classes in Edinburgh, while it remained the capital of Scotland, and which was then regarded as the standard of purity in diction, has now become barbarous, in consequence of the removal of the capital to London.

Vicissitudes in respect to such Standards.

Every one is familiar with the perpetual vicissitudes in dress, and everything, the chief recommendation of which is fashion. The remarks of Mr. Stewart on this point also, are so much to the purpose, and so well expressed, that I will venture another citation from him. "It is evident that, as far as the agreeable effect of ornament arises from association, the effect will continue only while it is confined to the higher orders. When it is adopted by the multitude, it not only ceases to be associated with ideas of taste and refinement, but it is associated with ideas of affectation, absurd imitation, and vulgarity. It is accordingly laid aside by the higher orders, who studiously avoid every circumstance in external appearance, which is debased by low and common use; and they are led to exercise their invention in the introduction of some new peculiarities, which first become fashionable, then common, and last of all are abandoned as vulgar." There is one circumstance which Mr. Stewart has not mentioned, which has perhaps quite as much influence in inducing these vicissitudes as that presented above. "The higher classes" are pleased with revolutions in society which are visibly produced by themselves, and which do not diminish, but increase and render manifest, to themselves and the world, their own controlling influence. In the perpetual vicissitudes of costume proceeding from and controlled by themselves, they are continually manifested to themselves as the "glass of fashion, and the mould of form." Thus a continued gratification of the love of power is enjoyed, a motive not the most commendable to be sure, but yet quite as real as that above presented

Peculiarities of Genius associated with Judgment, or correct Taste.

We are now able to state distinctly the pecularities of true genius, when associated with good Judgment. It consists in distinguishing those things which please simply in consequence of accidental associations, like those above referred to, from those which are correlated to the original and changeless principles of our nature, and in thus shadowing forth the real and permanent forms of beauty, sublimity, and fitness. Those forms of thought which stand correlated to the current opinions of the day, may have a wide-spread ephemeral popularity, after which they sink to a silent or dishonored grave, and a long oblivion. The productions of true genius, associated with good taste, on the other hand, will please as long as human nature remains what it is.

Influence of Writers and Speakers of splendid Genius, but incorrect Taste.

It is well known, that very strong conceptive and imaginative faculties (the peculiarities of true genius), sometimes exist in the absence of a well-balanced Judgment, and consequent good taste. The productions of such individuals will be characterized by surpassing excellencies, and glaring defects. Yet the mass of their admirers will, in time, become as well pleased with the latter as with the former; and the defects will be more frequently copied by imitators, perhaps, than the excellencies. The reason is this: The defects come to be associated with the feelings of interest and delight which the excellencies excite. The former are thus embalmed and consecrated by the latter. Every individual who would preserve his taste unvitiated, should be, in a special sense, on his guard under such circumstances.

Danger of vicious Associations.

Great genius and great vices, polished manners and corrupt morals, and productions the most finished in respect to style and imagery, and the most foul in respect to sentiment, are not unfrequently associated among men. The imminent peril of intercommunion with such minds and with such productions, is manifest, in the light of the law of Association above illustrated. The feelings of sublimity, beauty, and delight, awakened by the contemplation of great minds, polished manners, and the perfections of style and imagery, at first weaken, and finally entirely supplant the feelings of disgust, abhorrence, and repellency, which the contemplation of vice, and corrupt principle, in their unassociated grossness, excites. The final result is, the acquirement of polished manners and style, with the loss of virtue and virtuous principles. That "which cannot be gotten for gold," and for "which silver cannot be weighed as the price thereof," in comparison with which "no mention shall be made of coral or of pearls, and the price of which is above rubies," has been exchanged for that which might have been attained in much higher perfection without this irreparable loss; but which may exist in connection with the foulest morals, and an equal pre-eminence in guilt.

Unrighteous Prejudices, how justified.

Every individual is familiar with the fact, that persons and classes of men, placed in circumstances degrading in public estimation, often become the victims of cruel and unrighteous prejudice. Some circumstance, aside from condition, is fastened upon as the cause of this feeling, which is thus justified, on the assumption that it is natural, and therefore necessary, designed and sanctioned by Providence. Feelings connected with individuals by accidental association, are assumed as resulting from the original constitution of our nature, and are justified on that assumption.

Giving Individuals a bad Name, spreading false Reports, &c.

It is very frequently asserted as a proverb, that the evils resulting from giving persons a bad name, and spreading false reports respecting them, will ere long correct, and more than correct themselves, in consequence of a reaction of public feeling, as the truth comes to be known. This would be true, were men disposed to render impartial justice in all instances. But this is far from being the case. Pre-eminent virtues and endowments, together with a commanding influence, may often, under such circumstances, occasion a reaction of public feeling which will perfectly overwhelm the authors of the mischief. The standing of the mass of mankind, however, is not such as to occasion such reaction, even when the wrong done comes to be known. Hence it often happens that the feelings first awakened come to be permanently, to a greater or less degree, associated with them in the public mind. If this is not so, no thanks are due to those who first set the ball rolling.

Influence of the associating Principle in perpetuating existing mental Characteristics.

"To the pure," says the Sacred Writer, "all things are pure; but to the corrupt and unbelieving, there is nothing pure." In other words, a mind truly pure comes to be so correllated to objects in respect to not only the action of the voluntary power, but also in respect to the Sensibility and Intelligence, that all things awaken thoughts and feelings tending to perpetuate and increase that purity. The same is true with the vicious. Every object of thought and perception is brought into such a relation to their Minds, as to generate thoughts and feelings which tend only to develop and confirm existing tendencies to corruption. This law of self-perpetuation which virtue and vice respectively possess, is found in the associating principle. In a Mind which has long been the cage of impure thoughts and feelings, those feelings at last come to be associated with all objects of thought, and thus the entire current of thought and feeling is turned into an impure channel.

There are no limits to the application of the associating principle, as above illustrated. Its importance in mental science will be appreciated as it is understood in its endlessly diversified applications.

CHAPTER X.

MEMORY AND RECOLLECTION.

TERMS DEFINED.

MEMORY and Recollection are treated by philosophers only as important departments of the principle of Association. This, as we shall see, is demanded by sound philosophical analysis. The two terms above named are often used interchangeably, and never distinguished but by the following circumstances. In the process denominated Memory, notions, or conceptions of facts and events, are spontaneously recalled to the Mind. In that called Recollection, these Intellectual states are recalled by an effort of Will.

STATES OF MIND ENTERING INTO AND CONNECTED WITH THESE PROCESSES.

There are three distinct mental operations connected with each of these processes of Mind.

1. Some feeling or state of Mind which has formerly coexisted with the perception or apprehension of the object recalled — a feeling or state spontaneously recurring, or revived by some object of present thought, perception, or sensation.

2. A simple apprehension of the object or event itself — an apprehension attended with no belief or judgment whatever pertaining to the object.

3. A recurrence, in thought, of the circumstances of time

and place connected with the perception or apprehension of the object.

The above statement verified.

That objects of Memory and Recollection are not recalled directly and immediately, but are suggested, in the manner above described, is obvious from two considerations.

1. From universal Consciousness. Those who are least accustomed to analyze the operations of their own minds, as well as philosophers, have noticed this fact. Hence the common affirmations: "This reminds me of," or "This suggests to my mind such and such occurrences," clearly showing, not merely that such events are suggested, but that the subjects of them are conscious of it.

2. When we wish to recollect any events, or in the common phrase, to recall them, we do not attempt to do this directly, but by directing the attention to various objects, at present before the Mind, that they may suggest those which we wish to recall. Memory and Recollection are, in this respect, subject to precisely the same law, and the law which governs each is the same which governs the entire phenomena of Association. The above remark is so obviously true, that philosophers, as stated above, almost universally treat of these subjects in the same connection, Memory being considered only as one department of Association.

PRINCIPLE ON WHICH OBJECTS ARE REMEMBERED WITH EASE AND DISTINCTNESS.

Taking this position for granted, or as having been already proved, it will follow, as a necessary consequence, that the *ease* and *distinctness* with which any objects or events will be recalled to the Mind, will always be proportioned to the depth and intensity of the impressions formerly received from them, and with the number of objects and events with which such impressions have heretofore co-existed, or may hereafter co-exist. This conclusion we also find to be confirmed by universal experience. When you hear the declaration, "Such and such events I shall never forget," suppose you ask the reason for such an affirmation. The answer will invariably be, "It made such a deep IMPRESSION upon my Mind." On the other hand, if a person is asked for the reason why he recalls with such difficulty any particular event, he will uniformly answer, "It made such a feeble impression upon my Mind." Assuming that the state of the Sensibility is the regulating principle of suggestion, the fact is self-evident, that the ease with which any particular event will be recalled, depends not only upon the depth and intensity of the impression which it formerly made, but upon the number of objects or events with which such impression may have co-existed, and shall hereafter co-exist.

Deep and distinct Impressions, on what conditioned.

One inquiry, of no small importance in mental science, here claims our attention, to wit, the circumstances under which impressions received from objects of thought or perception are rendered deep and distinct. Among these I notice the three following, as the most important:

1. Attention. In former Chapters it has been shown that attention is the condition of distinct perception, both in respect to the phenomena of Sense and Consciousness. In walking, for example, we do not remember the particular acts of volition, which directed each particular step. Yet we know that we must have been conscious of such acts. The eye runs carelessly over a particular landscape, and nothing but the most general outline is remembered, while we know that each particular part must have been seen by us. For the

want of attention, however, these objects were not distinctly perceived. Of course no distinct and vivid impression was made upon the Mind, and consequently they are not remembered. The manner in which attention influences Memory is twofold. It not only impresses deeply and distinctly on the Mind particular scenes, each taken as a whole, but all the parts of such scenes. Hence the whole of such scenes will be recalled by the perception or suggestion of any particular part which may be met with in other scenes. That Memory, however, does not depend primarily upon attention, but on the *impression* made by an objects of attention, is evident from the fact, that the ease with which any particular event is recalled, is not proportioned to the degree of attention devoted to it, but to the vividness of the impression received from it.

2. The impressions made upon the mind by a particular event, and consequently the ease with which it will be remembered, depends upon the *circumstances* in which the event occurred — circumstances external to the Mind; such for example, as its occurrence at a time or place unexpected, in connection with other events deeply interesting to us, &c.

3. The impression which events make on the Mind, depends upon the *state of the Mind itself*, when they occur. Offices of kindness, when we little need them, make a comparatively slight impression upon the Mind. They are accordingly forgotten with comparative ease. But the stranger who watched over us when we were sick in a strange land, we never forget, for the obvious reason that such occurrences are deeply impressed upon the Mind. Who is not aware that the impression made upon the Mind in reading a book, listening to a discourse, or witnessing any scene, and consequently the ease and distinctness with which they are recalled, depends greatly upon the state of Mind at the time?

DIVERSITY OF POWERS OF MEMORY, AS DEVELOPED IN DIFFERENT INDIVIDUALS.

Assuming the principle, that those things of which we have formed distinct conceptions, and which have deeply moved and affected our Sensibility, will be easily and distinctly remembered, the diverse kinds of Memory, as they appear in different individuals, may be readily explained.

Philosophic Memory.

The philosopher is, above all things, interested in universal truths and general principles, and in facts which illustrate such truths and principles. With names, and minor circumstances of time and place, he has little or no interest. These, of course, he seldom recalls; while general principles and facts connected with, and illustrative of general principles, he never forgets. Here we have the peculiarities of what may be called Philosophical Memory.

Local Memory.

With general principles, however, the mass of men are very little interested. Events, as mere events, with all their circumstances of time, place, &c., are the things which chiefly interest them. In such cases, general principles, if understood at all, will readily pass from the Mind, while facts and events, with all their adventitious circumstances, will leave their permanent impress upon it. Here we have the characteristics of what is called Local Memory.

Artificial Memory.

The third and only kind of Memory which it is necessary to notice, is called Artificial Memory, a method of connecting things easily remembered with those which are recalled with greater difficulty, that the latter may be recalled by means of the former. The manner in which the principle of suggestion operates in this instance, may be readily explained. The two objects are brought into the relation of co-existence with one and the same state of Mind; and the familiar object, by exciting that state, recalls the one less familiar. The inexpediency of resorting to such associations, excepting upon trivial subjects, is so obvious as not to need any particular remarks.

MISCELLANEOUS TOPICS.

A few topics of a somewhat miscellaneous character, connected with our present inquiries will close this Chapter.

A ready and retentive Memory.

The distinction between what is called a ready, and retentive Memory, next demands attention. A philosophical Memory is known to be the most attentive and least ready. General principles are regarded by the philosopher, as above all price. These of course he never forgets. For the same reason, facts and events connected with, and illustrative of general principles leave an impress equally permanent upon his mind. The Memory of such a person however, will not, in ordinary circumstances, be ready, for the obvious reason that when he wishes to recall any particular fact, he finds it necessary first to recall the general principle with which it was associated. For the same reason, Local Memory will be more ready, but less retentive. The qualities in objects with which such persons are interested, exist alike in such an infinite variety of objects, that when this quality is met with, a great multitude of similar objects will be at once suggested. They will generally be those however, which have been most recently seen. Persons possessing Local Memory merely, will excel in common conversation, and in what may be called loose and rambling composition. Philosophical Memory displays itself in the laboratory, the hall of science, on the bench, in the lecture room, and pulpit.

The vast and diverse Power of Memory possessed by different Individuals.

The degree in which this faculty is developed in different individuals, may now be readily accounted for. It is owing, as I suppose, to two circumstances — natural diversities in which the power is possessed by different individuals, and an accidental direction of the power. Themistocles knew every citizen of Athens by name. Cyrus and Hannibal had each a similar knowledge of every soldier in his respective army. Their original endowments made them capable of such acquisitions. They made such acquisitions, because they considered them necessary to the end they designed to accomplish.

Improvement of Memory.

But for the faculty under consideration, the past would be to us, as if it had not been. No advantages could be derived from experience of our own or that of others. Existence, at each successive moment, must be commenced anew. The same errors and follies, which formerly occurred, must be repeated, without the possibility of improvement. Through this faculty, the past furnishes the chart and compass for the future. The progress of improvement is onward, with perpetually accumulating force. The question, therefore, How can this faculty be improved? presents itself, as of special importance. The following suggestions may not be out of place on this point:

1. The first thing to be kept distinctly in Mind, in all plans for the permanent improvement of Memory, is the *principle* on which its ready and retentive action depends, to wit, *deep*

and distinct impression. All our plans for the accomplishment of the object under consideration, should be formed with direct reference to this one principle.

2. As impressions depend very much upon distinctness of conception, in all efforts, to improve this faculty, we should habituate ourselves to *form distinct conceptions* of objects, especially of those which we wish to recollect. In this manner, the impression will not only be deep and permanent, but the notion associated with it being distinct, will, when recalled, possess a corresponding distinctness.

3. In thought, the object should be located, in distinct relation to the *circumstances of time and place* with which it is associated. In this manner the impression and conception both will not only be rendered deep and distinct, but each circumstance referred to, as it recurs in connection with other thoughts and perceptions will, by exciting the feelings under consideration, recall the object associated with it.

4. Knowledge, in order to be retained permanently, must be *systematized and reduced to general permanent principles.* Otherwise, it will be exclusively subject to the law of local Association which is so temporary in respect to retention.

5. To converse with others, and write down our thoughts which we wish to retain, contributes to permanency and distinctness of recollection. Knowledge, by this means, is rendered distinct, the corresponding impression deep and permanent, and the whole subject of thought most likely to be systematically arranged. All these circumstances tend to render Memory distinct and permanent.

6. Memory also, to be improved, must be trusted, but at the same time, not overburdened, as is the case when everything is committed to it, without the aid of a judicious diary of important thoughts and occurrences. That faculty which is not exercised will not be developed and improved.

Memory is not exempt from this law. At the same time, to overburden a faculty is a sure way to palsy its energies. Nothing but Reflection and Judgment, properly exercised, can fix upon the line where memory should and should not be trusted, without the aid of written records of our thoughts, and thus secure a proper development of this faculty.

Memory of the Aged.

One of the first indications of the approaching feebleness of age, is the failure, in a greater or less degree, of the power of Memory. A characteristic precisely the opposite is also sometimes presented in the experience of aged persons — a wonderful revival of the Memory of the occurrences of early life. A lady of my acquaintance, for example, aged about ninety years, had occasion to amuse some of her great-grandchildren one day. She thought she would, as a means to this end, relate to them the substance of a story, related in verse, which she had read, when quite young. She had never committed it to memory, and doubtless had thought little of it for more than half a century. As she commenced the story, the entire poem came fresh to her recollection. She could repeat it all, word for word. These two facts in the experience of the aged, the failure, on the one hand, and the wonderful revival of this power, on the other, need to be accounted for.

In respect to the first class of phenomena, two reasons may be assigned for their existence:

1. The failure of the faculty of perception and attention. As a consequence, distinct notions are not formed of objects of present thought and perception. Nor do they affect the Mind as they formerly did. For these reasons, the peculiar feelings which have co-existed with former thoughts and perceptions, and would, if revived, suggest them, are not revived.

2. In the failing of the perceptive faculty, there is a cor-

responding change in the correlation of the Sensibility to objects of thought and perception. Hence the same feelings precisely are not now excited by objects of thought and perception, as formerly, and consequently former intellectual states are not reproduced.

In respect to the second class, I would remark, that every one is aware, that amid the hurrying scenes of ordinary life, such crowds of associations rush upon the mind, at one and the same time, that no one entire scene of the past, is often distinctly recalled. On the other hand, when we are in a state of temporary isolation from the varying tide of events which is floating by and around us, then is the time when our recollections of the past become full and distinct. Now the aged are in a state of isolation of a more permanent character. Hence when a past scene is recalled, the Mind is in a state of comparative freedom from all diverting and distracting associations. Consequently the scene, in its entireness, is brought into full and distinct remembrance.

Duration of Memory.

If the law of Association illustrated in the preceding Chapter be admitted as true, it will follow, as a matter of course, that Memory is absolutely indestructible. Thought can never perish. If the impression with which any thought has co-existed, should, at any period, however remote, be in any form revived, the thought itself may be recalled. If any element of a given impression be reproduced, no reason can be assigned why a thought which co-existed with it, myriads of ages ago, should not thereby be recalled, as well as the one which co-existed with it but yesterday.

Numberless facts also, which lie around us in society, fully confirm the principle under consideration as a law of Memory. The case of the aged lady referred to above, presents a fact of the kind. The most striking one that now recurs to my recollection is given by Coleridge. It is the case of a German girl who had always labored as a domestic. While Coleridge was on a visit to Germany, and in the vicinity of her residence, she sickened, and if I mistake not, died. During her sickness, she began to utter sentences in languages unknown to all her attendants. Learned men, from a neighboring University, were called in. It was then found that she was reciting, with perfect correctness, entire passages from the Hebrew, Greek, Arabic and Syriac Scriptures, and also from the writings of the ancient Fathers. The occurrence was, by many, regarded as miraculous. A young physician in attendance, however, determined to trace out her past history, for the purpose of finding a clue to the mystery. He found at last, that when quite small, the young woman had lived in the family of an aged clergyman of great learning, who was in the daily habit of reading aloud in his study from the writings above referred to. As the child was at work in a room contiguous, she was accustomed to stop, from time to time, and listen to those strange sounds, the meaning of not one of which did she understand. There was the clue to the mystery. Those sounds were imperishably impressed upon the Memory. Hence their repetition, under the circumstances named. Cases of a similar nature might, to any extent, be adduced. They point with solemn interest, to the nature of the immortal powers within, as well as to facts of portentous moment in the future development of those powers.

CHAPTER XI.

IMAGINATION.

THERE is hardly any department of the present Treatise, in respect to which I feel a greater solicitude, than that upon which we are now to enter. I freely acknowledge, that I have not been satisfied with the views given upon the subject by authors held in general repute. It is by no means certain, however, that, when we have discovered real or apparent defects in the productions of others, we can produce anything more perfect ourselves. It not unfrequently happens, also, that the supposed defects lie in our own ideal, and not in that in which we suppose ourselves to have found them. All are aware that there is such a function of the Intelligence as the Imagination. When we meet with any of its real creations also, all recognize them as such. But then, when the questions are asked, What is this power? What are its functions? or, What are the laws of its action? a true answer does not so readily occur, as, at first thought, might be anticipated.

DEFINITION OF DISTINGUISHED PHILOSOPHERS.

In further remarking upon the subject, I will first present some of the definitions of this faculty, given by distinguished philosophers. I begin with the definition of Dr. Brown: — "We not only perceive objects," he observes, "and conceive and remember them as they were, but we have the power of combining them with various new assemblages — of forming, at our will, with a sort of delegated omnipotence, not a single universe merely, but a new and varied universe, with every succession of our thoughts."

"What is imagination," says Mr. Payne, "but Memory presenting the objects of pure perceptions (in a manner afterwards to be explained) in groups, or combinations which do not exist in nature?"

"In the exercise of the Imagination," says Abercrombie, "We take the component parts of real scenes, events or characters, and combine them anew, by a process of the mind itself, so as to form compounds, which have no existence in nature."

"But we have the power of modifying our conceptions," says Mr. Dugald Stewart, "by combining the parts of different ones together, so as to form new wholes of our own creation. I shall employ the word Imagination, to express this power."

"Imagination," says Professor Upham, "is a complex exercise of the mind, by means of which various conceptions are combined together, so as to form new wholes."

It will be perceived at once, that, according to some of these definitions, the Imagination has a primary reference to the objects of sense; and according to all, its creations are *fictions*, which have no corresponding realities in nature. Such creations are composed of elements of perceptions of real scenes; but yet these elements are so combined, that the creations, in all instances, have nothing corresponding to them in the universe within or around us.

OBJECTIONS TO THE ABOVE DEFINITIONS.

If these definitions be admitted as correct, and as presenting the entire and appropriate sphere of the Imagination, we must find some other faculty to which to attribute a large portion of the best poetry in existence. I will present a few familiar quotations, as examples.

Take, in the first instance, Wordsworth's description of the White Doe of Rylstone:

> "White she is as the lily of June,
> And beauteous as the silver moon
> When out of sight the clouds are driven,
> And she is left alone in heaven;
> Or like a ship, some gentle day,
> In sunshine sailing far away —
> A glittering ship that hath the plain
> Of ocean for its wide domain."

Nothing is here presented but what really exists in nature. Yet nothing but a creative Imagination, of a very high order, could have shadowed forth such a beautiful conception.

Take, as another example, the 19th Psalm, as given in our Bibles, or as thrown into verse in our common hymn books:

> "The heavens declare thy glory, Lord,
> In every star thy wisdom shines."

> "Thy noblest wonders here we view,
> In souls renew'd, and sins forgiven," &c.

Who will pretend that we have not here the creations of the Imagination, in its purest, highest flights? Yet in the first instance there are no new combinations of sensible objects presented, but a simple statement of facts in regard to objects perfectly familiar. In the second instance, no invisible object is referred to, but simple facts in regard to spiritual objects. Again:

> "Along the banks where Babel's current flows,
> Our captive bands in deep despondence strayed.

While Zion's fall in sad remembrance rose,
Her friends, her children, mingled with the dead.

"The tuneless harp, that once with joy we strung,
When praise employed, and mirth inspired the lay,
In mournful silence on the willows hung,
And growing grief prolonged the tedious day."

No one, surely, will pretend that here is a combination of objects of perception, which had no existence in nature.

Take the following lines from a poem, designed to present the scene which transpired in the wilderness where Elijah lodged, after he fled from the wrath of Jezebel:

"Amidst the wilderness, alone,
The sad, foe-hunted prophet lay;
And darkened shadows round him thrown,
Shut out the cheerful light of day.

"The winds were laden with his sighs,
As resting 'neath a lonely tree,
His spirit, torn with agonies,
In prayer was struggling to be free."

I make but one other selection, taken from Wordsworth's Boy of Winander Mere:

"Who
Blew mimic hootings to the silent owls,
That they might answer him. And they would shout
Across the watery vale, and shout again
With long halloos, and screams, and echoes loud,
Redoubled and redoubled, concourse wild,
Of mirth, and jocund din. And when it chanced
That pauses of deep silence mocked his skill,
Then sometimes in that silence, while he hung
Listening, a gentle shock of wild surprise
Has carried far into his heart, the voice

> Of mountain torrents; or the visible scene
> Would enter, unawares, into his mind,
> With all its solemn imagery, its rocks,
> Its woods, and that uncertain heaven, received
> Into the bosom of the steady lake."

Surely, in none of these instances, have the poets given to "airy nothing a local habitation and a name." Yet no one fails to notice in all of them the appropriate results of the Imagination.

I have still another objection to these definitions. A correct definition always gives at least the leading characteristic of the object to which it pertains. Now the simple recombination of the elements of thought into conceptions which have no corresponding realities in nature, if it be the exclusive work of imagination, is the action of that faculty in its lowest functions, a function in which its action is hardly to be distinguished from those of Understanding and Judgment. I have seen a man, and I have seen a horse. To conceive of the body of the man substituted in the place of the neck and head of the horse, gives the conception of a non-reality. It is hardly needful, however, to suppose the action of a new power, to account for such a creation as that. No one ever thinks of saying of a given conception, This is the work of Imagination, *because* no corresponding reality exists in nature. On the other hand, when the child Milton presented to the judges who were to award a prize to the pupil who should present the best poem on the miracle of turning water into wine, the single line,

> "The conscious water saw his God and blushed,"

it is no matter of wonder, that those judges looked at each other with astonishment, and instantly awarded the prize to the child-poet and genius before them. If they could not have given a correct definition of the Imagination, they could not fail to recognize themselves as in the presence of one of its sublime creations, and its author as possessed of a mind in which that peculiar faculty was energizing with wondrous power. The reason why they thus regarded this production was not the fact, that it presented "a new whole," but that in the creation itself there was the realization of a particular *idea*, and its realization in a form adapted to impress the mind with a *peculiar sentiment*. Hence we propose a new definition of this faculty.

ANOTHER DEFINITION PROPOSED.

It now remains to attempt, at least, an enunciation of the true conception of the Imagination. An object may sometimes be best explained by comparing it with another of which we have distinct apprehensions. Of the Understanding we have such apprehensions. The fundamental elements of all its conceptions are, as we have seen, substance and quality, cause and effect. It combines the elements given by the primary faculties *as* given, without modifying them at all. It is the faculty, in short, which takes cognizance of realities as they are. Now we have in our minds other ideas than those of substance and quality, cause and effect; such, for example, as the ideas of the beautiful, the grand, and the sublime. These ideas last named, do not respect objects as they really exist (for they may, or may not, exist in harmony with such ideas), but as arranged and combined in a given manner. We have in our minds, therefore, two entirely distinct classes of conceptions — those which respect objects just as they exist in the universe of matter and mind, within and around us, and those in which the elements of such objects are in thought combined, in harmony, more or less perfect, with fundamental ideas in the mind itself; as those of the beautiful, grand, sublime, &c., which do not respect objects as they are, but certain arrangements of such objects. The function of the Intelligence which gives us the former class of conceptions, we have denominated the Understanding. That which gives us the latter, that which "hovering o'er" all the elements of thought appearing upon the field of Consciousness, combines them into conceptions, more or less perfectly conformed to fundamental ideas, like those referred to above, is the Imagination. By Coleridge it is called the "Esemplastic, or into-one-forming power." It recombines the elements of thought into conceptions which pertain not to mere *existences*, but ideas of the beautiful, the perfect, the sublime, &c., in the mind itself. A conception of the understanding is perfect, when it represents its object as it is, whatever the object may be. A conception of the Imagination is perfect when it shadows forth forms of beauty, grandeur, sublimity, &c., which correspond with the *idea* in the mind. Understanding-conceptions are compared with the object. The only standard with which the creations of the Imagination are compared, is the idea.

IMAGINATION AND FANCY DISTINGUISHED.

Mr. Dugald Stewart is the first philosopher that I have met with, who makes a distinction between the Imagination and Fancy. I will give the remarks to which I refer, as it will prepare the way for the distinction which I wish to make. "It is the power of Fancy," he observes, "which supplies the poet with metaphorical language, and with all the analogies which are the foundation of his allusions. But it is the power of the Imagination, that creates the complex scenes he describes, and the fictitious characters which he delineates." According to the distinction here made, it was the Imagination of Milton, which created the whole scene and the particular characters presented in "Paradise Lost." His Fancy, on the other hand, furnished the figurative language, analogies, and illustrations with which it is adorned. The Fancy, as thus described is, as it will readily be perceived, nothing but a particular department of the operation of the principle of Association. It collects the materials from which the Imagination creates its scenes and characters, and then furnishes the attendant embellishments. In conformity to this view of the subject, Fancy is defined by Coleridge, as the "aggregate and associative power." Thus defined, while the Imagination is that function of the Intelligence which is correlated to ideas of the beautiful, the grand, the sublime, &c., the Fancy is that function of the associative principle, which is correlated to the same ideas.

Another Definition of the term Fancy.

There is another use of the term Fancy called "arbitrary Imagination," or Imagination not governed by the pure ideas of truth and beauty. In this use of the faculty of Imagination, instead of the beautiful being shadowed forth, grotesque images are produced with intentional violation of all laws of esthetics. In the present Treatise, the term Fancy will be used in conformity to the definition first given.

IMAGINATION AND FANCY ELUCIDATED.

Preliminary Remarks.

I will here introduce two remarks, which it may be important to keep in mind, in order to a full appreciation of what is to follow, and will then proceed to the illustration and elucidation of the subject before us:

1. The imagination pre-supposes the Fancy, as the aggregative power; while the latter does not pre-suppose the former.

2. Upon these distinctions are founded the epithets com-

monly applied to each, the Fancy being, in different individuals, denominated rich, luxuriant, or the opposite; the Imagination being denominated sublime, beautiful, or the opposite, according to the nature and character of its creations.

Elucidation.

We now proceed to a further elucidation of the nature of the Imagination, as distinguished from the Fancy, and of the characteristics of each. We will commence as the basis of our illustrations, with a work familiar to all, and for that reason the more to our purpose, to wit, 'Paradise Lost.' Before Milton existed, the various parts of the entire scene presented in this work, had been for ages before the minds of millions. Every one that had read his Bible was perfectly familiar with the revolt of Satan and his legions — the war in heaven — the creation of man, and his fall, through the wiles of Satan — the Eden of man's first abode, and his subsequent expulsion, &c. These scenes, by the aggregative powers of the Fancy had often been brought together in the same mind at the same moment. But here they remained in scattered fragments, "without form and void," as far as unity and identity are concerned, till a new creative power in the mind of Milton, "moving upon the face of the waters," brought all the disordered and scattered elements into one harmonious whole. Now what is this power which gave unity to all these endlessly diversified scenes? It is the Imagination. The Fancy first aggregates the materials — the elements. The imagination then calls into being the "new heavens and the new earth," formed into a harmonious unity out of the elements thus brought together. The same remarks apply to all the individuals, &c., real or imaginary, presented to our contemplation in the above poem. For the further illustration of these remarks I will now present a few extracts from the poem itself:

16

"He scarce had ceased when the superior fiend
Was moving towards the shore; his pond'rous shield,
Ethereal temper, massy, large, and round,
Behind him cast; the broad circumference
Hung on his shoulders like the moon, whose orb
Through optic glass the Tuscan artist views,
At evening, from the top of Fesole,
Or in Valdarno to descry new lands,
Rivers or mountains in her spotty globe."

The character and scene here presented, were created by the Imagination. The comparison of the shield to the moon, was the suggestion of the Fancy. Again:

"Which when Beelzebub perceived, than whom
Satan except, none higher sat, with grave
Aspect he rose, and in his rising seemed
A pillar of state; deep on his front engraven,
Deliberation sat, and public care;
And princely counsel in his face yet shone,
Majestic though in ruin; sage he stood
With Atlantean shoulders fit to bear
The weight of mightiest monarchies; his look
Drew audience and attention, still as night
Or summer's noon-tide air, while thus he spake."

The operation distinct and separate of the two faculties under consideration, is too obvious here to need any remarks.

To the same purpose I make one more quotation:

"He, above the rest,
In shape and gesture proudly eminent,
Stood like a tow'r; his form had yet not lost
All its original brightness, nor appear'd
Less than archangel ruined, and th' excess
Of glory obscur'd: as when the sun new risen
Looks through the horizontal misty air
Shorn of his beams: or from behind the moon,

In dim eclipse, disastrous twilight sheds
One half the nations, and with fear of change
Perplexes monarchs."

Here you perceive the propriety of the epithets, rich, and luxuriant, beautiful, and sublime, as applied to the Imagination and Fancy. — An imagination, the creations of which are beautiful, grand or sublime, is characterized accordingly. As the Fancy adorns such creations with analogies varied, multiplied, and appropriate, it is denominated rich, luxuriant, &c.

CHARACTERISTICS OF THE CREATIONS OF THE IMAGINATION.

The Imagination is exclusively a secondary faculty. It operates only upon elements which the other faculties furnish. As the laws which control the Imagination, are the ideas of unity, beauty, grandeur, sublimity, &c., it is by blending, in a peculiar manner, the elements of thought and feeling which lie under the eye of Consciousness, that this faculty shadows forth those forms which correspond to these ideas. My present object is to mark some of the principles in conformity to which a creative imagination blends, unifies, and shadows forth the forms of beauty, grandeur, and sublimity.

1. *Elements of Diverse Scenes blended into one new Whole.*

The first that I mention is that already noticed in the case of "Paradise Lost;" that in which the elements of different, and widely diversified scenes, are combined into one harmonious whole — into one beautiful, grand, or sublime conception. The character of the conception will depend upon two circumstances — the elements introduced into it — and the manner in which they are blended. To move upon the elements of thought, and blend them into form, in harmony with some one conception, is the principal law which controls the Imagination, in shadowing forth the beautiful, the grand, and the sublime. Nothing, almost, has greater influence in awakening in us the sense of the beautiful, the grand, or the sublime, than thus to contemplate parts of widely diversified scenes, which, in our thoughts, have lain in scattered fragments, all harmoniously blended into one grand conception. Thought is beautiful, and that which is brought into harmony with thought, has great power in awakening in us the sense of the same. To blend into one that which in thought has before been disconnected, and thus to unify our conceptions, and excite in us the sense of the perfect, the true, the beautiful, the grand, and the sublime, is the peculiar function of the Imagination.

2. *Blending the Diverse.*

The poet had heard, with feelings of awe and rapture, from the neighboring hills and mountains, the reverberations of the trumpet's notes, as they were sounded forth from some high cliff, on the mountain side. Amid similar scenes he had listened to similar sounds from the waterfall. His Imagination blends the two, and thus shadows forth the conception of the beautiful:

> "The cataracts blow their trumpets from the steep."

The Fancy, or associative faculty, may connect, but not blend. This is the peculiar function of the Imagination. Under the influence of the former faculty, the poet would have said,

> "The cataracts sound like trumpets from the steep."

> "The sunshine is a glorious birth."

To blend the conception of the production of light, with that of a birth, reveals the plastic power of the Imagination.

> "But now, when every sharp-edged blast
> Is quiet in its sheath."

It requires some reflection to appreciate the beauty of diverse thoughts here blended. Yet reflection will draw it forth. We have all conceived of the 'sharp-edged sword,' ceasing from the work of death, and lying quiet in its sheath. We have also heard the chill wind of winter spoken of as having a keen edge. As the poet walks forth amid the bland and mellow air of May, when the keen edge of winter has passed entirely from the atmosphere, his plastic Imagination unites the two conceptions above referred to into one. Hence the beautiful thought, "every sharp-edged blast is quiet in its sheath."

I might multiply examples of the kind under consideration to any extent. But these are sufficient to illustrate the principle.

3. *Blending Opposites.*

Another principle in conformity to which the Imagination shadows forth the forms of beauty, grandeur, and sublimity, is by blending things opposite to each other, such as the animate and inanimate, material and mental, the rational and irrational. I will give a few examples, the most of which will illustrate the principle under consideration with such obviousness as to render any particular remarks upon them unnecessary.

> "'Twas night: the sultry atmosphere
> Half palpable with darkness seemed,
> Save when the lightnings, quick and clear,
> Across wide heaven in grandeur gleamed,
> Rousing along the fields of air,
> *The growling thunders from their lair.*"

Every one is aroused to a deep sense of the grand and sublime on reading such a stanza. Two circumstances impart special grandeur and sublimity to the thought here presented — separating and presenting as opposites, things sustaining the relation to each other of cause and effect, as the lightning and the thunder — and blending opposites, the animate and inanimate, and thus representing the thunders as growling monsters in their lair, roused to rage and fury by the lightnings gleaming in grandeur across the fields of air.

I cite another passage from the same author — a poet *yet* unknown to fame. The language quoted, the poet has put into the mouth of an ancient Roman chieftain slave, dying in his humble shed, amid his comrades whom he was about to lead forth in a struggle for liberty, and who were assembled

"To hear his last and solemn charge,
Ere Death should set his soul at large.
Half-raising up his giant form,
With awful luster in his eye,
He spake:
'Ye spirits of the storm,
Careering chainless, through the sky,
Your thunder-trumpet peals for me
A glad and glorious jubilee.
Like you, unmock'd by man's control,
When on the clouds your chariots roll,
My free and disembodied soul
Soon makes the Elysian fields, long sought,
The play-ground of its deathless thought,'" &c.

I shall not spoil the passage, by particular comments. Every one will perceive, that it is combining things opposite, things in themselves grand and sublime, that imparts peculiar grandeur to this grand conception.

In similar strains the same writer represents the imprisoned eagle, as longing to

"Rise through tempest-shrouded air,
All thick and dark, with wild winds swelling,
To brave the lightning's lurid glare,
And talk with thunders in their dwelling."

Here the rational, in its sublimest forms, is first blended with the irrational, and then with the inanimate; and then one of these beings is represented as longing to rise amid scenes of fearful grandeur and sublimity, to converse with the other in his awful dwelling-place. Thus a creative Imagination evolves the forms of grandeur and sublimity.

It is the peculiar *manner* in which opposites are blended, that imparts such peculiar beauty to that most beautiful of almost all compositions, the 19th Psalm. The imagination of the poet represents the entire material universe, especially the luminaries of heaven, as all held in a blissful and devout contemplation and study of the perfection and glory of the Creator — all learning, and each imparting to the other a knowledge of the Infinite and Perfect. Day speaks to day, and night to night, of some new-discovered excellence revealed in the manifold works of God.

> "Hark! his hands the lyre explore.
> Bright-eyed Fancy hovering o'er,
> Scatters from her pictured urn,
> Thoughts that breathe, and words that burn."

Fancy, as a bright-eyed, embodied spirit, hovering over, breathing thoughts, and burning words — opposites, in themselves beautiful, so beautifully blended, are what impart such surpassing beauty to this beautiful thought.

> "But trailing clouds of glory do we come
> From God, who is our home."

By blending things so opposite as spirits and trailing clouds, does the poet impart an ineffable beauty to the idea of the soul coming from the hands of its Maker.

4. *Blending Things in their Nature alike.*

Sometimes the Imagination evolves the beautiful, by blending things in their nature identical. I will give a single example of this kind, the subjective influence of maternal affection, as the poet has presented it:

"Her love to me, in strong control,
  Form'd of her life the dearest part;
It seem'd a *soul within her soul*,
  The very *pulse within her heart*."

No comments are requisite here, in pointing out the blending, plastic influence of the Imagination, in thus evolving the forms of the beautiful.

5. *Combining Numbers into Unity, and dissolving and separating Unity into Number.*

Perhaps in no way does the Imagination more frequently body forth the forms of beauty, grandeur, and sublimity, than by "consolidating numbers into unity, and dissolving and separating unity into number."

"How beautiful are thy tents, O Jacob,
And thy dwelling-places, O Israel,
As rivers spread themselves abroad,
As gardens by the river side.

He coucheth and lieth down as a lion,
As a young lion, who shall rouse him up.
Blessed is he that blesseth thee,
And cursed is he that curseth thee."

The main force and beauty of this passage consists in the manner in which a vast number of people are presented as one venerable personage. Every one is so familiar with examples of this kind, that I need not multiply them.

I will give a single example or two of the opposite kind, that of dissolving and separating unity into number:

> "And too oft
> Even wise men leave their better sense at home,
> To chide and wonder at them when return'd."

No individual can fail to recognize the beauty of the thought here expressed. Yet it mainly consists in dissolving the unity of the Mind itself.

> "Between the acting of a dreadful thing
> And the first motion, all the interim is
> Like a phantasma, or a hideous dream:
> The genius and the mortal instruments
> Are then in council; and the state of man,
> Like a little kingdom, suffers then
> The nature of an insurrection."

6. *Adding to, or abstracting some Quality from, an Object.*

When a property is added to an object which it does not possess, the object then, as Mr. Wordsworth observes, "reacts upon the mind which has performed the process, like a new existence." This is one of the ways in which the Imagination delights us with the conception of the beautiful. For example:

> "O Cuckoo! shall I call thee bird,
> Or but *a wandering voice?*"

The cuckoo, though almost continually heard through the season of spring, is herself almost always invisible. This fact imparts a surpassing beauty to the conception evolved, in abstracting from her the idea of substantial existence, and representing her as a "wandering voice."

Examples of the former kind — that of blending with objects qualities which do not belong to them — have been given under the preceding topics. I will not forbear, however, the presentation of a single additional instance:

> "Sweet day! so cool, so calm, so bright,
> The bridal of the earth and sky:

> The dew shall weep thy fall to-night,
> For thou must die."

The beauty of this inconceivably beautiful thought, consists in representing the dew drop, which in itself is the pure result of physical causes, as a tear which Nature sheds over the fall of a bright and gladsome day. Adding this new quality to the dew-drop, makes it act upon us as a new existence.

7. *Blending with external Objects the Feelings which they excite in us.*

The Imagination often imparts a surpassing beauty to what is in itself beautiful, by blending with the object the feelings which the contemplation of it excites in our minds:

> "O then what soul was his, when on the tops
> Of the high mountains he beheld the sun
> Rise up, and bathe the world in light? He look'd—
> Ocean and Earth, the solid frame of Earth,
> And Ocean's liquid mass, beneath him lay
> In gladness and deep joy. The clouds were touch'd,
> And in their silent faces he did read
> Unutterable love."

> "The moon doth with delight
> Look round her when the heavens are bare."

No particular remarks, after stating the principle, are requisite, to show how that principle is illustrated by such creations.

8. *Abstracting certain Characteristics of Objects, and blending them into Harmony with some leading Idea.*

The same object, in respect to different features of it, may be contemplated relatively to different ideas in the mind. In the light of how many leading ideas, for example, may the bright worlds that hang around us, in the immensity of space, be contemplated. Now, the Imagination often evolves the forms of the beautiful, the grand, and the sublime, by throwing these objects before the mind, in harmony with one or more of these leading ideas. Take, as an example, the following stanzas from a poem entitled "A Psalm of Night:"

"Fades from the West the farewell light,
  Flung backward by the setting sun,
And silence deepens as the Night
  Steals with its solemn shadows on!
Gathers the soft, refreshing dew
  On spiring grass and flowret stems —
And lo! the everlasting blue
  Is radiant with a thousand gems!

Not only doth the voiceful Day
  The loving kindness, LORD! proclaim —
But Night, with its sublime array
  Of worlds, doth magnify Thy name!
Yea — while adoring seraphim
  Before Thee bend the willing knee,
From every star a choral hymn
  Goes up unceasingly to Thee!

Day unto Day doth utter speech,
  And Night to Night thy voice makes known;
Through all the earth where Thought may reach,
  Is heard the glad and solemn tone —
And worlds, beyond the farthest star
  Whose light hath reached the human eye,
Catch the high anthem from afar,
  That rolls along Immensity!"

Every one who contemplates the thought here embodied, aside from the sentiment of devotion awakened in his mind, will have a sense of beauty, majesty, and sublimity of the works of Divinity, unfelt before. In the stanzas, also,

"And beauteous as the silver moon,
When out of sight the clouds are driven,
As she is left alone in heaven,"

that beautiful orb is thrown before the mind in the light of one idea only, that of the beautiful. To blend thus into one conception, the elements of beauty, grandeur, and sublimity, existing in objects which may be contemplated in the light of other ideas, is one of the peculiar functions of the Imagination. In the light of the conceptions which it shadows forth, objects the most familiar put on new forms, and stand before the mind in an array in which we never contemplated them before. New fountains of thought and feelings are thus awakened in the depths of our own minds.

9. *Throwing the fleeting Thoughts, Sentiments, and Feelings, of our past Existence, into one beautiful Conception.*

I mention but one other form in which the Imagination delights us with the forms of the beautiful, the perfect, and the true, &c. It is by throwing into distinct and hallowed embodiment, those deep thoughts and sentiments which have had a fleeting existence in our experience, but which above all things, we desire never to forget. Who does not feel like dropping a tear of gratitude for that divine gift which enabled the poet thus beautifully to embalm, for eternal remembrance, what we have all experienced, but might otherwise forget?

"The tear, whose source I could not guess,
The deep sigh, that seem'd fatherless,
Were mine in early days."

Every one feels himself richer, when he has found such a thought as this. Of the same character is the following:

"To me the meanest flower that blows can give
Thoughts that do often lie too deep for tears."

Every one, also, who is familiar with Death as the "shadow of the rock Eternity," finds his own hallowed experiences embalmed in lines like the following:

> "The clouds that gather round the setting sun,
> Do take a sober coloring from an eye
> That hath kept watch o'er man's mortality."

I forbear further citations. To embalm in beautiful forms the hallowed experiences of the race, is one of the high prerogatives which he enjoys who has been favored by his Maker with the higher functions of the Imagination.

REMARKS ON THE PRECEDING ANALYSIS.

It is not professed that the preceding analysis has presented all the forms in conformity to which the Imagination moulds its creations. All that was designed, is to give a sufficient number of particular forms, to aid the student in his inquiries into the operations of this mysterious power.

Another remark is this: The examples presented in illustration of one particular form, often contain elements equally illustrative of other forms. This was unavoidable. It was enough for my purpose to present, in each example, the element illustrative of the principle to which it was referred.

REMARK OF COLERIDGE.

Coleridge has somewhere made a remark, which I regard as of great importance in guiding the judgment in detecting the peculiar operations of the Imagination, and separating them from the operations of other intellectual faculties. The amount of his remark is this: It is not every part of what is called a production of the Imagination, that is to be attributed to that faculty. Much often is mere narration, and much the mere filling out of the grand outline of the conception which the Imagination has combined, and which as properly belongs to the Understanding and Judgment, as the filling up of the outlines of any other discourse of which the Intelligence has conceived. With a great portion of the filling up of Paradise Lost, for example, Imagination had no more to do than with that of filling up the grand outline of a sermon, or oration. In the sublime conception itself, and in the mysterious blending of the elements of thought often met with, in throwing that conception into form, here we find the workings of this creative, plastic faculty. To evolve principles which would enable the student, under such circumstances, to discern the operations of this faculty, has, as before said, been the main object of the preceding analysis.

CREATIONS OF THE IMAGINATION, WHY NOT ALWAYS FICTIONS.

In the preceding part of this Chapter, it has been shown, that the creations of the Imagination are not always, as it has been often stated by philosophers, "new wholes which do not exist in nature." It becomes an important inquiry, when and why is not this statement true? It will be evident, at first thought, that when the elements of thought which enter into particular conceptions, are wholly recombined, the new wholes, thus produced, must exist purely in thought, without any corresponding existence. On the other hand, when the elements of beauty, grandeur, and sublimity exist in objects in connection with other and different elements, elements also related to other and different ideas, and when the Imagination, as in the Psalm of Night, above cited, blends these elements first named into some one beautiful, grand, or sublime conception, every element in the conception may be in strict correlation to realities. Take as a further illustration, a single stanza from a familiar hymn:

"His word of grace is sure and strong,
As that which built the skies!
The voice that rolls the stars along
Speaks all the promises."

Every element in this beautiful thought is strictly conformed to realities, as they are. Yet in the blending of these elements, particularly in the last two lines, we distinctly mark the plastic power of the Imagination, in its sublimest and most beautiful form.

The same is equally true, where, as shown above, the same power embalms, in similar conceptions, the hallowed sentiments and experiences of the past and present. Who that ever saw the tear of gratitude lying in the eye of affliction — a thing far more beautiful than the dew-drop, when it holds in its embrace the image of the morning sun — a tear started by some gift that eased, for a time, the pressure of woe, and then turned away with a sorrowful heart, that such worth should be crushed beneath such a weight, does not recognize the *truth*, as well as beauty, of the thought contained in the following stanza, especially in the last two lines?

"I have heard of hearts unkind, kind deeds
With coldness still returning:
Alas! the gratitude of men
Has oftener left *me* mourning."

In another sense, *all* the *proper* creations of the Imagination are true. They are true to *thought*. In the depths of our inner being, there lie thoughts too deep for any words which we can command. Nothing but an overshadowing Imagination can call them forth, and give them an external embodiment. Whether the forms in which they are embodied are correlated to substantial realities or not, they are true to thought, the most important of all realities. We feel grateful, therefore, when we find thoughts which we had vainly endeavored to express, moulded into form, and thus assuming "a local habitation and a name."

I mention one other, and a very important sense, in which the creations of the Imagination are true. They sustain, in many instances, relations to realities analogous somewhat to that sustained by general notions. In a very important sense, these last have no realities in nature corresponding to them; that is, there is no one object, that in all respects corresponds to a general notion, that is, that contains the elements it represents, and nothing more nor less. The elements belonging to it, however, are found in each particular ranged under it. Let us now, in the light of this illustration, contemplate the forms of the beautiful, for example, shadowed forth by the Imagination. We may not be able, in all instances, to find any one particular object which contains, and nothing more nor less, the elements which enter into this form. Yet, whenever we meet with an object containing the elements of beauty, we find that element represented in the forms of the beautiful bodied forth by the Imagination. In these forms, we do not find any one particular shadowed forth, but each particular blended in the universal. In the most perfect forms of statuary, for example, we do not find any one human form, in distinction from all others, represented, but we find whatever is beautiful in *every form* there embodied. As the Understanding there represents the particular in the general, so the Imagination represents all particulars relating to the beautiful, &c., in the universal.

SPHERE OF THE IMAGINATION NOT CONFINED TO POETRY.

Most of the examples introduced into this Chapter are poetical. From this I would not have it supposed, that, in my judgment, the Imagination is confined to this species of composition. We meet with its finest creations, on the other hand, in painting, in statuary, in prose, and in every kind of discourse in which the *elements* of thought can be blending in harmony with pure ideas. It admits, at least, of a doubt, whether the Imagination of Milton ranged with a more discursive energy in his highest prose compositions, or in his Paradise Lost.

LAW OF TASTE RELATIVE TO THE ACTION OF THE IMAGINATION.

It is, as we have seen, the peculiar province of the Imagination to dissolve, recombine, and blend the elements of thought. Its procedure in all these respects, however, is not arbitrary. Every thought cannot be blended with every other, without violating the laws of good taste. Here, then, an important question presents itself, to wit: What is the law which guides the Imagination, in blending the elements of thought? I will present my own ideas on this subject, by an example taken from the book of Job:

> "Hast thou given the horse his strength?
> Hast thou *clothed his neck with thunder?*"

The propriety of blending the two conceptions, that of the mane of the war-horse and of thunder, has been questioned by some, on account of the total dissimilarity of the objects of those conceptions. It is readily admitted, that no two objects are in themselves more dissimilar. Yet it is confidently maintained, that there never was a figure of speech more appropriate. The reason is obvious, and every one feels it, though he may not have an analytical consciousness of it. When two objects are, as objects of sense, totally dissimilar, the conception of each may excite precisely similar feelings. Hence the propriety and force of the figure employed by the sacred writer, in blending the two conceptions into one. This I conceive to be the universal law of good taste, relative to the action of the plastic power of the Imagination. *Whenever two conceptions sustain a similar relation to any one common feeling or sentiment, they may be blended into one.* The more diverse the objects of those conceptions, the more striking the figure, under such circumstances. I will give one other example:

"The twilight hours like birds flew by,
As lightly and as free;
Ten thousand stars were in the sky,
Ten thousand in the sea;
For every wave with *dimpled cheek*
That leaped upon the air,
Had caught a star in its embrace,
And held it trembling there."

Who is insensible to the exquisite beauty of the thought here? Yet the wave of the sea or lake, reflecting the stars of night, no more, as an object of sense, resembles the dimpled cheek of beauty, or the mother catching up her babe and holding it in her embrace, than the mane of the war-horse resembles thunder. Why, then, are we struck with such delight at the blending of conceptions, the objects of which, are, in themselves, so unlike? The answer is: These conceptions are mutually correlated to the same or similar feelings. When such conceptions are thus blended into a beautiful emotion common to both, there is shadowed forth the perfection of beauty. For this reason our hearts leap up, when we meet with such thoughts as the following, taken from the same effusion, as that above cited:

"I have heard the laughing wind behind,
When playing with my hair—
The breezy fingers of the wind,
How cool and moist they were!"

IMAGINATION THE ORGAN OF IDEALS.

Another important function of the Imagination now claims our attention; its functions as the organ of *Ideals*. In illustrating this function, the first thing to be accomplished is to distinguish between *Ideals* and *Ideas*.

Idea defined.

An Idea, properly defined, is a conception of Reason. As such it has the characteristics of universality and necessity, and is consequently incapable of change or modification. Thus when certain conditions are fulfilled, Reason evolves the ideas of time, space, substance and cause, which we have already considered, together with such as the beautiful, the right, the true, and the good, &c., hereafter to be considered.

Ideal defined.

An Ideal is a form of thought intermediate between an idea, and the conceptions or notions which the Intelligence generates of particular objects, and presents archetypes in conformity to which the elements of such conceptions may be blended in harmony with ideas. In the mind of Milton, for example, the ideas of the beautiful, the grand, and the sublime, &c., existed, as pure conceptions of Reason. When the varied conceptions, the elements of which are blended together in Paradise Lost, lay under the eye of his Consciousness, his Intelligence, brooding over those elements, at last blended them together into that grand conception, of which the poem itself is the external embodiment. This conception was the Ideal after which the poem was formed, to realize his ideas of the grand, the beautiful, and the sublime.

Ideals, Particular and General.

Ideals, like notions, are particular and general. Thus, in the mind of Milton, there existed a general ideal of what a poem should be, in order to realize, in greater or less perfection, the pure ideas of Reason. At the same time, there existed a particular Ideal of the manner in which the elements entering into that poem should be blended, in order in that particular production, to realize those ideas.

Ideals not confined to ideas of the Beautiful, the Grand, and the Sublime.

Ideals are not confined to any one class of ideas. Every individual, in all departments of human action, has an ideal of the form to which the objects of his action should be brought into conformity, and in the light of which he judges of all productions which meet his eye. Ideas of fitness, of the true, the perfect, and the good, are archetypes of Ideals, as well as that of the beautiful.

Ideals not fixed and changeless like Ideas.

Ideals, as compared with ideas, may be perfect or imperfect. They are consequently capable of continued modifications. We often hear it said of individuals, that their Ideals are imperfect or wrong. As intermediate archetypes between conceptions of particular objects, and pure ideas of Reason, Ideals may, in the future progress of the Intelligence, undergo endless modifications, always advancing towards the perfect and absolute, without reaching it.

Ideals the Foundation of Mental Progress.

As intermediate archetypes between particular conceptions, and universal and necessary ideas, Ideals constitute the foundation of endless progress in the development of the mental powers. Every new elevation which the Intelligence gains, presents new conceptions of particular objects, and consequently new elements of thought. Every new element of thought involves a new Ideal, more nearly approaching the perfect and the absolute, and thus lays the foundation for fresh activity, and further progress in the march of mind. Sometimes also Ideals degenerate, and thus the foundation is laid for the backward movements of society.

It is hardly necessary to add that the Imagination is the exclusive organ of ideals. To form such conceptions is not a function of Reason, nor of the Understanding or Judgment. It remains, then, as the exclusive function of the Imagination.

Ideals in the Divine and Human Intelligence.

In the Divine mind, the action of the Imagination is always in perfect and absolute correspondence to the Reason. As a consequence, there is a similar correspondence between the Divine ideal and idea. All of God's "works, therefore, are perfect." Not so with the finite. Man may eternally progress towards the infinite and perfect, but can never reach it.

ACTION OF THE JUDGMENT RELATIVE TO THAT OF THE IMAGINATION.

Taste defined.

Taste is that function of the Judgment by which the characteristics of productions, especially in belles-lettres and the fine arts, are determined in the light of ideals and ideas of beauty, order, congruity, proportion, symmetry, fitness, and whatever constitutes excellence in such productions. The Judgment may be exercised upon Ideals relatively to ideas, and upon particular productions relatively to both. Thus Milton when he apprehended the conception realized in Paradise Lost, might, and doubtless did, often compare that conception with his own idea, to determine the fact whether the former made a near approach to the latter. In filling out the conception, he would continually compare the external embodiment with the internal Ideal. In all such operations, he was exercising those functions of the Faculty of Judgment denominated Taste. The existence of good taste depends upon the existence in the Intelligence of correct Ideals, together with a well balanced, and well exercised Judgment pertaining to the ideas of beauty, fitness, &c. If a man's Ideal is false, his Taste is of course vitiated. If his Ideal were ever so correct, and he was not possessed of a well balanced, and well exercised Judgment, pertaining to such productions, he would also lack the characteristics of good Taste.

Productions of the Imagination when not regulated by correct Judgment or good Taste.

In some individuals in whom the Imagination exists and operates with a high degree of energy, its action is not guided and chastened by good Taste, or a well-regulated Judgment. In such cases we find the most perfect forms of beauty and sublimity shadowed forth in connection with the grossest deformities. The subject also will, in most instances, be wholly unable to distinguish the one from the other. In listening to such men, we, at one moment, are perfectly electrified with the forms of beauty, grandeur and sublimity which are shadowed forth to our ecstatic vision; but the next, perhaps, we are equally shocked and disgusted with images worse than grotesque, and forms of speech in strange violation of all the laws of good Taste. Under such circumstances we have special need of two things, Patience and good Judgment. The former will enable us to endure the evil for the sake of the good: the latter to separate the one from the other, that we do not receive the good and the bad, as is too often the case, as alike good, nor reject both as alike bad.

The most perfect of all human productions are the results of genius associated with good judgment. Of these the productions of Milton may be referred to as striking examples. Grandeur and sublimity are the pre-eminent characteristics of his genius. And how seldom are his sublime conceptions marred with violations of good Taste.

PRODUCTIONS IN WHICH THE ACTION OF THE FANCY OR IMAGINATION IS MOST CONSPICUOUS.

The productions of different authors we read with almost equal interest, but for entirely different and opposite reasons. I now refer to two classes of productions only, in one of which the operation of the Fancy is most prominent, and in the other, that of the Imagination. In productions of the former class, there will be an exuberance of metaphor, and beautifully appropriate comparisons and illustrations, and these will be the main source of the interest felt. In contemplating the productions of a creative Imagination, on the other hand, the grand conception will be the chief, and in some instances, the exclusive source of interest.

COMBINATIONS OF THOUGHT DENOMINATED WIT, AS DISTINGUISHED FROM THOSE RESULTING FROM THE PROPER ACTION OF THE IMAGINATION OR FANCY.

By the imagination different conceptions are *blended* on the ground of co-existence with similar feelings. The feeling into which they are blended will be the leading one with which each is associated. By the Fancy different conceptions are *associated* on precisely the same principle. Now Wit consists in blending and associating conceptions on the ground of remote and generally merely accidental elements found in them in common. Such combinations and associations therefore surprise and amuse us. When the Irishman, for example, replied to the question, what he would take to go, on a cold winter's night, a certain distance, in a state of nudity, "That he thought he should take a very bad cold," all recognize the reply as an example of genuine Wit. On an analysis we find that two thoughts are blended here, on the ground merely of an accidental element common to both. The term *take* is permanently associated with the phrase taking cold, and has a mere accidental association with the question proposed, since some other term (as what will you ask?) would have answered just as well. The blending of the two thoughts, in consequence of such an accidental element, is what surprises and amuses us, and constitutes the real wit involved in the reply.

A clergyman once delivered a discourse on the Divine works. In the progress of his remarks, he said that everything God had made was perfect in its kind. As the speaker descended from the pulpit, he was accosted at the door by an ill-formed hunchback of a man, who, looking him in the face, with a kind of malicious grin, asked the question, "What, sir, do you think of my form? Do you think that to be perfect? "Yes," replied the speaker, "you are a perfect hunchback." Here is genuine Wit. It consists, as every one will perceive, in assuming the idea of a hunchback as a conception of the perfect, and then classing the individual present under it as an embodied realization of that idea.

A combination, in its nature, not unlike the above, was made by a celebrated convict at Botany Bay, in respect to himself and associates:

"True patriots we,
For, be it understood,
We left our country
For our country's good."

Wit may not inappropriately be denominated shallow sense, being, in most instances, the antithesis of a blunder, or a blunder from design. As two Irishmen were walking together, for example, the one after the other, the individual foremost took hold of the limb of a tree, which extended across the path (the end being broken off), and holding it in his hand as he passed along, as far as his strength would allow, suddenly let it fly back. His companion behind receiving the blow in the forehead, was thereby thrown from a perpendicular to a horizontal position. On recovering his standing, however, as he was rubbing his eyes, he very gravely remarked to his associate, "In faith, it is well you held the limb back as long as you did. Had you not done so, it would probably have killed me." Here was a blunder. Now suppose that a bystander had witnessed the occurrence, and had made a remark precisely similar in respect to it. This would have been genuine Wit. I would here drop the suggestion, whether the most of what is denominated Irish wit, is not, after all, amusing blunders?

BOMBAST.

In the appropriate exercise of the Imagination, the elements of some important and deeply interesting subject lie out with distinctness under the eye of the mind. The Imagination, brooding over these elements, combines and blends them together into forms of beauty, grandeur, and sublimity, according to the leading idea in the light of which they are viewed. Now, when the Intelligence, in any department of the empire of thought energizes upon some subject of deep and glowing interest, it will never throw upon its conceptions the attire of bombast. It may shadow forth figures homely, and in opposition to the laws of good Taste. There will be no forms of expression, however, swollen or bombastic. But this presents the inquiry, What is bombast? There are three forms which this style of writing and speaking assumes.

The first is that in which an individual, without any object of thought before him, attempts to form and shadow forth some vast and sublime conception. Thus the subject attempts to grasp and express "some boundless thing," by a simple effort of self-inflation. If anything is generated under such circumstances, it will, of course, be windy, and inflated with "great swelling words of vanity."

"O," said a miscalled clergyman, as he rose to address a congregation amidst the solemnities of the Sabbath, "O that this very refined, polite, intelligent, and virtuous audience would soar — and soar — and soar with me — to some unknown — planet." He arose, of course, without thought, excepting the conception that he must say something very fine. In his efforts at self-inflation, the idea of *soaring* would most naturally suggest itself, and with that, the rhapsody that followed.

The second form is, when an individual endeavors to impart to a thought of trifling importance in itself, a very great interest, by arraying it in the attire of objects of great beauty, grandeur, or sublimity. We are all necessitated, from time to time, to speak of subjects of little or no great importance. We ought, in such circumstances, to show our good sense, by letting such thoughts pass from us "with the naked nature, and living grace," if they have any, which naturally belong to them. But no. Some individuals can never speak upon any subject, without showing their want of sense, by throwing around it a drapery which subjects really beautiful and sublime would be ashamed to wear. I will give a specimen from memory. I will attribute it to no individual, because I do not know that any individual ever said it. I give it as what a son of Erin is reported to have said: An individual who wished to express the simple conception, that he might have stayed in his native country, but chose to emigrate to this, and came accordingly; a conception, surely, which it required but few and very simple words to express. To him, however, it was a conception of vast interest. His Fancy was accordingly sent abroad for figures with which to adorn it, and thus the conception appears:

"Silent in some hermit's grot, and lulled to rest on mossy carpets, he might have spent his truant hours. But as he sped his trackless footsteps through the labyrinthian wastes of Fancy's rich, enchanted landscape, a voice re-echoed from the vaulted palace of the skies, and in sounds seraphic dwelt, and hung upon his ear. Obedient to the heavenly call, he bade adieu to fair Hibernia's hills, and with his staff, like Bunyan's Pilgrim, he followed the guiding star, till it shot its sparkling beams, and mingled with its mates around Columbia's banner."

The third form in which the vice we are considering appears, is when an individual has a very meager, feeble, and faint conception of a subject of great interest in itself, and when he attempts to inflate his conceptions to the vastness of his subject, by swelling words and pompous imagery and illustrations. How often is a great subject marred and defaced, by being daubed over with the "gloss and fustian" of minds who never had an adequate conception of it.

> "Poets and painters alike unskilled to trace
> The naked nature, and the living grace,
> With gloss and fustian cover every part,
> And hide with ornament their want of art."

I will not forbear doing myself the pleasure, nor the reader the profit, of the following quotation from the "British Spy," as it presents one of the sources of bombast in public speaking — the conception, that in some part of a discourse an individual must be pathetic:

"This leads me to remark a defect which I have noticed more than once in this country. Following up too closely the cold conceit of the Roman division of an oration, the speakers set aside a particular part of their discourse, usually the peroration, in which they take it into their heads that they will be pathetic. Accordingly, when they reach this part, whether it be prompted by the feelings or not, a mighty bustle commences. The speaker pricks up his ears, erects his chest, tosses his arms with hysterical vehemence, and says everything which he supposes ought to affect his hearers; but it is all in vain: for it is obvious that everything he says is prompted by the head; and, however it may display his ingenuity and fertility, however it may appeal to the admiration of his hearers, it will never strike deeper. The *hearts* of the audience will refuse all commerce, except with the *heart* of the speaker; nor, in this commerce, is it possible, by any disguise, however artful, to impose false ware on them. However the speaker may labor to seem to feel, however near he may approach the appearance of the reality, the heart nevertheless possesses a keen unerring sense, which never fails in detecting the imposture. It would seem as if the heart of man stamps a secret mark on all its effusions, which alone can give them currency, and which no ingenuity, however adroit, can successfully counterfeit." *

* When I listen to such an attempt at the pathetic as the above, I am reminded of a fact which an individual used to tell the students, when I was in college; — an individual who was accustomed to visit us statedly two or three times a year, and whose visits were not the most welcome to those of us who never were able to pay our bills, and others especially who had had money enough, and could not give a good account of the manner in which they had got rid of it. This individual,

BURLESQUE.

Burlesque sustains the same relation to bombast, that wit does to a blunder. Each copies its antithesis from design. The proper, and only proper object of burlesque, is bombast, and faults of a kindred character. To attempt to burlesque that which is in itself deserving of veneration, is to render one's self most criminal.

In genuine burlesque, the original will be copied to a certain extent, but yet with such variations as to leave no doubt of the design of the speaker or writer. One of the finest specimens of genuine burlesque, that I recollect to have met with, was given some years since in a foreign review of the works of an Irish orator of some celebrity, especially for what the reviewer termed bombast. He accordingly presents a speech professedly after the style of the orator, a speech designed to show the great advantages which the poor man has over the rich, in respect to happiness. I quote a single paragraph from the speech, as it occurs in memory:

"Happiness, Mr. Speaker, is like a crow seated upon the top of a mountain, which the hunter vainly endeavors to reproach. The hunter looks at the crow, Mr. Speaker, and the

notwithstanding his unwelcome errands, was accustomed to render himself very agreeable, by amusing anecdotes, which he would relate for the benefit of the students. Among these he was accustomed to relate the following, which he himself had heard: After the death of Washington, a Dutch orator in one of the villages on the Mohawk was appointed to deliver an oration on the character of that great man. The people assembled, and were entertained for about an hour and a half, with a most bathotic eulogy of the hero. At last the speaker came to a sudden and solemn pause. "Boys!" he exclaimed, "be very still now dere in de gallery; —now I be'sh come to de patetic.—Vashington died vidout a grunt, or a groan, or a grumble."

crow looks at him. But if he should attempt to reproach him, he banishes away, like the schismatic tints of the rainbow, which it was the sublime, and astonishing genius of Newton that developed and deplored."

SARCASM.

Analogous to burlesque is sarcasm. Its appropriate sphere is to burlesque false claims to merit — claims which may not be assumed in a bombastic style. It attributes to the individual his claims, but does it in such a manner, that the irony shall be visible. "No doubt ye are the people, and wisdom will die with you."

PROPRIETY OF USING THE IMAGINATION AND FANCY IN WORKS OF FICTION.

I close this protracted chapter with two or three suggestions of a general nature.

The first is, the propriety of employing the Imagination and Fancy in the production of fictitious composition. Of the propriety of employing such a noble faculty in bringing out such productions, some persons, whose opinions are deserving respect, have serious doubts. To me it appears that such doubts have been occasioned exclusively by an abuse of what is in itself proper. Suppose I am contemplating a statue. It presents all the forms almost of grace and beauty that appear in all beautiful human forms. I ask the question, What individual does this statue represent? The answer is, that it represents no one human form, but the statuary's own ideal of beauty and grace, as it may be embodied in a human form. Am I offended at the fact contained in the reply? By no means. Why may not an individual as properly embody, in external form, an Ideal in his own mind, as copy an object less beautiful without? The Ideal within is just as much a reality, as the object without, and may as properly be represented with the chisel, the brush, or the pen. To shadow forth conceptions more perfect than the real around, is to lay a foundation for human improvement. But let us suppose, that an individual, gifted with the power of thus blessing his race, employs that power, not in shadowing forth the forms of truth, beauty and perfection, but in throwing such attractions over vice and error, as tend to draw the young, the thoughtless, and the ignorant from the paths of truth, purity and peace; —such individuals deserve the deepest reprobation of the universe, as having abused and perverted one of the highest gifts with which any intelligent being has ever been intrusted. The individual also who will familiarize himself with the productions of such authors, subjects himself to an influence of all others, best adapted to sap the foundations of moral character. The maxim of ancient wisdom, "The companions of fools shall be destroyed," is no more true, than the maxim that the reader of impure books will himself become impure.

FALSE IDEA IN RESPECT TO THE INFLUENCE OF FAMILIARITY WITH THE POPULAR FICTITIOUS WRITINGS OF THE DAY.

A very common impression exists, that familiarity with fictitious writings, especially with the popular fictions of the day, tends to improve the Imagination, and that because they are fictitious. Now this is a grand mistake. It by no means follows, that because a work is fiction, and not sober history, the perusal of it tends to improve the Imagination. It may tend, on the other hand, to no other end, than to vitiate the Fancy, by generating impure associations. For myself, I am persuaded, that the study of such works as Prescott's 'Conquest of Mexico,' and 'Alison's History of Modern Europe,' tends incomparably more to develop the Imagination than the perusal of the great mass of fictitious works that are floating upon the surface of society. The question whether the perusal of a work tends to improve the Imagination, depends, not upon the fact whether it is fiction, but upon the manner in which the elements of thought are therein blended. Without departing at all from the path of truth in the narration of facts, the Imagination of the historian may be almost continually energizing, in blending into the forms of beauty, grandeur, and sublimity, the elements of thought which the narrative presents. In contemplating history, as its glowing facts are set forth in such forms, the Imagination may receive its most rapid development. The remark of Coleridge, that but a small part of even the best poems that we meet with, presents the appropriate creations of the Imagination, is pre-eminently true of fictitious writings. The question, then, whether the perusal of a particular work of fiction tends to improve the Imagination, depends not upon the fact that it is fiction, but upon the manner in which the elements of thought are therein blended.

IMAGINATION AND FANCY — HOW IMPROVED.

Every power is developed in one way only — in being exercised upon its appropriate objects. Each of the functions of the Intelligence under consideration, has its appropriate sphere. To develop the power, we must find its legitimate sphere, and in that sphere exercise it upon its appropriate objects. The Fancy is improved, by developing in the mind the sense of the beautiful, the true, the perfect, and the sublime, by furnishing the Intelligence with distinct apprehensions of the forms of beauty, grandeur, and sublimity, which the universe of matter and mind, nature and art presents.

The Imagination will be improved by familiarizing the mind with the true functions of the power itself, with the laws which regulate its action, in blending into form the elements of thought, and with its actual creations, as given in the works of minds most highly gifted with this function of the Intelligence.

CHAPTER XI.

REASON.

THE preceding Chapters have occupied more than the entire ground which is traversed in the common systems of Philosophy, so far as an analysis of the Intellectual Powers is concerned. Such an analysis, however, leaves untouched many of the more important phenomena of the human Mind. Consciousness and Sense, which lie at the foundation of all the faculties which have been the subject of the preceding analysis, can never give us infinite, eternal, absolute, universal, and necessary truths, nor can they account for the existence of the ideas of such truths in the Mind. Such ideas demand the admission of another power, not supposed in the existence of conceptions of contingent and relative phenomena. These last might exist in a Mind totally destitute of a knowledge of universal and necessary truths.

REASON DEFINED.

That faculty which apprehends truths, infinite, eternal, absolute, universal, and necessary, is the Reason. It bears precisely the same relation to such truths, that Consciousness and Sense do to contingent phenomena. Like those faculties, all its affirmations are direct and intuitive.

Coleridge's Characteristics of Reason as distinguished from the Understanding.

Coleridge has taken great pains to establish and elucidate the distinction between the Reason and the Understanding.

Before proceeding to a further analysis of the phenomena and functions of the former faculty, I will present some of the characteristics of these faculties — characteristics which he has given to distinguish the one from the other. In giving their characteristics, I shall use the term Understanding in the sense in which Coleridge himself appears to use it, as including the Judgment as well as the notion-forming power. I desire this fact to be kept distinctly in mind. In all other parts of this Treatise I use the Understanding and Judgment in strict accordance with the definitions given in preceding Chapters. Here I use the term Understanding in accommodation to the usage of the author whose distinctions I shall endeavor to elucidate. What then are the great distinctions between the Reason and Understanding, as laid down by this Philosopher?

1. "The Understanding, in all its judgments, refers to some other faculty as its ultimate authority." "The Reason in all its decisions appeals to itself." Take as an illustration of the above distinction the following proposition: "This is a book." "Space is, or exists." The first proposition supposes three things in the Mind — the conception designated by the term book — the perception of the particular object, a judgment that the object corresponds to the conception — and a consequent subsumption of the object under the conception. Now this judgment is an affirmation of the Understanding. Is it self-affirmed, or is it based upon the authority of some other faculty? Ask the speaker, how he knows that this is a book? He refers at once to Sense ("I see it"), and to a notion of a class derived from previous perceptions. The same may be shown to be true of every other affirmation of the Understanding, or generalizing power.

Let us now look at the second proposition — Space is. On what authority is this affirmation made? Upon no other authority than that of the faculty which apprehends the idea.

So of the proposition, "Every event has a cause." All men know it to be true. In all minds, however, the faculty which affirms it is the sole authority for the affirmation. The same principle holds in respect to all the judgments of the pure Reason.

2. "The judgments of the Understanding admit of degrees. Those of the Reason preclude all degrees." In reference to some particular object of the perception, for example, under certain circumstances, we conjecture that it is a man; under others, we believe it to be a man; under others, we are sure that it is; and under others still, we know it to be a man, &c. But who merely conjectures or believes that every event has a cause? We know it absolutely. In respect to this subject, the affirmation of the child and of the man, of the philosopher and of the peasant, are equally positive, and equally preclude all degrees.

3. The laws which govern the Understanding in all its judgments are imposed upon it by the Reason; while the laws of the Reason are self-imposed. I feel, for example, a painful sensation. Instantly I apply my Understanding to determine the particular cause. By what law is my Understanding governed, under such circumstances? By an idea or law, certainly, which exists, not in the Understanding itself, to wit, the affirmation of the pure Reason, that every event must have a cause. The same is true in regard to all other inquiries and affirmations of the Understanding, in regard to material substances. It obeys laws prescribed by another faculty. The Reason, however, obeys no laws but those which are self-imposed. When the Reason affirms absolutely that every event must have a cause — that succession supposes time — and that body supposes space, what law prescribed by another faculty or faculties does the Reason obey in such affirmations? None, surely.

4. All the judgments of the Understanding are contingent.

All the affirmations of the Reason are universal and necessary. I have before me, I will suppose, a right-angled triangle. I wish to know what relation exists between the square of the hypothenuse and the sum of the squares of the two sides. I first determine this question by actual measurement, and find that they are equal. I have now before me a particular fact. Why it is so, I know not, or whether this fact holds true in regard to other triangles, I know not. I repeat the experiment upon similar triangles of various sizes, and find that they all give me precisely the same result. I very soon begin to conjecture that this fact holds true of all similar triangles. Repeated experiments ripen this conjecture into such a conviction as to preclude all doubt. Still there is no absolute knowledge. Nor does there appear any necessity, from the nature of the subjects of these experiments, that the conclusions should not be different from what they are. Now let a person, in whose mind the principles of Geometry are developed, construct a figure and demonstrate the fact under consideration, in respect to that one particular triangle. What is the conclusion deduced from this demonstration? Not only that this fact holds in regard to this particular triangle, but that it does and must hold true in regard to all other similar triangles. In the former instance, we obtained a particular, contingent truth, as conceived by the Mind. In the latter we obtained a truth, universal and necessary.

5. The "Understanding is discursive." "The Reason is fixed." The judgments of the Understanding admit of degrees, and are perpetually passing and repassing from mere conjecture to positive affirmation; from doubt and disbelief to positive faith, and the opposite. The decisions of the Reason, however, have ever been characterized by the total absence of all degrees. They are, and always have been, positive, absolute affirmations.

6. The Understanding is the faculty of *believing*. The Reason is the faculty of *knowing*. Those who have never been in London or Paris, believe, with greater or less degrees of confidence, according to their knowledge of the facts, that there are such cities in existence. Yet they cannot, with strict propriety, be said to know these facts. But every person, in whose mind Reason exists at all, knows absolutely that space is — that every event must have a cause, &c.

The above distinctions, most of which are specifically stated, though none of them are illustrated, by Coleridge, not only distinguish the Understanding and Judgment from the Reason, but tend to elucidate the functions of each. I will now proceed directly to a further elucidation of the functions of Reason.

SECONDARY IDEAS OF REASON.

In former Chapters it has been shown, that Reason sustains this relation to the faculties of Sense and Consciousness: It gives the logical antecedents of phenomena affirmed by these faculties. Thus, on the perception of phenomena, we have the ideas of time, space, substance, personal identity, and cause.

Now Reason sustains a relation to the Understanding precisely similar to that which it sustains to Sense and Consciousness. It gives the logical antecedents of *notions* and *conceptions*, as well as of primary intuitions. The idea of right and wrong, of obligation, is not the logical antecedent of mere phenomena given by Sense and Consciousness. Before obligation can be conceived of or affirmed, the notion or conception, not of mere phenomena, but of an *agent* possessed of certain powers, and sustaining certain relations to other agents, must be developed in the Intelligence. The idea of obligation, then, is not the logical antecedent of phenomena affirmed by Sense and Consciousness, but of notions given by the Understanding. These considerations fully establish the propriety of the distinction between ideas of Reason as *primary* and *secondary*. The former are the logical antecedents of phenomena given by the primary contingent faculties. The latter sustain the same relation to those of the secondary faculties. The distinction here made seems hitherto, as far as my knowledge extends, to have escaped the notice of the analyzers of the human Intelligence. Its reality and importance to a correct understanding of the operations of the human Mind, will appear manifest, as we proceed with our analysis of the secondary ideas of Reason. An exposition of all the ideas comprehended under this class will not be attempted. All that will be attempted will be the induction and elucidation of a sufficient number of particulars to serve as lights to the philosophic inquirer, in his researches in the domain of mental science.

IDEA OF RIGHT AND WRONG.

Of the Secondary ideas of Reason, that which claims the first, and more special attention, is the one mentioned above, that of right or wrong, together with those dependent upon it, or necessarily connected with it.

This Idea exists in all Minds in which Reason is developed.

It is an undeniable fact, that in the presence of certain actions, the human mind characterizes them as good or bad, right or wrong; that the mind affirms to itself, that one class of the actions ought, and the other ought not to be performed; that when we have performed certain actions, we deserve reward, and that when we have performed others, we deserve punishment; and that when this takes place, there is moral order, and when it does not, there is moral disorder. Such judgments are passed alike by all mankind, the old and the young, the learned and the ignorant, the savage and the civilized. Should it be said, that mankind differ in different circumstances in their judgment of the moral qualities of actions, I reply:

1. This objection itself implies the universality of moral distinctions. As men may differ in referring particular effects to particular causes, while all agree in the judgment, that every event must have a cause, so it is with moral distinctions. Men may not always attribute the same moral qualities to the same actions; yet they universally agree in this, that actions are either right or wrong.

2. But when we refer to *intentions*, in which alone the moral quality of actions consists, we find a more extensive agreement among men than is generally supposed. A man wills the good of an individual possessed of moral excellence. Where is the intelligent being in existence who does or can regard such an act as any other than virtuous? Who is not aware, that men always justify wrong actions, if at all, by a reference to their intentions, showing by such reference, that in their judgment of the great law of love, all agree.

3. Vicious actions are seldom regarded as virtuous. Men may persuade themselves that it is not *wrong* to perform such actions, but never that they are *bound* to do them, or deserve a reward for having done them.

4. When an intention morally right is submitted to the contemplation of mankind, all agree in admitting it as virtuous and meritorious. Thus the sacred writer speaks of himself and associates, as through a "manifestation of the truth, commending themselves to every man's conscience." This could not have been the case, had not the consciences of all men been in fixed correlation to the moral law. The idea of right and wrong, then, is universal.

Idea of Right and Wrong necessary.

It is also necessary. When the Intelligence affirms an action or intention to be right or wrong, it is impossible even to conceive of it, as possessed of the opposite character. We can no more form such a conception, than we can conceive of the annihilation of space. It has the same claim to the characteristics of universality and necessity, that any other idea has.

Ideas dependent on that of Right and Wrong.

A moment's reflection will convince us, that the idea of right and wrong is the foundation of that of obligation; and this again, of that of merit or demerit; and this last of that of reward and punishment. When men would justify the bestowment of reward, or the infliction of punishment, they always refer to the *merit* or *demerit* of the individual. This judgment is sustained by a reference to the *obligation* of the same individual, and his obligations are shown by a reference to the idea of right and wrong. Such facts clearly indicate the relation of these ideas, the one to the other.

Chronological Antecedent to the Idea of Right and Wrong, &c.

It has already been remarked, that the ideas under consideration are the logical antecedents, not of the phenomena of the primary contingent faculties, but of Understanding-conceptions. Before we can conceive of ourselves as subjects of moral obligation, we must be conscious of the possession of certain powers, and of existence in certain relations to other beings. This knowledge is the chronological antecedent of the ideas of right and wrong, while these ideas sustain to these facts of Consciousness the relation of logical antecedents. The question now is, What are the elements of moral agency, necessarily pre-supposed, as the condition of the existence of the ideas of right and wrong, of obligation, &c., in our minds? They are the following:

1. Power to know ourselves together with our relations.

2. The actual perception of such relations.

3. Power to act, or to refuse to act, in harmony with these relations.

That the ideas of right and wrong sustain to such conceptions the relation of logical antecedent, is evident from the following considerations:

1. When we conceive of a being possessed of these powers, and existing in such relations, we necessarily affirm obligations of him. An intelligent being is revealed to me, as possessed of capacity for virtue or vice, together with susceptibilities for happiness or misery. I have a consciousness of the power to will his virtue and happiness, or his vice and misery. I instantly affirm myself under obligation to will the former instead of the latter. No other conceptions are necessary to the existence of this affirmation. These facts also being postulated, obligation must be affirmed. We can no more conceive it right to will the evil instead of the good, or, that we are not under obligation to will the latter, than we can conceive of the annihilation of space.

2. If any of these elements are not postulated, obligation cannot be conceived of, nor affirmed. If we deny of a creature intelligence to perceive his relations to other beings, we cannot conceive of him as under obligation to them. Whatever degree of intelligence be attributed to him, this involves, in our apprehensions, no obligation to one act of Will instead of another, in the absence of all power to put forth the required, instead of the prohibited act. Suppose a creature has any degree of intelligence whatever. This creates no obligation to locomotion in the absence of corresponding power. Suppose the mind located in a body totally destitute of the

power of locomotion. Would the existence of intelligence create obligation to locomotion? Certainly not. Such would be the response of universal Mind. Now the power to will is just as distinct from the Intelligence, as that of locomotion is. Hence, intelligence, of whatever kind or degree, can no more create obligation to one than the other, in the absence of corresponding power. To the conception of an agent, then, possessed of intelligence to know his relations, and power to act, or refuse to act, in harmony with those relations, the ideas of right and wrong, of obligation, &c., sustain the relation of logical antecedents.

IDEA OF FITNESS.

Every person who has attentively noticed the operations of his own mind, must have observed, that under certain circumstances, certain actions, or certain states of mind, appeared to him fit and proper. When asked to give a reason for such judgments, no other account can be given, than a simple reference to the nature of the thing itself, and to the circumstances supposed. For illustration, take the following passage of Scripture: "It was meet that we should make merry and be glad; for this thy brother was dead, and is alive again; and was lost, and is found." Suppose that father to have been required to give a reason for the judgment, that under the circumstances supposed, joy and merriment were fit or proper. What answer could he have given? No other answer than for the judgment, that no phenomena exist without a cause. In both instances, the mind knows absolutely that its judgments are, and must be true. No other reason for their truth, however, can be given, than this: The circumstances being given, they are self-affirmed.

This Idea synonymous with that of Right and Wrong, &c.

Now the idea of fitness, when applied to *moral relations,*

is identical with that of right and wrong. It is the foundation of the idea of merit and demerit; and consequently of that of reward and punishment.

It is also identical with the idea of moral order. When it is asked, Why is that state in which virtue is rewarded and vice punished, regarded as a state of moral order? no other reason can be assigned than this: Such a state is fit and proper.

IDEA OF THE USEFUL, OR THE GOOD.

Whenever we conceive of a creature capable of pleasure or pain, happiness or misery, we necessarily conceive of a state in which *all* the capacities of such a creature for pleasure and happiness are perfectly filled. This state we designate by the term *good*, a term sometimes used in another sense, as synonymous with that of right. Whatever tends to fill out the measure of pleasure and happiness, we designate by the general term, useful.

The ideas of the useful and the good, above defined, give birth to all the varied forms of human industry, such as agriculture, the mechanic arts, commerce, &c. All are moving on to the realization of one great leading idea, the filling up of the capacities of man for pleasure and happiness.

THE SUMMUM BONUM.

There is one idea of Reason, expressed by the words, *the great good*, the *summum bonum*, and the τὸ καλόν, about which philosophers have long disputed, and in respect to which they have been about equally divided in opinion. The question may be thus put: When we think of ourselves, or of the universe at large, what is that state to which our nature is correlated, so that we regard it as preferable to any other, actual or conceivable?

Some have placed the great good in happiness merely. To this position, however, we find that our nature is not exclusively correlated. If happiness were the only thing to which our nature is correlated, as in itself alone to be desired, if happiness exists, we should be totally indifferent in respect to the means, or conditions of its existence. We are not pleased, but pained at the thought, for example, that perfect happiness should be associated with great wickedness.

Others, in departing from this idea, have placed the great good in virtue. To this position, also, we find that our nature is not correlated. If virtue is the only thing that the Mind regards as good, it would be indifferent in respect to the condition in which it should exist; whether, for example, the virtuous agent were happy or miserable. We are pained, on the other hand, at the thought, that virtuous beings should not be happy. Happiness our Intelligence affirms to be the right of the pure and the virtuous.

The true solution is, no doubt, to be found in the blending of the two above given, or, as Cousin expresses it, "In the connection and harmony of virtue and happiness, as merited by it." If we conceive of a state of perfect virtue, associated with perfect happiness, this conception contains a realization of our idea of the *summum bonum*. Every department of our nature is correlated to that idea. We can conceive of no state so much to be desired as this. Nor can we perceive any element in this state to which the laws of our being do not fully respond.

RELATIONS OF THE IDEAS OF RIGHT AND WRONG AND OF THE USEFUL TO EACH OTHER.

We have seen above, that the ideas of right and wrong are the foundation of obligation, and this of merit and demerit, &c. The question has long been agitated among philosophers, whether there is any idea that sustains a similar relation to that of right and wrong, and of obligation By some it is maintained, that this is not an ultimate idea of Reason, but that it has its foundation in another, to wit, that of the useful. This question I regard as of such fundamental importance in mental and moral philosophy both, that I shall enter into a discussion somewhat protracted of it. The question then is, What is the foundation of moral obligation? Is utility this ground?

This purely a Psychological Question.

The object of Mental Philosophy, it should be borne in mind, is to explain human nature. When the Intelligence, for example, makes particular affirmations, the object of this science is, to ascertain the *reasons* in view of which such affirmations are made.

It is admitted by all, that in the presence of certain actions, the Mind does, as a matter of fact, affirm its obligation to perform them. The question, and the only question, for the philosopher to solve here is, What is the element or elements, in view of which this affirmation is made? The Utilitarian affirms that the *perceived utility* of the action, or its perceived tendency to promote happiness, is the only element in the action, and the only circumstance connected with it, in view of which obligation to perform it is, or can be affirmed. In view of nothing else, if this theory is true, can such affirmation be made? Now, as every one will perceive at once, the question whether this theory is true, is exclusively a psychological question. It can be truly answered, only by an appeal to Consciousness.

The theory under consideration is also given as a universal theory. If obligation is, in any instance, affirmed in view of any other consideration, this theory falls to the ground.

Further, if the Utilitarian, as is sometimes done, assumes the position, that PERCEIVED tendency is not the sole reason, why obligation is, in all instances affirmed, while it is in fact the only element which gives existence to obligation, his theory, instead of explaining the human Intelligence, convicts it of fundamental error, inasmuch as it asserts, that the Intelligence affirms obligation in view of considerations, which do not give existence to obligation. Having thus convicted the Intelligence of fundamental error, how is he afterwards, through the same Intelligence, to find out the truth? Now, at this point, we join issue with the Utilitarian. We assert that his theory does not correctly explain the human Intelligence relatively to the question under consideration, and is therefore wrong. To show this we will inquire,

Nature of Virtue.

In the first place, What is virtue? I answer, virtue is not a phenomenon of the Intelligence or Sensibility, but of the Will. As a phenomenon of Will, it must consist in *right willing.* This is a definition sufficiently explicit for the present argument. Should any one feel disposed to question the statement, that virtue consists exclusively in right willing, he will not deny that it is in part, at least, found here. This is all that is requisite to the present argument. The question then to be settled is this: *Is obligation to will in a given direction always affirmed, and affirmed exclusively, in view of the perceived tendency of thus willing?*

Happiness a Phenomenon of the Sensibility.

While virtue is, in this discussion, postulated as a phenomenon of the Will, happiness, on the other hand, is a phenomenon, neither of the Intelligence, nor Will, but of the Sensibility exclusively. This no one will deny.

Relation of Willing to Happiness.

Now the tendency of willing of every kind, to promote happiness, or its opposite, depends entirely upon the correlation between the nature of the Will and Sensibility. To understand, in this respect, the nature of willing, that is, its tendency to promote happiness, or its opposite, this correlation must be known. How can such knowledge be obtained? By experience only. This is self-evident. Prior to experience, I know not even that I have a Sensibility. Much less, if possible, can I know, prior to experience, the adaptation of any cause whatever, as for example, willing in one direction or another, in view of affirmed obligation, to produce in the Sensibility, happiness or misery.

Conclusion necessarily resulting from the Facts above stated.

Now as I can know from experience only, the tendency of willing in one way or the other, in view of affirmed obligation, to promote happiness or misery, it is demonstrably evident, that obligation must, in all instances, be in the first case affirmed, in total ignorance of such tendency. It must be affirmed, in view of other considerations exclusively. Perceived tendency, or utility, therefore, is not the exclusive reason in view of which obligation is affirmed. It is not the element which enters at all into original and primary affirmations of this nature. Utility, then, is not the exclusive ground of right.

Argument Expanded.

The above argument is as susceptible of absolute demonstration, as any proposition in mathematics. To show this, let A represent a moral action, B its results, the results which A *tends* to produce. As A is the cause of B, the relation of A as cause to B, as effect, must be learned exclusively from experience. For the same reason, A must be, in the mind, the chronological antecedent of B. Now as A is willing in view of affirmed obligation, it implies two things, obligation affirmed, and action or willing, in view of it. Let C then represent the former, that is, obligation affirmed, and D the latter, or willing in view of such affirmation. Now C must have been in the mind prior to D, because D is action or willing in view of C. But B is known subsequently to the existence of D, the former being an effect of the latter, an effect learned by experience alone. Now as D is known prior to B, much more must C have been known and affirmed prior to all knowledge of B. Because C is affirmed prior to the existence even of D, which is the chronological antecedent of B. Obligation, therefore, is in all instances, first affirmed in view of totally different considerations than the perceived tendency of action in view of such affirmation, and the theory of the Utilitarian falls to the ground.

Additional Considerations.

The nature of willing may be contemplated and known in another and different point of light still, not in relation to the phenomena of the Sensibility, but of the Intelligence. A mountain, we will suppose, is before the mind. Prior to experience, we cannot know, but that such is the correlation between our Wills and the mountain, that willing its removal to a certain place will cause its removal. In total ignorance of this relation, we may conceive of the removal of the mountain, and know what would be the effects of such an event, and understand perfectly what it is to will it. Our knowledge of the nature of willing in this respect, cannot be increased or diminished, by our knowledge of the tendency of willing in the other respect above mentioned. Now the question arises, whether, in total ignorance of the tendency of Willing to produce this result, the Intelligence may not affirm, and affirm absolutely, that it is proper or improper, right or wrong, for us to will the removal of the mountain? Suppose we know, that the removal of the mountain would occasion the death of a thousand individuals; but we do not know at all, whether our willing it has any tendency to produce the result. Would not the Intelligence under such circumstances affirm absolutely our obligation not to will the removal of the mountain? Who does not know, that it would make this affirmation? Obligation to right willing is therefore affirmed, in view of considerations entirely distinct and separate from the perceived tendencies of thus willing to promote happiness.

Argument stated in view of another Example.

God, we will suppose, is present to the contemplation of a rational being as capable of an infinite amount of happiness or misery. Before we can know whether willing God's happiness or misery has any tendency to produce the one or the other, we must understand the correlation between the nature of our Will and the Divine Sensibility. In total absence of this knowledge, however, we can understand perfectly the nature of willing in another respect, that is, what it is to will the infinite happiness, instead of misery of God. Now in total ignorance of the tendency of willing, to produce the result, and in view exclusively of its nature, in the other respect named, may not the Intelligence affirm absolutely the obligation of the creature referred to, to will the infinite happiness, instead of the infinite misery of God? If so (and who will deny that the Intelligence would, under the circumstances supposed, make the affirmation under consideration,) we have demonstrative evidence, that utility, or the perceived tendency of right willing, is not the reason in view of which obligation thus to will, is affirmed.

To bring this question to a final issue, let us suppose the being of God present, in the sense above explained, to the contemplation of one of his rational offspring, and that no other creature but this exists. In view of the divine capacities, this creature affirms absolutely his obligation to will God's infinite happiness, instead of his misery. In view of God's infinite excellence he affirms his obligation to love him. Now the question is, in view of the nature of willing, in which of the senses above named has this affirmation been made? In answering this question I remark, that the happiness of God may be assumed as an infinite quantity, incapable of any increase or diminution from any finite cause; or it may be assumed as a finite quantity, capable of increase or diminution from such a cause. Or (the only remaining supposition conceivable) the mind may be in doubt which of the above positions is true. Of these positions, the first, as I suppose, is the general impression of the race, and it certainly accords with the Bible.

Now, in whichsoever of these states the mind is, it affirms with equal absoluteness its obligation to will the infinite happiness, instead of misery, of God. When it holds that the happiness of God cannot be increased or diminished by any act of any finite will, still it affirms its obligation to will the infinite happiness of God, instead of his infinite misery. Now an affirmation made in the absence of a certain element cannot be based upon that element.

Further, the thing which this creature affirms himself bound to will, under the circumstances supposed, is the infinite happiness of God. Now it is demonstrably evident, that our willing cannot have any tendency to produce this result, a cause in its nature finite having no tendency to produce an effect that is infinite. The utmost that can be said of the tendency of willing is, that it is adapted to effect the happiness of God in a finite degree. Now, is it in view of such a result that we affirm our obligation to will a result that is infinite? Willing an infinite good derives, in our judgment, all its obligation from the perceived tendency of such willing to produce a finite good. Such is the doctrine of Utility.

Result of the Discussion thus far.

The result of the discussion thus far, is this: The perceived adaptation of willing the infinite happiness of God to promote that end, cannot be the reason of the affirmation that we are bound to will his infinite happiness, —

1. Because this affirmation is, as a matter of fact, made with the most perfect absoluteness, in the full belief that such willing has no tendency to effect his happiness at all.

2. Because that this affirmation is made with equal absoluteness, while the mind is in perfect suspense in respect to the fact whether our willing has any tendency to affect at all the happiness of God.

3. Suppose we adopt the conclusion that our willing has such tendency, this conclusion we can adopt only as the result of a process of reasoning. Before we have arrived at this result, the above affirmation was made with perfect absoluteness, and could not, therefore, have been based upon such conclusion.

4. When this conclusion is arrived at, the absoluteness of the affirmation under consideration is neither increased nor diminished.

5. To suppose that the obligation to will the infinite happiness of God is based upon the perceived tendency of thus willing to affect his happiness in a finite degree, is to abandon entirely the position that *intentions*, or what a man wills, determines moral character.

Other important Considerations.

Other considerations, bearing upon this point, now demand our attention.

1. No one is conscious of a reference at all to the tendency of our willing to affect the happiness of God, as the ground of the affirmation that we ought to will it.

2. When this tendency is pointed out and proved to exist, no one recognizes it as the reason of the affirmation under consideration.

3. No one who attempts to assign to others the reason why they are bound to love God, or to will his happiness, ever assigns this as the reason. Assuming the position, on the other hand, that we affirm ourselves bound to love God, or to will his happiness, for the sole and exclusive reason that the character of God is intrinsically excellent, and that his happiness is a thing in itself of infinite value, this assumption I affirm to be correct,

1. Because universal Consciousness affirms its truth.

2. When this fact is pointed out, universal Reason responds to it, as the real ground of the affirmation under consideration, and as an all-sufficient ground.

3. This fact is invariably referred to, when we attempt to convince others of their obligation to love God, or to will his happiness, and of their guilt in not doing it.

4. Upon this ground Utilitarians, as well as others, found their affirmations of obligation to will what is right, whenever their theory is not distinctly before their minds.

5. The more perfectly the mind is abstracted from all considerations but the simple relation of willing to what is intrinsic in the object presented, the more distinct and vivid will be the affirmations of Reason in respect to the moral character of our determinations. Of this every one is conscious.

The above Argument of universal Application.

The argument thus far has been based mainly upon one example, willing the happiness instead of the misery of God. It will readily be perceived, however, that this example is of universal application in respect to all duties which, as creatures, we owe to God. If obligation to will God's happiness is not based upon perceived tendencies of willing it, to produce that result, no more surely can obligation to love him, submit to his authority, or be grateful for his mercies, be based upon perceived tendencies of yielding to such claims to produce the same result.

Obligation not affirmed in view of the subjective Tendencies of Right or Wrong Willing.

Suppose the Utilitarian shifts his ground, and assumes the position that we affirm our obligation to will the happiness of God, or to love him, in view of the perceived tendencies of such willing to advance our own or the happiness of others. I reply —

1. That, as shown above, obligation must have been perceived, affirmed, and complied with, or transgressed, prior to the perception of any such tendencies. Such perceptions, therefore, cannot have been the basis of such affirmations.

2. The testimony of universal Consciousness is opposed to this supposition. When we affirm our obligation to love God, for example, nothing is further from our views than the thought, that this affirmation is based upon the perceived tendencies to make us happy.

3. No person ever assigns this as the reason why we are bound to will the happiness of God.

Another general Consideration.

I have one consideration further, of a general nature, in favor of the position which I am endeavoring to establish. It is this: The more perfectly a man is emancipated from the belief of the doctrine of utility, the more perfectly he is "rooted and grounded" in the belief of the opposite doctrine, the more sacred in his estimation does right, does duty appear. As proof of this assertion I appeal to the consciousness of those who have had experience of the influence of this belief upon their minds. That error should have such an influence, is the strongest anomaly in the history of human nature. "That which maketh manifest is light," and nothing, surely, but light can sanctify *duty* in our estimation.

Once more, according to the showing of Utilitarians themselves, the tendency of willing, as, for example, the happiness of God, is a consideration, in view of which, it is impossible for us to will. Now that fact in view of which it is impossible for me to act, is a fact in view of which I cannot affirm my obligation to act. On the other system, the very consideration, in view of which we affirm our obligation to will what is right, is the very consideration in view of which alone, as all admit, right willing is possible.

Mutable Actions.

The way is now prepared to consider a class of actions denominated Mutable. Here, at first thought, it would appear that utility must be the ground of right. For example, the parent says to his child, "You must not strike your brother or sister;" and the reason assigned for this prohibition is, "because it will hurt." Now this prohibited act is composed of two elements. 1. The physical part, or the motion of the hand. 2. The volition or act of the Will, as willing such motion. The real meaning of the prohibition is, "You shall not will this motion of your hand." The reason of the prohibition, and consequently the ground of obligation to comply, is the perceived connection between the motion and the well-being of the person exposed to its effects. Now here also it is demonstrably evident that utility is not the ground of the right. For the obligation to avoid willing arises from the perceived connection between the motion under consideration and its effects, and not from the perceived connection between willing and the motion itself. Because, when we suppose all such connection between willing and the motion destroyed, the obligation of the subject to avoid willing such motion remains equally sacred. The connection between willing and its effects is accidental. The character of willing, however, remains the same, whether this connection exists or not. This principle is of universal application. Whenever we are bound to will any end, we affirm ourselves under obligation to will every means which we judge adapted to secure that end. In neither instance is our obligation to will affirmed in view of the perceived connection between our willing and the object willed; but on account of what is intrinsic in the object itself.

I here close this protracted discussion of the relations between the ideas of obligation, and of the useful. It is not intended to be denied that perceived tendency is *a* ground of obligation, but that it is the exclusive ground. Less than I have said upon this subject, I could not have said, and satisfied my own mind. We will now proceed to the analysis of other ideas of Reason.

IDEAS OF LIBERTY AND NECESSITY.

Ideas defined.

These ideas, like those of right and wrong, are opposites.

The elements entering into one, are excluded from the other. The question is, What are the characteristics which separate and distinguish one of these ideas from the other? In answer, I would remark, that they represent two entirely distinct and opposite relations, which may be supposed to exist between an antecedent and its consequent. The first is this: *The antecedent being given, but one consequent is possible, and that must arise* This relation we designate by the term necessity. The second relation is, *The antecedent being given, either of two or more consequents are possible, and consequently, when any one does arise, either of the others might arise in its stead.*

These Ideas Universal and Necessary.

These ideas have the characteristics of absolute universality and necessity. Every antecedent and consequent, actual and conceivable, must fall under one or other of the relations which they represent. These ideas have nothing to do with the *nature* of antecedents and consequents. They simply and exclusively represent the *relations* existing between them. As representing such relations, they must bear the fundamental characteristics of all other ideas of Reason, inasmuch as no other relation, differing in kind from either of these, and not included in one or the other of them, is even conceivable.

Idea of Liberty realized only in the Action of the Will.

The relation between all antecedents and consequents, with the exception of motives and acts of Will, are conceived by the Intelligence as necessary. If the idea of Liberty is not realized in the action of the Will, it exists in the Intelligence without an object, or any element in any object corresponding to it, in the universe.

Chronological Antecedents of these Ideas.

No idea of Reason does or can exist in the Mind, without the appearance of some phenomena, through which it is revealed. The existence of the idea of Liberty can be accounted for only on the supposition of the appearance in Consciousness of the element of Liberty in the action of the Will. In all other phenomena of which the Mind is conscious, the element of necessity appears. The appearance of these phenomena, then, are the chronological antecedents of the ideas of Liberty and Necessity.

IDEA OF THE BEAUTIFUL AND SUBLIME.

Opinions of Philosophers.

All men agree in pronouncing some objects beautiful, and some sublime, and others the opposite. By many philosophers, the beautiful and sublime are contemplated as simple emotions. Some suppose, that all objects are to the Mind originally alike in this respect, that they are unadapted to awaken any such emotions in the Mind, and that these feelings come to be connected with particular objects by accidental association. Pleasing emotions are from some cause awakened in the mind. While in this state, we perceive, we will suppose, a rose. These emotions are thus associated with that object, so that when it is perceived again, they reappear. Hence, not because the rose is in itself more beautiful than any other object, but on account of the feelings thus associated with it, it is ever after regarded as beautiful. Now to this theory there exists this insuperable objection. Accidental association can never account for the absolute universality of judgment which exists among mankind, in respect to particular objects. Why, for example, do all the world agree in pronouncing the rose and lily more beautiful than the poppy or sun-flower? Accidents never produce perfect uniformity.

Others suppose, that there are in the mind ideas of Reason represented by the terms beautiful and sublime, and that objects are referred to one or the other, as they present corresponding characteristics. I will now present certain considerations designed to show, that this last is the true conception.

Considerations indicating the existence in the Mind of Ideas of Reason, designated by the terms Beautiful and Sublime.

One fact which has a very important bearing upon this question, strikes the mind at first view. It is this: No human form or countenance is regarded by any person as perfect. How can this fact be accounted for, except on the supposition, that every such judgment is based upon a comparison of the external object, with an idea more perfect, existing in the mind itself?

Again, the ancient sculptors and painters, when they attempted to give to the world, what all men would alike regard as the forms of perfect beauty, copied after no living model; but took from all the forms of beauty in the world around them, those parts which were most beautiful, and from these combined new forms more beautiful than any realities actually existing. Does not this show, that they were endeavoring to realize, not the forms of beauty actually existing in the universe around them, but an idea in their own minds more perfect than these forms?

With this supposition also, and with this only, consists the fact, that the pleasure derived from the contemplation of certain forms of beauty is permanent, and becomes more intense, the more intimate and protracted our acquaintance with them; while the pleasure derived from the contemplation of other forms ceases on a protracted and intimate acquaintance. The reason of this obviously is, that the first mentioned forms correspond very nearly, in all their parts, to the ideal in the mind. An intimate acquaintance with the others, however, gives us a knowledge of their defects, and in time destroys the pleasure which we felt when those defects were not perceived.

I will present one other consideration bearing upon the subject, which I regard as perfectly decisive. The particular elements which mark objects as beautiful or sublime, do in fact correspond with fundamental ideas. In respect to the sublime, all agree in fixing upon the Infinite as the chief source of emotions of sublimity. In finite objects one element only is correlated to these emotions, that of vastness.

The characteristics of the beautiful are determinate form, regularity, uniformity, and variety. A waving, instead of a crooked line, a line realizing the ideas of uniformity and variety, has universally been fixed upon, as the line of beauty and grace. Now that which proceeds according to fundamental ideas, must be itself the representative of such ideas.

Objection to the Universality of these Ideas.

An objection to the principle above elucidated, to wit, the different standards of beauty adopted by different nations, and by the same nations, at different periods, has sometimes been adduced. In reply, the following considerations are presented as deserving special attention :

1. It may be questioned whether the savage when he paints and tattoes his form, and the civilized person when he adorns his with the ornaments of civilized society, are endeavoring to realize the same idea. The one may be aiming to realize the idea of the beautiful, and the other (the savage), that of the terrible. The same holds true of architecture. The prominent idea in the Grecian style is the beautiful. That in the Gothic

is the grand, the solemn, the sublime. The former and the latter then, had not different standards of beauty. They were aiming to realize different ideas.

2. While the idea may exist alike in all minds, the *ideal*, that is, the *form* in which the idea shall be embodied, may exist in different minds, and among mankind at different periods, in different degrees of development. Consequently the *forms* in which they will embody the idea will be various.

3. In contemplating particular forms of beauty, in which many defects of course exist along with the beautiful, these may be mistaken for the particular features which are the source of the pleasurable emotions felt under these circumstances. These defects then will be copied instead of the actual beauties.

4. But in the midst of all this apparent variety, there is a more general agreement than is commonly supposed; an agreement that is fundamental to the inquiry before us. Introduce men of all ages, and of every nation into the same family, and ask them which of the children in that particular family is the most beautiful, and you will find but little diversity in their judgments, and no diversity which is not perfectly consistent with the supposition of a common ideal in their minds, while the striking coincidence in their judgments can be explained on no other supposition.

5. There are actual forms of beauty, in respect to which all men do agree. The most perfect specimens of ancient sculpture and painting may be adduced as an illustration. Also forms of beauty in the world around us; as the rose and the lily. Such circumstances we should find it difficult to explain on any other supposition than the one before us.

Chronological Antecedent of these Ideas.

The condition of the development of the idea of beauty

and sublimity in the mind, is the perception of the elements of the beautiful and sublime in some external object. In the Divine mind, these ideas, among others, existed eternally as the prototypes after which creation was formed and moulded. The human Intelligence is so constituted, that in the presence of objects, in the conformation of which the Divine idea is more or less nearly realized, the same idea is awakened in the mind of man. This idea then becomes the standard by which the external object is characterized as beautiful, grand, or sublime.

Illustration from Cousin.

Cousin thus beautifully explains the origin of the idea of beauty in the mind: "The idea of the beautiful is equally inherent in the mind of man, as that of the just and good. Interrogate yourselves, when a vast and tranquil sea, when mountains of harmonious proportions, when the manly or graceful forms of men or women, are present to your view, or some trait of heroic devotion, to your recollection. Once impressed with the idea of the beautiful, man seizes, disengages, extends, develops and purified it in his thought, and by the assistance of this idea, which external objects have suggested to him, he re-examines these same objects, and finds them inferior to the idea which they themselves have suggested."

Explanatory Remarks.

The remarks above made have directly respected the beautiful and sublime, as they are embodied in external form. By this I would not be understood as implying that nothing else is beautiful or sublime, or that this is their chief source. There are beauty and sublimity in thought, and if possible, higher still in action.

IDEA OF HARMONY.

The remarks and illustrations above presented, pertaining to the ideas of the beautiful and sublime, are equally applicable to that of harmony. The ear tryeth sounds, as the eye doth form and color. In harmony words and sounds are arranged according to fundamental ideas, just as other elements are in the beautiful and sublime. That this is the true explication of the subject will appear, I think, from the following considerations:

1. When highly excited by musical performances, those who attentively watch the operations of their own minds, cannot fail to notice, that under such circumstances they uniformly conceive of the same pieces as performed infinitely better; and that it is this conception which constitutes the main source of delight.

2. Persons in whose minds the principle of harmony is most fully developed, enjoy an exquisite piece of music quite as highly, when reading it alone, in the absence of all musical sounds, as when hearing it performed by the best trained choir, clearly showing that the idea in the mind far surpasses realities without.

3. Skillful performers on the organ or piano, who have lost the faculty of hearing, enjoy these instruments no less than before. I recollect to have read of a celebrated musician in Germany, who in his old age lost his hearing entirely. Yet, as his fingers would run over the keys of his piano, the instrument used being (a fact unknown to him) totally destitute of power to produce any sound whatever, he would rise in his feelings to perfect ecstacy of delight. In his own mind there was harmony deep and profound. It was harmony in idea.

4. The principles of harmony are all found to be reducible to mathematical formulas. These principles are not deduced,

in the first instance, from observation, irrespective of fundamental ideas. Such ideas must first be developed, before the principles of harmony can be understood.

REFLECTIONS.

Two reflections suggest themselves from the above analysis.

1. *Mind constituted according to fundamental Ideas.*

The first is, that a profound knowledge of mind clearly shows that our nature is constituted according to absolute principles of pure science, or of fundamental ideas of Reason. Nothing, at first thought, would appear to be at a further remove from the principles of pure science, especially of the pure mathematics, than the laws of harmony. Yet, when we have developed the laws of proportion in the pure mathematics, we find that we have developed those principles without the knowledge of which the laws of harmony could not be understood. The same results are equally applicable to external existences. In the study of pure science we have not departed from nature. We are only in the depths of our own Reason, developing the forms and laws to which nature, material and mental, is conformed. We are only developing those formulas and principles which enable us to understand the universe as it is. The more deep and profound our descent into the depths of pure science, the more profound and perfect is our knowledge of nature. What do such facts indicate in respect to the character of the Author of our being? He must be a pure Intelligence, in whose mind absolute science pre-existed as the patterns and laws after which all things, visible and invisible, are constituted. Hence, when the principles of the same science are developed in our own minds, we are then able to comprehend our own nature, and the constitution of things around us. Because we are from our nature scientific beings, for this reason alone it is that we can understand the works of God. Thus it is that

> "Trailing clouds of glory do we come
> From God who is our home."

How little is the student accustomed to reflect that in the study of the laws and principles of the triangle, the square, the circle, the ellipse, the parabola, and hyperbola, together with the science of number and proportion, he is developing in his own mind, those formulas and principles by which alone the wonders of astronomy, and the laws of attraction which bind the universe of matter in harmony together, &c., can be understood and explained by him. In our descent into the deep profound of the pure and abstract sciences, we find ourselves, whenever we come to recognize our position, in the deep profound of nature, and of the Infinite Intelligence of Nature's God.

2. *Poetry defined.*

We are now prepared for a definition of poetry, properly so called. A mere rythmical jingle of words at the end of lines of a given length, does not constitute poetry, according to the true signification of the term. Nor have I been satisfied with the popular definitions of the subject which I have met with. I will present, as an example, that given by Coleridge: "A poem is that species of composition which is opposed to works of science, by proposing for its *immediate* object pleasure, not truth; and from all other species (having this object in common with it) it is discriminated by proposing to itself such delight from the *whole* as is compatible with a distinct gratification from each component part." The great objection to this definition is, that many prose, as well as poetical compositions, would fall under it. I will now propose another and a different definition. Poetry, or more properly, perhaps, a poem, is the *creations of the Imagination embodied in language arranged in conformity to the idea of harmony.* I leave the definition to speak for itself.

IDEA OF TRUTH.

Idea defined.

Another fundamental idea of Reason — an idea which controls the Intelligence in all its movements — is the idea of truth. The term Truth may be contemplated *objectively* and *subjectively*. Objectively, it comprehends and expresses all realities, whatever they may be. Subjectively, it designates an intellectual conception in harmony with the *object* of the conception.

Chronological Antecedent of this Idea.

The chronological antecedent of this idea, or the condition of its development by the Reason, is the perception of phenomena, and the consequent development of the idea of substance. Then the great question, "What is truth?" becomes the leading idea in the Intelligence.

IDEA OF LAW.

The term law is used in a great variety of significations. Two general divisions, however, include all the meanings ever attached to this term, to wit, Natural or Physical, and Moral Law, words which are applied to the action of two distinct and opposite classes of powers.

In general, Law may be defined *as a rule of action.* Natural or Physical Law is that rule in conformity to which the *natural or physical powers* of the universe *do* act. Moral law is that rule in conformity to which *moral agents* are *re-*

quired to act. Natural or Physical Law is a rule *of* action. Moral Law is a rule *for* action.

The words Natural or Physical Law are used, among others, in the two following senses:

1. To designate the rule in conformity to which each particular power in nature acts, in the production of specific results. Between all material substances, for example, there exist two distinct and opposite principles, those of Attraction and Repulsion. The rules in conformity to which these principles act are called the Laws of Attraction and Repulsion. It is also a fixed and immutable principle, with such substances, that a body at rest, or in motion, will continue in the same state, till that state is changed by the action of some power external to the body itself, and that with such bodies, action and reaction are always equal. Here we have the laws of Rest and Motion, and of Action and Reaction. Every power in nature, mental and physical, has its laws. Thus we speak of theLaws of Matter and of the Laws of Mind.

2. To designate the rule in conformity to which certain powers of nature are or may be arranged for the production of certain results. The motion of the heavenly bodies, for examample, the balance of the material Universe, the phenomena of animal and vegetable life and production, &c., arise not from the original properties of the powers of nature, irrespective of their present arrangement and organization, but from the mutual action and reaction of those powers consequent on that peculiar arrangement and organization. Each particular power manifests many, to say the least, of its present peculiar qualities, in consequence of its present position and arrangement relatively to other powers around it. Thus we have that class of the laws of nature comprehended under the idea of Means and Ends. In this respect, the Universe is one vast whole, throughout all departments of which an absolute unity of de-

sign and arrangement obtains. Everything in nature exists and acts as a means to one all-comprehending whole. The wants of mind is the end. The entire arrangement and action of the powers of nature throughout, are subordinated as a system of means for the realization of this one end, and this is the law of nature, all particular principles pertaining to the arrangements of the powers of creation, such as those above referred to, being only particular parts of this all-comprehending whole. It is to this idea of law, that Coleridge refers in the following paragraph, to which I will append some illustrations:

COLERIDGE'S DEFINITION OF LAW.

"The first is that of Law, which, in its absolute perfection, is conceivable only of the Supreme Being, whose creative *idea* not only appoints to each thing its *position*, but in that position, and in consequence of that position, gives it its qualities, yea, it gives its very existence, as *that particular* thing. Yet in whatever science the relation of the parts to each other and to the whole, is predetermined by a truth originating in the *Mind*, and not abstracted or generalized from observation of the parts, there we affirm the presence of a *law*, if we are speaking of the physical sciences, as of Astronomy, for instance; or the presence of fundamental *ideas*, if our discourse be upon those sciences, the truths of which, as truths absolute, not merely may have an independent *origin* in the Mind, but continue to exist in and for the Mind alone. Such, for instance, is Geometry," &c.

To set the above definition in a clear and distinct light, take the following illustration: Let us suppose a body of men, say one hundred thousand in number, assembled together, all perfectly armed and equipped with all the implements of war, but without officers, without discipline, without order. Here is a congregated mass of powers, but the absence of law In other words, these powers act in conformity with no rule. What is the condition of this army? It is powerless, except for self-destruction, and that in exact proportion to its numbers. Contemplate now this army, officered, disciplined, and all brought into perfect order under some experienced commander. You have the same powers as formerly, but now acting in conformity with certain rules or laws. The army now becomes powerful, not for self-destruction, but for attack and defense. But what is the law which these powers obey, or in conformity with which they act? It is an idea in the mind of the commander. It is this idea which gives to each part of this army its particular position, and in consequence of that position, gives it its qualities, its very existence, as that particular part. The army receives its existence and qualities as that particular army from the law or idea which it obeys, or in conformity with which it acts.

You will now readily apprehend the meaning of the remark of Coleridge: "Law in its absolute perfection is conceivable only of the Supreme Being, whose creative *idea* not only appoints to each thing its *position*, but in that position, and in consequence of that position, gives it its qualities, yea, it gives its very existence, as *that particular* thing." The meaning, as far certainly as it is correct, is this: An idea in the mind of God appoints to every power in nature its particular position, and in consequence of that position, gives it its qualities, its very existence, as that particular thing.

In illustration, I would remark, that if we conceive of the powers of nature, as existing each one by itself alone, or as existing in different relations to each other from that which they now sustain, few of the peculiar qualities which they now exhibit would appear. All the phenomena of vegetation, for example, result from the peculiar *arrangement* of the powers of the material creation relatively to each other. Change this arrangement, and nothing but barrenness and universal desolation, or phenomena totally different from those which now appear, would appear. Each particular particle, therefore, receives its qualities, yea, its very existence, *as* the particular thing manifested to us, in consequence of its position relative to surrounding particles. Everything we behold or contemplate is to us what it is, in consequence of its existence, position, and consequent action in harmony with an *idea* in the infinite Intelligence.

Law, subjective and objective.

Law, in this sense, may be contemplated in two points of light, *subjective* and *objective.* In the first sense, it is an idea, in which powers are contemplated as arranged relatively to each other, so that their mutual action and reaction shall produce results in correspondence to a certain end conceived of, and chosen by the mind. In the second sense, it is the existence, arrangement, and consequent action of these powers, in harmony with that idea.

Conclusion from the above.

We come to this conclusion: that wherever powers act in conformity with law, they are acting in obedience to some idea existing in some intelligent mind. To illustrate this, let us suppose an army of one hundred thousand men all dressed and equipped alike, arranged in a given order, and all performing perfectly harmonious motions and evolutions. You here perceive the presence and all-pervading influence of law. Is it possible to conceive all this, and not suppose this law to be some idea in some intelligent mind — a mind that comprehends all the parts, and assigns to each part its position, &c.? If this could not be supposed of intelligent powers, much less could we suppose a similar action of necessary and unintelligent ones. The grand problem, then, the solution of which is the final object and distinctive character of philosophy, when once solved, leads the mind to the direct apprehension and contemplation of the Infinite, of God, whose creative idea is the law of all existences. The problem referred to is this: For all that exists conditionally (*i. e.* the existence of which is inconceivable, except under the condition of its dependency on some other as its antecedent) to find a ground that is unconditional and absolute, and thereby to reduce the aggregate of human knowledge to a system. Now, this ground can be found in nothing but in the mind of God.

Chronological Antecedent to the Idea of Law.

As Mind wakes into conscious existence, and contemplates the action of the powers of nature within and around it, it at once perceives all things existing and acting as a means to an end. Everywhere diversity blended with harmony, presents itself. Now, this presentation of the powers of nature is the chronological antecedent of the idea of Law in the Reason. Hence the great inquiry ever after imposed upon the Intelligence, to wit: What are the laws in conformity to which these powers act? In this inquiry, the Intelligence begins to "feel after" the Infinite, and it never rests until it finds itself in the presence of "that creative idea, which appoints to each thing its *position*, and in consequence of that position, gives it its qualities, yea, its very existence as that particular thing."

APPARENT MISTAKE IN RESPECT TO LAW.

Philosophers, as well as others, often *appear* at least to speak on this subject, as if, in their judgment, the powers of nature, with their present arrangement, on the one hand, existed, and Law on the other, as a separate something controlling their action. Coleridge maintains, that law (and by law, he means thought) is the only reality. Now, it should be borne in mind, that when we depart from ideas, nothing relative to the powers of nature exists, but the powers arranged in such a manner, that their mutual action and reaction shall produce results in harmony with such ideas. Look, as an illustration, at the steamboat. There is not here powers arranged in a given order, and then a something else, which controls their action. All the results we witness arise from the nature, and the peculiar arrangement of the powers here combined. So in all other instances.

THEORY AND LAW DISTINGUISHED.

The term theory is used in two senses somewhat different. The first meaning may be illustrated by a reference to what is denominated the Theory and Practice of Medicine. The end for which medicinal substances are used, in cases of disease, is the controlling of the disease, and its consequent removal. Now, when a certain disease appears, a particular course is adopted. The results are marked down. That course which, in given circumstances, is attended with the most favorable results, is set down as the course to be pursued in the treatment of this disease. The course becomes a Theory, to which medical practice is conformed. According to this usage, the term Theory supposes certain powers arranged under some one point of view, and certain principles of action adopted for the purpose of controlling these powers.

According to another usage, Theory means a certain hypothesis which has been adopted for the explanation of a given class of facts; an hypothesis, in conformity to which, it is supposed, the facts may be explained. In respect to a given class of facts, it frequently happens that all admit of an equally ready explanation, on either of two or more distinct and opposite hypotheses, and hence a corresponding number of Theories are adopted for their explanation. Thus we have two distinct and opposite Theories of electricity, all the facts presented being equally explicable in conformity to each.

Now Law, as distinguished from Theory, is an *hypothesis which sustains to a given number of facts the relation of a logical antecedent.* The facts being given, the hypothesis *must* be assumed as the ground of their explanation. The facts must not only be explicable by the hypothesis, but affirmed by it, in such a form as to contradict every other hypothesis which can be adduced for their explanation. This condition we find realized in the facts adduced by Newton, in demonstration of the law of attraction.

NATURE OF PROOF.

One thought suggested by the preceding analysis demands special attention — the nature of proof. No proposition is, properly speaking, proven, till facts or arguments are adduced, which not only affirm its truth, but contradict every opposite proposition. How often is this fundamental law of evidence overlooked and disregarded in almost every department of human investigation. In Theology, for example, how often is an hypothesis denominated a doctrine, which merely *consists* with a given class of passages of Holy Writ, assumed as absolutely affirmed by these passages, when, in reality, they equally consist with the contradictory hypothesis. Let it ever be borne in mind, that no passage or passages of Scripture prove any one doctrine which do not contradict every opposite doctrine. No facts affirm any one hypothesis which do not equally contradict every contradictory hypothesis.

FUNDAMENTAL AND SUPERFICIAL THINKERS.

Another suggestion which presents itself is this — the difference between *superficial* and *fundamental* thinkers. The former dwell only upon the surface of subjects, and having there found certain hypotheses which consist with mere exterior facts, they gravely conclude that they "have heard the conclusion of the whole matter." They have discovered all that can be known, and "wisdom will die with them." The latter class, on the other hand, retire into the interior of subjects, and taking their position upon some great central facts, announce the existence and operations of universal laws sustaining to exterior facts the relation of logical antecedents, and explaining them all. The reason why the positions assumed by such men are uniformly so impregnable is, that the error of every hypothesis, in opposition to that which they have assumed, as well as the truth of their own, becomes visible at once, in the light of the great central facts on which they have taken their stand.

THE PHILOSOPHIC IDEA.

The philosophic idea realized, or objectively considered, is the reduction of phenomena to fundamental ideas, the reduction of the sum of human knowledge to a system, the finding, amid the infinity of facts which are floating in the universe around us, some great central fundamental facts or laws, which are affirmed by all others, and explain them all.

This idea subjectively considered is a conception lying down in the depths of the Reason, that all substances exist and act in harmony with such ideas. Hence the questions perpetually imposed upon the Understanding and Judgment, in all departments of human research, to wit, what are the laws which explain the facts here presented? Science is everywhere now on the high road tending to the realization of this great idea. Happy the eyes that shall see it realized.

Chronological Antecedents of this Idea.

The chronological antecedents of this idea are the same as those which sustain a similar relation to that of law. Indeed this idea is but one form in which the idea of law manifests itself.

Other ideas of Reason will be considered, when we speak of matter and spirit, the soul, God, &c.

FIRST TRUTHS, OR NECESSARY PRINCIPLES OF REASON, AS DISTINGUISHED FROM CONTINGENT PRINCIPLES.

Contingent and necessary Principles defined and distinguished.

"Contingent principles," in the language of Cousin, "are those which force belief, though without implying any contradiction in the denial of them, and which are not therefore necessary, but irresistable, natural beliefs, actual, primitive, and instinctive, such as the belief in the stability of the laws of nature, the perception of extension," &c.

A necessary truth or principle, on the other hand, is one which not only forces assent, but which is always attended with absolute conviction of its necessity, of the total impossibility of supposing the contrary; such as the proposition, Every event must have a cause. The above distinction perfectly corresponds with those made by Dr. Reid. "Truths,' he observes, "which fall within the compass of human knowledge, whether they be self-evident, or deduced from those that are self-evident, may be reduced to two classes. They are either necessary or immutable truths, whose contrary is impossible; or they are contingent and mutable, depending upon some effect of Will or power, which had a beginning, and may have an end."

That a cone is a third part of a cylinder of the same base,

and the same altitude, is a necessary truth. It depends not upon the will or power of any being. It is immutably true, and the contrary impossible. That the sun is the center, about which the earth, and the other planets of our system, perform their revolutions, is a truth, but it is not a necessary truth. It depends upon the power and will of God.

First Truths defined.

First truths are those principles, whether contingent or necessary, which lie at the foundation of all science, of all reasoning. "They admit," says Dr. Reid, "of no other proof than the following: 1. All men do admit them, as a matter of fact in all their reasoning. 2. All men, even those who deny their validity, *act* upon them. 3. If denied, the validity of all reasoning fails."

Kind of Proof of which necessary Ideas or Principles admit.

The above remarks of Dr. Reid are strictly applicable to contingent principles. Necessary ideas and principles, on the other hand, admit of a kind of proof, that, as far as my knowledge extends, has escaped the notice of philosophers. All such ideas and principles sustain, as we have seen, to contingent phenomena and principles, the relation of *logical antecedents*, while the former sustain to the latter, the relation of *chronological antecedents.* Now, in addition to the kind of proof, adduced by Dr. Reid, necessary ideas and principles admit of this also: We can designate the phenomena or principles to which they sustain the relation of logical antecedents. Thus we may prove the reality of time, by refering to *succession*, of the reality of which every one is conscious. This is, in fact, the highest kind of proof of which any principle is susceptible.

Statement illustrated by a Reference to the Idea of God.

The idea of God is a first truth of Reason. In reference to the proof of the Divine existence, two errors, as it appears to me, have been committed by philosophers and theologians. Some have affirmed, that this truth is wholly insusceptible of any proof of any kind. Others have supposed that it admits of logical demonstration from given premises. Now the truth pertaining to the subject lies between the two errors above named. The Divine existence admits of the same proof that other necessary ideas of Reason do; that is, we may find the contingent phenomena or principles to which this great truth sustains the relation of logical antecedent. This, in common with the kind of proof common to all first truths, is the only kind of which it is susceptible; and when philosophical and theological research takes this direction, we shall find the highest kind of demonstration of the Divine existence. But this subject will claim attention in a subsequent part of this Treatise.

IDEA AND PRINCIPLE OF REASON DISTINGUISHED.

An idea of Reason is the pure conception of an object of Reason, irrespective of any other object; as the idea of space, time, substance, cause, &c.

A principle of Reason is the conception of the necessary *relation* of such objects to some other reality, as the principles, Body supposes space, succession supposes time, phenomena suppose substances, and events causes. Here the relation existing between contingent and necessary ideas is affirmed. This is what is meant by a principle of Reason.

AXIOMS, POSTULATES, AND DEFINITIONS.

An axiom is a first *principle* of Reason. Axioms which

are employed in particular sciences do not belong to those sciences exclusively. On the other hand, they pertain to all sciences, and are only in the form in which they are presented adapted to the particular science to be treated of. The axioms in Geometry, for example, The whole is greater than any of its parts, things equal to the same thing are equal to one another, &c., are not peculiar to Geometry, but are common to all sciences. The last named is the same thought expressed in a somewhat different form, as the axiom in logic, to wit, Where two terms agree with one and the same thing, they agree with one another.

Postulates are assumed axiomatic principles of Reason, which pertain exclusively to the particular sciences to be treated of. The postulate in Geometry, for example, that a straight line may be drawn between any two points in space, belongs exclusively to this and other cognate sciences.

Definitions, scientifically considered, give the *objects*, and the *qualities* of the objects to be investigated in the light of given axioms, and postulates. The conception, for example, of a straight line, a triangle, square, &c., of which the science of Geometry treats, are given by definition.

These principles are applicable to all sciences whatever.

IDEA OF SCIENCE, PURE AND MIXED.

Idea of Science defined.

The idea of Science, which of course is a pure conception of Reason, is *knowledge reduced to fundamental ideas and principles*; or *the properties and relations of objects, systematically evolved in the light of such ideas and principles.* Thus in Geometry, we have the proprieties and relations of particular objects systematically evolved in the light of axioms and postulates, which are, in reality, fundamental ideas of Reason. Whenever this end is accomplished, in reference to any phenomena, or objects, then we have the scientific idea realized.

Pure Sciences.

When the axioms, postulates, and definitions are all alike pure conceptions of Reason, and when the Judgment evolves the properties and relations of the objects of such definitions in the light of such axioms and postulates, then we have what are denominated pure sciences. Such is Geometry, and the mathematics generally.

Mixed Sciences.

When the axioms and postulates are ideas or principles of Reason, and when the definitions pertain to phenomena or objects contingent and relative, as in natural philosophy, and when the Judgment evolves the relations and properties of such objects in the light of such ideas and postulates, then we have mixed sciences.

FUNCTION OF REASON DENOMINATED CONSCIENCE.

Conscience defined.

Conscience is that function of Reason which pertains to the ideas of right and wrong, of obligation, of merit and demerit, &c. It is a testifying function of Reason, pertaining to the relation which *ought* to exist between the action of the Will and the idea of right and wrong.

General Remarks.

1. Conscience always commands us in the name of God. Her mandates are regarded as the voice of God speaking within us, and when disregarded, we always hold ourselves

amenable to the Divine tribunal. Conscience in the heathen is not only a law, but a law of God; and so it is regarded by them.

2. As Conscience is the voice of God within us, it follows that it can never, in its appropriate exercise, put right for wrong, and the opposite. In other words, no man acts conscientiously when doing wrong, nor in opposition to Conscience, when doing right. "Conscience," as Coloridge remarks, "in the absence of direct inspiration, bears the same relation to the will of God, that a good chronometer does to the position of the sun in a cloudy day."

Objection.

In opposition to the principle above stated, it is very common to refer to the contradictory standards of moral obligation adopted by different nations, communities, and individuals. The following considerations are deserving of special attention in reply to this objection:

1. To suppose that the heathen, for example, in all their rites and ceremonies, are endeavoring to realize the idea of right, is as absurd, as to suppose that the savage is endeavoring to realize the idea of the beautiful, when he is tattooing his body.

2. The Bible affirms that the heathen are actuated by *fear* and not by Conscience, "And deliver them who through *fear of death* were all their lifetime subject to bondage."

3. The judgment that a thing is not wrong, is often mistaken for the testimony of Conscience to its rightness.

4. When a reference is made to the intention, the only appropriate object of Conscience, we find a more universal agreement among men than is generally supposed, an agreement of such a nature as to demand the truth of the above

proposition, while every shade of difference may be explained in perfect consistency with it.

Term Conscience as used in the Scriptures.

A good conscience, as the words are used, in the Scriptures, is the testimony of the mind to the agreement of the Will, or moral action, with the moral law. An evil conscience is the opposite, the testimony of the mind to the fact of the disagreement of the action of the Will with that law.

GENERAL REMARKS PERTAINING TO REASON.

Relation of Reason to other Intellectual Faculties.

The relation of Reason to other functions of the Intelligence may now be readily pointed out. Of the phenomena, or truths affirmed by those faculties, Reason gives the logical antecedents. This is its exclusive function. The Judgment, in all its operations, is exclusively analytic. It simply evolves what is embraced in the affirmations of the other faculties. Reason is synthetic. It always adds to the affirmation of the other faculties something not embraced in the affirmation. The element added, however, always sustains to that to which it is added a fixed relation, that of logical antecedent. Thus when Sense or Conscience affirms phenomena, Reason adds to the affirmation an element not embraced in it, that of Substance, an element, however, sustaining to the affirmation a fixed relation, that of logical antecedent.

Through Reason Man is a religious Being.

As possessed of Reason alone is man a religious being. Through this awful power he attains to a knowledge of the soul, of moral obligations and retributions, of immortality, of

God, and enters into inter-communion with the Infinite and Eternal One.

Reason common to all Men.

Reason also exists in all men, and equally in all who possess it at all. This is evident from the fact that if an individual knows a truth of Reason at all, he does and must know it absolutely. There are no degrees in such knowledge. The difference, and only difference, between men lies in their perceptive and reflective faculties. Newton differed from other men not because he knew any more absolutely than they that events suppose a cause, that things equal to the same things are equal to one another, &c., but because he possessed powers of perception and reflection which enabled him to see (what they could not discover) the consequences involved in such truths.

Error of Coleridge.

Reason is not, as Coleridge maintains, an "organ identical with its appropriate objects." "Thus God, the soul, eternal truth," he adds, "are not the objects of the Reason, but they are the Reason itself." Space and duration he would admit are the objects of the Reason; but are they Reason itself? If God and the soul are the Reason, then they are identical, and Pantheism is eternal truth. Philosophers, as well as others, are accustomed to take many things for granted which need to be proved. We must, if we are not willing to be greatly misled, be careful what assumptions we permit them to make. Otherwise we may find ourselves under the direction of principles which may lead us we know not whither.

Paralogism of Cousin.

In order to do justice to this great philosopher, I must make quite a lengthy quotation from him, on the important point next to be considered. The extract is taken from his remarks on enthusiasm, and commences with a quotation from Locke.

"'Intuitive knowledge is certain, beyond all doubt, and needs no probation, nor can have any, this being the highest of all human certainty. In this consists the evidence of all those maxims which nobody has any doubt about, but every man (does not, as is said, only assent to, but) knows to be true as soon as ever they are proposed to his Understanding. In the discovery of and assent to these truths, there is no use of the discursive faculty, no need of reasoning, but they are known by a superior and higher degree of evidence; and such, if I may guess at things unknown, I am apt to think that angels have now, and the spirits of just men made perfect shall have in a future state, of thousands of things, which now either wholly escape our apprehensions, or which, our short-sighted Reason having got some glimpse of, we, in the dark, grope after.' I accept this statement, let it be consistent or not with the general system of Locke. I hold likewise that the highest degree of knowledge is intuitive knowledge. This knowledge, in many cases, for example, in regard to time, space, personal identity, the infinite, all substantial existences, as also, the good and the beautiful, has, you know, this peculiarity, that it is not grounded upon the Senses nor upon the Consciousness, but upon the Reason, which, without the intervention of any reasoning attains its objects and conceives them with certainty. Now, it is an attribute inherent in the Reason to believe in itself: and from hence comes faith. If, then, Intuitive Reason is above Inductive and Demonstrative Reason, the faith of Reason in itself in intuition, is purer and more elevated than an induction and demonstration. Recollect, likewise, that the truths intuitively discovered by Reason are not arbitrary, but necessary; that they are not relative, but absolute. The authority of Reason is absolute; it is then a characteristic of the faith attached to Reason, like Reason absolute. These are the admirable characteristics of Reason, and of the faith of Reason in itself.

"This is not all. When we come to interrogate Reason about itself, to inquire into its own principle, and the source of that absolute authority which characterizes it, we are forced to recognize that this Reason is not ours, not constituted by us. It is not in our power; it is not in the power of our Will to cause the Reason to give us such or such a truth, or not to give us them. Independent of our will, Reason intervenes, and, when certain conditions are fulfilled, gives us, I might say, imposes upon us, these truths. The Reason makes its appearance in us, though it is not in ourselves, and in no way can it be confounded with our personality. Reason is impersonal. Whence, then, comes this wonderful guest within us, and what is the principle of this Reason which enlightens us, without belonging to us? This principle is God, the first and the last of everything. Now, when the faith of Reason in itself is attached to its principle, when it knows that it comes from God, it increases not merely in degree, but in nature, by as much, so to say, as the eternal substance is superior to the finite substance in which it makes its appearance. Thus comes a redoubled faith in the truths revealed by the Supreme Reason in the shadows of time, and in the limitations of our weakness.

"See, then, Reason become, to its own eyes, divine in its principle. Now this mode or state of Reason which hears itself, and takes itself as the echo of God on the earth, with the particular and extraordinary characteristics connected with it, is what is called Enthusiasm. The word sufficiently explains the thing; Enthusiasm [Θεος εν ἡμιν] is the spirit of God within us; it is immediate intuition, opposed to induction and demonstration; it is the primitive spontaneity opposed to the ulterior development of reflection; it is the apperception of the highest truths by Reason in its greatest independence both of the senses and of our personality. Enthusiasm in its highest degree, in its crisis, so to say, belongs only to particular individuals, and to them only in particular circumstances; but in its lowest degree, Enthusiasm is as much a fact as anything else, a fact sufficiently common, pertaining not to any particular theory, or individual, or epoch, but to human nature, in all men, in all conditions, and almost at every hour. It is Enthusiasm which produces spontaneous convictions and resolutions, in little as in great, in the hero, and in the feeblest woman. Enthusiasm is the poetic spirit in everything; and the poetic *spirit*, thanks to God, does not belong exclusively to poets. It has been given to all men in some degree, more or less pure, more or less elevated; it appears above all, in particular men, and in particular moments of the life of such men, who are the poets by eminence. It is Enthusiasm, likewise, which produces religions, for every religion supposes two things: 1. That the truths which it proclaims are absolute truths; 2. That it proclaims them in the name of God himself who reveals them to it."

It requires a great philosopher to conceive of a great absurdity, and to give a professed demonstration of that absurdity by a great paralogism. In all these respects, I give it as my sober judgment, that the above passage is almost unequaled among the absurdities and paralogisms of modern times. What are the conclusions to which we are conducted in this strange rhapsody? They are the following: 1. Reason is in us, but belongs not to us. It constitutes no part of our personality. It is not a faculty of the soul, like the Understanding and Judgment, but is a light in the soul. 2. Reason is God, "the spirit of God within us." 3. In its own eyes Reason is God, "is divine in its principle."

What are the arguments by which these dogmas are affirmed to be proven? The following:

1. Knowledge by Reason is "intuitive knowledge." "Without the intervention of any reasoning, it attains its objects and conceives them with certainty." This peculiarity, I remark, Reason possesses only in common with Sense and Consciousness, with this advantage on their part, that intuitions through these faculties are prior, in the order of time, to any through Reason. If for such a consideration Reason is to be deified, and deemed no part of ourselves, much more should Sense and Consciousness.

2. "Truths intuitively discovered by Reason, are not arbitrary, but necessary; they are not relative, but absolute." Now what a leap in logic is that, to go from such a premise to the conclusion, that therefore Reason is God, "the spirit of God in us," and no part of ourselves. Cousin himself, in another place, has fully demontrated the fallacy of his own conclusions here. He has laid it down as a fundamental principle in mental philosophy, that the *fact* of knowledge of any kind in man, implies in him corresponding *powers* of knowledge. He himself affirms, that we do know by direct intuition, truths, absolute, universal, and necessary. The knowledge of such truths belongs to us, just as much as knowledge of any other kind, and implies in us corresponding power. If we had not the power to know such truths, the knowledge of them would never belong to us as phenomena of our intelligence. Now, the faculty by which, when certain conditions are fulfilled, we know such truths, is Reason, a faculty which belongs as much to us as any other functions of our Intelligence, and is no more impersonal than any of them.

3. His third and last argument is this, "Reason is not constituted by us. It is not in our power; it is not in the power of our Will to cause Reason to give us such or such a

truth, or not to give us them," &c. In view of such a consideration, to hear the philosopher exclaim, "See, then, Reason become, to its own eyes, divine in its principle." The man that, in such a premise, can see any such conclusion, must throw away his Reason, and see without his eyes. Reason, instead of deifying itself, and then falling upon its knees to worship its own image, exclaims,

> "for my single self,
> I had as lief not be, as live to be in awe
> Of such a thing as I myself."

No, Reason is too noble, too truthful a faculty to perform such an act of self-apotheosis. Reason stands in awe of nothing but the Infinite, which it apprehends, without ever confounding itself with that which it knows, adores, and worships.

He also whom Reason reveals, has said, "Thou shalt have no other gods before me." The man who deifies Reason, and gets upon his knees before that, is, in "Reason's eye," as well as in the light of inspiration, a heathen, as much as the man who worships devils.

In the paragraph above cited, Cousin himself furnishes us with a full demonstration of the fallacy of all his reasonings here. Reason, he says, "*when certain conditions are fulfilled*, gives us — I may say, imposes upon us — those truths." Now if Reason was really divine, God in us, knowledge through Reason would be unconditioned, as it is in God. Must the Divine Intelligence, as is true with ours, first perceive phenomena, before the Divine Reason can apprehend the idea of substance, space, time, &c.? Certainly not. We have Reason just as we have Free Will, because "we are made in the image of God." Yet Reason in us is not God, any more than Free Will is. Reason, too, has a sphere in the human Intelligence — a sphere which marks it as a function of that Intelligence, just as much as any other faculty, and as impersonal in no other sense than all other intellectual functions are.

TRANSCENDENTALISM.

Every one is surprised that, because, when certain intellectual faculties have given, by direct intuition, phenomena, another faculty should then give us the logical antecedents of such phenomena, philosophers should hence conclude, that this last faculty is God — is no part of our Intelligence, but the "spirit of God in us." Yet upon just such paralogisms is the entire fabric of German Transcendental Pantheism founded. When philosophers discover any power in nature before unrecognized, they are very apt to worship it as a God. Kant developed Reason as a function of the Intelligence — a function which philosophers had before failed to recognize. Germany at once raised the cry, "The gods have come down to us." Great is Reason. "God in us." There is no God but Reason, and Reason is everything. Everything, therefore, is God. Sorry am I to record the fact, that the great high priest of philosophy in France "has brought oxen and garlands" to do sacrifice to this new divinity.

REASON, IN WHAT SENSE IMPERSONAL.

From what has been said above, one thing is perfectly evident, to wit, in reason we are impersonal in the same and in no other sense, than we are in the exercise of all other intellectual faculties. What Cousin has said in respect to the action of Reason being independent of our Wills, is equally applicable to every intellectual faculty. "It is not in the power of our Will," he says, "to cause Reason to give us such or such a truth, or not to give us them." Nor is it in the power of our Will to cause Sense or Consciousness to give us such or such phenomena, or the Understanding or Judgment to give such or such notions or affirmations, or not to give them, when certain conditions are fulfilled. In one department of the Intelligence, we are impersonal in the same sense, and for the same reason, that we are in another.

REASON, IN WHAT SENSE IDENTICAL IN ALL MEN.

From the fact that, in all men, Reason gives precisely the same truths, it has been inferred that Reason does not exist subjectively in us, as other intellectual faculties do. It is like the atmosphere, it is said, which is in the lungs of all, but subjective to none. So Reason is a light in all, but a function of the Intelligence of none. Now it by no means follows from the fact, that the same phenomena appear in all men, that therefore, the power to perceive such truth, is subjective in none. The same phenomena appear in all, because the power to which they are to be referred is in all of precisely the same nature. Reason in all men is alike, in the same sense that powers which produce precisely similar phenomena are in their nature one.

CHAPTER XIII.

RECAPITULATION, WITH ADDITIONAL SUGGESTIONS.

THE last Chapter completes our analysis of the Intellectual powers. This analysis has led to the following classification of the powers, or functions of the Intelligence, distinguished as primary and secondary :

INTELLECTUAL FACULTIES ENUMERATED.

The former include Consciousness, the faculty which gives us a knowledge of whatever passes in the interior of our own minds, or *subjective* phenomena — Sense, the faculty which gives the qualities of external, material substances, or objective phenomena — and Reason, the faculty which apprehends and affirms the reality of necessary, universal, spiritual, infinite, and eternal truths.

The secondary faculties comprehend the Understanding, the conceptive or notion-forming power — the Judgment, the classifying, generalizing, and realizing power — the associating principle, with its varied functions, as simple association or suggestion, Memory, Recollection and Fancy — and the Imagination, or esemplastic power.

All these faculties we have found distinctly marked, and separated, the one from the other, by fundamental phenomena. Into these, we have found, that all the phenomena of human Intelligence may be resolved. These, then, we conclude to be the faculties of the human Intelligence.

Feeling a deep solicitude that the grounds of the above distinctions may be understood and appreciated, I have determined upon a cursory review of the various topics discussed in the preceding analysis. For particular reasons, I shall base this recapitulation upon the principle of classification of mental phenomena adopted by Kant in his Critick of Pure Reason — a principle, as we have seen, leading to the same classification of the intellectual powers, and to the advanced student, on some accounts, preferable to the one adopted in the preceding analysis.

"That all our cognition," he says, "begins with experience, there is not any doubt; for how otherwise should the faculty of cognition be awakened into exercise, if this did not occur through objects which affect our senses, and partly of themselves produce representations, and partly bring our Understanding-capacity into action, to compare these, to connect, or to separate them, and in this way to work up the rude matter of sensible impressions into a cognition of objects, which is termed experience? In respect of time, therefore, no cognition can precede in us experience, and with this all commences.

"But although all our cognition begins with experience, still on that account, all does not precisely spring up *out* of experience. For it may easily happen that even our empirical cognition may be a compound of that which we have received through our impressions, and of that which our proper Cognition-faculty (merely called into action by sensible impressions) supplies from itself, which addition we cannot distinguish from the former original matter, until long exercise has made us attentive to it, and skillful in the separation thereof."

All cognitions, or intellectual phenomena, are therefore divided by Kant into two classes — those derived from experience, and those not thus derived. The former he denominates empirical, the latter *à priori* cognitions. Cognitions *à priori* all have these fundamental characteristics, and by these they are distinguished from the empirical of every kind, to wit, *universality* and *necessity*. The proposition, for example, An event supposes a cause, is not only true of every event of which we have had experience, but we know absolutely that it must be true of all events actual and conceivable. These characteristics can never pertain to phenomena which have their source in experience, which is always limited, and in no instance can affirm anything more than that a thing really *is*, without ever affirming that it *must* be.

INFLUENCE OF THE ABOVE DISTINCTIONS.

The student who has followed this philosopher thus far, and has understood the ground of his classification, will never after, whatever his philosophic destiny may be, range himself as a disciple of Locke, maintaining and believing that all our knowledge comes from experience. He may fall into vagaries incomparably more wild and extravagant than ever appeared among the disciples of the sensual school. Yet between him and Empiricism "there is a great gulf fixed," and he will never pass over it to the school from which he has been separated. His destiny lies in another direction. Having discovered in the depths of his intelligence, cognitions bearing the characteristics of absolute universality and necessity, he never will, and never can, adopt the principle, that all our knowledge comes from sensation and reflection.

ERRORS OF KANT.

While we admit the reality and validity of cognitions *à priori*, as distinct from the empirical, it becomes a matter of fundamental importance in philosophy to settle definitely the *relations* between these two classes of phenomena thus distinguished. This point has been settled in the preceding analysis. Cognitions *á priori* universally sustain this relation to the empirical, that of *logical antecedents*, while the latter are the *chronological antecedents* of the former. Now these relations Kant overlooks entirely. Here lies his first error. On the other hand, he assumes, without argument or any attempt at proof, that there are cognitions *à priori* — cognitions more important than all others —which not only do not spring out of experience, but which transcend all experience, and extend the compass of our judgments wholly beyond its limits. "And exactly," he adds, "in these last cognitions, which transcend the sensible world, where experience can afford neither guide nor correction, lie the investigations of Reason, which we, as far as regards their importance, hold to be highly preferable, and in their object, far more elevated, than all the Understanding can teach in the field of phenomena, even with the danger of erring, rather than that we should give up such important investigations from any ground of doubtfulness, or disregard, or indifference. These unavoidable problems of pure Reason itself, are *God*, *Liberty*, and *Immortality*." The principle announced in this passage is this, That the cognition-faculty, once roused into action by experience, evolves through its own laws, and wholly irrespective and independent of what is given in experience, the conceptions above named — conceptions which sustain the relation of logical antecedents to no empirical cognitions whatever, and that the chief investigations of Reason pertain to these conceptions. Here lies the great error of this philosopher. From this single assumption flow out the most important peculiarities of his philosophy, together with all the wild vagaries of Transcendentalism. If these ideas are in the mind as logical antecedents of no empirical intuitions whatever, they are there as splendid conceptions to be sure, but with no claims whatever to objective validity — with no evidence that any corresponding realities exist. Yet as laws of thought, they determine our Understanding conceptions pertaining to ourselves, the external universe, and the origin of each. Such notions, therefore, as far as they depend upon and receive their character from these ideas, have no claim to objective validity. They are realities to us, simply and exclusively because our Intelligence, by virtue of its own inherent laws, has made them, relatively to ourselves, what they appear to be. Further, if these ideas of Reason exist in the Mind thus independent of experience, and at the same time exist there as regulative principles of experience-conceptions, should we not suppose, and does it not follow as a logical consequent, that all other *á priori* ideas have the same characteristics, and sustain the same relation to experience — such ideas, for example, as those of time, space, cause and substance?

These last ideas have the same characteristics of universality and necessity as those of God, Liberty, and Immortality; and, as laws of thought, sustain precisely the same relations to all Understanding-conceptions. All *á priori* ideas, therefore, exist in the Intelligence without any claim to objective validity. As those ideas, also, as laws of thought, determine the character of all Understanding-conceptions, these last are alike destitute of any claim to objective validity. Neither ourselves, nor the external world, nor that which our Intelligence gives us, as the cause of each, "are what we take them to be." They are all mere fictions of our Intelligence. Such Kant himself denominates them. Since this philosopher passed off the stage, his successors, such as Fichte, Schelling, and Hegel, have been laboring to build up the fabric of human knowledge upon the assumption above named, all agreeing in laying the foundation of their glorious temple upon "airy nothing," upon the wise assumption that the very temple they were building with so much toil and trouble was not "what they took it to be." Such, however, is the logical consequence of the assumption on which all their conclusions rest.

On the other hand, if we conceive the entire action of Reason to be in fixed correlation, in the first instance, to the intuitions of Sense and Consciousness, and in the second to Understanding-conceptions, giving the logical antecedents of such intuitions and conceptions, if we suppose that such intuitions and conceptions, in the order of actual development, precede the ideas to which they are respectively correlated, and are consequently unmodified by them, then we have an entirely different system of knowledge. On this topic I shall have occasion to speak again hereafter.

CLASSIFICATION OF THE PRIMARY MENTAL FACULTIES.

While the great principle which peculiarizes the system of Kant, and determines its destiny, is found to be a baseless assumption, his classification of the Intellectual faculties clearly designates him as one of the greatest analyzers of the human mind that has yet appeared. We will now proceed to a consideration of this subject. Knowledge, with us, commences not with *judgments*, but *intuitions*. This is evident from the fact that all judgments are composed of intuitions. Intuitions are of two classes, empirical, and *á priori*. The former also are subdivided as *subjective* and *objective*. This classification of intuitions gives us a threefold division of the primary faculties, or functions of the Intelligence, to wit, Sense, which gives us the qualities of external material substances — Consciousness, which gives us the qualities of the mind, or subjective phenomena — and Reason, which gives us intuitions *á priori*. This classification is sustained by phenomena fundamentally distinct from one another.

REMARKS UPON THE RELATIONS OF INTUITIONS TO ONE ANOTHER.

Before leaving the present subject it may be important to make a few remarks upon the relations of intuitions to one another, together with that of the faculties of intuition.

Intuitions cannot be opposed to each other.

My first remark is, that intuitions can never be in contradiction to each other. The intuitions of Consciousness, for example, can never be in contradiction to those of Sense, inasmuch as the exclusive office of the former, under such circumstances, is to give to the mind itself, what the latter faculty has affirmed of its object. For similar reasons intuitions *á priori* can never contradict the empirical of either class, because a logical antecedent can never, from the nature of the case, be contradictory to that to which it sustains such a relation. How can the idea of Time be in opposition to that of succession, or that of space to that of body, or the idea of phenomena be opposed to that of substance or cause? Nor can an *á priori* or empirical intuition be in opposition to another of the same class. The idea of substance, for example, cannot be in opposition to that of space, time, or cause; nor can the phenomena of extension be opposed to those of resistance or color. The same holds true in all other instances.

Different Intuition Faculties cannot contradict each other.

From the above principles the conclusion is irresistible, that the affirmations of no one faculty of intuition can be opposed to the other intuitions of the same faculty; nor can the intuitions of one faculty be opposed to the intuitions of another. For the same reasons it might be shown that, the affirmations of the primary and secondary faculties cannot be opposed to each other. These conclusions are so self-evident, that no remarks in confirmation are deemed requisite.

The logical Consequents of no one Intuition can be in Opposition to any primary Intuition, nor to the logical Consequents of the same.

Another conclusion is equally self-evident, to wit, That the logical *consequents* of no one intuition can be in opposition to any primary intuition, or to the logical consequents of the same. As the ideas of time, space, substance, cause, and of the infinite cannot be in contradiction to one another, nor to the intuitions of phenomena, so the logical consequents of any one of these ideas cannot be in contradiction to any other of these intuitions, or to the logical consequents of the same. If the ideas of substance and space, for example, are not contradictory to each other, how can the logical consequents of one contradict the other idea, or its logical consequents? So in all other instances.

ERROR OF KANT AND COLERIDGE.

We are now fully prepared to appreciate the theory of Kant, Coleridge, and the Transcendental school, generally, pertaining to the external world, or as Coleridge expresses it, pertaining to the "presumption *that there exist things without us.*" All these philosophers acknowledge, in the first instance, that through the faculty of Sense we have intuitions of the qualities of external material substances, and that by means of such intuitions together with the ideas of substance, cause, space, time, &c., the Intelligence gives us the external universe as a real existence. They then profess to find other intuitions of Reason, from which the necessary conclusion is, that "the things which we envisage are not that in themselves for which we take them." In other words, the logical consequents of one class of intuitions given by the Intelligence, are in opposition to other intuitions of the same Intelligence, and to the logical consequents of the same. Thus one series of intuitions devours others, together with all their consequents. The procedure of the Intelligence, according to this theory very much resembles that of the serpent in the fable, who seizing his tail in his mouth finally succeeded in burying his entire body so completely in his own stomach, that the body itself became wholly invisible. From the Intelligence in the first instance, proceed intuitions empirical and *á priori*, from which most logically result the apprehension, and knowledge of a vast and glorious universe of real existences. From the profound depths of the same Intelligence, there then proceed other intuitions through which the entire and before conceived substantial system of knowledge

> "Is melted into air, into thin air:
> And like the baseless fabric of a vision,
> The cloud-capp'd towers, the gorgeous palaces,
> The solemn temples, the great globe itself,
> Yea, all that it inherit, are dissolved;
> And like an unsubstantial pageant faded,
> Leave not a wreck behind."

Most sublime philosophy that, surely! And after these voracious intuitions have devoured all others that were before them, together with their consequents, "themselves still being so ill-favored that it cannot be known that they have eaten anything," it would be easy to find others by which these, in their turn, would be devoured, and so on interminably. Indeed this is the necessary procedure of the Intelligence, according to the system under consideration. For if, as this system maintains, all other objects of knowledge "are not what we take them to be," we must of necessity conclude, that this system of philosophy is not what we or its advocates take it to be. For the system itself is given by an intelligence, which, as they maintain, does not give things as they are, or as this same Intelligence "takes them to be."

On what, then, does this whole theory rest? On baseless assumptions, and nothing else. Coleridge directly acknowledges that his theory does rest upon assumptions. The same is true, however, he says, of the opposite theory. This is freely admitted, with this difference, however: His theory rests upon assumptions which are not affirmed as true by the Intelligence. The theory which gives us "things without us," rests upon assumptions affirmed as true by the Intelligence. There is a wide difference between a theory resting upon assumptions in opposition to intuitions, and one resting upon assumptions in harmony with such intuitions.

SECONDARY FACULTIES.

We are now prepared for a consideration of the secondary faculties or functions of the Intelligence.

Understanding.

After intuitions, the next class of phenomena which strikes our attention is notions, or Understanding-conceptions. Such notions are of two classes — those which pertain to individuals, and those which represent classes of individuals, or notions, particular and general. All such phenomena are found, on analysis, to be composed of intuitions given by the primary faculties. Now the act of combining intuitions into notions, particular and general, reveals an entirely new function of the Intelligence, a function not implied in the operation of either of the intuitive faculties, nor in all combined. This intellectual function we denominate the Understanding.

The Judgment.

As soon as an Understanding-conception appears on the theater of Consciousness, an intellectual process entirely new succeeds, a process by which, under the influence of the ideas of resemblance and difference, the particular elements which enter into the conception are separated from one another, and each is contemplated apart by itself. Here we have what is called the process of abstraction. When also one notion present in the Intelligence, suggests another of a similar character, by a similar process, to the one last stated, the qualities common to the two are separated. These the Understanding then combines into a general notion, a notion representing a class or classes of individuals. This notion being given by the process under consideration, the particular conceptions referred to, are subsumed, or classed under the general. Now this process differs entirely from the action of the notion-forming power. To combine intuitions into notions, particular and general, and in view of the ideas of resemblance and difference, to separate the elements of a given conception from one another, or in view of the same ideas, to separate the elements common to two or more conceptions, and finally when the Understanding has combined the elements thus separated into a general notion, to subsume the particulars under the general, are intellectual processes certainly entirely distinct from each other. The power to abstract and classify is not implied in the power simply to combine intuitions into notions, either particular or general. This function of the Intelligence, the power which separates things that differ, and ranges together under some common designation those that are alike, we denominate the Judgment. This is the faculty also chiefly employed in processes of reasoning. Reason furnishes principles, the Understanding terms, and the Judgment affirms, in the light of the principles of Reason, the agreement, or disagreement of the terms. If the student will attentively reflect upon what is passing in his own mind, he will clearly recognize the distinction above made between the Understanding and Judgment. Who ever confounds the formation of a conception of an object, with that action of the Intelligence which judges that such and such elements in the conception resemble, or are unlike each other? Who ever confounded the formation of general notions, such as are designated by the terms man, horse, &c., with that action of the Intelligence which affirms of individuals, This is a man, That is a horse? Such intellectual operations differ not in degree, but in kind, and suppose two functions of the Intelligence entirely distinct from each other.

The Associating Principle.

That principle of the Intelligence by which the presence of one thought in the mind recalls another which has formerly existed there, is so manifestly distinct from all other intellectual functions, that no philosopher has ever confounded it with any of them. As the object of the present recapitulation is to give the grounds of the distinctions made in this Treatise between the different intellectual faculties, a simple allusion to the principle of Association is all that is requisite in this department of our subject. It remains only to speak of the

Imagination.

A reference to a distinction made in a preceding Chapter, between the ideas of Reason, as primary and secondary, will enable us to explain very distinctly our own conception of the nature of this function of the Intelligence. With the former class of ideas, such as those of time, space, substance, and cause, objects exist in full and perfect harmony. The sphere of the Understanding, therefore, is actualities as they are. With most of the secondary ideas of Reason, however, such as those of the right, the just, the good, the beautiful, the grand, and sublime, realities may or may not exist in correspondence. Now we find a power of the Intelligence which is perpetually laboring to combine, in thought, the endlessly diversified elements of objects given by the other faculties into harmony with those ideas last named, especially those of the beautiful, the grand, and sublime. This function of the Intelligence we denominate the Imagination. The Ideal generated by this faculty, incomparably superior as it is to what the Understanding conceives in the sphere of realities, finds an external embodiment in poetry, sculpture, painting, and in all the varied adornments of art. The peculiar sphere, as well as phenomena of the Imagination thus clearly distinguish it from all other intellectual faculties.

Such is the classification of the intellectual faculties presented in this Treatise. Of two things pertaining to it, the author himself is fully persuaded — that the distinction here made between the intellectual faculties is real, being sustained by fundamental phenomena — and that the classification is complete, inasmuch as there is no intellectual operation, actual or conceivable, which may not be resolved into the appropriate action of one or more of these faculties.

CHAPTER XIV.

SPONTANEOUS AND REFLECTIVE DEVELOPMENTS OF THE INTELLIGENCE.

HAVING completed our analysis of the intellectual powers, other important questions pertaining to the action of the Intelligence next demand our attention. We are all aware, that objects of observation and reflection are distinctly apprehended on one condition only, to wit, that we give *attention* to them. But we observe and reflect upon that, and that only, which has been given in the Intelligence prior to all acts of attention. When we give attention, it is to some definite thing, as this or that particular object. Now the object must have been given prior to the act of attention; else the direction of the act would be wholly indefinite, and without respect to any particular object. The inquiry which will occupy our attention in the present Chapter is this: *What is the state of the Intelligence, what are the characteristics of its affirmations relative to objects of knowledge, prior to observation and reflection? and what are the relations of such affirmations to the state of the Intelligence, in observation and reflection?* The former we denominate the *spontaneous*, and the latter the *reflective* developments of the Intelligence.

GENERAL CHARACTERISTICS OF ALL OBJECTS OF KNOWLEDGE, AND OF OUR KNOWLEDGE OF THE SAME.

Before proceeding further, I would invite special attention to two or three preliminary observations:

1. All objects of thought are finite or infinite, and each of these bears the respective characteristics of contingency or necessity.

2. All finite substances comprehend ourselves, and that which is not ourselves. The infinite substance sustains the relation to each of unconditioned and absolute cause.

3. Consequently, all our knowledge consists in apprehending the nature of the finite and of the infinite, together with the relations of the finite to the finite, and of the finite to the infinite. The Intelligence can never go beyond these; because these comprehend all possible existences, and all the modes and relations of existence.

DISTINCT APPREHENSION CONDITIONED ON ATTENTION.

But these things, as I have remarked, we distinctly know only on one condition — that we attend to them; in other words, observe and reflect upon them. Yet they must, in some sense, have been apprehended before observation and reflection, because the objects of observation and reflection must have been previously given in Sense, Consciousness, or Reason.

SPONTANEOUS DEVELOPMENT OF THE INTELLIGENCE.

The question again returns upon us, What is the state of the Intelligence, as developed, previous to attention, *i. e.* previous to observation and reflection? To attend, to observe, and reflect, are acts of the Will, directing the action of the Intelligence. But, as before observed, the objects must have been in some sense apprehended previous to attention. For when we will to attend to anything, the act implies that the thing itself was in some sense in the mind, as an object of thought. How came this thought here? Certain conditions are requisite to its existence. But when these conditions are fulfilled, how does this thought arise? I answer, by a spontaneous action of the Intelligence, a spontaneity previous to all acts of the Will. "When Intelligence manifested itself for the first time," says Cousin, to whom I am indebted for almost everything I now say, "it is evident that its manifestation could not have been a voluntary act. It manifested itself, nevertheless, and you possess a consciousness of it, more or less vivid. Endeavor to take your thought unawares, in the act of thinking without having wished to think; and you will find yourself at that point which the Intelligence takes as its point of departure; and thus you may at the present moment observe, with more or less accuracy, that which did occur, and must necessarily have occurred, in the first act of your Intelligence, at a time which is no more, and which can never return." Now what is contained in this primitive intuition, this spontaneity of human intelligence? All that will subsequently be found in observation and reflection; but as Cousin observes, "If all is there, all is there on certain conditions."

CHARACTERISTICS OF THIS SPONTANEITY.

The next inquiry demanding attention is the characteristics of this spontaneity. The most important are the two following:

1. It is in all instances a positive affirmation, and not a negation. "To think," says Cousin, "is to affirm. The first affirmation into which nothing of volition has entered, and by consequence, nothing of reflection, cannot be an affirmation mingled with negation; for our first acts are not denials. It must therefore have been an affirmation without negation, an instinctive perception of truth, an entirely instinctive development of thought."

2. The other characteristic of this primitive intuition is,

that although it contains all that is subsequently found in observation and reflection, it contains them obscurely. In observation and reflection, and there only, all things are distinct, because that there, and there only, do we find not only affirmations, but negations.

Characteristics illustrated.

I have said, that in this primitive spontaneity there is contained all that is subsequently found in observation and reflection, but somewhat obscurely. Consequently, there was a time when indeed mind was, and the universe also; but to itself, as an object of knowledge, neither the mind, nor the universe, nor God existed. At the next moment, by a spontaneous development of the Intelligence, the mind was revealed to itself. At the same moment that which is not itself, and the cause of itself, and of that which it perceived as not itself, was also revealed. In other words, the mind apprehends but obscurely the finite and the infinite, with a mysterious consciousness of the relation of the one to the other. "We do not commence," says Cousin, again, "with seeking ourselves, for this would imply that we already know that we exist, but on a certain day, at a certain hour, at a certain moment, a moment solemn in existence — without having sought ourselves, we find ourselves; thought, in its instinctive development, discloses to us that we are; we affirm our existence with profound assurance — with an assurance unmingled with any negation whatsoever. We perceive our existence, but we do not discern, with all the distinctness of Reflection, our proper character, which is that of being limited and bounded; we do not precisely distinguish ourselves from the world, nor do we precisely discern the character of this world; and besides these, we perceive the existence of something different from those, to which naturally and instinctively we refer both ourselves and the world; we distinguish all this, but without very strictly discriminating between its component parts. Intelligence, in developing itself, perceives all that is; but it is not able to perceive it in a reflective, distinct, and negative manner; and although it perceives it with perfect assurance, it perceives it somewhat confusedly." Again — "Spontaneous and instinctive thought enters upon its functions by virtue of its own nature; and first of all, it gives us ourselves, the world, and God; the world and ourselves, with boundaries confusedly perceived, and God, without bound — the whole in a synthesis, in which clear and obscure ideas are mingled together."

But while these truths are thus revealed and affirmed, they are not, I repeat, clearly, but confusedly apprehended. The nature of the self, and of the not-self, which was the immediate object of perception, together with that of the cause of each, was not distinctly given. Yet all were given, and given in such a manner, that observation and reflection would separate the one from the other, and render each distinct and palpable to the mind. But the *basis* of observation and reflection is given in this primitive spontaneity. Observation and reflection may separate these elements, and determine their relative characteristics; but they can add no new element to the composition, unless it be themselves as facts of Consciousness, which, as facts, must also be first given in the manner above referred to.

Some additional remarks, designed to elucidate still further the subject before us, are here required.

CATEGORIES OF SPONTANEOUS AND REFLECTIVE REASON.

I begin with noticing the distinction between the categories of spontaneous and reflective Reason, and with such illustrations as will enable us to distinguish them. The categories of the reflective Reason are all abstract, universal, and necessary. Those of spontaneous Reason, are necessary, but concrete, and particular. With this difference, they are identical. In other words, the categories of spontaneous Reason, are those of reflective Reason in a concrete and particular form. For example, the principle of causality, as a category of the reflective Reason, is this: Every event must have a cause — a truth, universal, necessary, and absolute. Now this principle, as a category of spontaneous Reason, is this: This particular event, — this particular sensation, for example, must have a cause. The principle of space, as a category of reflective Reason, is, Body supposes space. As a category of spontaneous Reason it is, This particular body is somewhere, or in space. Thus by determining the categories of reflective Reason, we can readily determine those of spontaneous Reason. For the former are the latter in a necessary, to be sure, but concrete and particular form.

RELATION OF OBSERVATION AND REFLECTION TO THIS ORIGINAL SPONTANEITY.

The relation of observation and reflection to the original spontaneity of the Intelligence, next claims attention. Their exclusive object is to determine the nature, character, and relations of that, the reality of which has been previously affirmed. With the reality itself they have nothing to do. For example, what has reflection to do with determining the question whether I really exist, or not, the very truth which must be assumed as the basis of all reflection? Reflection may determine my nature and character, but my existence must be first affirmed, and then assumed, before reflection becomes possible. The same remarks apply equally to external existences. Observation and reflection may determine their character, but never their reality. Hence the reason of the universal inquiry in respect to external objects, which inquiry is, not whether this particular object EXISTS; but what are its nature, character, and relations? the reality of the object being necessarily assumed as the ground of all such inquiries. Observation and reflection, then, assume an entirely wrong direction when we attempt by them to determine the reality of our own existence, or of the existence of the external world, or of that to which we necessarily refer ourselves, and the external world. The reason or ground of such affirmations we can know only by falling back upon the original spontaneity of the human Intelligence. There no man is or can be a skeptic, and he that makes himself such by observation and reflection, is, in the language of Inspiration, a fool. Yes, he is more than a fool; he is supremely wicked.

CONFIDENCE REPOSED IN THE FIRST TRUTHS OF REASON, HOW WEAKENED.

You see how it is, that the confidence of men, in the first truths of human Reason, is often weakened. They expect, by a process of reasoning, to demonstrate the reality of those very truths which must be assumed, or all reasoning becomes impossible; and which, as the ground of such reasoning, have been previously affirmed with absolute certainty, in the primitive spontaneity of the human Intelligence. They expect also to have their convictions strengthened by the demonstration, an expectation not realized, of course. The result is, that the conviction is weakened, instead of strengthened. The man who expects to have his confidence in the reality of his own existence, or in that of the external world, or of God, increased by any process of reasoning, is, in my judgment, seeking for truth in the wrong direction. Whenever we fall back upon the spontaneity of our own Reason, we find ourselves intuitively affirming each of these truths with equal absoluteness, and assuming them as the ground of all our inquiries. When we contemplate our own existence, and that of the external world, as we necessarily do, as conditioned and relative, we never inquire whether there is an existence unconditioned and absolute, to which the former may be referred; but what is the character of that unconditioned and absolute existence, to which, by a previous, spontaneous, intuitive, and absolute affirmation of Reason, all that is conditioned and relative has been referred.

USE OF THE COMMON DEMONSTRATIONS OF THE DIVINE EXISTENCE.

Of what use, then, it may be asked, are the common demonstrations of the existence of God? Of none, I answer, in satisfying our own minds of the reality of the Divine existence. If this is expected from them, our confidence will be rather weakened than strengthened, and that, for this reason: The mind begins the investigation by suspending its belief in the reality of the Divine existence, upon the validity of the demonstration. It also expects and demands, as above remarked, that the demonstration shall be such as to increase its previous confidence in the reality of the Divine existence. But such expectation will not be realized. Hence the demonstration will, under such circumstances, rather diminish than increase our confidence in this fundamental truth. The most delightful feature of our holy religion, to my mind, is this: its great fundamental truths are all suspended, not upon the validity of demonstrations, but placed at the foundation of all demonstration, among the primitive, absolute, and necessary intuitions and affirmations of Reason; intuitions which no one can deny without violating the fundamental laws of his own being, and rendering himself a fool, not only, but infinitely impious. For no man can possibly become so impious and wicked as the skeptic. The man who enters a family and seduces every female there, but leaves a consciousness of guilt as a foundation for repentance, and reformation to virtue, is a saint, compared with the man who, without actual seduction, annihilates in the minds of such females, all regard to chastity, as a virtue, and to its opposite as a sin. This the skeptic does when he has obtained his object. Of what use then, the question returns upon us, are such demonstrations? Of no use but this, to turn the weapons of the enemy against himself. To substantiate his position, he appeals to science. Now science, when pressed into the field, must be shown to be on the side of his opposers. Till thus pressed she remains silent, because her influence is not needed.

CONCLUSIONS ARRIVED AT BY A PROCESS OF REASONING, WHEN FALSE.

We see when it is, that any conclusions to which we come by a process of reasoning are, and must be false. When they contradict any of the necessary and spontaneous intuitions of human Intelligence, as for example, the reality of our own existence, or that of the external world. Every step in a process of reasoning must be intuitively certain. Now to bring a conclusion to which we have arrived by a series of intuitions, against another primitive intuition, is to affirm the falsity of one intuition upon the authority of another; and the non-reality of the primitive upon the authority of the derivative. This is precisely what Coleridge has done, or rather, promises to do. He first acknowledges that the belief in the reality of things without us is an intuition, primitive and necessary, and then promises, by a series of intuitions, to demonstrate the non-reality of such existences. — *See Biog. Lit.* p. 153.

REASONS OF THE DIVERSITY AND DIFFERENCE OF THE OPINIONS OF MEN.

In *judgments*, men differ, not in the spontaneous, but reflective developments of their Intelligence. In the former state, all put essentially the same inquiries, and all believe the same things. There is no doubt or disbelief here. In this inner sanctuary of the Intelligence, skepticism has no place. In respect to the results of observation and reflection, here diversity and contradiction appear. The reason is, that in the former state, nothing but the pure affirmations of the Intelligence are met with. In the latter, *assumptions* mingled with such affirmations, together with the logical consequents of assumptions, present themselves.

SOURCES OF ERROR.

Error has no place among the spontaneous affirmations of the Intelligence, for the obvious reason that here nothing but pure intellectual affirmations appear. The same would be true in the reflective operations, but for the fact, that *assumptions* are here mingled with such affirmations. When men contemplate one class of facts, for example, various hypotheses may present themselves as grounds of the explanation of the facts, hypotheses none of which are affirmed as true by the Intelligence. The Will, however, may assume some one as true, which is not so. The assumption, together with all its logical consequents, is now mingled with the facts, and all together present a confused mass of error and truth. Here is the source of error of every kind, and in connection with all subjects of thought. Pure thinking, unmingled with assumptions, is never adulterated with error.

CHAPTER XV.

ORIGIN OF IDEAS.

In all our inquiries hitherto, one question has been left almost wholly untouched, the question in respect to the ORIGIN OF OUR IDEAS. To this question special attention is now invited.

THE TWO SCHOOLS IN PHILOSOPHY.

Two great schools have, for the last century or two, divided the philosophical world, in respect to the question before us. These schools have been denominated the Sensual, and Ideal or Transcendental school. At the head of the former is Locke. At the head of the latter is Kant. A few remarks explanatory of the principles of these schools, may prepare the way for a more distinct elucidation of the present subject.

Principles of Locke.

I begin with Locke. According to him, all ideas existing in the mind, are derived from two sources, *Sensation* and *Reflection*. To establish his principles, he first proves that there are no *innate ideas* in the mind, that is, ideas previous to experience. Having disposed of this question, he starts the following as the great problem in philosophy:

"Let us suppose," he says, "the mind to be, as we say, white paper, void of all characters, without any ideas, how comes it to be furnished? Whence comes it by that vast store which the busy and boundless fancy of man has painted on it, with an almost endless variety? Whence has it all the mate-

25*

rials of Reason and knowledge? To this I answer," he adds, "in one word, from experience; in that all our knowledge is founded, and from that it ultimately derives itself."

In a subsequent section, he shows that the sources of experience are twofold, as observed above, Sensation, and Reflection or Consciousness.

"Our observation," he says, "employed either about external, sensible objects, or about the internal operations of our minds, perceived and reflected on by ourselves, is that which supplies our Understandings with all the materials of thinking. These two are the fountains of knowledge from whence all the ideas we have, or can naturally have, do spring." Experience being the watchword of the school of Locke, and of his system, the system itself has been denominated Empiricism.

It should be borne in mind, that Locke does not speak of experience, as the mere *condition* of all our knowledge. In that case, his system would be undoubtedly correct. Nor would his principles be doubted by any school in philosophy. On the other hand, he speaks of experience, as furnishing the *materials* of all our knowledge. All knowledge is exclusively constituted of elements furnished by experience.

Theory of Kant.

In opposition to Empiricism, Kant and the Transcendental school maintain that experience is so far from giving us necessary truths, that these truths themselves lie at the foundation of all experience.

To understand the principles of Kant correctly, it is necessary to keep in remembrance the fact, that he evidently uses the term experience in two senses — in respect to the Sensibility and the Intelligence. When he says that all our cognition begins with experience, he then refers to the Sensibility;

for he speaks of the "faculty of cognition being awakened into exercise," by this experience. To suppose that by experience here, he refers to the action of the Intelligence, would make him say, that the "cognition-faculty is awakened into exercise" by the action of the cognition-faculty. He supposes, and very correctly, that the condition of the primary action of the Intelligence, is some effect from some cause upon the Sensibility. By the term experience here, he refers to this effect.

On the other hand, when he affirms that *à priori* or necessary ideas, are the condition and ground of all experience, he here uses the term under consideration with reference to the Intelligence exclusively. His meaning is, that ideas *à priori* are the condition and ground of all other mental perceptions and affirmations. In conformity with this statement, he first attempts to show that the ideas of time and space are the necessary condition of all affirmations of Sense and Consciousness pertaining to the qualities of all substances subjective and objective. When, for example, a certain effect is produced upon the Sensibility by some unknown cause — a cause, as his theory affirms, existing nowhere and in no time — the ideas of time and space are developed, while the effect is postulated as the quality of some cause external to the mind, and existing in time and space. This mental act postulating a subjective effect as the quality of some external cause, is what he calls perception. But for these ideas, no such perception could have taken place.

He then goes on to show (and, as we shall see, he is here correct), that other *à priori* ideas are the condition of all Understanding-conceptions and affirmations of the Judgment.

Such are the principles of these schools. In their fundamental affirmations, both are alike wrong. This I will now attempt to show.

PRINCIPLES OF LOCKE TESTED WITH REFERENCE TO NECESSARY IDEAS.

We begin with Empiricism — the proposition that all our knowledge, all ideas now in the mind, come from experience, from sensation and reflection. Take as an example the idea of space. Here I lay down this proposition as self-evident, that that which cannot give the essential fundamental characteristics of an idea, cannot give the idea itself. Now the fundamental characteristics of the idea of space, are *infinity* and *necessity*. The Reason apprehends space as infinite, and not only affirms that it is — that is, that it exists, but that it must be. On the other hand, everything of which we are conscious and which we perceive, is finite, and as we have seen in former Chapters, is also contingent. Nor can these faculties reach beyond the finite. But the idea of the infinite is in the Mind, because the idea of space is there, which is infinite. The idea of space, then, cannot come from Sensation or Reflection. But suppose that Sensation or Reflection, or both together, could give space as infinite. They could merely affirm that it is, not that it *must* be. The system of Locke, and of the entire sensual school, falls to the ground, when tried upon the idea of space. The same fact might with equal distinctness be shown to be true with respect to all ideas which lie beyond the limits of the contingent. Thus far and no further can Empiricism go. Necessary, universal, absolute, and eternal truths, can never be derived from experience, for the obvious reason that they are not the objects of experience. They lie entirely beyond the limits of Sense, and Consciousness or Reflection, which constitute the sole ground and source of experience.

PRINCIPLES OF LOCKE FAIL IN RESPECT TO UNDERSTANDING-CONCEPTIONS.

But Empiricism not only fails entirely, when tried upon all necessary truths, but also upon all the phenomena of the Understanding. Every notion existing in the Understanding, is composed, as we have seen, of two classes of elements, the phenomenal and the rational, the contingent and the necessary. These elements are given by faculties entirely distinct the one from the other. The phenomenal are given by Sense and Consciousness. The rational by the Reason. The first elements only are given by experience. The last lie beyond the bound of experience. Example: Sense perceives the quality of some external substance. No notion can be formed till the idea of substance is developed, by conceiving of this quality as belonging to some substance. So of all the notions of the Understanding. As they all embrace elements *necessary* as well as *contingent*, and as the latter only are derived from experience, all such notions include elements which were never given by experience.

ERROR OF KANT.

The fundamental error of Kant, understanding the proposition, that necessary ideas are the condition and ground of all experience, as he employs it — that is, in its universal form, as including all intellectual affirmations — has been made sufficiently manifest in preceding Chapters. The intuitions of Sense and Consciousness, instead of being conditioned on the prior existence, in the mind, of the ideas of time and space, are themselves the necessary chronological antecedents of these ideas. Using then the term *experience* as pertaining to the intuitions of these faculties, the proposition of Kant is demonstrably false. All necessary ideas sustain to the contingent the relation of logical, while the latter sustain to the former the relation of chronological antecedents. It is the height of absurdity to represent the logical antecedent as the condition and ground of the existence of the chronological.

POSITION OF KANT TRUE IN RESPECT TO UNDERSTANDING-CONCEPTIONS AND AFFIRMATIONS OF THE JUDGMENT.

If we admit that contingent intuitions are the chronological antecedents of necessary ones, still it may be asked, is there not an important sense in which the proposition, that ideas *á priori* are the condition and ground of all experience, is true? It is strictly true, I remark, if the term experience be used with reference, not to the phenomena of Sense and Consciousness, but as it is sometimes used, with reference to the Understanding and Judgment. There is a wide difference between merely *perceiving* and *understanding* an object. An object is *perceived* when it is presented to the mind as an object of Sense. It is *understood* when, and only when, such questions as these have been resolved in respect to it, to wit: When and where does it exist? what are its qualities, its nature, substance, quantity, and relations? But the resolution of these questions necessarily pre-supposes the existence of the ideas of time, space, substance, quantity, quality, and relation, in the mind. Using the term experience in the sense of understanding objects, how perfectly manifest is the fact, that necessary ideas are not derived from experience, but are themselves, together with the perceptions above referred to, the condition and ground of experience. Some object must first be perceived, not understood, but perceived — before necessary ideas can be developed in the mind. Perception and Consciousness, then, in the sense now explained, are the chronological antecedents of all necessary ideas, and these again are both the logical and chronological condition and ground of experience — that is, of *understanding* objects. But Perception and Consciousness do not give necessary ideas, only in this sense: when any object or phenomenon is perceived by Sense or Consciousness, the Reason, on occasion of such perceptions, enters into immediate and spontaneous exercise, and apprehends the ideas of space, time, substance, cause, quantity, quality, relation, &c. These ideas are not derived from, but merely occasioned by such perceptions. These ideas thus developed, then become the laws of thought, under the influence and guidance of which all our knowledge of objects is derived — that is, all our experience, using the term in the sense of understanding objects.

Now if we understand the word experience as mere Sense and Consciousness, then, I repeat, it is the chronological condition or ground of all ideas in the mind. In this sense of the term Locke is, no doubt, right in the affirmation, that all our knowledge is derived from experience. But this is evidently not the sense in which the term was understood by him. But if experience be understood, as designating the notions (contingent and relative) formed in the mind, of objects of Sense and Consciousness, then I affirm that such notions, instead of being either the logical or chronological *antecedents* of necessary ideas, are themselves both the logical and chronological CONSEQUENTS of such ideas.

TRUE EXPLANATION.

Intuitions.

The question in respect to the origin of our knowledge, together with its progress from its commencement to its development in its present form, now admits of a ready explanation. Knowledge, in all instances, commences (certain conditions being fulfilled) with the intuitions of Sense and Consciousness. Reason then intervenes, and affirms the logical antecedents of each empirical intuition, as it is given.

Notions.

The next class of phenomena that appears is Understanding-conceptions, in which the intuitions referred to are combined into notions of particular things. At first all such notions are concrete and particular. The elements of the abstract, the general, and the universal exist, but they exist only in the concrete.

The Judgment.

The Judgment now intervenes, and under the influence of the ideas of resemblance and difference, separates the elements of the abstract, general, and universal, from the concrete and particular. Then notions, abstract and general, and ideas of Reason in their abstract and universal form, appear on the theater of Consciousness. A new action of the Judgment now takes place — an action in which the particular is subsumed under the abstract, the general, and the universal.

Associating Principle and the Imagination.

In the midst of all this movement, the associating principle is perpetually active, and over all the great deep of thought thus set in motion, the Imagination then hovers, and blends the endlessly diversified elements of mental conception, feeling, and action, into forms more perfectly harmonizing with the ideas of the just, the good, the beautiful, the sublime.

Scientific Movement.

The last movement of Mind is the scientific movement — a movement in which the properties and relations of the varied objects of thought are systematically evolved in the light of fundamental ideas and principles of Reason. Such is the origin of knowledge. Such, too, is the movement of Mind from the beginning, as it rolls on towards its final consummation in pure and universal science. In beauty, grandeur, and sublimity, nothing can be compared with the movement of Mind. All that is external and visible but feebly reflects it.

MANNER IN WHICH THE GENERAL, ABSTRACT, AND UNIVERSAL ARE ELIMINATED FROM THE CONCRETE AND PARTICULAR.

But one additional topic, connected with the present subject, requires elucidation, to wit: The manner in which notions, general and abstract, and ideas and principles, universal and necessary, are eliminated from notions and judgments, concrete and particular.

General Notions.

In answering this inquiry, I begin with general notions. We will take for example and illustration, the notion designated by the word mountain. It is admitted, that in the first development of the Intelligence, there was no such general notion in the mind. The Intelligence began not with the general notion, but with the conception of some particular mountain which had before been an object of perception. How then is the general eliminated from the particular? Another mountain becomes an object of perception. Under the influence of the associating principle, the first notion is recalled. The Judgment, as these perceptions are present on the theater of Consciousness, separates the elements common to the two. The Understanding now combines these common elements into a new conception, under which the Judgment subsumes the two particulars. On the perception of a third mountain, the general notion, in a manner like that just described, undergoes a new modification, by which it embraces those elements only common to the three particulars, while each particular is again classed under the general. Thus the process goes on, till the notion under consideration assumes its most general form. This is the process by which general notions are, in all instances formed, a process so particularly elucidated in a former Chapter, that nothing further need be said upon it here.

Abstract Notions.

We will now consider the origin and genesis of abstract notions, such as are designated by such terms as redness, sweetness. These are distinguished from general notions, and also from necessary and universal ideas, by this characteristic: They designate some single quality of particular substances without reference to those substances.

To form general notions, more than one object must be given. To form abstract notions but one is required. Example: This apple is red. When we have separated the quality designated by the term red, from the subject to which it belongs, we then have the abstract notion designated by the term redness. The same holds in all other instances.

Universal and Necessary Ideas.

In explaining the origin and genesis of universal and necessary ideas, in their abstract and universal form, we will take as the basis of our explanation and illustration the principle of causality, to wit: Every event has a cause.

It is admitted, that originally, this principle is not given in this form. What is given? Some particular event, and the affirmation of the Reason, This particular event had a cause. It is also admitted and affirmed, that the universal principle is not here, as is true of contingent general principles, given by the succession of particulars. For if you suppose the event repeated a thousand or a million times, all that you have in each instance is the particular event, and the particular affirmation, This event had a cause. How then shall we account for the formation of the idea or principle under consideration? Let us recur to the individual fact above alluded to — the fact composed of two parts; the empirical and absolute parts. We will leave out of view the idea of succession, and confine ourselves to the one fact before us.

By immediate abstraction let us suppose the separation of the empirical, and the disengagement of the necessary and absolute. We then have the pure idea of the absolute and necessary. This idea thus developed we find it impossible not to apply to all cases, real or supposed. We have then, and in this manner, the universal, necessary, and absolute idea or principle.

This process might perhaps be more distinctly explained by a reference to the ideas of body and space. These ideas are not originally given in their present simple abstract form. They are given in such proportions as this: This particular body is somewhere, or in space. Here you have the empirical part, body, and the necessary and absolute part, space. Separate the two, and you have the contingent idea of body, and the necessary and absolute idea of space. Hence the principle, universal, necessary, and absolute: Body supposes space.

ERROR OF COUSIN.

I have now a word to say upon a favorite principle of Cousin, that most necessary ideas, such as the idea of time, cause, &c., have their origin in Reflection, and what he calls a sentiment of the Will. The first succession of which we are conscious, he says, is some act of the Will, for the reason that we perceive nothing only on the condition that we attend to it, and the condition of attention is the Will. To this I reply: It is admitted that we know nothing, *i. e.* have a distinct knowledge of nothing, only on the condition of attention, and that the condition of attention is the Will. But from this it does not follow, that the act of attention is the first thing of which we are conscious. It may be some feeling or thought, it being impossible for us to become distinctly conscious of the act of attention, till we attend to that. Equally false is his conclusion that the consciousness of our own proper causality precedes any conception of the principle of causality. We are not conscious of our Will as a cause, but of the acts of the Will as mere phenomena. Succession within and without is nothing but succession. The first phenomenon that is observed by the mind, whether it is within or without us, develops the principle of causality, or we can never account for its existence in the mind.

CHAPTER XVI.

LAWS OF INVESTIGATION.

INVESTIGATION AND REASONING DISTINGUISHED.

ONE department of inquiry of great importance still remains. When we have done with this, our inquiries in regard to the intellectual powers will have closed, only as far as we may find their operations combined with that of the other faculties or susceptibilities of the mind.

The department to which I refer, is the employment of these powers in what is called a process of Investigation and Reasoning. These processes, though intimately connected, are entirely distinct, and should be carefully distinguished the one from the other. In the former process our exclusive object is the *discovery* of truth. In the latter, the object equally exclusive is, to *prove the truth* already discovered.

Your attention in the present Chapter will be directed to the first process. Our inquiry is, What are the laws which govern the mind, or ought to govern the mind, in a process of Investigation of truth?

SUBSTANCES, HOW KNOWN.

All substances are revealed to us by their respective phenomena. Their *existence*, not only, but their *nature*, *character*, and *powers*, are revealed to us in this manner, and this manner exclusively. The induction of phenomena therefore lies at the basis of all our investigations pertaining to substances.

INDUCTION OF PHENOMENA, FOR WHAT PURPOSES MADE.

There are four purposes entirely distinct, for which an induction of phenomena is made:

1. For the purpose of discovering the nature, characteristics, and powers of some particular substance.

2. For the purpose of classification, into genera and species.

3. For the purpose of discovering some general fact, or order of sequence.

4. For the purpose of discovering universal laws, in conformity to which the action of substances is subordinated.

Now the principles which should guide us in the induction of phenomena, depend upon the *object* we have in view in such induction.

INDUCTION PERTAINING TO PARTICULAR SUBSTANCES.

In the induction of phenomena for the purposes of determining the characteristics and powers of some particular substance, the following principles are of fundamental importance in guiding our investigations:

1. In marking the phenomena which appear, or the characteristics of particular phenomena, omit none which do exist, and suppose none which do not exist.

2. In determining the particular powers of the substance in the light of phenomena thus classified and characterized, undeviatingly adhere to the following principles: Phenomena, in their fundamental characteristics alike, suppose similar powers. Phenomena, in their fundamental characteristics unlike, suppose dissimilar powers. In strict conformity to those principles, an attempt has been made, in a preceding part of the present Treatise, to determine, among other things, the different

functions of the human Intelligence. Whether the effort has been successful, time will determine.

INDUCTION FOR PURPOSES OF CLASSIFICATION INTO GENERA AND SPECIES.

In the induction of phenomena for the purpose of classification into Genera and species, the following principles should be strictly adhered to:

1. Fix definitely and distinctly upon the *principle* of classification, whatever it may be.

2. With a rigid regard to principle, range with the given class every object, whatever its diversities in other respects, which bears the characteristic mark.

3. Strictly exclude from the class, every individual in which the characteristic mark is wanting.

The correctness and apparently easy application of the above principles are so obvious, that it would seem every one would find it very easy to apply them in all cases. But their rigid application, in cases where it is often most demanded, requires an intellectual integrity, and sternness of virtue, which the mass of mankind "very little wot of." Every one almost would readily apply them to shells, and rocks, and earths, and beasts, and fowls, and fishes, and even to the objects in the firmament above us. But let us suppose that an individual has before him a correct definition of treason, murder, theft, and of kindred crimes punishable by the law, and that he should discover upon an only son, a dark spot, which, if carefully examined, would mark him as a subject of one of the crimes above named; it would require the stern virtue of a Brutus, to be willing to have inquisition made according to the principles of immutable justice. Cases which thus try the virtue of mankind are of very frequent occurrence.

FINDING A GENERAL FACT, OR ORDER OF SEQUENCE.

A general fact, as we have seen, is a quality which attaches itself to each individual of a given class. Sometimes it may be peculiar to this one class; sometimes it may be common to it and other classes. In other instances, it may be an essential quality of one class, and a mere accident in connection with another. When we have ascertained a fact to be general, then when an individual of a given class appears, we know, without particular investigation, that the quality is also present. In determining the question whether a fact is strictly general, the only difficulty which presents itself, is in distinguishing between an essential and accidental quality. These two principles should determine our conclusions under such circumstances:

1. The existence or absence of perfect uniformity of experience.

2. Experience in such decisive circumstances, as to render it certain that the fact is or is not an essential, and not an accidental quality of the class. Nothing but good judgment can enable one to distinguish between decisive and indecisive facts under such circumstances.

One of the most fruitful sources of error is based upon uniformity of experience in certain circumstances. The absence of such uniformity is certain evidence that a fact has an accidental, and not a necessary connection with a certain class. Its presence, however, may constitute no certain ground for the opposite conclusion. The king of Japan, for example, reasoned very inconclusively, from an experience perfectly unvarying in his circumstances, to the conclusion, that water never, under any circumstances, exists in any other than the fluid state. To separate the decisive from the indecisive, and rest our conclusions upon the former class of facts only, is the distinguishing characteristic of strong perceptive powers associated with good judgment.

The Probable and Improbable.

Between the perfectly certain and uncertain lie the probable and improbable. If, as has been already said, a fact has been ascertained to have a necessary connection with a given class, its presence, when any individual of the class is met with, becomes perfectly certain. But if its connection is accidental, its existence in connection with a particular individual of the class becomes probable or improbable in proportion to the uniformity or want of uniformity of experience under similar circumstances. Many, very many of the most serious transactions of life rest upon a calculation of probabilities.

ORDER OF SEQUENCE.

The object of investigation here is to ascertain, in reference to given effects, those things which sustain to such effects the relation of real causes. The difficulty to be overcome, often consists in this: The real cause of a given effect may exist in connection with such combinations of powers, that it may be difficult if not impossible for the beholder to determine which produced it. Under such circumstances, careful experiments, in connection with close observation, can alone determine the real order of sequence. There are four important principles which should be strictly adhered to, as tests of all our conclusions in relation to such investigations:

1. When in each experiment, the combination has been different, with this exception, that one element has been present in all, and the given effect has in each instance arisen, we then conclude that this element is the real cause of the effect.

2. When, on the removal of a certain element, the given effect disappears, while it remains, this being present when

each of the others is removed, we then conclude that this particular element is the particular cause.

3. When the given effect is the invariable consequent of the addition of a new element to a given combination, while the effect does not appear, when this antecedent is not added, we then fix upon this particular antecedent as the real cause.

4. When a number of consequents exist in connection with a number of antecedents, and when a particular consequent invariably disappears on the removal of a given antecedent, we fix upon the latter as the real cause of the former.

THE DISCOVERY OF UNIVERSAL LAW.

In the induction of phenomena for the discovery of universal law, three important principles are to be strictly adhered to.

1. The phenomena must not merely *consist* with this particular hypothesis, but *demand* it as their *logical antecedent.*

2. Consequently such phenomena must contradict, with equal positiveness, every other contradictory hypothesis.

3. All phenomena to which the given hypothesis does not sustain the relations of logical antecedent, must be left wholly out of the account, as having no bearing upon the subject.

But this subject has been so fully treated of in the preceding Chapter, that nothing further upon it is demanded here.

TESTIMONY.

It often happens, and that in reference to subjects of the greatest importance, that the facts which constitute the basis of our inquiries after truth, have never been given to us as objects of Sense or Consciousness. We are compelled to receive or reject them on the testimony of others. From this source the greatest part of our knowledge, and of the most important of our knowledge, is derived.

The great inquiry here presents itself: What are the laws of evidence under the influence of which we judge ourselves bound to receive and act upon phenomena revealed to us through the affirmations of other minds? Testimony is used for the same purpose that the faculties of Sense and Consciousness are used, to wit, for the ascertainment of facts, or phenomena, which constitute the basis of judgment in regard to a given subject.

CHARACTERISTICS OF THE STATEMENTS MADE BY A WITNESS.

The statements made by a witness may be contemplated in three points of light.

1. In the light of the idea of possibility or impossibility. If an individual should affirm that an idiot, remaining such, had given a scientific demonstration of some of the most abstruse problems in the higher mathematics, we should give no credit at all to his statement, on the ground of a perceived impossibility of the occurrence of such a fact. If, on the other hand, the witness should affirm that an individual remaining an idiot up to a certain period, did, from that period, manifest a high degree of mental energy, we should pronounce the statement highly improbable, though not absolutely impossible in itself. The statement, therefore, is capable of being established by testimony.

2. The statement may also be contemplated in reference to the question whether in itself, aside from the character of the witness, it is credible or incredible. A statement characterized as impossible, is absolutely incredible. No weight of testimony can render it worthy of belief. An event also may be contemplated as possible, and yet the statement that it has actually occurred may be almost wholly wanting in respect to credibility. If it should be said that a pure spirit before the throne had, without any form of temptation from without or

within, violated his duty to his God, we should hesitate to pronounce the occurrence impossible in itself. Yet we should deem it hardly credible. A statement, to be credible, must assert what is in itself perceived to be possible. It must also fall within the *analogy* of experience. Thus, to the great mass of mankind, there is wanting entirely any experience of a direct revelation from God. Yet the existence of such a revelation for the good of the race, is analogous to what all have experienced of the Diviue beneficence to man. There is, therefore, nothing incredible in the statement, that such a revelation has been made. A statement, then, which affirms the occurrence of an event in itself possible, and which falls within the analogy of experience, is capable of being rendered worthy of all confidence by testimony.

3. A statement is in itself probable or improbable, when it does or does not accord with general experience in similar circumstances. A thing may be possible, and, at the same time, very improbable. No one would say that it is absolutely impossible that a die, when thrown, should fall twenty times in succession with the same number uppermost. Yet all would pronounce such an occurrence in an extreme degree improbable. An improbable event may be rendered worthy of belief by testimony. A much higher degree, however, is demanded to establish such an occurrence, than one which accords with what we have had experience of in similar circumstances.

CIRCUMSTANCES WHICH GO TO ESTABLISH THE CREDIBILITY OF A WITNESS.

We will now consider the circumstances which go to establish the credibility of a witness. Among them I will specify the following, without enlarging upon any of them:

1. The most important characteristic is a *character for veracity.*

2. The next is a capacity to comprehend the particular facts to which he bears testimony.

3. Full opportunity to have observed the facts, together with evidence that adequate attention was given to them at the time.

4. Evidence that the occurrence was of such a nature that the individual was not deceived at the time, and that it sustains such a relation to the individual, as to preclude the reasonable apprehension that his memory has failed him in respect to it.

5. An entire consistency between the statements of the witness and his conduct in respect to the events, the occurrence of which he affirms. If an individual affirms his entire confidence in the veracity of a certain person, and his entire treatment of him is in full harmony with his statements, we are bound to admit the truth of what the witness testifies in relation to his own convictions.

CORROBORATING CIRCUMSTANCES ASIDE FROM THE CHARACTER OF THE WITNESS.

But there are circumstances often attending the testimony of a witness, totally disconnected with the question of his veracity, which demand our confidence. Among these, I specify the following:

1. The entire absence of all motives to give false testimony. This principle is based upon the assumption, that men do not act without some motive, and that consequently they will not ordinarily violate the principles of truth without some temptation to do it.

2. When no assignable motives exist to induce an individual to make a given statement, if he is not convinced of its truth, and when strong motives impel him to deny it, especially if it be false, then we recognize ourselves as obligated to

believe his statements without reference to his moral character at all.

3. Another circumstance which tends strongly to corroborate the statements of a witness is this: When the facts affirmed lie along the line of our own experience in similar circumstances. This, however, is not a safe principle to rely upon, in the absence of other circumstances of strong corroboration. Villains often throw their statements into harmony with experience, for the purpose of covering their dark designs.

4. When, though new, they accord with the known powers of the agent to whom they are ascribed.

5. When these facts stand connected with the development of laws and properties in the agent, before unknown.

Under such circumstances, the further removed from experience the facts are, the greater the probability of their being true. Because the greater the probability that they would, if not true, have been unknown to the witness.

CONCURRENT TESTIMONY.

The confidence which we repose in the affirmations of a witness is greatly strengthened by the concurrent testimony of other individuals. Here the following circumstances should be especially taken into the account:

1. When each witness possesses all the marks of credibility above refered to.

2. When there is an entire concurrence in their statements, or a concurrence in respect to all material facts.

3. When the characters of the several witnesses are widely different, as friends and enemies, &c., and who of course must be influenced by widely different motives, and even by those directly the opposite; especially when their character, motives, and relations to the subject, are so different as to preclude the supposition of a collusion between the witnesses.

4. When one witness states facts omitted by others, and when all the statements together make up a complete account of the whole transaction.

5. When there are apparent contradictions between the statements of the witnesses, which a more enlarged acquaintance with the whole subject fully reconciles. Such occurrences in testimony preclude the supposition of collusion, and present each individual as an independent, honest witness in the case.

6. Coincidences often occur in the statements of witnesses which, from the nature of the case, are manifestly undesigned. When such occurences attend the testimony of various individuals, all affirming the same great leading facts, they tend strongly to confirm the testimony given. This principle is most beautifully illustrated by Dr. Paley, in his Horæ Paulinæ — a work deserving more attention than almost anything else the Doctor ever wrote.

Great care and sound judgment are requisite in the application of the principles above stated. When they are fulfilled in the case of testimony pertaining to any subject, it would be the height of presumption and moral depravity in us not to act upon it as true. Infinite interests may be safely based upon the validity of such testimony. We are often necessitated to decide and act, however, in the absence of testimony thus full and complete, and often upon testimony failing in many respects of the marks of credibility above laid down. To discern between the valid and the invalid — to determine correctly when to trust and when to withhold confidence, requires stern integrity of heart, and a Judgment, "by reason of use exercised" to distinguish the true from the false.

CHAPTER XVII.

REASONING.

THE distinction between Reasoning and Investigation was made plain in the last Chapter. The former process has nothing to do with the *discovery* of truth. Its exclusive object is the establishment of truth already discovered. It belongs to Intellectual Philosophy to develop the laws of Reasoning—that is, to develop those laws which control the action of the Intelligence, when drawing conclusions from premises laid down.

THE SYLLOGISM THE UNIVERSAL FORM OF REASONING.

I will introduce what I have to say upon this subject by the following quotation from Whately's Logic:

"In every instance in which we reason, in the strict sense of the word, *i. e.* make use of argument, either for the sake of refuting an adversary, or of conveying instruction, or of satisfying our own minds on any point, whatever may be the subject we are engaged on, a certain process takes place in the mind, which is one and the same in all cases, provided it be correctly conducted." Again: "In pursuing the supposed investigation, it will be found that every conclusion is deduced in reality from two other propositions (thence called premises), for though one of them may be, and commonly is suppressed, it must nevertheless be understood as admitted; as may be made evident by supposing the denial of the suppressed premise, which will at once invalidate the argument."

Hence this author affirms, in opposition to the opinion of some on the subject, that the syllogistic is not a particular kind of reasoning, as distinguished from moral or inductive reasoning, for example, but the sole and universal process.

The above Principle verified.

That this author is correct in the principle above stated, a very few considerations will render evident.

That all reasoning, purely demonstrative, is strictly conformed to the law of the syllogism, none will deny. As an example and illustration of this kind of reasoning, we may take the following: "Things equal to the same thing, are equal to one another. A and B are each equal to C. Therefore they are equal to one another. The major premise, in all such processes, is either an intuition of Reason, or some proposition previously demonstrated.

But *inductive* Reasoning has by some been supposed to be an exception, because that, in the syllogism, we go from the general to the particular; whereas, in the inductive process, we reason from the particular to the general. This objection, if valid, would equally exclude almost the entire mass of demonstrative reasoning. Here also we do in reality go from the particular to the universal—that is, the minor premise is particular. This objection assumes also what is not true of the syllogism — that is, that in all instances, in the syllogistic form, we reason from the general to the particular. All reasoning is strictly conformed to the laws of the syllogism, wherein a conclusion is legitimately drawn from two premises, a major and a minor. In induction, as well as everywhere else, these two premises appear, the major being almost universally suppressed. In no form of reasoning legitimately conducted is the conclusion more extensive than the major premise. When we reason from the particular to the general, we always do it under the assumption (and this assumption is the suppressed major) that what is true of the particular, is also true of the class to which the individual belongs.

FORMS IN WHICH THE MAJOR PREMISE APPEARS.

There are three forms in which what is called the major premise, that which asserts the universal or general fact, is expressed; a circumstance which has led others to suppose that there are three kinds of reasoning, of which the syllogism is one. These forms are the categorical, in which the general fact is directly affirmed or denied — the hypothetical, in which the general principle is hypothetically affirmed or denied, as in the proposition, If A is B, C is D — and the disjunctive, in which a fact is affirmed to attach to some one of a given number, without determining which, as in the proposition A is either in C or D.

The categorical we have already considered. It remains to consider the last two. Now a moment's reflection will convince us, that a hypothetical premise is nothing but a universal put into the form of a particular. The proposition, for example, If Cæsar was an usurper he deserved death, is nothing more than the universal proposition, All usurpers deserve death, expressed in a concrete and particular form. The same holds in respect to all propositions of a similar character. A hypothetical proposition is nothing but a general or universal principle hypothesized in respect to a particular case.

A careful analysis will show that a disjunctive proposition, also, is in reality nothing but a general, or universal proposition, expressed in a concrete and particular form. When, for example, we say, A is either in B or C; it is not in B, therefore it is in C, we find, on analysis, that the first premise contains a universal principle, expressed in a concrete and particular form. The principle is this — when an element must exist in connection with some one of a given class, to prove that it does not attach to some one or more of the members, is to prove that it does belong to those, be they one or more, that remain. The syllogism, therefore, might be thus expressed: If C is not in one of the two, it is in the other. It is not in one, to wit, B. Therefore it is in C. The syllogism then is not a particular form of reasoning, but the universal and exclusive form.

PRINCIPLES WHICH LIE AT THE BASIS OF ALL CONCLUSIONS FROM A PROCESS OF REASONING.

All conclusions in a process of reasoning are, of course, either affirmative, as A is B, or negative, as A is not B. Such conclusions rest upon two distinct and opposite principles, on which all reasoning, legitimately conducted, rests.

1. All terms which agree with one and the same term, agree with one another.

2. All terms which agree with a particular term, differ from all others which disagree with the same term.

Remarks upon these Principles.

On the former principle all *affirmative*, and on the latter all *negative* conclusions rest. All reasoning strictly conformed to these principles, must be right, and all which transgresses them, must be wrong.

It will be perceived also, that these principles are nothing more than particular forms of the axioms common to all sciences, as the axiom in mathematics, "Things equal to the same thing are equal to one another," &c.

In the celebrated dictum of Aristotle, these two principles

are expressed in one formula, to wit: *Whatever may be affirmed or denied of any term distributed (i. e. taken universally), may be affirmed or denied of every particular comprehended under that term.*

REMARKS ON ARISTOTLE'S DICTUM.

The two principles under consideration, thrown into this form, are not rendered more distinct and simple than they were before; nor, in my judgment, are they rendered as distinct as when they appear in their separate form, the form in which they are announced in connection with all other sciences. Throwing them into this form has also, I believe, induced two quite common mistakes connected with the science of logic.

The first is the impression noticed above, that the syllogism is exclusively confined to one kind of reasoning, to wit: that in which we proceed from the universal to the particular. From the form of the principles, as announced in the dictum, we should suppose that this must be the case in respect to all reasoning conformed to the syllogism; whereas no such difficulty even apparently attaches to these principles, when announced in their distinct and separate forms.

The second mistake is found in the somewhat harmless, but very useless labor, which we meet with in the common Treatises on Logic, of *reducing* all the syllogisms in the last three figures to the first. This is done because that in this last-named figure only, is the dictum *directly* applicable to the syllogism. Now what is the real use of these reductions? Are the two terms more fully compared with one and the same third, or is their agreement or disagreement with that term, and consequently with each other, more distinct, in the first figure, than in all the legitimate moods in either of the others?

By no means. Take, as an illustration, the following syllogism in Camestres, in the second figure. Every X is Z. No Y is Z. Therefore no Y is X. This syllogism reduced to Celarent in the first figure, would stand thus: No Z is Y. Every X is Z. Therefore no X is Y; the converse of the conclusion above obtained, and which, by simple conversion, may be changed into the same, to wit, no Y is X. Now I ask, is the proposition, No Y is X rendered any more evident by all this process than it was before? Are X and Y more distinctly compared with Z, or is the fact that one agrees, and the other disagrees with that term, and consequently that they disagree with each other, more distinct and palpable, in the last instance, than in the first? If any person can see the difference between them, they can see what I cannot. Of what use then is all this labor at reduction? This only: the student is taxed with much labor in the conversion and transposition of propositions, under the promise of additional light upon the correctness of conclusions previously obtained upon principles undeniably legitimate. The result is, that his conclusions are rendered not one whit more distinct or valid to his view than they were before. No science should be burdened with useless labor. Logic, like all other sciences, with these principles in their distinct and separate forms, is far better off without the dictum than with it.

DIFFERENT KINDS OF REASONING.

We are now prepared for a contemplation of the different kinds of reasoning resulting from the nature of the different subjects upon which the Intelligence is employed in such processes. I will introduce my remarks upon this department of our inquiries, with the following quotation from Coleridge:

"Every man must feel, that though he may not be exerting different faculties, he is exerting his faculties in a different way, when in one instance he begins with some one self-evident truth (that the radii of a circle, for instance, are all equal), and in consequence of this being true, sees at once, without any actual experience, that some other thing must be true likewise, and that, this being true, some *third* thing must be equally true, and so on, till he comes, we will say, to the properties of the lever, considered as the spoke of a circle; which is capable of having all its marvelous powers demonstrated even to a savage who had never seen a lever, and without supposing any other previous knowledge in his mind, but this one, There is a conceivable figure, all possible lines from the middle to the circumference of which are of the same length: or when, in the second instance, he brings together the facts of experience, each of which has its own separate value, neither increased nor diminished by the truth of any other fact which may have preceded it; and making these several facts bear upon some particular project, and finding some in favor of it, and some against the project, according as one or the other class of facts preponderates: as, for instance, whether it would be better to plant a particular spot of ground with larch, or with Scotch fir, or with oak in preference to either. Surely every man will acknowledge that his mind was very differently employed in the first case from what it was in the second, and all men have agreed to call the results of the first class the truths of *science*, such as not only are true, but which it is impossible to conceive otherwise: while the results of the second class are called *facts* or things of *experience:* and as to these latter we must often content ourselves with the greater *probability*, that they are so, or so, rather than otherwise — nay, even when we have no doubt that they are so in the particular case, we never presume to assert that they must continue so always, and under all circumstances. On the contrary, our conclusions depend altogether on contingent *circumstances.* Now when the mind is employed, as in the case first mentioned, I call it *Reasoning,* or the use of the pure Reason; but, in the second case, the *Understanding* or *Prudence.*"

Without reference to the propriety of the peculiar use here made of the terms Reasoning, Understanding, and Prudence, I would observe, that no one can doubt the reality of the distinction between the *kinds* of reasoning designated in this passage. The question arises, What is this distinction? What are the peculiarities which distinguish the one kind of reasoning from the other?

Distinctions Elucidated.

1. One ground of distinction is found in the nature of the objects of ratiocination in the two instances referred to. In the first example the objects are pure and necessary conceptions of Reason. In the second, the objects are realities contingent and particular.

2. In the first instance no elements exist in the objects but what are perfectly known to the mind. No unknown elements exist to vitiate our conclusions. In the second instance what is known exists in connection with elements of which we are totally ignorant, and which may operate in the production of results precisely opposite to the conclusions which we have drawn from what we do know.

3. Consequently, in the first instance, our conclusions involve nothing but universal, necessary, and absolute knowledge. In the second instance, the utmost that we obtain is, conclusions more or less probable, according to the degree in which the known may be affected by the unknown, to wit, conclusions not necessary but contingent.

DISTINCTION BETWEEN DEMONSTRATIVE AND PROBABLE REASONING.

The distinction between *demonstrative* and *probable*, or as it is sometimes improperly called, *moral* reasoning, can now be readily pointed out. When the properties and relations of objects embracing no elements which are not perfectly known, are systematically evolved in the light of axioms and postulates, which are the intuitions of Reason, the result is absolute demonstration. If the objects themselves are pure ideas of Reason, the conclusions will be universal and necessary. If the objects are contingent, such will be the conclusions. The result, however, is pure demonstration, in both instances alike. The syllogism, for example, every X is Y, every Z is X, and therefore every Z is Y, is perfect demonstration, whatever the objects represented by the terms may be.

On the other hand, when we attempt to determine questions pertaining to events depending in part upon circumstances which we know, and in part upon others which we do not know, and in a state of ignorance of the influence of that which is unknown in determining the result, or when we attempt, in the light of fundamental principles, to determine the relations and properties of substances embracing elements known and unknown, and while we are ignorant of the extent in which these relations and properties depend upon the unknown elements, then our conclusions are in no sense demonstration, but partake of probabilities greater or less, according to the degree in which the known or unknown elements preponderate. Thus we have a distinct view of the broad distinction between the two kinds of reasoning under consideration. It does not lie in the *nature* of the objects to which such reasoning pertains, but in the *relations* of the objects to our Intelligence. Were all objects as perfectly known to the mind, as the objects treated of in the mathematics, then all reasoning would be alike demonstrative.

COMMON IMPRESSION IN RESPECT TO THE EXTENT OF DEMONSTRATIVE REASONING.

"If," says Mr. Dugald Stewart, "the account which has been given of demonstrative evidence be admitted, the province over which it extends must be limited almost entirely to the objects of the pure mathematics." With this statement there is quite an extensive agreement, I believe, among philosophers. The reasons assigned for the above conclusion are the following:

1. The fact that the basis of all mathematical demonstrations, are axioms and postulates which are intuitively certain.
2. That every step from these axioms and postulates to the remotest conclusions, is equally intuitive.
3. That the terms employed are so few, and distinctly defined, that they cannot be misapprehended.

The principle assumed is, that no other science is capable of possessing the above characteristics, and consequently that no other science can so properly be called demonstrative.

Let us first inquire, whether the mathematics is the only science based upon axioms and postulates intuitively certain. Take as an illustration the following axiom in mathematics: The whole of a thing is greater than any of its parts, and compare it with the following affirmation of Reason: Every event has a cause. Which is the least certain? Neither. Thus I might show by an induction of many particulars, that all the fundamental principles of morals and religion are as intuitively certain as any of the primary intuitions of the mathematics.

Permit me in the next place to ask, whether there are no

important truths resulting with as intuitive certainty from the primary truths of morals as from those of the mathematics? Take the following intuition in morals: "Thou shalt love thy neighbor as thyself," and consider the following proposition based upon it: "Love worketh no ill to his neighbor." Consequently the man that does his neighbor a deliberate injury cannot be actuated by the principle of love. The above conclusion is of great practical importance, and yet I shall not hesitate to pronounce it as absolute a demonstration as can be found in Geometry. So of the numberless other truths based upon the primary intuitions of morals and religion.

In regard to the last peculiarity of mathematics I have only to say that when the principles of morals are as definitely settled as those of the mathematics (and no reason but a false philosophy can be assigned why they have not been thus settled long ago), we may expect the same precision in morals as in any other science.

METHOD OF PROOF.

Having shown that all reasoning resolves itself into two classes, demonstrative and probable, another topic demanding attention is the *method of proof*, or the general mode to be adopted in proving a proposition, the truth of which has been already ascertained. In the last Chapter I endeavored to develop those laws of belief which should guide the mind in its inquiries after truth. Now when truth has been discovered and adopted in conformity with those rules, and we wish to present arguments for the purpose of conveying to other minds the same convictions which exist in our own, one rule of fundamental importance presents itself. Present those considerations by which our own mind has been convinced. This rule might, at first thought, seem to be so obviously proper, and so manifestly of universal application, as to render its statement entirely unnecessary. But there is no rule which is more frequently transgressed, and for the obvious reason, that few persons practice self-reflection sufficiently to render themselves distinctly conscious of the real ground of their assent to a vast majority of the truths which they believe. Hence it very commonly happens, that when individuals are called upon to assign reasons for propositions which they most firmly believe to be true, they for the first time, perhaps, begin to doubt the reality of the objects of their faith. This most frequently happens, perhaps, in reference to truths the most obvious, and with which the mind is most familiar. The reason of this most singular fact is obvious. We seldom recur to the grounds of our belief in truths so obvious and familiar, that they have been universally admitted. The evidence of such truths has come into the mind unsought. The reverse is the fact with respect to truths less obvious and familiar.

Real proof found in no other Method.

On reflection, it will appear evident, that in no other method of argumentation is real proof to be met with. We may show an individual that the truth of a given proposition necessarily results from principles which he admits. But this (the *argumentum ad hominem*) is merely hypothetical, and not real proof. For if the principles of the individual are false, the argument is good for nothing, as far as the real establishment of truth is concerned. The same may be said of every other kind of proof but that of which we are speaking.

SOURCES OF FALLACIES IN REASONING.

Assuming the proposition which I have endeavored to establish as true, to wit: That every conclusion in a process of reasoning is based upon two propositions called premises, the place where fallacies in reasoning are to be found, if they exist, may be readily pointed out. They must be found in one or both of the premises, or in the conclusion. Hence, in examining any particular process of reasoning, such questions as these are of fundamental importance.: What is the proposition which the author is aiming to establish? What principles has he assumed as previously established or as self-evident? Are these principles legitimately assumed? What statements does he propose as matters of fact? Are they authentic? Do they belong to the principle to which they are applied? Do his conclusions legitimately result from the premises laid down? By such questions as these, fallacies, if they exist, may commonly be detected. Four great questions, I repeat, should be asked, if we would determine correctly whether a proposition has been proved by a given process of argumentation, to wit: What is the precise nature of the proposition which is the subject of the argument? What are the premises or arguments by which the proposition has been sustained? Are these premises sound? And does the conclusion legitimately result from the premises? If fallacies have been introduced into the process, we shall thus discover their particular hiding-places, and know how to bring them into the light.

CONCEPTION OF LOGIC.

The object of the present and preceding Chapter has been to lay down certain great principles, in respect to the discovery of truth, and its establishment by a process of argumentation. In this department of our investigations, it remains to speak of but one additional topic, the *Conception of Logic.*

ALL THINGS OCCUR ACCORDING TO RULES.

"Everything in nature," says Kant, and this is one of his most important thoughts, "as well in the inanimate as in the animated world, happens or is done according to rules, though we do not always know them. Water falls according to the laws of gravitation, and the motion of walking is performed by animals according to rules. The fish in the water, the bird in the air, moves according to rules."

Again: "There is nowhere any want of rule. When we think we find that want, we can only say that, in this case the rules are unknown to us."

The exercise of our Intelligence is not an exception to the above remark. When we speak, our language is thrown into harmony with rules, to which we conform without, in most instances, a reflective consciousness of their existence. Grammar is nothing but a systematic development of these rules. So also when we judge a proposition to be true or false, or to be proved or disproved by a particular process of argumentation; or when we attempt to present to ourselves, for self-satisfaction, or to others for the purpose of convincing them, the grounds of our own convictions — that is, when we reason, our Intelligence proceeds according to fixed rules. When we have judged or reasoned *correctly*, we find ourselves able, on reflection, to develop the rules in conformity to which we judged and reasoned, without a distinct consciousness of the fact. In the light of these rules, we are then able to detect the reason and grounds of Fallacious judgments and reasonings.

Logic defined.

The above remarks have prepared the way for a distinct statement of the true conception of Logic. *It is a systematic development of those rules in conformity to which the universal Intelligence acts, in judging and reasoning.* Logic, according to this conception, would naturally divide itself into two parts — a development of those rules to which the Intelligence conforms in all acts of correct judgment and reasoning, and a development of those principles by which false judgments and reasonings may be distinguished from the true. A Treatise on Logic, in which the laws of judging and reasoning are evolved in strict conformity to the above conception, would realize the idea of science as far as this subject is concerned. Logic, to judging and reasoning, is what Grammar is to speaking and writing. Logic pertains not at all to the particular objects about which the Intelligence is, from time to time, employed, but to *rules* or *laws* in conformity to which it does act, whatever the objects may be.

RELATIONS OF LOGIC TO OTHER SCIENCES.

In the chronological order of intellectual procedure, Logic is preceded by judging and reasoning, just as speaking and writing precede Grammar. In the logical order, however, it is the antecedent of all other sciences. In all sciences the Intelligence, from given data, judges in respect to truths resulting from such data. We also reason from such data for the establishment of such truths. Logic develops the laws of thought which govern the action of the Intelligence in all such procedures. As a science, it is distinct from all other sciences, yet it permeates them all, giving laws to the Intelligence, in all its judgments and reasonings, whatever the objects may be about which it is employed.

CHAPTER XVIII.

MISCELLANEOUS TOPICS.

THERE are a few topics of a miscellaneous character connected with our previous investigation, which I have reserved for a distinct and separate Chapter. The first to which I would direct attention is,

THE BEARING OF THE PHILOSOPHY OF LOCKE UPON SCIENCE PROPERLY SO CALLED.

In the philosophy of Locke, *axioms* have no place, except as objects of ridicule and contempt. He directly denies that any science whatever is founded upon them. Equally removed from his philosophy are all ideas of pure Reason. All the objects of knowledge are qualities external and internal. Now in what sense and in what form is science pertaining to any subject possible, according to the fundamental principles of this philosophy? The answer which I give to this question is this: In no form whatever is science of any kind possible, according to the fundamental principles of this philosophy. We will take in illustration the science of external and material substances. All that we know of these substances, according to this philosophy, is by sensation — that is, qualities, and nothing else. Now the first step in a scientific process pertaining to these qualities, is that of making abstraction of them, in thought separating those which differ, and uniting those which agree. On what condition can this process take place? On one condition only, to wit: that we have in our minds the ideas of resemblance and difference. But these ideas are pure conceptions of Reason, and are not given by sensation at all.

Sensation may give the colors red and yellow, for example; but it can never give the fact, that the one color differs from the other. This judgment is conditioned on the prior existence in the mind of pure conceptions of Reason, the ideas above named. But the reality of such ideas this philosophy denies. It thereby, in its fundamental principles, renders the first step in a scientific process impossible.

But let us suppose that this philosophy did admit of abstraction. Simple classification and generalization would be possible — that is, these qualities, as they exist in combination, might be classed into genera and species, and then qualities, common to all individuals of given classes, might be found. This would be the utmost limit of scientific procedure, according to this philosophy, and this comprehends the limits of the sphere of the Intelligence as presented in the school of Locke. But this is the starting point of real science, properly defined. When substances have been classified and generalized, the Intelligence is then brought into circumstances to evolve their properties and relations in the light of fundamental ideas. This is science — a thing impossible according to the philosophy of Locke.

In the denial of the axioms, also, as the foundation of science, Locke renders science of all kinds impossible. Suppose we did not know the axiom, Things equal to the same thing are equal to one another, how could we affirm that because A and B are equal to C, therefore they are equal to one another? It would be impossible to make such an affirmation. The same holds in respect to every step in all the sciences, pure and mixed. Take away the axioms, and "darkness all, and ever-during night" enshrouds the sun of science. Whenever we meet with scientific Treatises in the school of Locke (and we meet with many), they exist in spite of his philosophy, and not as a consequent of it.

KANT'S DISTINCTION BETWEEN ANALYTICAL AND SYNTHETICAL JUDGMENTS.

I have reserved for this place, the consideration of the distinction above named, a distinction which constitutes one of the fundamental peculiarities of the philosophy of Kant, and which laid the foundation for the various systems which have risen out of the principles and fragments of his philosophy.

Analytical and Synthetical Judgments defined and distinguished.

The first thing to be done is to define these judgments, as given by our author, and to distinguish the one from the other. All judgments pertain to the relation between a subject and predicate. This relation, he affirms, is possible only in two ways. Either the predicate is really contained in the subject, and the judgment evolves, or designates it as a quality necessarily embraced in our conception of the subject; or the predicate lies completely out of the subject, although it sustains a certain relation to it. Thus when we affirm that all bodies are extended, the predicate is really embraced in our conception of the subject; since it is impossible to conceive of a body which is not extended. The judgment in this case simply designates the quality named as thus embraced in the conception. All such judgments proceed on the principle of contradiction. No individual, for example, can deny the proposition, All bodies are extended, without contradicting the essential conception which every one has of body. All such judgments Kant denominates *analytical.* To find them, we have only to analyze our conceptions and find the elements essentially embraced in them.

On the other hand, when we say all bodies are heavy, the predicate does not, as in the former case, lie within the subject, as an essential element of our conception of the subject. We cannot conceive of body which is not extended. But we can conceive of body as extended, without including in the conception the idea of weight. That all bodies have weight, we learn from experience alone. Through experience this element is added to our notions of body. All judgments of this character, Kant denominates synthetical.

All pure experience-judgments are synthetical, that is, when, by investigation, we have discovered, as connected with an object, or an essential element of it, some quality unknown before, we then, in thought, add that quality to our former conception of the object.

But we find, on analysis of our judgments, that we have not only empirical, but *á priori* judgments, which are synthetical. Of this character are all the primary principles of Reason-judgments, such as, Body supposes space: succession time; events causes, &c. In all such judgments the predicate is not contained in the subject, as an essential element of our conception of that subject, but lies wholly without it, and the Judgment affirms the relation between them.

Consequences which Kant has deduced from the above judgments as defined and distinguished by himself.

At first thought, it would appear that the principles above elucidated would be very harmless, at least in their results (and so they will be found to be when legitimately applied), and that they would lead to no disastrous conclusions pertaining to the validity of our knowledge relative to realities within and around us. Yet upon these principles, this philosopher has founded most of his conclusions, in which the validity of our faculties, in reference to all affirmations pertaining to realities, material and mental, finite and infinite, is denied. The conclusions to which he pushes these principles, may be thus stated:

1. Not only are all experience-judgments synthetical, but also all judgments of pure science, such, for example, as mathematical judgments.

2. As in all such judgments, the predicate lies wholly out of the subject, such judgments have no claim whatever to objective validity. They are entirely foundationless. In themselves the ideas represented by both the subject and predicate have no claim whatever to objective validity, and as the predicate lies wholly out of the subject, it can have no foundation in that.

3. As such judgments are themselves without foundation, so also must be all sciences founded on them as principles.

4. As all pure sciences rest exclusively upon such judgments, and as all judgments pertaining to such sciences, such for example, as mathematics, are purely synthetical, such sciences, with all judgments pertaining to them, are wholly without any objective validity.

5. As synthetical judgments, *á priori*, precede as laws of thought, and determine the character of all experience-judgments, and all conclusions based upon them, these last judgments, like the former, are wholly destitute of all claims to objective validity. The entire fabric of human knowledge, consequently, falls. Our Intelligence is exclusively a faculty of cognizing as real, what has no existence out of the cognition-faculty itself. The universe, material and mental, God, liberty, and immortality, are the unreal objects of foundationless conceptions. Yet they are objects which we are bound to treat as real, because our cognition-faculty presents them as such, and practical Reason, that function of Reason which teaches what we ought to do, affirms our obligation thus to treat them.

6. On no other supposition than that such is the nature and procedure of the cognition-faculty, can we account for the possibility of *à priori* synthetical judgments of sciences all of whose judgments are synthetical, together with the relations above stated of synthetical judgments to experience. The existence of synthetical judgments reveals the nature of the cognition-faculty, and determines the character of its whole procedure. The basis of the whole system of knowledge is synthetical judgments, having no claim to objective validity. The entire superstructure receives its form and dimensions from such judgments. The building, therefore, cannot be more substantial or real than the foundation on which it rests.

Errors of Kant, in defining and applying the distinctions which he has made between these judgments.

Such is the system of this philosopher, a system moulded from the airy materials, and built upon the airy foundation under consideration. It now remains to point out some of the errors into which he has fallen on this subject.

1. It may be questioned whether he has rightly *defined* these judgments, and consequently given the true criterion by which the one class may be distinguished from the other. We will propose another definition. When the connection between the subject and predicate in any given proposition is such, that we have no occasion to go beyond the proposition itself, to determine its validity, then the judgment expressed in that proposition is analytical. When, on the other hand, this connection is such, that we have to go beyond the sphere of the proposition, that is, to bring in other propositions, to determine its validity, then the judgment is synthetical. Take the two following propositions in illustration, the first of which is analytical, and the second synthetical, according to Kant: Body is extended; and Body supposes space. Why should the judg-

ment expressed in one of these propositions, be denominated analytical, and that in the other synthetical? In neither instance have we occasion to go beyond the sphere of the proposition or judgment itself to discern its validity; and it is exclusively by analysis and not by synthesis, that is, by an analysis of the nature of the subject and predicate, and of the necessary relations between them, and not by the introduction of other judgments, that that validity is in both instances alike and equally discerned. Both judgments also have precisely the same characteristics of absolute universality and necessity, and this universality and necessity are in both cases alike and equally discerned within the sphere of the judgments themselves. Nor is the predicate contained in the subject, in the former proposition, and not contained in it, in the latter, in any such form, as to make any fundamental difference between the judgments themselves. In the one instance we compare the idea of body with that of extension, and perceive intuitively that if body is, it must have extension. In the next instance, we compare the same idea, that of body, with that of space, and perceive, with the same absolute intuitiveness, that if body is, space must be. No important reasons can be assigned why one of these propositions should be denominated analytical, and the other synthetical.

By Kant's own fundamental characteristic of analytical judgments also, the validity of our definition of these two kinds of judgments, and the error of his own, is rendered self-evident. The truth of all analytical judgments, he affirms, is discerned, on the principle of contradiction, that is, if you deny them, you deny what is necessarily involved in the very idea of the subject and predicate. Now this holds equally true of the two judgments above adduced. It is no more a contradiction of our idea of body, to affirm, that body is not extended, than it is to affirm, that body does not suppose space.

If then *all* judgments, the truth and necessity of which may be discerned on the principle of contradiction, are to be reckoned as analytical judgments, and they are according to Kant himself, and also according to all principles of sound science, then all of his *à priori* synthetical judgments are, in fact, analytical and not synthetical judgments at all.

2. Hence I remark, in the next place, that Kant errs fundamentally, in his assumption, that all the pure sciences, the mathematics for example, have their exclusive basis in synthetical judgments. All basis principles of such sciences, on the other hand, the axioms, I mean, are exclusively analytical judgments. There is not a single axiom in any of these sciences, the truth and necessity of which is not discerned exclusively on the principle of contradiction, the distinguishing characteristic of analytical judgments, according to Kant himself. The axioms, for example, things equal to the same things are equal to one another, and the whole is greater than any one of its parts, and equal to all its parts together, are discernible upon the principle of contradiction, and upon no other principle. So of all the basis principles of all the sciences without exception.

3. But incorrect classification is not the only error of Kant, in respect to *à priori* synthetical judgments, synthetical judgments as he has himself defined them. He has failed to mark the *real relations* between the subject and predicate in such judgments. Had he done this, a failure to do which is a capital omission in philosophy, he would have perceived at once that no such conclusions as he supposed, can be drawn from those judgments. In an *à priori* synthetical judgment, as defined by Kant (the *à priori* analytical judgment according to our definition), the predicate lies out of the subject, and is not included in it, as in empirical analytical judgments, the only analytical, according to

Kant.* In the former judgments, the predicate to be sure is not contained in the subject as an essential element of the same. On the other hand, the former sustains to the latter the relation of *logical antecedent.* Now such a judgment is self-evidently as valid for things in themselves, as a judgment which affirms of a subject an element embraced in the conception of that subject. The propositions, for example, If body is, there must be real extension and if body is, space must be, are in themselves equally self-evident, and equally valid for things in themselves. We have then, even granting that one of these judgments is analytical and the other synthetical, no more occasion to question, as Kant has done, the validity for things in themselves of one of these judgments, than we have to do the same thing in respect to the other.

4. Another great error of Kant, in the use which he has made of the Judgments under consideration, is found in the affirmation which he makes, that in all the pure sciences, the pure mathematics for example, all judgments alike are exclusively snythetical; when, in fact, they are all alike, as actually discerned, analytical. This is evident from the fact, that all such judgments are discerned on the principle of contradiction. In the mathematics, for example, the truth of all the axioms is discerned, exclusively on the principle of contradiction, and every conclusion is so deduced, that it must be admitted, or

* The distinction between an empirical and *a priori* analytical judgment here becomes perfectly manifest. In the first case, the predicate is really contained in the subject as an essential element of the same, as in the judgment, Body is extended. In the latter case, the predicate lies out of the subject, but sustains to it the relation of *logical antecedent*, as in the judgment, Body supposes space. Both classes of judgments are analytical, for the fundamental reason, that their truth and necessity are alike discerned on the principle of contradiction.

the axioms denied. In other words, the whole procedure of such sciences is on the principle of contradiction — Kant's own criterion of analytical judgments. He himself admits, that all derivative judgments, in the mathematics, do proceed on the principle of contradiction, and yet affirms, that such judgments are, in fact, synthetical and not analytical. "Although," he says, "a synthetical proposition may at all times be discerned by means of the principle of contradiction, yet only in this way, inasmuch as another synthetic proposition is pre-supposed from which it can be deduced — but never of itself." Now here are two important mistakes. The first is, that *no* synthetical proposition understood as he has defined it, is discerned of itself on the principle of contradiction; when, as we have already seen, all of his *à priori* synthetical propositions are thus discerned, and that exclusively. On no other principle do we, or can we, discern the truth of the axioms, things equal to the same things are equal to one another, if equals be added to, subtracted from, multiplied or divided by equals, the products will be equal, and the whole is greater than any one of its parts, and all the parts together are equal to the whole, &c. Being thus discerned, they should, as already shown, be ranked as analytical and not as synthetical judgments. Being also ranked by Kant as synthetical judgments, he is undeniably in error, in affirming that no synthetical judgments as defined by himself, are discerned, of themselves, on the principle of contradiction. The second error into which he has fallen, is found in the affirmation, that all derivative synthetical propositions are discerned through some other synthetic proposition, when in the pure sciences, the mathematics, for example, all such propositions are discerned analytically through analytical and not synthetical propositions properly defined, that is, through propositions which are themselves and of themselves, discerned, on the principle of contradiction.

5. Hence, I remark finally, that Kant, for the reasons above stated, gives an entirely and fundamentally false account of the procedure of the Intelligence in the sciences. According to him, the Intelligence, in all the Sciences, begins with synthetical judgments, judgments in which the predicate lies wholly out of the subject. From this predicate, as a subject, the next step is to another predicate lying in a similar manner out of that, and so on, each step being like the first purely synthetical. If this were the case, we should have, in none of the sciences anything like demonstration; for this in all instances, rests exclusively upon the principle of contradiction. All demonstrative sciences are truly analytical, and not synthetical. Their basis principles are all analytical propositions, that is, propositions whose truth is discerned exclusively, on the principle of contradiction. Every deduction from these propositions is made exclusively on the same principle. No philosopher, therefore, has more fundamentally erred, on any subject, than Kant has, in his definitions of analytical and snythetical judgments, and in the use which he has made of those judgments.

THE TRUE AND FALSE SYSTEMS OF PHILOSOPHY.

We are now prepared to contrast the system of Philosophy taught in this Treatise, with what we will take the liberty to denominate false systems, systems to which it stands opposed. All systems of philosophy take form and receive their fundamental characteristics from the ideas which their respective advocates entertain in respect to the question of Ontology, that is, in respect to the question, What shall we regard as real? This question resolves itself into another, to wit, What do we *know* to be real? The true answer to each of these questions must be found in one of these three systems, to wit, Realism, as taught in this Treatise, Materialism, or Idealism in one of its forms. As no other theories of Ontology are conceivable or possible, and as but one of these can be true, that one, whichsoever it may be, must be true, in which the true answer to the questions under consideration is found. We will now consider these diverse systems in the order above named.

CRITERION OR TESTS BY WHICH WE MAY DISTINGUISH THE TRUE FROM ALL FALSE SYSTEMS.

Before proceeding, however, it may be well to fix definitely in mind some sure *tests* by which the true theory may be known and distinguished from all false ones. The following principles I lay down as involving such tests :

1. The true theory will take into account *all* the facts of Consciousness with *all their essential* characteristics, just as they are, supposing nothing which does not exist, and omitting nothing which does exist.

2. The *principles* of this theory will readily account for all these facts with all their characteristics, and that without exception.

3. The *principles* of this theory will be *necessarily supposed* by these phenomena, and all its *deductions* will be necessary logical *consequents* of these principles and phenomena, so that it will be manifest not only that this one system is true, but that all contradictory ones must be false.

Every theory possessing these characteristics, it will readily be seen, cannot be false, and every one wanting or contradicting all or any of them, cannot be true. Suppose, for example, a theory is constructed which accords only with a part of the real facts of Consciousness, that one circumstance is an absolute demonstration of the fact that such theory is founded in error; for if it were true, it would not only accord with but be demanded by the facts referred to. We are now prepared to consider the systems before us.

THE SYSTEM OF REALISM.

1. Knowledge, according to the teachings of the system of Realism, implies two things, — an *object* of knowledge and a *subject* possessed of the *power* of knowledge. Between the nature of the subject and object such a correlation exists, that when the appropriate conditions are fulfilled real knowledge of such object arises, as the necessary consequent of this correlation.

2. Between mind and realities within and around it, this correlation exists. It is relatively to them a *power*, and they are relatively to it, *objects* of real knowledge.

3. As a faculty of knowledge, the action of the Intelligence is, and must be, as the *essential characteristics* and *relationships* of the *objects* of knowledge.

4. There are two classes of realities known as such, with equal absoluteness to the Mind — Spirit and Matter, on the one hand — and Time, Space, and God, &c., on the other. Of the real fundamental qualities of the first class, the Mind has a direct and immediate, or presentative knowledge, through Consciousness and Sense. The second class it knows as real, as necessarily supposed by the actual facts of which it has an absolute presentative knowledge.

According to this system, "the things which we envisage *are* that in themselves for which we take them," and "their relationships are so constituted as they appear to us." All "our intuition is" not "nothing, but the representation of phenomena," but that of real qualities of objects which have not a mere ideal, but a real existence. "Every quality," "all relationships of objects in space and time," and time and space themselves would remain what our Intelligence now affirms them to be, "whatever changes might take place in the subjective qualtiy of our senses," or if the Sensibility and Intelligence both should be done away with. Matter and Spirit, in their essential characteristics, are realities in themselves. The universe, material and mental, and God as the free, intelligent, self-conscious author of each, are realities also. Mind knows not only its own manner of perceiving such objects, but the objects themselves, and has to do with each alike, because each alike is real. According to this theory, Mind is not in a universe of fictions of its own creation, but of realities, realities finite and infinite, realities which it knows because they are objects and it is a faculty of knowledge, and to which it sustains relations infinitely solemn and momentous. That this is the true and only true theory, I argue from the following considerations:

THEORY OF REALISM VERIFIED.

1. It, and it alone, accords with the intuitive and necessary convictions of the universal Intelligence on the subject. All men do and must believe, whatever their speculative theories may be, that they have an actual knowledge not only of their *manner* of perceiving, but also and equally of the *objects* of perception themselves. To this statement there is absolutely no exception. Either the universal Intelligence is a lie, or this is the true theory of knowledge.

2. By no possibility can this theory be shown to be false, and any one of an opposite character true. Suppose an individual should undertake to prove that "the things which we envisage are not that in themselves for which we take them." How could he do it? He has in the whole procedure to employ the very faculty which he affirms to "take things" and and their "relationships for that in themselves" which they are not. Then, by the fundamental demands of his theory, we

are bound to say, that his arguments and their relationships and bearings are not that in themselves for which he takes them. Nor is his theory of knowledge that in itself for which he takes it. No theory of knowledge, the opposite of that under consideration, can be devised, which does not render real knowledge on all subjects alike impossible. Now a theory which undeniably accords with the intuitive convictions of the universal Intelligence must be held to be true, until it is demonstrated to be false.

3. All the *facts* and *operations* of Mind, in all its needlessly diversified procedures, can be *explained* in perfect accordance with this theory, and cannot, as we shall hereafter perceive, be explained in accordance with any other. The actual procedure of the Intelligence will be the same, whether we suppose the objects of knowledge to be real or not. Nothing in the supposition of such reality therefore can lie in the way of such explanation, though it may appear, as hereafter it will, that on any other theory, the facts of mind could not be what they now are.

4. All the *activities* of universal humanity, the entire procedure of the Intelligence in all the sciences mental and physical, have their actual basis in the truth of the theory of knowledge under consideration, and are the height of absurdity on any other assumption. The science of Mind is based throughout upon the assumption, that the phenomena of spirit, as given in Consciousness, phenomena which lie at the basis of that science, are to the Intelligence real objects, and it is to them a real power, of knowledge. The science of natural Philosophy and Astronomy, and all the natural sciences, procede entirely upon the assumption that a relation precisely similar exists between the Intelligence, on the one hand, and the qualities of external material substances, on the other. The same is true of the Mathematics, and all the activities of

humanity. All have their basis in one assumption exclusively, to wit, that Mind, as a faculty of knowledge, knows things and their relationships as they are, and are the perfection of absurdity on any other supposition. How infinitely absurd was it in Kant, for example, to spend his life in writing books to convince the world that "things which we envisage are not that in themselves for which we take them;" when, according to his theory, there was no such world as he was writing to; there were no real beings, such as he took them to be, to be convinced; no real beings holding any theory at all; nor was his own theory that in itself for which he took it. So of all the activities of humanity, whatever their objects or directions.

5. As a final reason for holding this theory, we remark that it is involved in no difficulties which are not common to all others, and rests upon the very principle, as far as the *mode* of knowledge is concerned, upon which, in the last analysis, all others must rest. If Intelligence be given, as in its nature a faculty, and realities as in their nature objects of real knowledge, all difficulties, as far as the facts of knowledge are concerned, disappear, and that totally. The reason for knowledge is that the Intelligence is a faculty, and realities within and around it are objects of real knowledge. Now the same reason precisely must be assigned, if we assume that such a relationship does not exist between the Intelligence and realities. Why is it, that they are not to it objects, and it to them, a faculty of real knowledge? The answer, and the only answer, that, in the last analysis, can be given, is that such is the nature of Mind, on the one hand, and of realities on the other. Why is it that the Intelligence takes things and their relationships to be that in themselves which they are not? The answer is, such is the nature of the Intelligence as a faculty, and of realities as objects of real knowledge. Why is it, finally, that the Intelligence, in the first instance, envisages things and

their relationships as possessed of given real characteristics, and then the same Intelligence envisages the same things to be not that in themselves which it had previously envisaged them to be? But one answer can be given, to wit, that such is the nature of the Intelligence, as an envisaging faculty. As this is the reason which, in the last analysis, must be given for all the procedures of the Intelligence, whatever their nature may be, it is surely infinitely more reasonable to stop just where the universal Intelligence, in fact, does stop, to wit, with the principle, that Mind is a faculty, and realities around it are objects of real knowledge. We are then involved in no difficulties not common, and escape those which are perfectly fatal to all others.

MATERIALISM.

Materialism assumes Matter to be, to the mind, the only possible object of knowledge, and consequently as the only reality. It is also a system of absolute Atheism. It admits and can admit of no overruling power, of no power whatever which is not itself a result of material development and operation. All the facts of the universe, material and mental, it resolves into the necessary results of such development and operation. Now the material hypothesis can be sustained but upon the following conditions:

CONDITIONS ON WHICH THE MATERIAL HYPOTHESIS CAN BE SUSTAINED.

1. It must be admitted, that Matter, with all its qualities, properties, and laws, has existed from eternity, and has, from eternity, contained within itself, as an inherent property of its own nature, and that without change or modification, the unconditioned and absolute cause of all its own dispositions,

arrangements and operations; yes, of all the phenomena of Mind, and of all the facts of the universe just as they actually occur.

2. All our reasonings and deductions must be based exclusively upon the *known* properties of matter. We are not to assume, as the basis of our explanations of any of the facts of the universe, any unknown properties in this substance, unless the reality and character of such unknown properties are most clearly indicated and affirmed by those that are known.

3. It must be shown, that nothing but the *known* properties of Matter need be assumed to account for the entire facts of the universe, material and mental, just as they are, and that these facts can be better accounted for, by a reference to said properties, as the unconditioned cause of these facts, than to any other conceivable hypothesis.

4. It must be admitted that all the known properties of matter are comprehended in its Primary, Secundo-primary, and Secondary qualities, as elucidated in the Chapter on Sense. The known properties of Mind, on the other hand, are undeniably thought, feeling, and voluntary determination, and nothing else. Mind is given to itself as an absolute unity wholly incapable of composition. Matter is given as a multiple always existing as a compound, and capable of an endless diversity of compositions, and in every new composition exhibiting properties wholly unknown before. Mind everywhere exists as the *end*, and Matter, in all its known dispositions and arrangements, exists as the *means* to this one end — the wants of Mind. Matter, so far forth as known to us, possesses no inherent power of *originating* animal or physical organizations, such as now exist, the only power which, in this respect, it apparently possesses, being that of *perpetuating* organizations already existing, and that according to fixed and immutable laws of propagation. The power of origination from a state

of total unorganization, of any real or conceivable forms of animal or vegetable organization, has never yet been proven to exist in Matter. No known facts indicate in it the existence of such a power, much less the power to originate the leading forms of organization actually existing on earth. Yet the fact is absolutely undeniable, that the time was when no such organizations did exist, nor any of the embryo principles from which they *now* result. If science has established anything, it has established the fact, that the present order of things throughout the universe had its beginning in time. The time was, when the heavens as now organized, had no existence, when "the earth was without form," and when neither vegetables nor animals, rational or irrational, had any existence upon it.

Mind, also, in all the higher and spiritual departments of its nature, is constituted in fixed and immutable adaptation to one all-overshadowing idea, that of God, as the unconditioned cause of all that conditionally exists, who, as a free, intelligent, self-conscious personality, presides over the entire movements of the universe, who, in absolute wisdom and righteousness, exercises a moral government over all moral agents in being, and who, as the creator, proprietor, and governor of all, is in himself possessed of all the attributes involved in the ideas of absolute infinity and perfection. The instinct of worship and prayer are absolutely universal principles of Mind, and the only appropriate object of these principles, is a *personality* possessed of the attributes above referred to. We never pray to a principle, a blind, unconscious truth, whatever its nature may be, but to a *person* upon whom we recognize ourselves as dependent, and who has the power to grant or withhold our requests. Worship, when directed to any other object than infinity and perfection, tends undeniably to limit and degrade the mind, and when directed towards a personality possessed of these attributes, as undeniably tends to expand, elevate and ennoble it. These facts clearly indicate, that such a personality is the only appropriate object of these immutable principles of universal Mind.

Mind, also, is fundamentally constituted to act under a system of moral government, presided over by such a personality. In all the circumstances of its existence, the Mind cannot but have a consciousness of actions as morally right and morally wrong. By the law of its conscience also, it cannot but feel impelled to do the one and avoid the other. When the voice of conscience is seconded by a positive command and prohibition from lawful authority, the Mind is under a much higher influence in favor of the right and against the wrong, than when left to the unseconded behests of conscience. Now suppose the Mind, under these circumstances, should regard itself as under an absolute command from a being possessed of absolute infinity and perfection, a being to whom it owes its existence, and upon whom it hangs in absolute dependence for all the blessings of that existence, and to whom it is bound by all the ties actual and conceivable, that can bind a creature to its creator, suppose the Mind, in the presence of the right and the wrong, ever regards itself as subject to a solemn command from such a being to do the right and avoid the wrong, it is then undeniably subject to the highest moral influence, and all in the right direction, of which we can possibly form a conception. Under precisely such an influence is the Mind while acting under the omnipresent conviction of the being and perfections of God. This is enough to show, that in all the higher and spiritual departments of its nature, it is constituted in fundamental correlation to the idea of such a supreme being.

5. I remark finally, that it must be admitted that throughout the wide domain of Nature, one law obtains with absolute universality, unless the higher and spiritual department of our

nature be an exception, to wit, that *wherever there is a fundamental want of sentient existence, there is a corresponding provision, and wherever there is a fundamental adaptation, there is a corresponding object or sphere of action.* This statement will be universally admitted, as all science pertaining to nature is based upon the assumption of its truth. With these conditions and facts in mind, I urge against Materialism the following considerations:

OBJECTIONS TO MATERIALISM.

1. It has not a shadow of *positive evidence* in its favor, evidence either *à priori* or *à posteriori.* The reality of an IMMATERIAL substance, endowed with the power of thought, feeling, and voluntary determination, is to the Intelligence just as conceivable, and therefore possible, in itself, as that of a material substance possessed of the attributes of extension and form. From none of the known attributes of Mind can we derive the remotest evidence that it possesses any of the known attributes of Matter. Mind is an absolute unity, with not a solitary phenomenon indicating in it the properties of extension, form, solidity, or color, of any indeed of the Primary, Secundo-primary, or Secondary properties of Matter. Nor does Matter exhibit a solitary phenomenon indicating in it the remotest likeness to any of the properties of Mind. Nor do its powers indicate in it any unknown properties from which the phenomena of Mind can result. The proposition, then, that Matter is the only reality, is not only wholly incapable of being proved, but is absolutely unsustained by any form or degree of positive evidence whatever.

2. The dogma that Matter is the only reality, is opposed to the *intuitive convictions* of the race. All mankind, however ignorant or barbarous, have a conception of two orders of existence. The rudest savage in being, no more confounds his

soul with his body, or any of its phenomena with any of those of Matter, than he does night with day. Now this conviction indicating, as it does, the presence to the universal Intelligence of phenomena in these substances, phenomena which affirm them to be distinct and opposite in their nature, the one to the other, must be held as true, till the opposite is proven, which, as we have seen, can never be done. The burden of proof is with the materialist.

3. We have precisely the same evidence of the reality of *Mind* as something *not material*, that we have of *Matter*, as something not *spiritual*. We have the same evidence of the reality of the phenomena of Mind, that we have of those of Matter, and we have as distinct a knowledge of one class of phenomena as we have of the other. We can as readily resolve the phenomena of Matter, solidity, extension, and form, into those of Mind, thought, feeling, and voluntary determination, as we can the latter into the former. We can, with the same propriety and logical consistency, assume spirit to be the only reality, and deny the existence of all solid and extended substances, as we can assume Matter to be the only reality, and deny the reality of Mind, and we have absolutely no evidence whatever in favor of either of these exclusive assumptions.

4. It is absolutely impossible, from the fundamental characteristics of Matter, to deduce those of Mind, or to conceive *how* those of the latter can proceed from those of the former, any more than we can conceive how that creation itself can be the result of a power inhering in empty space. There is no resemblance or analogy between the one class of phenomena and the other. They are, in every conceivable respect, total opposites. How can phenomena, which are totally void of the characteristics of solidity, extension, and form, result from the phenomena last named? How can a compound extended and

solid substance, every particle of which is absolutely void of thought, feeling, and free will, produce an absolute simple, which is totally incapable of composition, which, as a simple, exhibits none of the known properties of that from which it is derived, and in which the power of thought, feeling, and voluntary determination, as its sole and exclusive known properties, inheres? Can any one *perceive* any *intelligent* adaptation in any or all of the known properties of Matter to produce those of Mind? Or do the known properties of the former substance indicate in it any unknown properties from which those of the latter substance can by any possibility result? Certainly not, and no one will pretend the opposite. Here is the burden that lies upon Materialism. Before it can lay the least shadow of claim to validity, it must take the known properties of Matter just as they are, on the one hand, and those of Mind on the other, and then show an *intelligent* adaptation in the former to produce the latter. Or it must show from the known properties of Matter, that those which are unknown do inhere in it from which those of Mind may result. Now no one ever did or ever will even attempt to accomplish any such object, and until it is accomplished, Materialism must be regarded, not only as utterly void of all evidence to sustain its claims, but as contradicted by the highest possible evidence.

5. Materialism also rests upon the assumption, that Nature, in the very highest departments of her creations, is fundamentally constituted in fixed and immutable adaptation to the *unreal* instead of the *real*, and that the principle that for all the necessities or demands of the nature of sentient existences, there are corresponding provisions, and for every fundamental adaptation of such existences, there is a corresponding sphere of action, is totally false, as far as the highest wants and adaptations of such existences are concerned, and this system must be false, unless that assump-

tion is true, an assumption also unsustained by the least shadow of evidence of any kind. Mind, as we have seen, is, in all the higher departments of its nature, fundamentally constituted in fixed and immutable correlation to one all-overshadowing reality, that of a personal God, endowed, as the creator and governor of the universe, with all the attributes involved in the ideas of absolute infinity and perfection. Materialism takes away this greatest of all actual or conceivable realities, and thus assumes, that the great basis principle of all Science pertaining to the relations of sentient existences, is totally false as far as the highest wants and adaptations of such existences are concerned, to wit, the moral and spiritual nature of Mind. *Nature never vibrates to the unreal.* Why should we assume this principle to be false, in reference to the highest of all the wants and adaptations of that to which all things else sustain the exclusive relation of a means? Should we grant the assumption without absolute demonstration of its validity? Materialism demands this assumption of us, without producing the least shade of evidence of its truth, and Materialism must fall unless this foundationless assumption is granted.

6. Nor is it possible, in accordance with the principles of this system, to account for the *great leading facts of the Universe.* Those of Mind, of all others the great central facts, we have already considered. To an explanation of not one of these facts, can this system make the least approach whatever. Equally impotent is it, in its attempts to explain the facts of the external material creation. If Matter is the only real substance, it must contain within itself, as an immutably inherent law of its own nature, the unconditioned and absolute cause of all organizations animal and vegetable, in existence, and of the entire mechanism of the universe. As that cause existed from eternity, it must have acted from eternity, and that with all possible force. It must have thus acted, or it could never

have acted at all. Those internal principles which prevented its acting from eternity up to any given or conceivable period, must have prevented its acting at all to eternity. Creation, then, the general organization of the universe, and all vegetable and animal organization, must have been from eternity, or it could, by no possibility, have occurred at all. Creation is not from eternity, but had its origin in time. Its cause, then, can be no inherent law of Matter. The materialist may deny the fact of the origin of the present order of things in time, and then he is confronted by all the known leading facts of the universe; or he may admit the fact under consideration, and then his own system is demonstrably false. It can no more be true, than that the same thing can exist and not exist, at the same time. That which, from eternity to a given period of time, had no existence, and then began to be, as is true of the present order of things throughout the universe, can, by no possibility, owe its existence to any inherent law of Matter. If this proposition is not self-evident, none other is, or can be.

The time was when the earth existed with a total destitution of all forms of vegetable or animal organization, and of all the embryo principles from which such organizations now result. Such are the absolute teachings of Science upon this subject. From what known law of Matter (and we are permitted to reason from such laws only), could existing and past organizations have originated? With Matter given in a state of total and universal unorganization, and of corresponding destitution of all embryo principles from which animal or vegetable organizations now arise, let the Materialist designate the known law of Matter from which he can deduce the organizations which do exist. Unless he can do this, every principle of true Science requires, that we refer the origin of such effects to a cause out of Matter and above it.

It is also a well ascertained fact of Science, that the general organization of the universe, as revealed by the science of Astronomy, is an event of time, and not a reality existing from eternity. The time was when Matter was not organized into systems of suns and worlds as it now is. As now organized, there are two classes of facts which demand special attention, those which result from the *inherent laws* or *properties* of Matter, and those which pertain to what may be called its *accidents.* The attraction of bodies towards a common center results from the inherent properties of Matter. Motion, on the other hand, and especially in any given direction, is not such a property, but a pure accident of this substance. The harmony of the movements of the heavenly bodies results from a perfect equality of two opposite motions, one of which results exclusively from the inherent properties of Matter, and the other, both in its *degree* and *direction* is, as exclusively, a pure accident of the same substance. I refer, of course, to the centripetal and centrifugal forces, by the perfect equality of which the planets are held in their orbits, as they move about their central suns. Now this centrifugal force, both in its degree and direction, must have existed from eternity, or it can never be accounted for by a reference to the inherent properties of Matter: because it in no form results from such properties. Separate this motion in either form from Matter, and by no conceivable possibility, but by a power out of Matter, can that motion ever be attached to it. If this motion did eternally attach to this substance, the system of worlds, as they now exist, must have been from eternity. So of the world which we inhabit, with all its animal and vegetable organizations. The Materialist may take the ground, that this motion, in both forms, did attach to Matter from eternity, and then he is confronted by all the teachings of Science, and by all the great leading facts of the Universe. Or he may admit that these accidents did not thus attach to this substance, and then his system leaves him no principles by which he can account for the organization of the system of creation. Upon one or the other of these rocks his system must be fatally impaled.

7. Materialism, I remark finally, must fall to pieces upon its own favorite principle, to wit, that the laws of nature are absolutely *uniform* and *invariable* in their operation. We grant this principle as of fundamental authority in interpreting the facts of the universe. But what are the laws of nature? This question cannot be answered *à priori*, but exclusively *à posteriori*. Nature's laws can be discovered only by careful observation of her actual operations. When we have discovered those laws, if we can find any undeniable facts in nature which could not have been produced through those laws, then we know absolutely that a power out of and above nature does exist, and that these facts are the result of the action of that power. Let us now notice some of these laws: 1. Every species of vegetables and animals has an independent existence, that is, was not derived by transmutation from any other species. Not a solitary fact can be adduced, in the present or geological history of the earth contradictory to, and not confirmatory of this law. No advocate of the Development theory pretends to find, in the present or past facts of the earth's history, a solitary intermediate formation from which the truth of his theory can be deduced. The above then must be regarded as a law of nature, or no such law stands revealed through the known facts of the universe. 2. Every individual vegetable and animal derives its existence, as such a vegetable or animal, through a fixed and immutable law of *propagation*. Every plant is derived from a seed, and every seed from a plant of its own species, and every animal is derived through the prior union of two individuals, a male and a female. If this is not a law of nature, no such law can be revealed to us through nature's operations. 3. Another

equally manifest and universal law of nature is this, that all animals, and vegetables too, commence their existence in an embryo state, and that all the leading species of the former class can arrive at maturity but through parental care and sustenance.

Now if it is true (and no fact can properly be adduced as a fact of science, if this cannot), that the time was when no vegetables or animals, or any embryo principles from which such organizations now originate, did exist, then the following conclusions are undeniable: 1. Every species of vegetable and animal existence owes its origin, not to the laws of nature, but to a power not only out of and above Matter, but nature also. 2. The original pair from which all leading species of animals was derived, was originally produced, not in an embryo state, but in a state of maturity, a state in which they were capable of self sustentation. 3. The laws of nature, in accordance with which such species now derive their existence, owe their origin, not to nature herself, but to the very power above referred to. How can Materialism avoid these conclusions? We affirm, that it cannot avoid them, and therefore, that it must fall to pieces upon its own principles. I have just alluded to a few of the considerations which lie against this theory, a theory not only not sustained by any form or degree of evidence whatever, but also confronted by all the great central facts of the universe. I have said enough, however, to enable the reader to estimate duly its real claims to his regard, a theory which has no higher merit than the infinitely absurd attempt to resolve the highest conceivable orders of substances into the lowest, and to deduce from the lowest conceivable phenomena those which are absolutely the highest. Matter and Mind stand at the widest extremes of conceivable existence. To resolve the latter into the former, is an absurdity no less than the affirmation, that the whole is always less than any one of its parts.

SYSTEMS OF IDEALISM.

While Materialism resolves all substances into Matter, Idealism denies all reality of Matter, and resolves all realities into different forms of spiritual existence, or manifestation. All that the Mind knows or can know, according to this system, is its own operations. Nothing out of the Mind, therefore, can be to it an object of knowledge. Now the various forms of Idealism, to an elucidation of which special attention is here invited, take their rise wholly from the different principles on which the facts of Consciousness are explained.

IDEAL DUALISM.

One system assumes the reality of two unknown and unknowable substances, called Noumena, to wit, the *subject* which thinks, and the *object* which, in some unknown and unknowable manner, affects the thinking something, and sets the machinery of thought in motion. This is the system of Ideal Dualism, of which Kant is the great representative and expounder. The effect which the external object produces in the thinking subject, is denominated *sensation.* This sensation, through the idea of substance and phenomena, is given in Consciousness, as a phenomenon of the subject, the Me, and thus we have the idea of ourselves. At the same time, the same phenomenon, the sensation, is, in the same Consciousness, through the ideas of time and space, perceived as a quality of a substance external to the mind, a substance having extension, form, &c., the sensation constituting, as we have seen in former chapters, the *content* of the perception, while the ideas of time and space give it *form,* and make the object, the sensation itself, appear as a reality wholly external to and diverse from the Mind. Through ideas pre-existing in the Reason, the Understanding forms notions of this and other objects similarly envisaged in the Mind, and the Judgment, through the ideas of resemblance and difference, abstracts, classifies and generalizes them. Thus we attain to our conceptions of the universe, material and mental. No real objects corresponding to these conceptions exist. "The things which we envisage," in the language of Kant, "are not that in themselves for which we take them; neither are their relationships so constituted as they appear to us. If we do away with our subject, or even only the subjective quality of the senses in general, every quality, all relationships of objects in space and time, nay, even space and time themselves would disappear, and cannot exist as phenomena in themselves, but only in us." We ourselves, and all things which we take as real, are mere phenomena to which no corresponding realities do, or, as we shall see must be the case according to the fundamental principles of the theory, can exist.

WHAT ARE REALITIES ACCORDING TO THIS SYSTEM?

Such is the system of Ideal Dualism. While, according to its fundamental teachings, we can have no *positive* knowledge of noumena, that is, of things as they are in themselves, we can make some important declarations *negatively* in regard to them, declarations which cannot but be true. For example:

1. According to the principles of this system, there can be no substances, or noumena, having real *extension* or *form*. If space has no real existence, as this system affirms that it has not, and the system cannot be true if it has, then, by no possibility can any objects exist which really and truly have extension and form.

2. Nor, according to the principles of the same system, can there be any intelligent or sensitive existences which really

have any *successive* experiences, that is, thoughts, or feelings, or purposes, which really succeed each other, nor can there be anywhere any really *successive* events? Time as well as space, is nothing in itself, according to this system. Then there can be no succession of events, or experiences, mental or physical.

3. Neither can there be any God sustaining to this or any other universe, to noumena or phenomena of any kind, the real relation of creator or governor. Creator and creature, ruler and subject, of necessity, suppose events as really successive. No such realities can exist, according to this system The only idea of God that it can admit as valid, is that of an unknown and unknowable something, sustaining unknown and unknowable relations to unknown and unknowable noumena existing nowhere and in no time, and which have in themselves neither extension, nor form, nor successive phenomena.

4. According to the principles of this system also, it is totally unphilosophical to suppose a real Divinity of any kind. The supposition of such a reality is wholly unnecessary to account for the facts of Consciousness as given in the system, or any other facts whatever. This Kant himself perfectly understood. He was in theory, in consistency with the principles of his system, as blank an atheist as David Hume, though not as far from the just charge of hypocrisy. Kant gave out to the world that the doctrines of the evangelical faith would be immutably established by his system, that "only by means of this Critick can the roots themselves be cut off from Materialism, Fatalism, Atheism, Free-Thinking, Unbelief, Fanaticism —and Idealism and Skepticism," and then taught positively that God is nothing, but like time and space "a regulative idea," "in many respects a very useful idea," that when we think of God, "it is only a being in idea that we think," and that in reference to the order and harmony of the universe, "it must be the same thing to us where we perceive this, to say,

God has so wisely decreed, or nature has so wisely ordered it." Practically we are to treat the idea of God as valid, just as we should that of nature; but neither is to be intellectually regarded as representing anything whatever that is real. It is enough to say, however, that if Kant was not a blank Atheist, it was because he refused to admit the necessary logical consequences of his own fundamental principles. Ideal Dualism is, and can be, in itself, nothing more than a system of absolute Atheism.

REMARKS UPON THIS SYSTEM.

In demonstrating, as we have done in former chapters, that all the fundamental principles of this system are false, and totally so, we have shown undeniably, that the system itself cannot be true.

1. The system of Ideal Dualism, or that of Kant, rests fundamentally upon the assumption that *all* of our knowledge of Matter is exclusively through sensation, and therefore mediate, or representative. We have shown that but a *part* of our knowledge of Matter is through sensation, and therefore representative; that, on the other hand, our knowledge of all its essential qualities is really and truly presentative, and therefore just as valid for the reality of its object as is that of our own mental states. 2. Kant maintains, that the ideas of time and space give form to Sense-perceptions, and that those ideas are, consequently, the chronological antecedents of such perceptions. We have shown that these ideas, on the other hand, are the chronological consequents of such perceptions, that we do not have these perceptions because we have these ideas, but that we have these ideas, because we first have the perceptions, and that these ideas instead of being laws of Sense-perception, are in fact, categories of Understanding-conceptions. 3. Kant, in the next place, bases his system upon a distinction which he

makes between analytical and synthetical judgments. We have shown that he has fundamentally erred, first, in his definition of these judgments, and secondly, in the application which he has made of them even as defined by himself, and consequently, that none of the conclusions which he deduces from them are valid. 4. Kant maintains, that all our ideas of an external material universe are self-contradictory, and therefore that no such universe can exist. We have shown, that his whole argument upon this subject is based upon a very gross psychological error, mistaking an idea of Reason for an Understanding-conception, and that no such contradictions as he professedly adduces do or can exist. 5. Kant maintains that *none* of the ideas or principles of Reason are valid for things in themselves. We have shown that *all* such ideas and principles must be thus valid. Ideal Dualism cannot be true, unless all the above-named principles of Kant are true, and, as we have seen, not one of them is or can be true.

In addition to the above, I would here remark, that this system is totally *self-contradictory*. It maintains, that *no* ideas of Reason are valid for things in themselves, and then rests wholly upon the assumption, that *some* at least of these very ideas are thus valid. To explain the facts of Consciousness, it assumes the reality of two entities, the *subject* and *object*. Here then we have the idea of substance and quality as valid for things in themselves. Kant affirms also, "that all our cognition occurs through objects which affect our senses, and partly of themselves produce representations, and partly bring our Understanding capacity into action." Here we have the idea of cause and effect assumed as valid for things in themselves, and also that of time; for cause and effect imply real succession, and consequently the objective validity of the idea of time. Now if these ideas of Reason should be regarded as valid for things in themselves, all others would be.

Further, the entire system of Ideal Dualism is based upon the assumption, that knowledge has a *real beginning* and a *real progress.* But this not only assumes the reality of succession, and consequently the objective validity of the idea of time, but also bases the explanation of the facts of Consciousness upon an assumption which this philosophy denies, which cannot be true, if this philosophy is true, and which Kant himself formally denies in his Critick of pure Reason, page 41, to wit, that human knowledge has a real beginning and real progress. A system thus self-contradictory cannot be true.

The system of Ideal Dualism also rests upon an assumption, the truth of which, as Kant himself admits, we cannot even conceive to be possible, and that system cannot be true unless the validity of this assumption be granted, to wit, the pure ideality of space. "We can never make to ourselves," he says, "a representation of this, — that there is no space, although we may very readily think, that no objects therein are to be met with." In a few pages subsequent, he tells us, that "if we should do away with our subject, or even only the subjective quality of our senses in general, every quality, all relationships of objects in Space and Time, nay, even Time and Space themselves, would disappear, and cannot exist as phenomena in themselves, but only in us." In other words, that which we cannot but conceive of as real, whether we ourselves, or anything else exists or not, would, according to this philosophy, be totally annihilated, if even the subjective quality of our senses was changed. The same idea is given in this philosophy, as unconditionally necessary and absolute, on the one hand, and as purely contingent on the other, and Ideal Dualism cannot be true, unless the same thing in itself cannot but be, and at the same time may or may not be, that is, unless the same thing can, at the same time, exist and not exist.

This philosophy also rests upon the assumption, that *all*

departments of our nature, intellectual, sensitive, and voluntary, are immutably correlated to the *unreal*, instead of the *real*, and that in respect to ourselves, the universe, and God. For a personal God whom, according to the fundamental demands of our higher nature, we can love, worship, pray to, and confide in, it substitutes a mere "regulative idea," an infinite nonentity, without substance or real attributes. For a substantial and glorious universe, material and mental, to which as such a reality, as Kant admits, our nature is correlated, it substitutes an "airy nothing," without "a local habitation or a name." In other words, according to the fundamental teachings of this philosophy, our entire nature is immutably correlated to the unreal, instead of the real. Unless nature vibrates exclusively to the unreal, this philosophy must be false.

The entire deductions of this philosophy, I remark again, are immutably opposed to the necessary intuitive convictions of the universal Intelligence. This Kant himself admits. This philosophy gives the universe as a non-reality, but it can never, as he affirms, make that universe appear to the Intelligence as anything else than real. "For," he says, "we have to do with a *natural and unavoidable illusion*, which itself reposes upon subjective principles," an illusion which, as he subsequently affirms, "irresistibly adheres to human reason." In other words, his philosophy gives, as only true, what, as he himself affirms, human reason irresistibly affirms to be false. Need we any further demonstration of the fact, that such a philosophy must be "science falsely so called?" Other considerations bearing upon this system are reserved till we come to speak of the general characteristics of Idealism in all its forms.

SUBJECTIVE IDEALISM. — SYSTEM STATED.

Ideal Dualism, as we have seen, affirms the reality of two unknown and unknowable entities (noumena), the one sustaining to certain phenomena (sensations) in the other, the relation of a cause. This admission, as we have also seen, affirms the validity of certain ideas of Reason, for things in themselves, an admission perfectly fatal to the claims of Idealism in every form, a system which, in no form, can be true, if *any* ideas of Reason are thus valid. To avoid this fatal rock, Fichte, who was at first a disciple of Kant, and who, as finally dissenting from him, became the author of Subjective Idealism, in its modern form, took away the external object entirely, resolving all realities, the universe, and God into the subject, "the Me." Kant took for granted the validity of sensation for an external object or cause. The unity of scientific truth, as Fichte maintained, requires that nothing should be taken for granted, that beginning with self-evident truths, every subsequent step should be taken with absolute demonstrative certainty. Of what then has the Mind an absolute knowledge, a knowledge so absolute, that no skeptic ever questioned its validity? Of its own operations, its sensations, desires, perceptions, judgments, ideas, &c. These then are to be assumed as the only known realities, and whatever else is to be admitted as real, must be shown from these to be such, and that with demonstrative certainty. In the center of this one circle, therefore, — the mind's own operations, — Philosophy must take its stand. All without this circle must be held as unreal. Yet in this very circle, the Mind, the only reality according to this system, apprehends itself, as encompassed by an external universe, as the grand theater and cause of its own operations. How shall we account for such phenomena? We must find their cause wholly within the subject.

In the subject, according to this system, two distinct and opposite principles exist — the principle of spontaneous self-activity and expansion — and that of certain "inexplicable limitations." In its spontaneous activities, its efforts after self-development and expansion, the Mind, through laws and principles inherent in its own nature, finds itself limited and confined. In itself, therefore, it experiences the feeling of resistance to its own activities, of confinement within certain limits beyond which it vainly endeavors to expand itself. This feeling may be called a *sensation* As seen by the eye of Consciousness, it is in the first instance, through the idea of substance and phenomena, postulated by the Intelligence as a phenomenon of the Mind itself, and thus the idea of "the Me" is attained. In the next instance, this same feeling, as seen by the eye of Consciousness, in its exterior function, is perceived, through the ideas of Time and Space, as the quality of an object external to the Mind, an object having extension, form, &c. Thus we attain to the idea of a "Not-me," an external material universe, and to that of God, as the creator and governor of this universe. As the universe is no reality in itself, and has no existence out of the Mind, so God is nothing but an ideal of the Mind's own formation, an idea of moral order formed by the Mind, and in conformity to which it realizes its own development. God is not the creator of "the Me," or of "the Not-me," but is himself created by "the Me," a favorite form of expression with certain leading disciples of this school.

Ideas and principles of Reason have the same place in this system, that they have in that of Ideal Dualism, that of principles and laws which have no objective validity. Such is subjective Idealism. On this system I remark:

REMARKS UPON THIS SYSTEM.

1. That it is throughout irreconcilably self-contradictory. Its fundamental principle is this, that nothing is to be taken for granted, and then it bases its entire explanation of the facts of Consciousness upon a pure assumption which is taken for granted, to wit, the existence within the Mind of certain "spontaneous activities," on the one hand, and of certain "inexplicable limitations," on the other. These entities, if they be such, lie as much without the circle of the Mind's conscious operations as the external universe. The latter may just as properly be taken for granted as the former. Further, this system rests upon the assumption that no ideas of Reason are valid for things in themselves, and then assumes that some of these ideas are thus valid, those of cause and effect, phenomena and substance, &c.

2. The explanation of the facts of Consciousness, as given in this system, is based wholly upon mere assumptions, which are not only not self-evident, but whose validity can, by no possibility, be established by evidence. The reality of these "spontaneous activities," and "inexplicable limitations," cannot be shown to be either the logical antecedent or consequent of any one, nor of all of the facts of Consciousness together. In other words, this system is wholly based upon an hypothesis which is not only not self-evident, but which is wholly incapable of being established by any form or degree of evidence whatever.

3. But granting this hypothesis as true, it is absolutely impossible to deduce from it the entire facts of Consciousness just as they are, what every valid hypothesis must and will do. Take these activities and limitations, and how can it be shown, that from them, in connection with the known laws of mind, just the thoughts, feelings, and voluntary determinations

actually given in Consciousness, would arise, and that none others could arise. There is no conceivable connection between the antecedent and consequent, in this case, and no such consequent can be shown to exist. Yet such a connection must be shown to exist, or Subjective Idealism is void of all claims to our regard.

4. This system also rests upon an assumption which we have already shown to be false, the assumption that the Mind has no absolute knowledge of anything but of its own operations. We have already seen, that the Mind has the same direct, presentative knowledge of the qualities of Matter, that it has of its own operations. It would be no more a denial of the palpable facts of Consciousness to affirm the non-reality of the former than it would to deny that of the latter. This system cannot be true, unless Consciousness is "a liar from the beginning."

5. The legitimate logical results of the fundamental principles of this system, is absolute Nihilism, a denial of the reality of all substances, objective and subjective, finite and infinite. Everything without the circle of absolute knowledge is, according to these principles, to be held as unreal, and nothing but the Mind's own operations are objects of this form of knowledge. These, then, should be assumed as the only realities, and the reality of all else denied. This is pure Idealism, or Nihilism, a system which must be true, if the fundamental principles of that under consideration are true.

6. This system, I remark finally, is fundamentally subversive of all the principles of morality and religion. As far as God is concerned, it is a system of absolute Atheism. Equally subversive is it of all forms of obligation, arising from the civil, social and domestic relations of life. Nonentities have no moral claims upon us. All is unreal according to this system, without the circle of "the Me." "The Me" is the only

reality. "The Me" begets its own parent as well as creates its own God, and things begotten and created are absolute nonentities. To whom, then, does it owe its moral allegiance? To itself alone. There is not, and cannot be, any religious, social, civil, or domestic moral tie, if this system is true. These are its legitimate logical consequents, the total subversion of all the principles of morality and religion.

PANTHEISM, OR THE SYSTEM OF ABSOLUTE IDENTITY.

Subjective Idealism assumes the subject, "the Me," as the absolute principle of all things, thus resolving the universe and the Infinite into the Finite. Each individual being has this principle in himself, and hence there are as many such principles as there are men. The unity of Science requires that there should be but one Absolute. Hence the assumption, that the Absolute, in the language of Morell, "is not the individual 'Me' that resides in every man, but the divine 'Me' of which every man is the image or reflection." Fichte, to escape certain insuperable difficulties involved in the system of Kant, took away the *object*, and resolved all realities into the subject. Schelling, the author of the system of Absolute Identity in its modern form, to escape similar difficulties in the system of Fichte, took away all subjects but one, the Infinite and the Absolute, and resolved all realities into that. The grand consummation to be sought, the Absolute unity of Science, required, that a principle should be found in which there should be an absolute identity between the Finite and the Infinite, the subject and the object, between *being* and *knowing*. The following propositions will present the fundamental elements and characteristics of this system:

ELEMENTS AND CHARACTERISTICS OF THIS SYSTEM.

1. Being and knowing are in fact one and identical. There

is no such thing as an *object* to be known, and a *power* of knowledge, and then an *act* of knowledge consequent on the mutual correlation between the object and power referred to. The *act* of knowing and the *thing known*, on the other hand, are one and identical.

2. The universe, material and mental, is nothing but the Infinite and Absolute in a state of development. Before creation commenced, an infinite mind, essence, or thought—these words, according to this system, being identical in their meaning—filled the immensity of space. This infinite something is the only reality. All individualities, all finite objects, or personalities, are nothing but the diverse *forms* which this one sole substantiality assumes, in the process of self-development. In the Infinite and Absolute, two opposite forces, each infinite and indestructible, exist, one tending to expand infinitely, and the other seeking to know itself in this infinity. The result of these two forces interpenetrating each other, each being infinite and indestructible, is a finite generation. Hence individualities finite and limited, arise. These individualites are not separate existences, but only forms in which the Infinite and Absolute develops itself. In the finite the same contradiction, the same conflict of opposing forces, is repeated — the finite seeking to expand itself, and to know itself in this expansion. In this act of self-consciousness, the finite is present to itself as *subject* and *object*. The object is the external creation. The subject is the being who knows this creation. Yet the subject and object are not two, but one and the same. Neither is distinct from the Infinite and Absolute, but only a form in which the postulate *I am* in the Infinite is repeated. The I in the Finite and Infinite, in order to know itself, must see itself in the act of perceiving an object. For how can we know what perception is, that is, know ourselves as percipients, only by knowing ourselves in the act of perceiving something, that

is, some object? But the object known cannot be different from the subject which knows, since being and knowing are correlative, and must meet in the same subject. The subject, then, knows itself by seeing itself as its own object, an object postulated as external to the self, in order that the I may know itself in the act of perceiving something which to itself, that is, to the philosopher (since, as Coleridge remarks, none but philosophers who have a *peculiar* philosophical talent can descend to such depths), is both itself and not itself. In thus seeing ourselves in all things, and finding all things in ourselves, we at length, as streams in the ocean from whence they came, lose ourselves and all things in the Infinite and Absolute. The infinite projects itself into the finite in order to know itself in producing and perceiving the finite. The finite loses itself again in the Infinite, as bubbles in the ocean from which, for a moment, they appear as separate, without being in reality distinct existences. God is the sole reality, creation the mirror in which he sees himself, by an act of self-projection in the finite. This is the Pantheistic System, which resulted as the "natural daughter" from the philosophy of Kant. I do not say, that I have made myself understood, in the hints above given, of this strange philosophy. How can that be rendered intelligible which its great expounder affirms can never be symbolized by words, which must be *thought* in order to be understood, which can be thought only by the peculiarly gifted, and to these has no other claims to truth, than that it is thought?

3. Prior to development in the universe, God exists in a state of undeveloped, unconscious impersonality, and exists simply and exclusively as the absolute *essence* from which all things, by a necessary law of development in said essence, proceed. As developed in the universe also, the Absolute attains

to Self-Consciousness, that is, to the exercise of real Intelligence, only in the consciousness of humanity.

4. Creation, while it proceeds according to laws of Intelligence, is not the result of intelligent foresight, and of a corresponding act of Will, but, as said above, of a necessary law acting potentially in the Absolute. This law renders it impossible that this process should not occur, or that it should take on a differet form from what it actually does.

5. This system, as a matter of fact, leaves us with no higher object of intelligent worship, and no more perfectly meets the demands of the religious sentiment in man, than does that of Subjective Idealism. An undeveloped unconscious impersonality is surely no object of intelligent worship, and this is God, as originally given in the system. Then, if the Absolute, in a state of development, is to be worshiped at all, it should be most undeniably, in the highest form in which He is therein presented, and that is the state in which He attains to self-conscious personality, that is in the Consciousness of man. Humanity, and that only, is God, in a state of development. Humanity, then, is to itself the only proper object of worship — humanity as the Absolute developed. But the same thing appears, only under another name, in the system of Subjective Idealism. Any system which presents the universe in a state of development, or undevelopment, as God, is really and truly a system of blank Atheism, and nothing else.

6. The necessary logical consequence of this system is that of Absolute Idealism, with a denial of the existence of all substances, finite and infinite. If being and knowing are one and identical, then, undeniably, thought without subject or object, is the only reality. Creation is nothing but a process of thinking, and God is only an infinite thought in a state of undevelopment.

REMARKS UPON THIS SYSTEM.

Such is the system of Absolute Identity or Pantheism. That it is utterly false and foundationless, I argue from the following considerations:

1. While it professedly gives a perfectly scientific system of knowledge, a system based upon self-evident axioms and postulates, it actually rests upon no form or degree of evidence whatever. The only claim set up in its behalf by Schelling himself, is a special faculty of *intuition,* inborn only in the few, and absolutely wanting in the general Intelligence, a faculty of intuition which, in the language of Morell, "affords us a species of knowledge which does not involve the relation of subject and object, but enables us to gaze at once by the eye of the Mind upon the eternal principle itself, from which both proceed, and in which thought and existence are absolutely identical." The reality of such a faculty, and its absolute authority in philosophy is wholly taken for granted in the system, without any attempt to establish either by evidence. In other words, this system rests upon unathorized assumptions, and upon nothing else. All real science has its exclusive basis in axioms and postulates, self-evident not only to the few, but to the universal Intelligence. Such would be the basis of this system, were it founded on the rock of truth.

2. The system is, in itself, intrinsically absurd and self-contradictory. The idea that that which is in itself already both infinite and absolute, has in itself the principle of self-development and self-expansion is intrinsically absurd and self-contradictory. We might, with the same propriety affirm, that infinite duration and boundless space contain in themselves the same principles, and that the action of these principles in these realities is the cause of all the facts of creation. The idea of development pertains to the finite alone. The Infinite and

Absolute are already developed, or they never can be. Then the idea of an infinite and absolute thought (for being and knowing are identical, according to the system) seeking self-development, or having in itself such a principle, is, of all things, intrinsically absurd and self-contradictory, and the Mind cannot but thus regard the subject, the moment the idea is suggested.

3. There is an absolute want of intelligible *connection* between the *principles* of the system and the *results* deduced from them. We will first present these principles as set forth by Coleridge. "Descartes," he says, "speaking as a naturalist, and in imitation of Archimides, said, Give me matter and motion, and I will construct you the universe. We must of course understand him to have meant: I will render the construction of the universe intelligible. In the same sense the transcendental philosopher says, Grant me a nature having two contrary forces, the one of which tends to expand infinitely, while the other strives to apprehend or *find* itself in this infinity, and I will cause the world of intelligences, with the whole system of their representations, to rise up before you. Every other science pre-supposes Intelligence as already existing and complete. The philosopher contemplates it in its growth, and, as it were, represents its history to the mind, from its birth to its maturity." Again, "It is equally clear, that two equal forces acting in opposite directions, both being finite, and each distinguished from the other by its direction only, must neutralize or reduce each other to inaction. Now the transcendental philosophy demands, first, that two forces should be conceived which counteract each other by their essential nature; not only in consequence of the accidental direction of each, but as prior to all direction, nay, as the primary forces from which the conditions of all possible directions are derivative and deducible: secondly, that these forces should

be assumed to be both alike infinite, both alike indestructible. The problem will then be to discover the result or product of two such forces, as distinguished from the result of those forces which are finite, and derive their difference solely from the circumstance of THESE DIRECTIONS. When we have formed a scheme or outline of these two different kinds of force, and of their different results, by the process of discursive reasoning, it will then remain for us to elevate the Thesis from notional to actual, by contemplating intuitively this one power, with its two inherent, indestructible, yet counteracting forces, and the results or generations to which their interpenetration gives existence, in the living principle, and in the process of our own self-consciousness."

Now, in the name of the universal Intelligence, we may ask, and we may ask it at the risk of being told that the "philosophic talent is not yet inborn in us," Can any Intelligence like ours, either by intuition, or by any process of discursive reason, calculate the results of the action of two such forces as these? Can he show the results, let him conceive these infinite and indestructible forces to meet in what direction he will? Above all, can he show, or conceive, that the result of the action of such forces, begun in the Infinite and repeated in the finite, shall and must be the system of which we are conscious, and nothing else? This he must do, or his conclusions are not scientific. Must not a philosopher be, "not *in himself*, but *beside himself*," who can suppose that the system of mental operations of which we are actually conscious, is the real result of the action of two forces, one of which tends to expand infinitely, and the other to know itself in that expansion, and especially that he can logically deduce from the action of such forces, as the necessary result, this system just as it is? Even Hegel could not digest such absurdities; and hence, he rejected the system which rested on them as a system of monstrosities.

We will next contemplate these principles as given by Schelling. We have given an infinite being, essence or thought, an undeveloped, unconscious infinite impersonality, having in itself the law or principle of self-development. These are the sole principles of the system. Can any one *conceive* how that the necessary results of the process of self-development in such an unconscious, undeveloped, infinite impersonality, would be the facts of human Consciousness pertaining to the universe of Matter and Mind just as they are, and nothing else? that from such a process in such an impersonality, an infinite number of self-conscious personalities, such as man is, with all his experiences, external and internal, would arise, and that none others can arise? Such a connection as this must be shown to exist between the principles of a system, and these facts, or it has no claims whatever to our regard. No such connection can be conceived or shown to exist between the principles of the system under consideration, and the facts attempted to be deduced from them.

4. There are undeniable facts of human Consciousness which could not exist at all, if the principles of this system were true. If being and knowing, as this system teaches, are one and identical, then thought is the only reality, and there cannot be in the Infinite and Absolute, developed or undeveloped, or in any of the forms of its development, anything like a Sensibility or Free Will, or any of the phenomena pertaining to either of these faculties. But we have the same evidence of the reality of the phenomena of these faculties, that we have of those of thought. We might, with the same propriety, assume, that Sensibility or Will is the only reality, as to assume that Intelligence is, as this system does. This

system can give us but a part of the facts of Consciousness, and these not as they are. It therefore must be false.

5. The idea of God as going through the process of self-development, attributed to Him in this system, a process in which He finally attains, from a state of unconscious impersonality, to self-consciousness and personality only in man, degrades the Infinite and Perfect infinitely below religious worship or veneration, and thus does the most fatal violence to the religious principles and sentiments in the human mind. The entire moral and spiritual departments of our nature are wholly correlated to the unreal, or this system must be false. Every feature of the divine character given in the system, tends to degrade infinitely the Divinity in our estimation, on the one hand, and the character of humanity, in entertaining such ideas of God, on the other. Take this process as described by Morell: "This Infinite being, containing everything in itself potentially which it can afterwards become actually, strives by the law which we have above indicated, after self-development. By the first movement (the potence of Reflection), it embodies its own infinite attributes in the finite. In doing this, it produces finite objects, *i. e.*, finite reflections of itself, and thus sees itself objectified in the forms and productions of the material world. This movement, then, gives rise to the *philosophy of nature.* The second movement (potence of sub-sumption) is the egress of the Finite into the Infinite; it is nature, as above constituted, again making itself absolute, and resuming the form of the eternal. The result of this movement is *mind*, as existing in man, which is nothing else than nature gradually raised to a state of consciousness, and attempting in that way to return to its infinite form. This gives rise to transcendental idealism, the philosophy of *mind.* The combination of these two movements (Patur der Vernunft) is the reunion of subject and object in the divine reason; it is God,

not in his original or potential, but in his unfolded and realized existence, forming the whole universe of Mind and Being. This is the proper view of Schelling's pantheism, and is fully unfolded in the philosophy of the Absolute." In other words, the Infinite and Absolute, the undeveloped, unconscious infinite Impersonality, attempts in the process of self-reflection to develop itself, that is, to see and know itself as it is, and not as it is not. The result is certain sensations which it sees as phenomena of a not-self, and hence the generation of the external material universe, or rather perceptions of it, the seeing and the thing seen being, according to the system, one and identical. The Infinite and Absolute having thus seen itself as it is not, that is, as finite instead of infinite, and thus having got out of itself and beside itself, attempts a regress through the Finite back into the Infinite, that is, back into itself again. In this process the Infinite and Absolute attains, for the first time, to the exercise of self-consciousness, and here it appears transformed into an indefinite number of self-conscious individualities (men), not one of whom knows himself as he is, that is, as Deity developed, but conceives of himself as a self-conscious finite personality, surrounded with finite impersonal realities, wholly separate from itself, the material universe, and owing its existence to an infinite self-conscious personality, God. The Infinite and Absolute now having got wholly out of itself and beside itself, and hopelessly so, by any process of intuition or induction hitherto generated in any form which it has assumed, as a last and desperate resort, generates in a few reflections of itself, "an intellectual intuition" through which the Infinite and Absolute perceives the whole process by which it got out of itself and beside itself, and thus it gets back into itself again, not however as it was originally, but in a state of complete development. This is no caricature. It is this system developed as it is, and who can entertain sentiments of respect for the Infinite and Absolute when contemplating him as necessitated by the laws of his own being, to go through an endless round of such processes as these, and in none of them attaining to any higher forms of development, or to the exercise of any higher degrees of intelligence than appear in the consciousness of man?

6. There are other respects in which this system does violence to all the laws of the higher, spiritual and religious nature of universal Mind. For a self-consciousness personality, endowed with all the attributes of infinity and perfection, and to whom we can look with sentiments of love, veneration, confidence and hope, the only idea of God to which our nature is correlated, it substitutes, in the first instance, an undeveloped, unconscious impersonality that neither knows itself nor any other object, and in the next, the universe itself as this God developed in the highest form to which he can possibly attain, an idea of Divinity that meets not a solitary demand of the religious sentiment in humanity. For fellowship and intercommunion with God, a fundamental demand of the sentiment under consideration, it substitutes the union of absolute identity. For moral purity, as the exclusive condition of this union, it substitutes science, "intellectual intuition." Every feature of Divinity presented in the system is in absolute antagonism to the demands of the religious principle in universal Mind.

7. This system is also equally subversive of morality, in every form or degree. All realities in existence are, according to its fundamental teachings, nothing but the Infinite and Absolute developed or undeveloped. All acts and events that actually occur, are only different forms and developments of the necessary activity of God himself. Unless God himself, and the necessary activity of the divine nature, are moral evil, there can be no such thing as moral wrong in the universe.

Now a system that thus subverts fundamental and immutable morality, and belies the Universal Conscience, is not hastily spoken of, when it is denominated "science falsely so called."

8. I remark finally, that there is not, in a single principle or deduction of the system, anything good, or useful, or tending, in any form, in that direction. Upon the procedure of none of the sciences does it throw a solitary ray of light, nor present a principle which can be a guide in morals, religion, or in any department of human activity. The system stands before us simply as a lasting monument of illustrious talents wholly misdirected, talents laboring undesignedly, it may be hoped, for the subversion of every useful idea and principle pertaining to God, to humanity, and the universe.

PURE IDEALISM.

All forms of Idealism which we have yet contemplated, involve absolute contradictions, at the same time affirming and denying the same things. They are all based upon the exclusive assumption, that *no* ideas of Reason are valid for things in themselves, and then fundamentally base their explanation of the facts of Consciousness, upon the assumption, that some of these very ideas are thus valid, the ideas of substance, for example, cause and effect, antecedence and consequence, &c. To escape such fatal rocks, Pure Idealism — the last and only other form which Idealism itself ever assumes — takes away all substances, all subjects and objects, all real entities of every kind, and resolves all things into pure thought without subject or object.

Thought has been supposed to imply two things, a subject and object. If either is assumed as real, then ideas of Reason are valid for things in themselves. To escape this difficulty, Hegel — the author of Pure Idealism in its modern form — took away both the subject and the object, and affirmed thought itself to be the only reality. Creation is nothing but a process of thinking, and the law of development inherent in thought itself, and giving existence and direction to the process of its development is God, God the Infinite and Absolute. According to the process of ordinary thinking, every thought implies the reality of a subject and object, with a perceived relation between them. The subject and object, Hegel affirms to be nothing: and the *relation*, as existing in thought, to be the only reality. The universe, therefore, is constituted wholly of *relations*, relations with no real objects related to each other. God is not a self-conscious personality, but, as we have said, a law of development in thought itself, and attains to self-consciousness only in man, the divine Consciousness being identical with the endlessly progressing Consciousness of humanity. In the system of Hegel, God, as an object of thought, occupies no higher place than in that of Schelling. In that of the latter, he is, as we have before shown, an infinite, unconscious, undeveloped Impersonality, who attains to development only in the Universe, and to self-consciousness only in man. In the former system He is an infinite and eternal principle, or law inherent in thought itself, an endlessly progressive principle of development which attains to Consciousness only in man, and is itself synonymous with the ever-advancing Consciousness of Humanity. From what is said above, the reader will form a conception sufficiently distinct of the principles, essential characteristics, and bearings of this system, and that is all that is requisite for our present investigations. The details are left to other writers, whose object is to present the system in its entireness, in its principles and deductions. A few remarks only are requisite to demonstrate its total invalidity.

1. The system, in its essential principles and logical deductions, is in direct contradiction to undeniable and fundamental facts of Consciousness. No system, as we have before said,

can be true, whose essential principles do not, as their necessary results give, and whose logical deductions do not perfectly accord with, those facts, just as they are. Now assuming thought to be the only reality, the principle and cause of all things, what can be deduced from it? Absolutely nothing but forms and developments of pure thought itself. Nothing approaching the phenomena of Sensibility or Will, can, by any possibility, arise. But these phenomena are realities as fully attested as such, as thought itself. We have the same authority for affirming feelings or voluntary acts to be exclusive realities, and to resolve all things into forms which such feelings or acts assume, as to postulate the same thing pertaining to thoughts. If these phenomena are not real, nothing is, and if they are, the system of Absolute Idealism must be founded wholly in error.

2. This system is perfectly self-contradictory in its fundamental principles. The assumption on which the entire superstructure rests is this, that nothing shall be assumed as the basis of philosophy which is not given in Consciousness, as contained in thought itself. The systems of each of his predecessors was rejected by Hegel for this reason, that in all of these systems, alike, something not given in thought, and as one of its essential elements, was assumed, as the ground of the explanation of the process of thought. After rejecting such a principle, as wholly unphilosophical and fatal to the system based upon it, what does Hegel do, in the construction of his own system? He has, to be sure, not assumed the reality of an infinite and absolute *substance* from which all things proceed, a substance lying out of thought, but he has assumed, as the condition and ground of explaining the process of thought, the reality of an infinite, eternal, and absolute *law*, a law inherent in thought itself. Now this law is no more given in Consciousness as an element of thought, than the finite and

absolute substance above referred to. Both alike, and one just as much as the other, lie without the circle of Consciousness, and both are assumed for the same reason precisely, the explanation of the facts of Consciousness. If such an assumption is fatal to one system, it is to another; the system of Absolute Idealism falls to pieces upon its own principles. Besides, if we are allowed to assume anything lying without thought itself, as the condition and ground of explaining the facts of Consciousness, we should make that assumption which is in itself the most reasonable, and which best accords with the laws of human nature, and the facts of the universe. Now the reality of an infinite *Being*, as the cause of all things, is in itself just as conceivable as that of an infinite *Law*, and the former assumption infinitely better accords with the facts of Consciousness, the fundamental demands of our entire moral and spiritual nature, and with the facts of the Universe within and around us. The system under consideration is not only fatally self-contradictory, but is based upon a principle the most unreasonable in itself.

3. The validity of the principles on which this system is exclusively founded, is absolutely inconceivable and impossible. Thought without a thinker, without subject or object, relations without realities related, and phenomena without substance, we can no more conceive to be possible or real, than we can conceive of the annihilation of space. Yet these constitute the entire basis and substance of this theory. Well has one of his own countrymen remarked, that "Hegel's philosophy is nothing in itself, and by itself, nor was its author in himself, but beside himself."

4. The legitimate bearings of this system upon morality and religion must claim our attention. If thought, with its developments, is the only reality, then of nothing but thought can any form of moral obligation be predicated; and unless

thought can affirm of itself, that it ought not to develop itself according to the necessary operations of an infinite, eternal, and absolute law, residing within itself, morality has and can have no place in the universe. Unless thought also can be to itself an object of self-worship, thought which attains and can attain to no higher forms of development than appear in the Consciousness of humanity, there can be no religion, no sphere whatever for the action of the religious sentiment. Yet Absolute Idealism speaks of God, of Morality, Religion, Sin, Holiness, Redemption, and Immortality; and professes to solve all the great problems of thought pertaining to all these high themes. But what are its actual teachings on these subjects? Let an individual from the country, from whence this system proceeded, answer. "Hegel has a God without holiness, a Christ without free love, a Holy Ghost without illumination, a Gospel without faith, an Apostacy without sin, Wickedness without conscious guilt, an Atonement without remission of sin, a Death without an offering, a religious Assembly without divine worship, a Release without imputation, Justice without a judge, Grace without redemption, Dogmatical Theology without a revelation, a This Side without a That Side, an Immortality without existence, a Christian Religion without Christianity, and in general, a Religion without religion." This is no caricature, but a valid statement of facts. Take the principles of the system, and no other or higher forms of thought on any of these subjects can be deduced from it. This system, together with that of Absolute Identity, does idealistically what Polytheism does materially. It "changes the glory of the Incorruptible God, into an image made like unto corruptible man, and to birds, and four-footed beasts, and creeping things."

GENERAL REMARKS UPON THE SYSTEMS OF IDEALISM.

I shall conclude what I have to say upon Idealism, with a

few general remarks upon its diverse forms which we have contemplated. All these systems, as we have seen, rest upon common assumptions, and perfectly harmonize in certain fundamental particulars, in the assumptions, for example, that no ideas of Reason are valid for things in themselves, that neither ourselves, the universe, nor God, time, space, cause, nor substance, are in themselves, or their relationships, "that for which we take them," &c. Hence it is that there are certain remarks which are equally applicable to every form of development which this system has assumed, or can assume. Among these remarks I would direct special attention to the following:

1. All these systems alike rest upon mere *assumptions* unsustained by any form or degree of positive evidence whatever. Not one of their basis principles are intuitively evident, nor can their validity be established by any process of discursive reasoning. This has been rendered perfectly evident in our preceding investigations. All real science, all true systems of knowledge have their basis in principles having apodictical certainty, principles whose validity is self-affirmed. Not one of these systems rests upon any such principles, and consequently not one of them has any claim whatever to a place in the firmament of the sciences.

2. All these systems are perfectly *self-contradictory*, and rest upon the assumption, that the same identical principles are both true and false at the same time. They all rest upon the assumption, that *no* ideas of Reason are valid for things in themselves, and must be false, unless that assumption is true. Then they all alike base their explication of the facts of the universe upon the assumption, that *some* of these ideas have this validity, and not one of these systems can be true, unless this assumption also is valid. They all agree, for example, that there is somewhere an ultimate reason why the facts of Consciousness are what they are, and not otherwise, that there

is in these facts a real *process*, a *beginning*, and a *progress*, a process which results from a real cause inherent in thought itself, in the substance of the Mind, or in the Infinite and Absolute. Here we have the assumption of the validity of the ideas of substance, cause, antecedence and consequence, succession and time. But none of these systems can be true, if any of these ideas have objective validity, and they cannot be true unless these same ideas have this validity. They all rest upon the assumption that nothing without the circle of the Mind's conscious operations is to be assumed as real, and then base their explication of these very facts upon the assumption of the validity of principles lying wholly without the circle of Consciousness. Now systems thus fundamentally self-contradictory must be false.

3. From the principles of none of these systems, nor of all together, can we explain the facts of Consciousness, as they are. On the other hand, it can be rendered demonstrably evident, that if these principles were true, these facts could not, by any possibility, be what they are. If, for example, there is in the human Mind the power of Will, of voluntary determination, not one of these systems can be true, and if such a power does not exist, no facts of Consciousness should be assumed as real. If either of the systems last elucidated is true, there not only cannot be any such power as that of Will in man, but not even a sensibility: for if being and knowing are really and truly one and identical, as they both alike affirm, and cannot otherwise be true, then thought is the only reality. There can be no Sensibility or Will in any being. No system can be true which does not explain *all* the facts of Consciousness as they are. Not one of the systems under consideration can give us but a part of these facts, and not even these as they are.

4. According to all these systems, there is a necessary and

irreconcilable antagonism between the *natural* and *scientific* procedures of the Intelligence. In the former, we attain, as they all teach, to a knowledge of ourselves as endowed with the powers of thought, feeling, and voluntary determination, of the external material universe, of Matter, as a substance possessed of the qualities of extension, form, &c., and of God, as the creator and governor of all things, and as such, as possessed of all the attributes involved in the ideas of infinity and perfection. In the latter procedure, we discover that all these great pre-affirmed realities are nothing but splendid nonentities. Thus science and nature are and must be eternally at war with each other, the exclusive function of the former being to destroy and dissolve what the latter constructs and builds up. Now the exclusive function of real science is, not to annul, but to enlarge and perfect the natural procedures of the Intelligence. Idealism, in all its forms, is based exclusively upon the assumption, that the exclusive direction of the natural and unavoidable procedure of the Intelligence is towards the unreal and nothing else, an assumption just as absurd and self-contradictory as the idea of an event without a cause.

5. Hence, I remark, that there is a precisely similar antagonism between the *theoretical* and *practical* sides of all these systems. Practically, as they all teach, we are to treat ourselves, the world and God, as given in the natural procedures of the Intelligence, as most real and substantial verities. Theoretically we are to hold and treat these same verities, as nothing but absolute nonentities. Such are the fundamental teachings of all these systems. Now what man in his senses can believe that there is any such antagonism between true theory and right practice? What is the province of true theory or science, but to give to practice its most perfect direction? What must we think of systems of philosophy whose fundamental assumptions are, that all right forms of human activity

are in the exclusive direction of the unreal? Such is Idealism, whatever form it assumes.

6. Idealism, in all its forms alike, totally confounds all *distinction between truth and error*, and annihilates all *tests* by which the one can be distinguished from the other. If mental operations are the only objects of real knowledge, and all else is to be held as unreal, as all these systems maintain, then as one form of cognition is, in itself, just as real as another, it is consequently just as true. The wildest vagaries of the maniac are in themselves just as real, and consequently just as true, as the most sober deductions of the philosopher. One system of philosophy is as real a development of the Ego, of the Absolute, or of the law of thought, as another, and consequently has precisely the same claims to be received as true. These are the legitimate consequences of Idealism, and can, by no possibility, be separated from it. There is no such thing as truth as distinguished from error, if any of the forms of Idealism are true.

7. I remark finally, that Idealism in all its forms, is utterly subversive of all the principles of morality and religion. It takes from God every attribute to which the religious sentiment in humanity is correlated, and from humanity every element on which moral obligation can be based, and every principle by which the right can be distinguished from the wrong. By it the universe is unpeopled of all proper subjects of moral government, and left itself as a nonentity without a divine sovereign to rule over it. This is Idealism in its "naked nature," and "living grace." Much more might be said of it, but nothing good. There is not a principle in it which tends in that direction. It takes from humanity its universe, its God, its redeemer, its guide of life, and the vista of immortality, and leaves it to satisfy the longings of its immortal nature with the empty shadows of absolute nonentities.

I would not here be understood as affirming that none of the teachings of the advocates of Idealism are true and worthy of regard. What I do say is this, that what they have said that is true, has not grown out of their theories, and is not to be found among the basis principles of the same. Not a solitary proposition that is true can be found among those principles, or can be logically deduced from them. We say this in sorrow, not in anger. We commenced our inquiries into the German philosophy, confidently expecting to be thereby enriched with priceless treasures of wisdom and knowledge. We take leave of it, with the fullest persuasion, after fathoming its depths, that it is nothing but an abyss of darkness and error.

MODERN TRANSCENDENTALISM.

The procedure of the systems of philosophy, which we have been considering, has been very much like the "endless wars of Chaos and old Night," described by Milton. Each new sect in philosophy demolished the system of their predecessors, and then erected another, to be demolished by a third more foundationless, if possible, than any that preceded; and the last that appears is the most baseless of all, and leaves the great questions in philosophy more in the dark than they were before. As a consequence, the public mind has been fast becoming somewhat skeptical in respect to the *possibility* of philosophy itself. This circumstance apparently has given rise in Europe and this country to a new sect, it would hardly be proper to say of philosophers, since they systematically reject all philosophy. They *assume* as true, the general principles of Cousin, Hegel, Schelling, &c., and then reject and denounce all philosophy, everything like consecutive reasoning, or logical deduction. Action purely instinctive, they hold, is by far the most perfect form of activity. The same holds of the Intelligence. Philosophical reflection, logical deduction, and systematic treatises, especially in respect to Mental Philosophy, Theology, or Morals, only trammel thought and darken the spiritual vision. Thought, purely spontaneous and instinctive, is the most true, and the most perfect.

When Reason is permitted to develop itself freely, untrammeled by logic; when men, in short, think, speak, and act from pure instinct, without system, there is the most perfect system. The most perfect demonstration is the simple enunciation of spontaneous mental conceptions, without argument. Hence, they never reason, never explain, never discuss, but, as oracles of Reason, simply announce her dicta. If you call in question any of their enunciations, they have one reply, and that is always at hand, to wit, You are not spiritual. The truly spiritual is not developed in you. How can a man that never saw, discriminate between colors? You ask of them a particular explanation of their principles. This only occasions the retort, You are not spiritual — the truly spiritual is not yet inborn in you. They talk much of religion, and complain that all the world lacks it; and yet religion is, with them, "without form and void;" for almost all of them deny of God everything but an ideal existence. They speak of Christ as the incarnation of divinity; and then, in the language of one of their great leaders, represent his character as essentially defective, on account of the lack of "fun" in its composition. They talk much of sin, regeneration, atonement, redemption, repentance, faith, holiness, purity, and love, &c. All the vocabulary of evangelical religion is introduced as familiar terms into their discourses: yet all such terms find themselves there in such strange company, and in the midst of such new and bewildering associations, that they cannot even know themselves. The following passage will give, perhaps, as correct a view of the meaning which they attach to terms like the above, as any that is often met with in their writings. It is from one of their leading writers, in an article found in the Dial, the organ of the sect:

"Holding, as they do, but one essence of all things, which essence is God, Pantheism must deny the existence of essential evil. All evil is negative — it is imperfection, non-growth. It is not essential, but modal. Of course, there can be no such thing as hereditary sin — a tendency positively sinful in the soul. Sin is not a willful transgression of a righteous law, but the difficulty and obstruction which the Infinite meets with in entering into the finite. *Regeneration* is nothing but an ingross of God into the soul, before which sin disappears, as darkness before the rising sun. Pantheists hold also to the *Atonement*, or at-one-ment, between the soul and God. This is strictly a unity, or *oneness of essence*, to be brought about by the incarnation of the Spirit of God in us, which is going on in us as we grow in holiness. As we grow wise, just, and pure — in a word, holy — we grow to be one with him in mode, as we always were in essence. This atonement is effected by *Christ*, only in as far as he taught the manner in which it was to be accomplished more fully than any other, and gave us a better illustration of the method and result in his own person, than any one else that has ever lived."

Now, if any one should ask this writer to explain the meaning he really attaches to such terms and phrases as "non-growth," the "Infinite entering into the finite," and "the incarnation of the Spirit of God in us," and especially if we should ask of him a reason of his belief in Pantheism, his only reply, no doubt, would be: You are not spiritual; the spiritual is yet to be inborn in you. And then he would go on with most pitiful lamentations over the want of religion, of spirituality, in all the world; of the melancholy decay of the god-like spirit of faith, and spiritual vision, and inspiration, that existed in Moses, and Christ, and Paul, and Mahomet, and among the heroic spirits of the Reformation. Now, the philosophic observer is not at a loss to perceive, that all this complaining of the non-growth, and absence of spiritual vision in all the world but themselves, is nothing but a feint, to keep from view a mass of foundationless assumptions, the validity of which they themselves dare not seriously examine, nor have distinctly exposed to public view, lest their baselessness should become so manifest, that even their abettors would be ashamed to avow them any more. Mysticism is the consummation, the last development, of false philosophy. Men who are on the track of error, will reason and philosophize, as long as they can hope to convince the world of their principles by reasoning based upon the result of philosophic investigation. When this hope fails, the last resort is assumptions, attended with the usurpation of direct spiritual vision, and superior divine insight and illumination.

ECLECTICISM OF COUSIN.

System stated.

From the chair of Philosophy in Paris, Cousin has pronounced Eclecticism as constituting the distinguishing characteristic, the perfection of the philosophic movement of the ninteenth century. Before admitting this enunciation as true, it becomes us to inquire diligently into the meaning of such an imposing term. The attentive reader of the works of this great philosopher will not be at a loss to determine the meaning which he attaches to the term, nor the doctrine represented by it. This philosopher professes to have obtained a point of observation, from which he has brought all previous systems of philosophy into complete harmony with each other. All possible questions in philosophy have been solved in these different systems. Each system has moved in the direction of some one great question, and has attained its object in the solution of that question. It now remains to take from all these systems the principle on which each rests, and which each has developed, and resolve the whole into one harmonious unity. The following passages will show that I have not misconceived nor misstated the principles of this philosopher:

"You may perceive the tendency of my discourse. After the subjective idealism of the school of Kant, and the empiricism and sensualism of that of Locke, have been developed, and their last possible results exhausted, no new combination is, in my opinion, possible; but the union of these two systems, by centering them both in a vast and powerful eclecticism." Again: "Our philosophy, gentlemen, is not a melancholy and fanatical philosophy, which, being prepossessed with a few exclusive ideas, undertakes to reform all others on the same model; it is a philosophy essentially optimistical, whose only end is to comprehend all, and which therefore accepts and reconciles all. It seeks to obtain power only by extension; its unity consists only in the harmony of all contrarieties."

Remarks upon this System.

For myself, I would say, that I wholly dissent from the system of Eclecticism as above announced. I do it for the following reasons:

1. It is, as a system, totally unlike the procedure of the Intelligence in reference to every other science. No science whatever that has stood the test of time has been evolved in conformity to this principle. What if some astronomer, for example, should arise, and profess to have found some point of observation from which he could show that all systems of astronomy were essentially correct, and should proclaim that the true system is found in all, as the general in the particu-

lar, and should be so evolved as to include all other systems? He might say, in the language of this great philosopher, "Our astronomy, gentlemen, is not a melancholy and fanatical astronomy, which, being prepossessed with a few exclusive ideas, undertakes to reform all others upon the same model; it is as an astronomy essentially optimistical, whose only end is to comprehend all, and which, therefore, accepts and reconciles all. It seeks to obtain power only by extension; its unity consists only in the harmony of all contrarieties." All this is well said, and looks well on paper. But who would expect to find, in a system constructed in conformity to such an hypothesis, the true "Mécanique Céleste?" In every other science, each school has found its point of observation, from which it has attempted a solution of the great questions pertaining to that particular science, and which was its object to solve. One school has succeeded another, till some one has evolved a system which has stood the test of time. So, I venture to predict, it will be in respect to the Philosophy of Mind. If the true system has not yet been developed, the time is coming when it will be. And that philosopher will have the happiness of attaining this great end, who shall find, not some point of observation from which he can reconcile all the jarring antagonistic systems which have claimed the credence of man, but some great central position, in the depths of our inner being, from which he can solve the diversified questions of philosophy pertaining to the facts of universal Consciousness.

2. The assumption on which Eclecticism, as above defined, rests, is totally false in point of fact: the position that the essential element in each system is true. Take, as an illustration, the system of Pantheism. Now that system is either totally right or wholly wrong. It either correctly explains every fact pertaining to the universe, or it totally falsifies every fact professedly explained by it. It either rightly explains, or

totally misrepresents all things. Further, if this system is right, every other system is totally wrong, and misrepresents everything which it professedly explains. There is no blending of this system with any other which does not assert its fundamental principle; and then it is not another, but one and the same system.

The same holds true of the systems of Hegel, Kant, and Locke. Either thought is the only reality, and then Hegel is totally right, and all other systems wholly false, or thought is not the only reality, and then in nothing is Hegel right. This system either correctly explains or totally misrepresents every fact in the universe.

Either ideas of Reason are valid for things in themselves, and then Kant is wholly wrong, or they are not thus valid, and Kant is wholly right. His fundamental principle either rightly explains or totally misrepresents every idea of Reason. There is no position midway between these extremes.

Either all ideas do come from experience, and then Locke is wholly right, and all systems denying this are so far wholly wrong, or all ideas do not come from experience, and then Locke is wholly wrong. It does not help the matter to say, that *some* ideas come from experience, and therefore Locke is partly right. Locke and all the world knew, long before his celebrated Essay was thought of, that *some* ideas came from experience. It was only as an *universal* proposition that Locke affirmed his position. If that proposition is not strictly universal, Locke is wholly wrong, and so he himself regarded the subject.

Nor, in my judgment, was it becoming in a great philosopher to attempt to show, as Cousin has done, in conformity to the spirit of Eclecticism, that the great principle of Locke's philosophy is right, by attributing to him a principle that he never held, or conceived of; to wit, that ideas of experience are the *chronological antecedents* of all other ideas. The individual who has ever read Cousin's Psychology, translated by Prof. Henry, a work presenting one of the finest specimens of philosophic reasoning to be met with in any language, will recollect the frequency with which the remark is made in that work, that there is an important sense in which the propositions of Locke, that all ideas come from experience, is true. Locke's whole system rests upon this one proposition. Cousin, after proving the proposition false, must show that after all it is true, or the fundamental position of his own Eclecticism would fail entirely. How does he accomplish his object? By the affirmation that there is a sense in which the proposition, that all ideas are derived from experience, is true; that is, such ideas are the *chronological antecedents* of all other ideas. But this, I repeat, is a sense in which Locke never presented the proposition under consideration, and never thought of doing it. Did it become a great philosopher to attempt to save his own hypothesis, by attributing to another a principle which all the world know he never held, or, at least, never avowed?

In the remarks made above, I would by no means be understood as advancing the sentiment, that if Pantheism or any other system is wrong, that therefore nothing which the abettors of such systems may say, is true. Nothing is further from my intention than this. This whole Treatise presents proof sufficient of the fact, that no such thing is intended. What I do mean is this, That whatever truths exist in connection with false systems, and many such often are therein found, exist in them not in consequence of the systems, but in spite of them, and are totally misrepresented by them. The true Eclecticism, as I understand it, is this, To search for truth in connection with every system, without assuming beforehand, that it does or does not exist there. "Prove all things; hold fast that which is good." This is an Eclecticism, which is infinitely preferable to that which "consists only in the harmony of all contrarieties."

3. In his position as an Eclectic, Cousin has fallen into the very error which he has charged upon Locke, as so greatly vitiating his *method* as a philosopher. The error is this: Beginning with an hypothesis, before carefully analyzing and classifying the facts of Psychology as the basis of an hypothesis. Locke, as Cousin has shown, by assuming at the outset a particular hypothesis respecting the origin of Ideas, was led to misrepresent (an error perfectly natural under the circumstances) the most important facts of human Consciousness. So Cousin, by assuming, that the fundamental elements of all systems are right, must, to be consistent, be a sensualist with Locke, a spiritualist with Fichte, a pantheist with Schelling, and a nihilist with Hegel. These considerations are abundantly sufficient to show the claims of Eclecticism to the regard of philosophers.

COMMON SENSE.

There are few words in more common use than the above. Common Sense is everywhere appealed to as a standard and test of truth and error. Yet it would be somewhat difficult, without the most careful reflection, to define correctly the words under consideration. Dr. Reid regards Common Sense as a distinct faculty of the mind. Philosophers generally have rejected this assumption. This they have done, however, without themselves attempting to tell us what this something is, the reality of which they all acknowledge. My object will be, to state distinctly the real meaning of the words under consideration.

Common Sense defined.

Every one is aware, that, in the presence of certain facts,

the universal Intelligence invariably makes particular affirmations. With such affirmations, numberless assumptions, together with their consequents, may be mingled. Hence, in reference to almost all subjects of thought, diversity of opinion appears. Yet, in the midst of all this diversity, there are judgments common to all minds who have apprehended the same facts.

Now these affirmations, common to all minds in the presence of the same facts, affirmations in their concrete and particular form, is what is meant by the words Common Sense. The words designate the *real* affirmations of the universal Intelligence, in view of given facts, as distinguished from assumptions, and the logical consequents of the same, pertaining to the same facts. Common Sense, then, is not, as Dr. Reid supposes, a special faculty of the Intelligence. It designates, I repeat, the real affirmations of the general Intelligence, in distinction from assumptions and their logical consequents.

Common Sense a Standard of Truth.

Common Sense, then, may be properly appealed to, as a decisive standard of truth. Its responses must be true, else the universal Intelligence is a lie. No conclusions in philosophy and religion, no results of processes of investigation and reasoning which are in contradiction to its decisions, will stand the test of time. I will here confess, that the principle under consideration has been a leading idea which has guided my Judgment in respect to the great facts and principles announced in the present Treatise. That philosophy, which, disregarding all assumptions and their consequents, shall announce the real convictions of the universal Intelligence, is the true philosophy. Philosophy and Common Sense the Author of our existence has joined together. Philosophy runs mad with the wildest conceivable delusions, when divorced from Common Sense as a light, and authoritative guide.

Philosophic Principles — why rejected by the mass of Mankind.

Philosophy (falsely so called) has at various periods denied the reality of Mind, of Matter, or the external world, and of God, the author of the two former. Yet the mass of mankind have continued to believe their own substantial existence, together with that of the external world, and of God. The reason is, that philosophers have rested their investigations upon baseless assumptions; while the mass of mankind, more fully influenced by the philosophic spirit in respect to such subjects, have followed the dictates of Common Sense. Universal materialism, on the one hand, or spiritualism on the other, together with kindred systems, such as Pantheism and Idealism, can never become the sentiments of the race. The Common Sense of mankind is at war with all such principles. Suppose, for example, an individual announces as a truth of philosophy, what Pantheism affirms, that all individualities in the universe are not real, but only apparent, that they are all the phenomena of one common substance. Such a dogma can never become the belief of the race; for the obvious reason that it contradicts the fundamental affirmations of the universal Intelligence pertaining to phenomena and substance. The reason is that *separateness*, and not absolute unity, is the fundamental phenomenon which all individualities present in respect to each other. When things *appear* as separate, we must admit that they are separate; in other words, that Pantheism is false, or deny the fundamental convictions or Common Sense of the race, pertaining to their ideas of substance.

Dictates of Common Sense — how known and distinguished.

One important question arises here, to wit: How can we determine, whether a given fact or principle is or is not a dictate of Common Sense? This question we can answer, not by an appeal to tradition, to books, or to the responses which the race at large might formally give, if required to respond to the inquiry. For with all such responses, numberless assumptions would no doubt be mingled. On the other hand, every one who would understand the dictates of Common Sense must enter into the depth of his own Mind, and there notice the real affirmations of his own Intelligence, in view of given facts. Such affirmations he may trust in and announce, as the real dictates of the Common Sense of the race. He that will most correctly interpret the real dictates of his own Intelligence, is the most perfect oracle of the universal Intelligence. In retiring, then, from the outward world into the depths of our own Minds, and there receiving the real dictates of our own Intelligence, we find the true facts and principles of Common Sense.

Characteristics of Men distinguished for Common Sense.

We often hear individuals spoken of as wanting in, or possessed of a great degree, of Common Sense. The characteristic which distinguishes the latter from the former class, is a well-balanced Judgment, particularly in respect to the common transactions of life — a Judgment by which they detect and announce at once the real affirmations of the Intelligence in the presence of given facts. The mass of men — a fact to which philosophers as a body are by no means exceptions — are so blinded by assumptions, and theories founded thereon, that, in respect to the most important subjects, they do not recognize the real affirmations of their own Intelligence. In the presence of given facts, they see in them what all the world sees. Yet under the influence of false assumptions and theories, they disregard what their own Intelligence really affirms. Men, on the other hand, distinguished for Common Sense, in the presence of the same facts and convictions, announce and rely upon, not in their abstract and universal, but in their concrete and particular form, their own judgments, just as they lie in their own Intelligence—judgments which all the world really pass in the presence of the same facts; but which, for reasons above stated, philosophic minds especially, in many instances, totally disregard. Of the latter class we say, they are destitute of, or rather do not *use*, their Common Sense.

After writing the above, I was much interested to find that the sentiments expressed so fully, correspond with those of Jouffroy, in respect to the same subject. I will present, as a further elucidation of this important subject, two extracts from the writings of the philosopher above named:

"The history of philosophy presents a singular spectacle; a certain number of problems are reproduced at every epoch; each of these problems suggests a certain number of solutions, always the same; philosophers are divided; discussion is set on foot; every opinion is attacked and defended, with equal appearance of truth. Humanity listens in silence, adopts the opinion of no one, but preserves its own, which is what is called *Common Sense*.

"Thus, to refer to examples, all philosophical epochs have produced upon the stage the opposite theories of Materialism and Spiritualism in metaphysics, and those of Stoicism and Epicureanism in morals. None of these doctrines has permanently prevailed: none has perished; all have found sincere and illustrious partisans; all have exerted nearly the same influence; but, in the end, the human race, which has witnessed their debates, has become neither Materialist nor Spiritualist, neither Stoic nor Epicurean; it has remained what it was prior to philosophy, believing at once both in matter and spirit, respecting duty and pursuing happiness at the same time."

Again: "Everybody understands by Common Sense a certain number of principles or notions evident of themselves, from which all men derive the grounds of their judgment and the rules of their conduct; and nothing is more correct than this idea. But it is not sufficiently known that these principles are merely positive solutions of all the great problems which philosophy agitates. How could we regulate our conduct, what judgments could we form, if we could not distinguish between good and evil, truth and falsehood, beauty and deformity, one being and another, and reality and nullity; if we did not know what we should hold to, concerning that which we see with our eyes, perceive with our Consciousness, and apprehend with our Reason; if we had no idea of the purpose and the consequences of this life, of the Author of all things and of his nature? What would be the light of Intelligence, how would society proceed, if there were even the shadow of doubt on the notions which we possess in regard to most of these points? Now what are these notions, so firmly and so necessarily established in the Intelligence of all men, but a series of responses to these questions: What is the true? What is the good? What is the beautiful? What is the nature of things? What is being? What is the origin and certainty of human knowledge? What is the destiny of man in this world? Is his entire destiny accomplished in this life? Is this world the production of chance, or of an intelligent cause? And, we ask, are not these the questions with which philosophy is occupied? Do they not contain, in their germs at least, all the questions of logic, metaphysics, morals, politics, and religion?

"Common Sense, therefore, is nothing but a collection of

solutions to those questions which philosophers agitate. It is another philosophy prior to philosophy properly so called, since it is found spontaneously at the bottom of every Consciousness, independently of all scientific research. There are accordingly two votes on the questions which interest humanity, namely, that of the mass and that of the philosophers, the spontaneous vote and the scientific vote, Common Sense and systems."

CHAPTER XIX.

THE INTELLIGENCE OF MAN, AS DISTINGUISHED FROM THAT OF THE BRUTE.

It has been very common with philosophers to represent all created existences, from the highest Intelligences in heaven to the crude forms of matter, as successive links in one great chain, each link in the chain, commencing with the lowest, differing mainly in *degree* from that which immediately succeeds it. The highest forms of brute, and the lowest of rational Intelligence, for example, differ, it is asserted, not in *kind*, but only in *degree*. Of late, the reality of orders of existences, as successive links of a great chain, has come to be seriously doubted. The intelligence of man and of the brute, it is said, differs not in degree, but in kind. If we conceive of the highest forms of brute intelligence increased to any degree whatever, as far as degree is concerned, still it makes no approach at all to real rationality. The different orders of brute instincts do constitute, it is thought, different links of one chain. Those of rational Intelligences constitute another and totally different chain, a chain none of the links of which are connected, in any form, with any of those of the other. This last is the opinion entertained by the author of this Treatise. I will now proceed to state the grounds of this opinion. I will introduce what I have to say upon this subject by two extracts, somewhat lengthy, from Coleridge. In the first, we have a classification of the different forms of brute Instinct; in the second, we are presented with two instances of Instinctive Intelligence, in their highest manifestations.

BRUTE INSTINCTS CLASSIFIED.

"It is evident that the definition of a genus or class is an *adequate* definition only of the lowest *species* of that genus: for each higher species is distinguished from the lower by some additional character, while the general definition includes only the characters common to *all* the species. Consequently it *describes* the lowest only. Now I distinguish a genus or *kind* of powers under the name of adaptive power, and give, as its generic definition, the power of selecting and adapting means to proximate ends; and as an instance of the lowest *species* of this genus, I take the stomach of a caterpillar. I ask myself, under what words I can generalize the action of this organ; and I see that it selects and adapts the appropriate means (*i. e.*, the assimilable part of the vegetable *congesta*) to the proximate end, *i. e.*, the growth or reproduction of the insect's body. This we call VITAL POWER, or *vita propria* of the stomach; and this being the *lowest* species, its definition is the same with the definition of the *kind*.

"Well, from the power of the stomach I pass to the power exerted by the whole animal. I trace it wandering from spot to spot, and plant to plant, till it finds the appropriate vegetable; and again on this chosen vegetable, I mark it seeking out and fixing on the part of the plant, bark, leaf, or petal, suited to its nourishment; or (should the animal have assumed the butterfly form), to the deposition of its eggs, and the sustentation of the future larva. Here I see a power of selecting and adapting means to proximate ends *according to circumstances.* And this higher species of adaptive power we call INSTINCT.

"Lastly, I reflect on the facts narrated and described in the succeeding extracts from Huber, and see a power of selecting the proper means to the proximate ends, according to *vary-*

ing circumstances. And what shall we call this yet higher species? We name the former, Instinct; we must call this INSTINCTIVE INTELLIGENCE.

"Here then we have three powers of the same kind, Life, Instinct, and Instinctive Intelligence; the essential characters that define the genus existing in all three. But in addition to these, I find one other character common to the highest and lowest, viz.: that the purposes are all manifestly pre-determined by the peculiar organization of the animals; and though it may not be possible to discover any such immediate dependency in all the actions, yet the actions being determined by the purposes, the *result* is equivalent: and both the actions and purposes are all in a necessitated reference to the preservation and continuance of that particular animal or of the progeny. There is a selection, but not *choice* — volition rather than Will. The possible *knowledge* of a thing, or the desire to have the *thing* representable by a distinct correspondent *thought*, does not, in the animal, suffice to render the thing an *object*, or the ground of a purpose. I select and adapt the proper means to the separation of a stone from a rock, which I neither can, nor desire to make use of for food, shelter or ornament: because, perhaps, I wish to measure the angles of its primary crystals, or, perhaps, for no better reason than the apparent *difficulty* of loosening the stone — *stat pro ratione voluntas* — and thus make a motive out of the absence of all motive, and a reason out of the arbitrary will to act without any reason."

MANIFESTATIONS OF INSTINCTIVE INTELLIGENCE.

"Huber put a dozen humble-bees under a bell-glass along with a comb of about ten cocoons, so unequal in height as not to be capable of standing steadily. To remedy this, two or three of the humble-bees got upon the comb, stretched themselves over its edge, and with their heads downwards fixed their fore feet on the table on which the comb stood, and so with their hind feet kept the comb from falling. When these were weary others took their places. In this constrained and painful posture, fresh bees relieving their comrades at intervals, and each working in its turn, did these affectionate little insects support the comb for nearly three days, at the end of which they had prepared sufficient wax to build pillars with. But these pillars having accidentally got displaced, the bees had recourse again to the same manœuver (or rather *ped*œuver), till Huber pitying their hard case, &c.

"'I shall at present describe the operations of a single ant that I observed sufficiently long to satisfy my curiosity:

"'One rainy day, I observed a laborer digging the ground near the aperture which gave entrance to the ant-hill. It placed in a heap the several fragments it had scraped up, and formed them into small pellets, which it deposited here and there upon the nest. It returned constantly to the same place, and appeared to have a marked design, for it labored with ardor and perseverance. I remarked a slight furrow, excavated in the ground in a straight line, representing the plan of a path or gallery. The laborer, the whole of whose movements fell under my immediate observation, gave it greater depth and breadth, and cleared out its borders: and I saw at length, in which I could not be deceived, that it had the intention of establishing an avenue which was to lead from one of the stories to the under-ground chambers. This path, which was about two or three inches in length, and formed by a single ant, was opened above and bordered on each side by a buttress of earth, its concavity *en forme de gouttière* was of the most perfect regularity, for the architect had not left an atom too much. The work of this ant was so well followed and understood, that I could almost to a certainty guess its next proceeding, and the very fragment it was about to remove. At the side of the opening where this path terminated, was a second opening, to which it was necessary to arrive at by some road. The same ant engaged in and executed alone this undertaking. It furrowed out and opened another path, parallel to the first, leaving between each a little wall of three or four lines in height. Those ants who lay the foundation of a wall, a chamber or gallery, from working separately, occasion now and then a want of coincidence in the parts of the same or different objects. Such examples are of no unfrequent occurrence, but they by no means embarrass them. What follows, proves that the workman, on discovering his error, knew how to rectify it. A wall had been erected with the view of sustaining a vaulted ceiling, still incomplete, that had been projected from the wall of the opposite chamber. The workman who began constructing it, had given it too little elevation to meet the opposite partition upon which it was to rest. Had it been continued on the original plan, it must infallibly have met the wall at about one-half of its height, and this it was necessary to avoid. This state of things very forcibly claimed my attention, when one of the ants arriving at the place, and visiting the works, appeared to be struck by the difficulty which presented itself; but this it as soon obviated, by taking down the ceiling and raising the wall upon which it reposed. It then, in my presence, constructed a new ceiling with the fragments of the former one.'" — *Huber's Nat. Hist. of Ants.*

The facts above cited, every one will acknowledge, may be assumed as representing Instinctive Intelligence, in its highest form. The question to be settled is, In what respects is this like rationality, as it exists in man? In what respects do these forms of Intelligence agree, and disagree?

PRINCIPLE ON WHICH THE ARGUMENT IS BASED.

In conducting our inquiries on this subject, the first thing to be settled is, the *principle* on which our conclusions shall be based. On all hands it is agreed, that there are points of resemblance between the manifestations of Intelligence in the brute and among mankind. At the same time, there are points of dissimilarity equally manifest and important. Now let A represent the mental phenomena which appear in man, and never appear in the brute. If we can find the power or powers in man from which the phenomena represented by A result, we have then determined fully the faculties which man possesses and the brute wants. The faculties thus asserted of man, are to be wholly denied of the brute, and all the manifestations of brute intelligence are to be accounted for by a reference to what remains, after the former have been subtracted. All must admit, that this is the true and the only true principle to be applied in the case. It now remains to apply the principle to the solution of the question before us.

POINTS OF RESEMBLANCE BETWEEN THE MAN AND THE BRUTE.

That brutes, such as are supposed in the present argument, possess the faculty of external perception, such as sight, hearing, taste, smell, and touch, that such perceptions are followed by feelings of a given character, and that these feelings are followed by external actions which are correlated to the perceptions referred to, and that all these manifestations are common to man and the brute both, will be denied by none who have, however carelessly, observed the facts which have presented themselves to their notice. Such are the phenomena common to man and the brute.

HYPOTHESES ON WHICH THESE COMMON FACTS MAY BE EXPLAINED.

There are two distinct and opposite hypotheses on which these common facts may be explained. When man has an external perception, Reason at once suggests certain fundamental ideas in the light of which he explains to himself the phenomena perceived, and passes certain judgments upon them. Action with him has special reference, not to the phenomena, but to the judgments thus passed. All these things we know from Consciousness, to be true, in reference to man.

As far as the facts under consideration are concerned, it may be that the same is true of the brute. All the phenomena of brute action, however, are equally explicable, on an entirely different hypothesis. When a brute has a perception of some object, without the presence of any fundamental ideas in the light of which he can explain to himself what he sees, and consequently form notions and judgments of the object perceived, and then act in view of judgments thus formed, it may be, that such perceptions are followed by certain feelings, and that from these, as necessary consequents, external acts, such as the brute puts forth, arise. All that would be intellectual with the brute, on this hypothesis, would be the simple power to *perceive* the object, without the capacity to recognize himself as the *subject*, or the thing perceived as the *object* of the perception, so as to form any conceptions or judgments pertaining either to the subject or object. The feelings which attend such perceptions, together with such as arise from the internal organism of the brute, such as hunger and thirst, are followed necessarily by external actions in harmony with the sphere for which the creature was designed. The action of the brute would be in fixed harmony with law — law, however, which has no subjective existence in the Intelligence of the creature, but which exists as an idea in that of the Creator. Action, in such a case, would be purely mechanical, the propelling force being the feelings generated as above supposed, while the law of action would be an idea which the subject of the action never apprehended, but in conformity to which the organism of the brute is formed.

A case stated in the public prints, a case, whether true or false, at least conceivable, and therefore proper to be used in illustration, will fully illustrate the hypothesis under consideration. A lady, some time before the birth of a child, was struck at by a rattlesnake, and barely escaped with her life. As a consequence of the fright of the mother, the child, when born, had upon parts of its body the marks of the serpent. His eyes had the fiery and vengeful appearance peculiar to the reptile. One arm, also, lay coiled upon its side in a manner perfectly serpentine. As the child grew up, and came into the presence of certain objects, despite of all efforts of his Will to the contrary, his eyes would roll in their sockets, with the fiery vengeful appearance peculiar to the serpent when attacked by an enemy. At the same time, the arm referred to would strike at the object perceived, in exact conformity to the motions of the reptile in similar circumstances. In connection with the physical organization of this individual, two classes of actions, each equally conformed to ideas, appeared; the one class, however, the consequents of *volition* in harmony with conceptions and judgments, and the other caused by *feelings* generated by external perceptions. Now, in conformity with the fact last named, we can explain all the phenomena of brute action, however intelligent in appearance. All such phenomena may be the exclusive result of the peculiar feelings and organism of the animal, in the total absence of the Intelligence peculiar to man. The question is, Are there any facts peculiar to brute and human action, verifying this hypothesis? This question I will now endeavor to answer, in the light of the principle I have laid down as the basis of our conclusions on this subject.

POINTS OF DISSIMILARITY BETWEEN MAN AND THE BRUTE.

In order to test the validity of the hypothesis under consideration, we will now attend to the fundamental phenomena which distinguish man from the brute. Among these, I will specify only the following:

1. Man, from the laws of his Intelligence, is a *scientific being*. The main direction of the human Intelligence is not merely towards phenomena, but towards the *scientific explanation* of phenomena. This is one of the great wants of human nature, the scientific explanation of phenomena. All mankind agree in the assumption, that in the brute there is a total absence of this principle. Brute intelligence pertains exclusively to mere phenomena. The creature never seeks an explanation of what he sees. He acts from feelings generated by perceptions, without ever seeking an explanation of what he sees or feels.

2. Man, as a race, is progressive. The brute is perfectly stationary. For six thousand years, each race has been spectators of precisely the same phenomena. The commencement of observation with man, was the commencement of intellectual progress, which has been onward from generation to generation. With all his observations, the brute has never advanced a single step. He is now just where he was six thousand years ago. The beaver builds his dam, lives and dies, just as did the first that ever appeared on earth. The same is true of the action of every brute race.

3. Man is the subject of moral obligation, and consequently of moral government. In other words, man is a moral agent. All this is universally denied of the brute. He is

never, except when man acts towards him, as all acknowledge, irrationally, regarded or treated as the subject of moral obligation or of moral government. I might cite other points of dissimilarity, equally manifest, and equally fundamental. But these are sufficient for the present argument.

FACTS APPLIED.

It now remains to apply the facts above stated to the solution of the question under consideration. When we have determined the faculties necessarily supposed, as the condition of science, progress, and moral agency in man, we have determined the faculties which we are totally to deny of the brute. For it should be borne in mind, that the facts above named do not exist in one degree in man, and in a smaller degree in the brute. The difference is not that of degree, but of total dissimilarity. What various individuals of our race, in the respects under consideration, possess in different degrees, the brute *totally* wants. The faculties, therefore, which are to be affirmed of man as the condition and ground of these facts, are to be totally denied of the brute.

1. I ask, then, in the first place, What faculties constitute man a *scientific being*, those in the absence of which he cannot possess science, and in the possession of which he is, of course, scientific? Sense, the faculty of external perception, man, as we have seen, has in common with the brute. But this a creature may possess in any degree, and make no approach whatever to science. Other faculties in addition are supposed as the condition and ground of such developments. What, then, are these faculties? I answer, they are of the primary faculties, Reason, and Self-Consciousness; and of the secondary, Understanding and Judgment. In the absence of Reason, fundamental ideas, in the light of which phenomena may be explained, are totally wanting, and consequently Science be-

comes impossible. Without Reason also, Self-Consciousness would, properly speaking, be impossible, or if possible, absolutely useless, and therefore not supposable, as originating from perfect Intelligence. Without Reason, too, conceptions, notions, and judgments would, as we have seen in former Chapters, be absolutely impossible. Notions cannot be formed without ideas of Reason, such as substance, cause, time, space, &c. Judgments, also, and consequently classification and generalization, cannot take place without the ideas of resemblance and difference. In other words, without Reason, the exercise of the Understanding and Judgment is impossible. The existence of these faculties is therefore not to be supposed. If, then, as we are logically bound to do, we take from the brute Reason, Self-Consciousness, Understanding, and Judgment, what remains to him? Just what we have attributed to him, to wit, the power of external perception, together with corresponding feelings and susceptibilities, and an external organism, the action of which is in necessary conformity to the feelings thus generated.

It should be borne in mind, that science in man does not depend upon the *degree* in which the faculties above named are possessed by him. The degree of the scientific movement will be, other things being equal, as the degree in which these powers are possessed. When they exist in any degree, there will be real science. The total absence of science in the brute, indicates most clearly a total absence of the scientific faculties, faculties which are so connected with each other, that if one be conceived of as wanting, the others also must be.

The question, I repeat, is not whether the action of the brute is not in harmony with fundamental ideas, but whether these ideas have a *subjective* existence in his Intelligence. The bee, for example, builds its cell in conformity to pure ideas of Reason. But does it not thus build, not because it knows such ideas, but because of the peculiarity of its perceptions, sensations, and physical structure, all of which render its thus building mechanically necessary? The facts before us show clearly that it does.

2. In the next place, we will raise the inquiry, What faculties in man render him a *progressive being?* They are evidently the same as those which render him scientific, with the addition of the Imagination. It is because that where phenomena appear, mankind are able, in the light of ideas of Reason, to explain to themselves these facts, and thus find the fundamental principle involved in them, that, as a race, we are progressive. For this reason, also, mankind gain important knowledge from accidental experience, a fact which never appears in the brute. A man and a brute are swimming together across a river. They become exhausted, and when about to sink, meet with something like a plank floating by. They both get on to it and are saved. The brute passes on without being a whit wiser from his experience. The occurrence constitutes an era in the history of the human race. Man reflects upon the occurrence, and hence arises all the wonders of ship-building and navigation. All these had their origin in accidental occurrences like that above supposed. In the knowledge obtained from occurrences similar in their nature, the art of printing, and all the results of steam-power, &c., originated. Man and the brute also hear melodious sounds. Each alike copies what he hears. On the part of man, these sounds are recombined into strains still more melodious. Hence the science of music. The brute copies what he hears, but never, in a solitary instance, recombines, in the least, what he hears. The mocking-bird presents a striking illustration of the truth of this statement. It will copy almost every melodious sound it ever hears. Yet it was never known to produce a single new combination of sounds. Such facts most indubitably

indicate in the brute the total absence of all the faculties which lay the foundation for progress in man, the faculties of Reason, Self-Consciousness, Understanding, Judgment, and the Imagination. With these in any degree, creatures are in a corresponding degree progressive. Without them, whatever else they may possess, they are perfectly stationary. Nothing is more unphilosophical and illogical, than the conclusion often drawn, in the presence of progress on the one hand, and its total absence on the other, that brute Instinct and human Intelligence differ only in degree. How demonstrably evident is the conclusion, that they differ not in degree, but in kind.

3. In respect to the inquiry, What faculties in man exist as the condition and ground of *moral agency* in him? the answer is ready. They are the faculties above named, together with that of Free Will. The absence of those first named, in the case of the brute, has already been established. Shall we still attribute to him that of Free Will? The following considerations perfectly satisfy my own mind on this point:

(1.) The action of Free Will, in the absence of conceptions and judgments, is impossible. Till I have conceptions of A and B, and judge that one differs from the other, or at least, that one is not the other, I cannot choose between them. There may be selection, but not choice; nor can there be selection such as implies the action of Free Will.

(2.) None of the phenomena of brute action necessarily suppose the presence of Free Will in the subject. All such phenomena are just as explicable on the opposite hypothesis as on this. Now a power is never to be supposed, when its presence is not affirmed by positive facts, or necessarily supposed by the known sphere of the subject. No such considerations demand the assumption of Free Will in the brute. Such an assumption therefore is wholly illogical.

(3.) All the phenomena of brute action clearly indicate the

absence of the power under consideration. Place the brute in any circumstances whatever, and there let particular sensations be generated in him, and his action will be just as fixed and uniform, as that of any mechanical power whatever. As often as the experiment is repeated, it will invariably be attended with the same results. With such facts before us, how illogical the assumption of Free Will in the Brute.

(4.) Such a power as that under consideration would be a totally useless appendage to the brute, contemplating him in reference to the sphere for which he is designed. When the intellectual faculties above named are denied him, what a useless appendage to the brute, and how worse than useless to man, in respect to the use to be made of the animal, would such an appendage as Free Will be. The creation of such a power, under such circumstances, would be a wide departure from all the manifestations of wisdom visible in all the Divine works beside.

(5.) Finally, the power under consideration constitutes one of the most essential elements of the Divine image in which man was created. Why should we suppose an element so fundamental in that image to exist in a creature, in whom all the other elements are totally wanting, and that without any solid basis for that conclusion?

Thus, by the most logical deductions, we have determined the powers of the brute, as distinguished from those of man. Taking from the former, what fundamental phenomena require us to do, to wit, the powers of Reason, Self-Consciousness, Understanding, Judgment, Imagination, and Free Will, we leave him with the powers of external perception, with a sensibility, and physical organization, of such a nature, that under the varied circumstances of his being, his action is in necessary harmony with the ends for which the all-wise Creator designed him. All the phenomena of brute action can be accounted for on this hypothesis, and its truth is also affirmed by fundamental phenomena. In this lower creation man stands alone. There is nothing like him "in the heavens above, nor in the earth beneath, nor in the waters under the earth." There he stands, "the image and glory of God." Fallen though he is,

> "his form has yet not lost
> All its original brightness, nor appears
> Less . . . . than the excess
> Of glory obscured."

GENERAL REMARKS.

1. We are now prepared to explain the ground of the misjudgment so common in respect to the action of the brute. Men judge of brute action in the light of their own consciousness, pertaining to similar actions in themselves. When men and brutes are placed in similar circumstances, and the external actions of both are similar, men often conclude that the brute acts in view of the same conceptions and judgments, in view of which they are conscious of acting themselves. Now such conclusions are wholly unauthorized. The external manifestations of instinctive and rational Intelligence may be, in many important respects, similar, yet there may be a total dissimilarity in the nature of these different kinds of Intelligence.

2. We are also prepared to state the conclusion which the facts connected with brute Intelligence force upon us. It is one of these two: Either the Intelligence of the brute is incomparably more perfect than that of man, or, aside from the power of external perception, he has no Intelligence at all, such as man possesses. The first manifestations of Intelligence in man, how imperfect and feeble! How rude and ill-shaped, for example, the first habitations built by man! How slow the progress of human architecture from such rude beginnings to

its present perfection! On the other hand, the first production of the brute bears the stamp of perfection. The first dam built by the beaver, the first nest built by the bird, have never been surpassed. The first cell built by the bee can hardly be improved, even in thought. Now suppose that such actions of the brute are, as is the case with man, the result of the carrying out of an idea, a plan, previously developed in his Intelligence, what must we conclude? Why, that the first race of brutes that ever appeared on earth, had a degree of Intelligence which man, after six thousand years of laborious progress, has hardly reached. This or the opposite one forces itself upon us.

3. Another consideration to which I would direct attention is this — the facts on which the conclusions of individuals have been based, in respect to the existence of the higher powers of Intelligence in the brute, as contrasted with others in the same connection, which have been totally overlooked. A distinguished naturalist, for example, states that the wild ass, when he begins to flee from a man, will first turn one ear, and then the other, backwards towards the object of his terror. From this fact, he concludes that the animal is deliberating what course he shall take; and, as a consequence, attributes to it the possession of the powers of deliberation and Free Will. A grave conclusion, surely, to infer from the leering of an ass, the existence of such powers. How often have the actions of the elephant been proclaimed, as proof of the existence of the higher powers of Intelligence in that animal? Now let us contemplate another class of facts in connection with the same animal. Those who have visited menageries are familiar with the dancing of the animal at the "sound of the lyre," actions as indicative of superior Intelligence as any he ever puts forth. How was the creature taught such an act? Did he take lessons, as men do, and thus acquire it?

It was by a process very different from this. When the keepers wish to have the animal acquire the art under consideration, they place him upon a floor covered with plates of iron. These plates are gradually heated, till the creature, beginning to feel pain in his feet from the heat, lifts first one foot and then the other. As soon as such motions begin, the music commences, which is made to become more and more lively as the animal steps with greater and greater rapidity. When this process has been continued for a sufficient length of time, the music ceases, and the animal is instantly taken from his painful condition. These experiments being repeated a few times, such an association is established between the sound of the lyre and the Sensibility of the animal, that as soon as he hears the music he begins to dance, and continues the pace till the music ceases. Thus we have the elephant dancing in his wisdom, as many suppose. Now had the animal the real Intelligence possessed by any individual of our race, who is in any degree removed above absolute idiocy, such an imposition could not be practised upon him for a single hour.

The actions of the creature, in this case, in conformity to Intelligence, are not, as all perceive, a manifestation of Intelligence in him, but in the keeper. So whatever Intelligence the animal manifests in any instance, is not an indication of Intelligence in him, but in the Creator. The same is true of all other animals.

4. The form in which memory exists in brutes, may now be readily pointed out. Memory, in man, is the recalling of the fact that we were, in particular circumstances, the subjects of such and such thoughts, feelings, &c. In the brute no such recollections can occur. When the brute has been affected in a given manner, in given circumstances, the same sensations are reproduced in him when he comes into similar circumstances again, and hence the same actions are repeated.

5. Finally, we notice the error of some who attempt to account for the diversities of intellectual manifestations between men and brutes, on the ground of diversities of phrenological development. To suppose that the soul of a dog, if placed in connection with the brain of a Newton, would manifest the Intelligence of that great philosopher, is as illogical as to suppose that gold and water will exhibit the same phenomena, when subjected to the same influences. The manifestations of substances diverse in their nature will, under the same circumstances, be as diverse as their nature. The brute, in any circumstances, is still a brute, and not a man, nor an angel. Diversities of phrenological development may account for the diverse intellectual manifestations among men; but not for those between man and the brute. The brute must become another being, before he can manifest the intelligence of man.

CHAPTER XX.

MATTER AND SPIRIT.

PRINCIPLES ON WHICH THE ARGUMENT IS BASED.

ALL legitimate reasoning, in respect to the nature of any substance, is based upon the assumption, that all substances are as *their essential phenomena,* that substances all of whose phenomena are totally and fundamentally unlike, are as totally and fundamentally diverse from each other in their nature, and that so far as the fundamental phenomena of any substances differ, there is, and must be, a corresponding difference in the nature of the substances themselves.

All reasoning, also, pertaining to substances, must be based upon their *known* qualities. No qualities known to exist must be overlooked or disregarded, and no unknown qualities must be supposed to exist, unless the reality and the character of the unknown are clearly indicated by those that are known, and then the former are no longer unknown, but positively discerned. Such are the principles on which the argument pertaining to these two substances — Matter and Spirit — must be based.

PRINCIPLES APPLIED.

We have already, in a former Chapter, said all that need be said on this subject. In showing, as we think we have done, that the material hypothesis cannot account for all the facts of the universe — that of Mind especially — we have shown that Matter is not the only substance; in other words, that Spirit or Mind is not Matter. All that is requisite on the present occasion, is to indicate simply the nature of the argument bearing upon this subject. The reality of a fundamental distinction between these two substances, can be denied but upon one of two hypotheses — the Material hypothesis which resolves the phenomena of Mind into those of Matter, or the Spiritual hypothesis which resolves the phenomena of Matter into those of Spirit. Against each of these hypotheses I urge the following fundamental objections:

1. Each alike stands opposed to the absolute intuitions of the universal Intelligence. That Intelligence no more confounds one of these substances with the other, than it does substance with space, or scarlet color with the sound of a trumpet. It has separated them as opposites. Now this conviction must be held to be true until it has been demonstrated to be false. The universal Intelligence has separated Matter and Spirit, as diverse and opposite substances. The burden of proof lies upon him who would convict that Intelligence in this separation of fundamental error.

2. No positive evidence of any kind or degree can be adduced in favor of either of these hypotheses. Each hypothesis alike must rest, as we have seen in a former Chapter, upon mere assumptions wholly unsusceptible of proof, and as totally unsustained by any form or degree of positive evidence. This, we are quite sure, will not be denied.

3. The truth of either of these hypotheses is absolutely inconceivable and impossible, excepting upon the assumption that our knowledge of the qualities of these two substances is not valid. If we admit that thought, feeling, and voluntary determination, are the *real* qualities of the Mind, we must admit that the substance in which these qualities inhere is an absolute unity, wholly incapable of division or composition on the one hand, and as utterly void of solidity, extension, and form, on

the other. We cannot divide a thought, feeling, or act of Will. Neither of these phenomena has a this side, a that side, a top or a bottom, length, breadth, thickness, taste or color. The substance, itself, thus assuming that its real qualities are known, must be an absolute unity, as absolutely void of all the properties of Matter. So if•we assume that the qualities of Matter are really known to us, and that the substance itself is as its qualities, then we can, by no possibility, conceive of it as anything else than a compound, extended, solid, and figured substance, that is, as not being an absolute unity, void of extension and form, and endowed with the powers of thought, feeling, and free Will. Suppose we assume that our knowledge of the qualities of these substances is not valid, then the substances themselves are absolutely unknown to us, and we cannot reason about them at all. We should also deny the validity of all knowledge of every kind: for if we know not the qualities of Mind, on the one hand, and of Matter, on the other, it is absolutely impossible for us to know anything. Assuming our knowledge of the qualities of these substances to be real, the truth of the doctrine of Materialism or Idealism, each alike, is absolutely inconceivable and impossible. Assuming this knowledge to be invalid, then neither of these hypotheses can be held as true, because we know nothing, and can know nothing, upon this subject or any other. The doctrine of the immateriality of the soul, then, can be denied but upon one hypothesis, a denial of the integrity of the Intelligence as a faculty of knowledge in respect to all subjects alike.

COMMON OBJECTIONS.

A few of the common, and most important objections to the above argument, demand a passing notice:

1. It may be said, that for aught we know, there may be phenomena yet unknown to us, common to both these substan-

ces. To this I reply, that when such phenomena are discovered, we will acknowledge that so far, and so far only, their natures are alike. Such a discovery, however, would not affect the above demonstration; for it would still remain true, that, as far as the phenomena under consideration are concerned, they are wholly unlike.

2. It may also be objected, that these two substances have always, so far as our knowledge extends, existed together. This objection supposes us ignorant of the Eternal mind, an admission which we shall by no means grant. But suppose we yield even this. Does co-existence, and even necessary co-existence, suppose a common nature? Body and Space always co-exist, as far as Body is concerned, and as far as our experience goes; but to supppose them, for this reason, identical in their nature, is absurd.

3. The mutual influence of these two substances, the one upon the other, is often adduced as proof of the identity of their ultimate essence. But this fact equally consists with both hypotheses, and of course can prove neither. Before it can be shown to possess any force, it must be shown that no two substances can mutually affect each other, only on the single condition of a common nature. But this can never be done.

These are the principal and only objections, as far as my knowledge extends, to the above demonstration. Their weakness shows the weakness of the hypothesis they are designed to sustain.

CHAPTER XXI.

IMMORTALITY OF THE SOUL.

THE relations of spirit to the eternal future before us, present questions of greater moment to us, as intelligent beings, capable of investigating the question of our own destiny, than any other of which we can conceive. Indeed, all real interests with such beings are involved in such a question. In the volume of Inspiration, this doctrine is, as we should expect, set with the greatest possible distinctness before our minds. The individual who confides in the truth of that sacred record, needs no other foundation on which to rest the question of his own Immortality. The examination of the truth of this doctrine, however, pertains not merely to those who are privileged with the knowledge of Inspiration. This conviction may properly be presented as the great phenomenon of the race, of the universal human Intelligence. It belongs to Philosophy to investigate the grounds of this universal conviction.

PRELIMINARY CONSIDERATIONS.

Before proceeding to a direct consideration of the grounds of this conviction, a few preliminary considerations demand our special attention:

1. The first that I notice, is the fact above stated, that the conviction of the truth of this doctrine is co-extensive with the race of man. It belongs to no age, to no form of religion, to no nation, to no race of men, as a peculiarity. It is the common element of all religions, the common conviction of

the race, in all ages and conditions. To the wild son of the forest, to the ferocious cannibal of the isles of the Pacific, to the wanderer among "Afric's sunny mountains," and the inhabitants of "India's coral strand," as well as to that portion of the race to whom Christianity has imparted the blessings of civilization, the conviction of an endless existence after the closing up of the concerns of this mortal sphere is an omnipresent reality. "Simple nature" has imparted this expectation to the race, as the common boon of Heaven, irrespective of rank or condition.

2. This conviction does not exist in the universal Intelligence as the result of *investigation*, of *logical deductions* from processes of reasoning. This is evident from the fact, that it exists among races of men totally unaccustomed to reason on any such subject. Here, also, it exists with as much strength as among those who are most disciplined in logical deductions. It lies in the mind as one of the great primary intuitions of the universal Intelligence. It has precisely the same claim to a place among such intuitions that the belief of our own existence has.

3. This conviction lies in the Intelligence in such a form, as to be, in reality, incapable of increased confirmation by any process of reasoning. When we fall back upon the primary intuitions of our minds, we find it there, as one of the great starting points of the Intelligence. We find it, not as a point to be reached after we have left the sphere of primary intuitions, but as one of the seven pillars on which the temple of truth, reared by investigation and reasoning, must rest. Like all other primary intuitions, this conviction is incapable of essential confirmation by any process of logical deduction.

4. While this conviction, as a primary intuition of the universal Intelligence, is incapable of essential confirmation from logical deductions, it remains equally proof against all

apparent demonstrations to the contrary. An individual may pile what he may deem demonstration upon demonstration upon this conviction, in order to crush and annihilate it, till he triumphs in the terrible assumption, that its light is for ever extinct in his mind. Still, in a moment, it will rise before him again, in all the strength and vigor of immortal youth. He again knows the truth of that conviction, with an assurance with which he hardly recognizes his own existence. This apparent resurrection is not the result of logical deductions. In that moment the Intelligence looks down into the depths of its inner being, and there again finds this intuition unmoved from its eternal foundations, as the moveless rock beneath the billows of the ocean. The individual who thinks that he has demonstrated to himself the fact, that as a brute he shall live and die, should remember, that however secure he may think himself from the conviction of, to him, the unwelcome truth of his own immortality, the terrible reality will hereafter leap upon him again, as an armed man. He will never escape from it. It will and must be to him as a guardian angel, or a specter of darkness.

5. In the facts above stated, we have the highest possible evidence of the truth of the doctrine under consideration. What the universal Intelligence affirms, in view of certain facts, must have its foundation in these facts, or we must assume that the Intelligence itself is a lie; and then to reason on any subject becomes the perfection of folly.

6. As a primary conviction of the universal Intelligence, the exclusive province of philosophy pertaining to it is, to investigate the *grounds* of this conviction, and not to attempt to establish the truth of it by any other process of logical deduction. Here, I think, lies the error in the common demonstrations, or attempted demonstrations, of the doctrine of Immortality. The assumption in all such demonstrations is, that the truth

of this doctrine is to be found as some distant point in a process of logical deduction, instead of recognizing the conviction of the truth of the doctrine as one of the primary intuitions of universal Reason, and then falling back upon the intuition itself, to discover its foundation, or chronological antecedent. One fact should be kept in mind here. In falling back upon any primary conviction of the Intelligence, for the purpose of finding the foundation of the same, the validity of that conviction does not depend upon the success of our endeavors. Reflection may fail of its object, "yet the foundation of truth standeth sure."

PRINCIPLES ON WHICH THE PRESENT ARGUMENT RESTS.

There are two foundation principles on which the entire argument pertaining to the doctrine of Immortality rests:

1. The first is this, that every sentient being is formed for a particular destiny. To fill the sphere of existence for which each creature was formed, that constitutes his destiny. That each creature is thus formed and adapted to a particular sphere, the filling up of which constitutes his destiny, is a fundamental conviction of the race.

2. There is in the constitution of each being, and order of beings, a fixed adaptation to his or their particular destiny. To suppose the opposite, would be to suppose that the Creator lacks wisdom, or goodness, or both.

Hence, if we would determine the destiny of any being, or order of beings, we must investigate their powers and susceptibilities, and from these learn what their real destiny is. The great French naturalist, from a single bone belonging to an animal of an extinct species, could determine at once, in view of that single part, the genus or species of the animal, and the main features of its physical structure. So true is Nature in the adaptation of one part of her works to another.

Equally real and perfect is the adaptation of the constitution of each creature to his particular destiny. Of this all men are convinced. All men believe that the destiny of the bee differs from that of the horse, and that that of man differs from that of either of the former. The ground of this conviction is the fundamental difference of their nature and constitution

We must admit the validity of the above principles, as the ground of the argument pertaining to the doctrine of Immortality, or deny wholly the validity of all conclusions based upon the laws and constitution of Nature. If we deny the propriety of reasoning from the fundamental laws and constitution of a being to his destiny, it becomes perfect folly for us to reason from or about creation at all. If the voice of Nature is false in this instance, he is guilty of infinite folly and absurdity who will trust her anywhere.

DIRECT ARGUMENT.

We are now prepared for a distinct statement of the ground of the universal conviction of the truth of the doctrine of Immortality. *It is the conscious adaptation of the powers and susceptibilities of the soul to that great idea, or to its realization, as the appropriate destiny of man.* Our godlike powers and susceptibilities are in conscious adaptation to the realization of that idea as our appropriate destiny, and to none other.

1. The universal conception of the idea, as one of the primitive ideas of Reason, indicates in man powers adapted to its realization. For who should realize an idea but the being who has conceived of it? The conception of the idea of Paradise Lost indicated, in Milton, powers adapted to the production of that immortal poem. So the universal conception of Immortality, as one of the fundamental phenomena of the

human Intelligence, indicates, in man, powers adapted to the realization of that conception.

2. But when this conception arises in the human mind, we find our powers and susceptibilities in conscious adaptation to it. The realization of the idea becomes the great object of desire, and our whole being shrinks back with horror at the thought of annihilation. How true to nature, as the truth lies revealed in the depths of universal mind, is the sentiment which Milton has put into the mouth of a fallen spirit:

> "For who would lose,
> Though full of pain, this intellectual being
> These thoughts that wander through eternity,
> To perish rather, swallowed up and lost
> In the wide womb of uncreated night,
> Devoid of sense and motion?"

Unless the fixed direction of universal nature is towards the unreal, Immortality is the destiny of man. Now it is the conscious adaptation of his powers to that idea, together with the principle, that the destiny of each being and race of beings is as their powers and adaptations, that constitutes, as it appears to me, the chief ground of the universal conviction of the truth of the doctrine of Immortality. What other conviction should arise in the conscious presence of such facts?

3. But there is another fundamental fact which lies at the basis of the universal conviction of which we are speaking— a fact of which every one becomes sufficiently conscious, as soon as he knows himself, to lay the foundation of the conviction under consideration, although the fact may not, in most minds, possess all the distinctness of reflection. It is the fact, so undeniably and universally manifest, that all the powers of the soul are capable of and adapted to a state of *endless progression.* The powers of thought involve the elements of end-

less progress in knowledge. So all our capacities are in their nature adapted to a state of limitless expansion. What is the conviction which forces itself upon the mind in the presence of such powers? The answer is, that the doctrine of Immortality reveals the destiny of man, or the fundamental tendencies of nature are towards the unreal and untrue. Which conclusion is most reasonable, that powers and susceptibilities adapted to endless expansion are just to begin to open to the light and influence of truth, and then descend into the abyss of non-existence, or that "the eternal years of God are theirs?" What excuse can a rational being have, in the presence of such faculties, for not assuming his own Immortality as the great goal towards which all his plans and purposes shall be directed?

4. There is another important fact bearing upon this topic — a fact of which every one is conscious as soon as he comes to recognize himself as a *moral* agent. It is a fact, that we do violence to our moral nature, and render ourselves really incapable of the virtues to which our nature is adapted, when we reject the doctrine of Immortality. When we contemplate ourselves as the creatures of a day, our nature shrinks to the dimensions of its own withering, contracted conceptions, and thus becomes incapable of great thoughts and noble aspirations. "The grander my conceptions of being, the nobler my future. There can be no sublimity in life without faith in the soul's eternity." It is only in the presence of such conceptions and anticipations, that great virtues, such as render us pure and blessed even here, become possible to us. The individual who does not "dial on time his own eternity," cannot become truly great, nor greatly good. His aspirations and his virtues, if he could have any, would, of necessity, be as contracted and groveling as his conceptions of his own destiny, and that of the race with which he is connected. Now this feeling of suicidal violence done to the higher departments of

our nature, in the denial of this doctrine, is one of the chief sources, as I suppose, of the universal conviction of the truth of the soul's eternity.

5. I mention another fact as the ground of this conviction. It is the fact, that every one becomes aware of as soon as the fact presents itself to his mind, that no real reasons whatever exist against the doctrine of which we are speaking. On the one hand, the truth of the doctrine stands forth as a primary, fundamental intuition of universal Reason. On the other, no reasons at all present themselves against this intuition. What reason, for example, does the dissolution of the physical organization, with which the soul is now connected, and the consequent disappearance of any manifestations of the soul's existence to us, afford against this doctrine? This fact is just as consistent with the soul's Immortality, as with the opposite supposition. It may be but one of the necessary steps in the progress of its future development.

The same holds true of the loss of mental vigor which often attends the approach of dissolution under consideration. When from weariness and exhaustion, we approach a state of sleep, we find the same want of vigor; yet we know that the real powers of the soul are not the less, under such circumstances. The same may hold true in the case above referred to. It may be, and no doubt is, one circumstance which attends our mortal state, while it has no bearing whatever against the soul's Immortality. With such evidences as that above stated, and in the total absence of all evidence to the contrary, every one feels that it would imply infinite guilt in him not to assume the doctrine under consideration as true.

6. There is one fact which science has developed, as confirmatory of the universal conviction under consideration, though from its being a fact of science, it cannot constitute a ground of that conviction At death, not a particle of the

physical organization, with which the soul is here connected, perishes. How unreasonable and absurd the supposition, that the soul, for which all else was made, is the only reality that then ceases to be? As the particles of the body immediately enter into new combinations, how reasonable the conclusion (and how unreasonable and absurd the opposite conclusion), that the soul also passes away from the present scene to the sphere of its future existence!

FUTURE RETRIBUTIONS.

There is one element of the doctrine of Immortality which should not be passed over without special attention. I refer to the question, whether the soul, in the eternal future, is to exist in a state of moral retribution. The following considerations may be presented as having a decisive bearing upon this question:

1. Wherever, throughout the wide world, the idea of Immortality is met with, we find it connected with the belief and anticipation of a state of moral retributions. There is not an age or nation where an exception to this belief can be met with. Such a fact marks the doctrine of future retributions, as one of the primary intuitions of universal Rason.

2. All our ideas of moral fitness are met in this doctrine, and are perfectly reversed by every other hypothesis. No individual can contemplate a life of self-sacrificing virtue, and of flagrant wickedness and crime unattended with repentance, as terminating in the same condition hereafter, and retain his sentiments of moral esteem for the "Judge of all the earth." Every individual does as fatal violence to his moral nature, who entertains the sentiment that God does not, in eternity, hold deserved retributions in readiness for the virtuous and vicious, as the man does who denies the soul's immortality. I feel perfectly safe in venturing the affirmation, that there is

not an individual on earth, who holds that God has prepared the same rewards hereafter for the virtuous and the vicious here, that does, or can, in the depths of his own mind, entertain feelings of esteem and reverence, and is inspired with feelings of delight and praise, for the Eternal One.

3. I mention one other very decisive fact bearing upon this question. Every observer of the facts that lie all around him in the universe, cannot have failed to notice an invariable tendency, common to the practice of both virtue and vice; it is a tendency to changeless fixedness of character in the one specific direction in which an individual accustoms himself to act. Now, what does such an unvarying and universal fact indicate, in respect to the character of the future destiny of moral agents? Certainly this, and this only, that the moral universe is advancing, not only in the line of immortal existence, but to a state of fixed and changeless moral retributions. What other convictions do such considerations tend to impress upon the Mind of all who seriously throw their thoughts upon the eternal future before them? How thoughtfully, then, does it become us to walk along the borders of that "undiscovered country," across whose bourne we are so soon to pass.

CHAPTER XXII.

THE IDEA OF GOD.

We come now to a consideration of the last and most important subject to be investigated in the present Treatise — *the idea of God.*

PRELIMINARY CONSIDERATIONS.

In the commencement of my remarks upon this subject, special attention is invited to the following preliminary considerations:

1. The idea of God, like that of Immortality, is in all Minds in whom Reason is in any considerable degree developed. This will be admitted by all who are at all acquainted with the history of the race. The idea of God is a common phenomenon of the universal Intelligence.

2. Like the doctrine above named, it is not in the Mind as the result of logical deduction; yet it is there with such weight of conviction, that every one feels that he involves himself in infinite guilt, in denying, or entertaining a doubt of its objective validity. This is evident from the fact, that every skeptic, in the depths of his own mind, believes that, if there is a God, he has forfeited His eternal favor, in the denial of His existence, a fact clearly evincing the consciousness, that in doubting, instead of adoring and worshiping, he has done fatal violence to the laws of his own being.

3. This idea is naturally in the Mind with such weight of

conviction, as to be apparently incapable of any considerable increase or diminution by any process of logical deduction. Arguments in favor of its validity, do not, in most instances, really increase the weight or force of this conviction. They simply develop in the Mind a distinct and reflective consciousness of what it was absolutely assured of before. Nor can professed arguments to the contrary erase this conviction from the Mind; a fact fully evinced by the force with which the assurance of the being of God often leaps upon the Mind of the skeptic, in moments of solemn thought, of sudden calamity, or unexpected exposure to death.

4. As this conviction is thus in the Mind, and not there as the result of logical deduction, it must be ranked among the *primary* intuitions of Reason.

5. As a first truth of Reason, the Divine existence is susceptible, in the first instance, of the kind of proof common to all first truths, and in the second, of that which is peculiar to all necessary intuitions.

In the light of the above observations, we will now proceed to a consideration of the ground of the universal conviction of the reality of the Divine existence. There are two fundamental forms in which the idea of God exists in the Mind, to each of which special attention will be directed, to wit, God, the unconditioned cause of all that exists and acts conditionally — and God, the Infinite and Perfect.

GOD THE UNCONDITIONED CAUSE OF ALL THAT EXISTS CONDITIONALLY.

Whatever ideas mankind may entertain of the universe, whether they resolve all substances into Matter or into Spirit, or whether they regard thought as the only reality, there is one point in respect to which they all in fact do, and must perfectly harmonize, to wit, that there is an *ultimate reason why the facts of the universe, whatever their nature may be supposed to be, are what they are, and not otherwise.* Now if the term God be employed to designate this ultimate Reason, or unconditioned Cause, then all mankind do really and truly believe in God, and none doubt, or profess to doubt his existence. It is no more possible for us to doubt the reality of such ultimate Reason, than it is to doubt the validity of the principle, that every event must have a cause. As thus defined, the question, and only question, at issue between the Theist and anti-Theist is, not whether God *exists,* but *what is his character?* that is, What is the nature and character of this final, unconditioned Cause, the reality of whose existence all admit, and none can, by any possibility, doubt?

POSSIBLE HYPOTHESES ON THIS SUBJECT.

On a moment's reflection, it will be perceived, that there are but a certain number of possible hypotheses on this subject, and that some one of these, to the exclusion of all the others, must be true. It is self-evident, that this cause must exist as an inherent law of nature, or it must exist out of and above nature, as a power exercising an absolute control over it. If the latter supposition be granted, then, as all will admit, the Theistic hypothesis, as above defined, must be true. If, on the other hand, the former supposition be granted, then the unconditioned Cause must exist as an inherent law of Matter, or of Spirit, or of pure thought, no other supposition being conceivable or possible. The true answer, then, to the question, What is the nature and character of the ultimate Reason or unconditioned Cause under consideration, will be found in the hypothesis of Theism, of Materialism, or in that of some one of the forms of Idealism. This must be true, because these include all conceivable hypotheses.

None but the Theistic Hypothesis can be true.

If it be admitted, that there are two orders of finite substances — Matter and Spirit — and that they possess the attributes, and sustain to each other the relations which we have attributed to them, then the truth of the Theistic hypothesis is undeniable. Indeed, it has never been denied, but upon the assumption of the non-reality of Spirit as distinct from Matter, or of Matter as distinct from Spirit, or of all substances whatever. The Unconditioned must be an inherent law of thought, of Spirit, or of Matter, or the free, intelligent, self-conscious personality of Theism. The truth of these statements is so self-evident, that no one was ever known to deny it.

Now it has already, we think, been rendered perfectly evident, that neither the hypothesis of Materialism, nor any one of those of Idealism can be true. That of Theism, then, must be true. We might with perfect safety rest the argument here. The paramount importance of the subject, however, requires that we give to the argument bearing upon that subject, a still more extended elucidation.

THE THEISTIC HYPOTHESIS ESTABLISHED AS A TRUTH OF SCIENCE.

The relation of the Divine existence considered as the Ultimate Reason or Unconditioned Cause of the facts of the universe, is an absolutely necessary truth, the opposite being inconceivable, and in itself, impossible. Hence, as we have already remarked, it is a truth universally admitted. Now whatever attributes are necessarily implied in the idea of such a cause, on the one hand, and in the facts of the universe, on the other, must be affirmed of God. This all will admit. The process of the argument, in the first instance, is wholly *à priori*, and in the next *à posteriori*.

ATTRIBUTES NECESSARILY IMPLIED IN THE IDEA OF THE UNCONDITIONED.

The following may be enumerated as the attributes necessasarily implied in the idea of God considered as the Unconditioned Cause, to wit, Eternity, absolute Immutability, and full and perfect adequacy and adaptation to produce the facts of the universe, and render them what they are, and not otherwise. If this Cause did not exist from eternity, it would itself be an effect of some other and prior cause, and therefore not itself the ultimate or unconditioned Cause. If it were not absolutely immutable, its condition and states would be determined by some other cause, in which case also, it would not be the ultimate Cause. If it did not possess perfect adequacy, and adaptation to produce the facts of the universe, it could, in no sense, be the cause of those facts. These attributes then must pertain to God, as the Unconditioned. As necessary corollories from these truths, the three following propositions may be affirmed of the Unconditioned:

1. The cause assigned, in any given hypothesis, must have, to possess any claims whatever to our regard, an *intelligent* adaptation to produce the facts of the universe, and render them what they are. If it has no apparently adequate adaptation to such an end, the hypothesis containing it, is intrinsically absurd, and may be properly rejected on the ground of impossibility.

2. The cause assigned must not rank lower in *kind* than the effect attributed to it; otherwise such cause could have no *intelligent* adaptation to produce the effects attributed to it.

3. The Unconditioned Cause assigned for the facts of the universe, must be one which possesses in itself the power of self-originating activity, that is, of commencing action from a state of rest, and that from the influence of no cause out of

itself. The facts to be accounted for are not a series of events existing from eternity, but one having, as we shall see hereafter, its beginning in time. The Unconditioned must be a cause then, having in itself the power of pure self-originating activity. It must be one possessing a creative, or formative energy, which remained inactive from eternity up to a certain moment in time, and then, from no cause out of itself, commenced such activity. The truth of these statements, the first two, to say the least, will not be denied. How the last can be is hardly conceivable.

ATTRIBUTES OF THE UNCONDITIONED NECESSARILY SUPPOSED IN THE FACTS OF THE UNIVERSE.

We now come to a consideration of the attributes of the Unconditioned, necessarily supposed in the facts of the Universe. To proceed intelligently in this department of our inquiries, we must first classify the facts from which these attributes are to be deduced. Among these facts, I notice the following:

Facts of creation bearing upon our present inquiries.

1. These facts, that is, the present order of things throughout the universe, *had their origin in time,* and are not a series of events existing from eternity. This statement is affirmed as true by the intuitive convictions of the race, by all the deductions of science bearing upon the subject, is assumed as true in all the theories of the universe invented by the ingenuity of man, and is contradicted by no known facts in existence. We therefore assume the truth of the proposition as universally granted.

2. The present state of the earth is the result of a series of *independent creations,* each having its beginning in time. The earth has existed under the reign of Fishes, under the

reign of Reptiles, under the reign of Mammals, and it now exists under that of Man. Not a solitary fact can be adduced presenting the remotest indication, that any one of these orders of existence originated by transmutation from any one that preceded it. All the known facts of creation, on the other hand, affirm, and that most absolutely, the opposite supposition. I simply announce here the teachings of science on this subject, and assume the truth of its uncontradicted teachings as the basis of the present argument.

3. Every distinct species of animals or plants that now exists, or ever has existed on earth, has an *independent* existence, that is, did not derive its existence by transmutation from any pre-existing species. If science has not established this fact, it may truly be said to have established nothing.

4. Creation, from its commencement, has been progressive in one direction exclusively, from the *less to the more perfect.* The truth of this proposition is affirmed directly by all the teachings of science pertaining to the facts of creation, and is assumed as true in all the theories of the universe, of every kind. This fact, which is in itself of fundamental importance, also implies, that the series of creations had a beginning; else there could be no progress in the direction referred to.

5. No evidence whatever can be adduced of the existence of any power inhering intrinsically in nature, of originating from a state of total and universal inorganization, any, much less the leading, orders of animals or vegetables that now exist, or ever have existed on the earth. The only power pertaining to this subject, even apparently inhering in nature, is that of *perpetuating* species already existing, and that according to a fixed and immutable law of *propogation.* Nothing can be affirmed as a law of nature, if this proposition is not true.

6. All the material elements of which the earth is now constituted, once existed in a state of total unorganization,

with no animals or vegetables upon it, and no embryo principles from which such organizations now originate. An individual must close his eyes to all the facts of Geological science, to doubt the truth of this proposition.

7. Two orders of finite substances, Matter and Spirit, are to the Mind, as the basis of its reasonings on this subject, objects of absolute knowledge. These substances are in all their known qualities not only diverse the one from the other, but perfect opposites. Mind, rational Mind, I mean, everywhere stands revealed with the attributes of a free, intelligent, sensitive, self-conscious personality. Matter exhibits none of the properties which make any approach whatever towards the idea of such a personality. Undeniable and fundamental phenomena place an impassable gulf between them, as far as unity of nature is concerned. No one will question at all these statements, but upon one assumption, that their real qualities are wholly unknown to us. This is a formal impeachment of the validity and integrity of the Intelligence, as a faculty of knowledge, and then all inquiry after truth becomes an absurdity. Hence, I remark:

8. That while these substances are in their nature fundamental opposites, a fixed and undeniable relation exists between them, which imparts an absolute *unity to creation.* Mind is the center about which the entire material universe revolves. Mind is the end, to which the entire organization and movements of the universe sustain the exclusive relation of a means. Creation is thus an absolute whole, in which there is a place for everything, and everything is in its place, as far as the great, all-comprehending law of means and ends is concerned.

9. Creation, throughout, is constructed upon principles of *pure science* as developed in the Intelligence. Everything within and without us, seems, to say the least, to be the realization of a *plan*, which had a pre-existence in the Intellect of

the great Architect of nature. In the constitution of our nature, mental and physical, in the general structure of the universe, as developed in the science of Astronomy, and in the organization of animals and plants in the world around us, ideas and principles of pure science, as they exist in the Intelligence, are everywhere realized. Creation, throughout, wears this one exclusive aspect, and this is one of the fundamental facts that bear upon our present investigations.

10. Mind is constituted in fundamental and immutable correlation to one idea of the Unconditioned, the idea exclusively presented in the Theistic hypothesis. Two absolutely universal instincts noticed in a preceding Chapter, point, as thus shown, exclusively in this one direction — those of *worship* and *prayer*. To these I may add a deep and universal sentiment, from which, indeed, those just named take their rise, that of profound dependence upon a power out of and above itself. Man, also, is fundamentally constituted as a subject of moral government. In the interior of his Mind there is a perpetual revelation to him of the idea of right and wrong, or of the law of duty; through his conscience he ever recognizes himself as in the presence of a solemn behest to do the one and avoid the other. At the same time, he feels deeply impressed with the sense of the moral desert of good or ill, as he does the one or the other, and he instinctively anticipates from a power out of and above himself corresponding retributions. It is, finally, an immutable demand of the moral nature of universal Mind, that all the interests of the moral universe should be finally adjusted according to the principles of eternal and immutable justice. All the above-mentioned principles and instincts of our rational nature, are immutably correlated to but one idea of the Unconditioned, that of a free, intelligent, self-conscious personality, ruling the universe in absolute wisdom and righteousness. Whether such a being exists, is not now the question.

We might, however, as well deny that Mind, or any of its operations exists at all, as to deny the facts of its constitution above referred to.

11. Finally, throughout the entire domain of nature, one fixed and immutable law obtains, as far as the observation of man extends, to wit, For every fundamental want of sentient existence, there are corresponding provisions, and for every fundamental adaptation a corresponding object, or sphere of activity. Human observation has never yet discovered a solitary exception to this principle. Nature never vibrates towards the unreal. Nor is there, we may safely conclude, throughout the wide domain of her creations, such a chasm as there would be, were the above principles untrue.

THE THEISTIC HYPOTHESIS INTUITIVELY CERTAIN FROM THESE FACTS.

Such are the great leading facts of the universe bearing upon our present inquiries, facts against none of which will any well-informed and candid mind venture a denial. Now we affirm, without fear of contradiction, that from these facts the truth and necessity of the Theistic hypothesis, in opposition to every other, actual or conceivable, is intuitively evident. We cannot deny the facts without impeaching the validity and integrity of the Intelligence itself, as a faculty of knowledge, and then all inquiries after truth of every kind become absurd. We cannot, on the other hand, admit the facts, without affirming, as self-evident, the truth of this one hypothesis, and the total invalidity of every other. But the truth of this one hypothesis, as affirmed by these facts, needs a still more particular and special development. To accomplish this end, I remark —

TRUTH OF THIS HYPOTHESIS MORE PARTICULARLY DEVELOPED.

1. The Unconditioned can, by no possibility, be any law *inhering in nature*, any law, as affirmed by the material hypothesis on the one hand, or the Idealistic, in any of its forms, on the other. This I affirm for the following reasons:

(1). As we have already seen, not one of these hypotheses can be true, and some one of these must be true, if the Unconditioned is an inherent law of nature. We need not repeat the argument, by which the truth of these statements has already been demonstrated.

(2). On no such hypothesis can we account for the undeniable fact pertaining to the Unconditioned, that of *commencing activity*, or putting forth of creative power *from a state of inaction*. Creative energy in the Unconditioned remained inactive from eternity up to a given period, and then it commenced action. Now this could not possibly be true of any law inhering in nature. Any such law remaining inactive, from eternity to any one period, must remain so to eternity, unless roused to action by some power out of itself, and then this law would not itself be the Unconditioned. The idea of a law of nature remaining from eternity to a given period inactive, and then commencing action from no cause out of itself, is just as inconceivable and impossible as an event without a cause, or the annihilation of space.

(3). Hence, I remark, that on no such hypothesis, can we account for the undeniable fact of Creation, that of its *origin in time*. The Unconditioned, as we have seen, must be immutably the same, from eternity to eternity. If it were an inherent law of nature, it must have acted as a creative energy from eternity, or it never could have acted at all. Creation, then, could not have been a fact having its origin in time. It is such a fact, and therefore the Unconditioned is no law inhering in nature.

(4). The element of progression from the less in the direction of the more perfect, an element which undeniably constitutes a fundamental characteristic of creation, can be accounted for on no hypothesis that the Unconditioned is in any form a law inhering in nature. Progression proceeding from such a law must have been from eternity, and would already have attained to infinity. It has not thus attained, and therefore cannot proceed from such a law. The hypothesis, under consideration, then, cannot be true.

(5). The facts of the *origin* of *animal* and *vegetable organizations,* such as really appear on earth, from a state of universal unorganization, cannot be accounted for on the hypothesis under consideration. Matter was once exclusively in this state, with no embryo principles or conditions from which such organizations now originate, or by any known law of nature can originate. This is absolutely undeniable. Now from what known (and we must reason only from the known) inhering law of nature can the origin of all the species of animals and vegetables that have existed and now exist on earth, be accounted for? No such law can be designated, and therefore the facts before us must be attributed to a power out of and above nature.

(6). This hypothesis can be true, also, but upon the validity of one assumption, to wit, that nature, in all the higher departments of her works, is immutably correlated to the *unreal,* instead of the *real* in the Unconditioned. I refer, of course, to the higher and spiritual departments of Mind. These, as we have seen, are in fixed correlation to the Theistic hypothesis, in opposition to every other. The great fundamental principle of science, that for every fundamental want of sentient existence there is a supply, and for every fundamental adaptation a corresponding sphere of action, is totally false, if the hypothesis under consideration is true. It cannot be true, for the reason that for the facts of the universe it assigns a cause, which makes nature opposed to herself, and from which such facts can, by no possibility, arise.

2. The Unconditioned can be no cause *acting from necessity*. This is absolutely evident from considerations already presented. A necessary cause must act, as soon as the conditions of its activity are fulfilled. This is the fundamental element of our idea of such a cause. With the Unconditioned these conditions must have been fulfilled from eternity, or not at all. The opposite supposition involves the assumption that the action of the Unconditioned depends upon a cause out of itself, in other words, that it is not the Unconditioned. Creation, then, would be from eternity, and could not be an event of time. To account for creation as having had its beginning in time, a cause must be assigned, that could have acted as a creative energy, at that one moment, and need not to have thus acted at any preceding one, and that cause remaining from eternity to eternity absolutely immutable and determined in its activity by no other cause. Now the idea of necessitated causation does not, and cannot answer these conditions. It has no power from a state of inaction to commence activity, but from causes out of itself. From one state it cannot assume a new form of activity, but from the occurrence of new conditions which render continuance in the former state, and non-action in the new direction, equally and absolutely impossible. Now no such new conditions could have arisen with the Unconditioned, at the moment referred to, the very supposition of their occurrence implying a self-contradiction, to wit, that the Unconditioned is not the Unconditioned. No reasons existed for the commencement of creation at the moment referred to, rather than at any other moment, each period being in itself

in all respects absolutely like every other, and as equally distant from the eternity past and the eternity to come. The fact of creation as an event of time, a fact undeniable, cannot be accounted for upon the supposition, that the Unconditioned is any form of necessitated causation.

Every objection also, almost without exception, that lies against the idea that this cause is any inhering law of nature, lies with equal force against the idea, that it is any other form of necessitated causation. It is just as impossible to account for the facts of creation on one supposition as on the other.

3. The Unconditioned must be a *free Cause*, in opposition to all forms of necessary causation. On no other supposition is the undeniable fact of creation as an event having its beginning in time, a conceivable or possible event. On this hypothesis, it is both conceivable and possible. If the Unconditioned is a free and not a necessary cause, then at each successive moment from eternity, he might or might not put forth his creative energy. Its non-exercise at each previous moment, and its exercise at the moment when it was put forth, is conceivable, and therefore possible. On no other conceivable supposition can the fact, that the effects of the Divine agency are in time and not from eternity, be accounted for.

A cause that acts from necessity must, as we have seen, act as soon as it exists, and the conditions of its activity are fulfilled, which must have been true of the Unconditioned from eternity. The effects of the Divine agency, then, if the *Unconditioned* is a necessary cause, must have been from eternity, and not, as in fact they are, in time. If the human race, or the universe of mind around us, had their origin from a necessary cause, their existence must have been from eternity, or they could never have existed at all. That which rendered it impossible for the Unconditioned to create such beings from eternity up to any one moment, would have rendered it impossible for him to have created them to eternity. There can be no possible escape from this supposition.

To suppose the Unconditioned to be a necessary and not a free cause, is also self-contradictory. What is the fundamental element of our idea of a necessary cause? It is this: a cause which can act only as it is acted upon by something which necessitates its action. A necessary cause, therefore, in its action, must be conditioned, and not unconditioned and absolute. If God, then, is not a free, he is not the unconditioned cause of all conditional existences. Besides the supposition that the unconditioned and absolute is under the law of necessity, implies that the necessitating power acted *antecedently* to the unconditioned. This is equivalent to denying that God is the *first*, as well as the unconditioned and absolute cause.

4. As an unconditioned and absolute cause, God must be possessed of Intelligence. This follows as a necessary consequence of the fact, that he is a *free*, and not a *necessary* agent. Free agency, in the absence of Intelligence, is an absolute impossibility. We cannot possibly conceive of such an agent. Further, the universe to which God has given existence is *one*. Every object and element in the universe exists as a part of the great whole. The whole is in perfect adaptation to each and every part, and every part is in adaptation equally perfect to the whole; and the great whole, with all its parts, exists in perfect harmony with fundamental ideas of the Intelligence. Now to suppose that a free cause without Intelligence has created and constituted a universe, all the parts and departments of which, as parts of one great whole, exist in perfect harmony with fundamental ideas of the universal Intelligence, is an absolute impossibility. It is, in reality, the gross absurdity of affirming an event without a cause.

5. As the unconditioned and absolute cause of all that conditionally exists, God is a *spiritual*, and not a *material* existence. This follows, as the logical consequent of the fact, that he is a free and intelligent, and not a necessary and unintelligent agent.

6. God also must be a *moral* agent. This likewise is a logical consequent of the fact that he is an intelligent and free agent. Intelligence and free agency cannot be postulated of any being without, as the logical consequent of that supposition, attributing to him moral agency.

7. As the unconditioned cause, God exists and acts as the moral legislator and governor of the moral universe, exercising the functions of moral government in perfect harmony with the laws of absolute wisdom and rectitude. The basis of the universal and necessary conviction that God thus exists and acts, is found, I suppose, in the conscious laws and operations of our own mental and moral nature. Here we are conscious of the actual establishment of a moral government in perfect harmony with the immutable principles of justice and goodness. Conscience reveals the right and the wrong, and demands implicit and absolute obedience to the one, and corresponding avoidance of the other. Nor can we do the one or the other without experiencing in ourselves corresponding retributions. Here is moral government established, and no one can mistake its character. What is without may present apparent disorders, in the midst of which, however, we cannot mistake the fact, that all things are tending towards an ultimate adjustment, in accordance with the principles of absolute truth and justice. The revelations in the interior of our own mental and moral being, however, we cannot mistake, the revelations of "God as the judge of all," ruling the moral universe in absolute wisdom, justice, and beneficence.

8. I remark, finally, as a necessary deduction from all that we have previously established, that as the Unconditioned, God is a free, intelligent, self-conscious *Personality*, in opposition to the impersonal god of Pantheism and kindred hypotheses. Freedom, intelligence, spirituality, and moral agency must, as we have seen, be affirmed of God. Now these attributes necessarily imply Personality in the Godhead. With this position the entire facts of the universe, material and mental, perfectly accord, and they accord with none other. Our entire mental and moral nature are immutably correlated to the unreal, if God is not such a personality. Man also exists as such personality. To suppose that the Unconditioned is not a person, but a thing, as in that case he must be, is to assign for the effect a cause which ranks infinitely lower in kind than that which it produces. From what has already been established, however, the truth of the proposition before us is self-evident. No further enlargement of the argument is demanded in this connection.

GOD, THE INFINITE AND PERFECT.

We come now to consider the second form in which the idea of God is revealed in the human Intelligence, to wit, God, the *Infinite and Perfect.*

This a First Truth of Reason.

That this form of the idea of God is a first truth of Reason, is evident from this one consideration. Should any one attribute to God an acknowledged imperfection of any kind, he would know in himself, that he had thereby involved himself in infinite guilt. Men may, without conscious guilt, impute to the Most High real imperfections, but not as such. Whatever individuals regard as necessarily implied in the idea of the Infinite and Perfect, they universally conceive themselves as under the highest obligation to attribute the same to God. Further, there never was a time, since the idea of God first arose in our minds, when we did not thus regard him. There never was a time since the period under consideration, when we would not regard ourselves as infinitely guilty in attributing to God any acknowledged imperfection, or in not affirming of him whatever we regarded as involved in the idea of the Infinite and Perfect. God, then, the Infinite and Perfect, is a first truth of universal Reason. It now remains to designate the grounds of our conviction of the objective validity of this form of the idea of God.

DOES CREATION INDICATE THE CHARACTER OF GOD AS INFINITE AND PERFECT?

At the outset of our inquiries here, an important question arises, to wit: Does creation reveal its author as Infinite and Perfect? Can an effect acknowledged to be finite reveal its cause as infinite? If so, this revelation cannot be found in the mere *extent* of the Divine works. Suppose that the creation of *one* world only would have revealed its author as finite, how many such worlds would it take, to reveal him as infinite? Nothing short of a number absolutely infinite, which is an absurdity. It is the height of absurdity, therefore, to reason, as is commonly done, from the mere *extent* of creation, which is still acknowledged to be finite, to the absolute infinity and perfection of its author. Yet we cannot say, *à priori*, that God may not stand revealed in his works, as the Infinite and Perfect. That he is thus revealed therein, has been shown above. The fact we are bound to admit, although we may not be able to designate the grounds of our convictions in respect to it. It not unfrequently happens, that in the presence of certain facts, our Intelligence affirms absolutely particular conclusions, as the logical antecedents of the facts, while we may be at a loss to determine the particular elements in view of which those conclusions are affirmed. For such a reason, the conclusions ought to be to us none the less valid. I once read of a painting which presented with great perfection of execution, a human countenance. Every one that contemplated the countenance, felt, as his eyes were fixed upon it, a sort of horror creeping over him. Let us suppose that no one could designate the elements in the picture, which sustained to those feelings the relation of cause. No one would, for that reason, doubt the existence of such elements in the object. So, in the presence of the universe, God stands revealed to our minds as the Infinite and the Perfect. Though we may not be able to find those elements in his works, which thus reveal him, shall we, for that reason, doubt the reality of the revelation? In the case of the painting referred to, it was found that the author had produced it, after perpetrating the crime of murder. Hence he had penciled in the countenance, the internal feelings of his own mind. So God, for aught we can know, *à priori*, may have somewhere in his creation, penciled out the indications of his own Infinity and Perfection, pencilings which the universal Intelligence discovers and correctly interprets, without, in most instances, being able to distinguish. This I believe to be the real state of the case. God, in his works, stands revealed as the Infinite and Perfect. The elements in his works, by which he is thus revealed, may not yet have been designated. Yet they will be. It becomes us, as philosophers and Christians, to continue our observations till the elements under consideration are recognized and presented to the world.

REASONS WHY THESE ELEMENTS HAVE NOT YET BEEN DESIGNATED.

Permit me here to suggest the inquiry, whether, mainly for the three following reasons, almost, if not quite all efforts to find the ground of the conviction under consideration, pertaining to the Divine Infinity and Perfection, have proved unsuccessful:

1. The two forms above designated, in which the idea of God is developed in the Intelligence, have not been recognized and separated from each other. Hence, considerations adapted only to reveal God as the unconditioned and absolute cause, have been adduced to prove his Infinity and Perfection. Failing to establish this last point, they have been rejected, as having no bearing whatever upon the question of the Divine existence.

2. An attempt is always made to demonstrate the reality of the Divine existence and perfections by a formal process of logical deduction, instead of recognizing the belief of these truths as among the primary and necessary intuitions of Reason, and then falling back upon those intuitions to find their chronological antecedents, in other words, the grounds of such affirmations of Reason pertaining to God.

3. The argument for the Divine Infinity and Perfection has almost invariably taken a wrong direction, to wit, the element of *immensity* in the external creation. This immensity is limited, finite. The infinite is not found here. Hence, many have concluded, that no evidence at all exists in creation, of the Infinity and Perfection of God. So Kant reasons; and because this one element of creation does not reveal God as the Infinite and Perfect, he argues, that creation presents no evidence at all, even of the Divine existence, — a most strange and illogical conclusion. Where, then, should we ex-

pect, *à priori*, to find those pencilings in view of which the Intelligence affirms the Divine Infinity and Perfection? Not surely in the external material universe, but in that "which is made in the image of God," the universe of Mind. Among the laws of its inner being, Mind will find the indications of the Infinity and Perfection of its Author, if it finds them at all.

FOUNDATION OF THE CONVICTION THAT GOD IS BOTH INFINITE AND PERFECT.

We are now prepared for a direct consideration of the grounds of the affirmation of the Intelligence, that God is both Infinite and Perfect.

1. The first that I notice is a fundamental element in the idea of God, as the unconditioned and absolute cause of all that exists conditionally. Whatever the Intelligence necessarily apprehends as finite, it as necessarily regards as conditioned. In tracing back every chain of causes and effects to the first, or unconditioned and absolute cause, we naturally and necessarily ask, in respect to everything given as finite, What caused that? We put this question with no more doubt that it had a cause, than we have that no event exists without a cause. The Intelligence does not, and cannot recognize itself, as in the presence of the unconditioned and absolute, till it finds itself in the presence of the Infinite and Perfect. This I believe to be one of the chief sources of the conviction in our minds in respect to God as the Infinite and Perfect.

2. In the presence of this idea of God, the Intelligence intuitively and absolutely affirms the total absence of all evidence, that God is finite and imperfect. Hence the Intelligence cannot affirm either of God. Further, from the depth of our inner being there proceeds a solemn prohibition against imputing to God any imperfection, natural or moral, without

positive evidence. Every one feels the presence and force of that prohibition, who attends properly to the admonitions of his own nature.

3. To the idea of God, as the Infinite and Perfect, our entire mental constitution is in conscious harmony. It is only in the presence of this idea that the Mind is capable of the degree of virtue and happiness which its nature consciously demands. We cannot exist without a consciousness of such facts pertaining to the fixed correlation between the changeless demands of our own nature and the reality of God, as the Infinite and Perfect. Our nature shudders and shrinks back with horror at any other conception of God than this. The idea of God, as the Infinite and Perfect, is the great want of universal Mind. To every other want, in the universe within and around us, a corresponding reality exists. To know the demands of the nature of any being, is to know with perfect certainty the reality of corresponding objects in creation around. Shall we suppose that the great overshadowing want of universal Mind is the only necessity to which no corresponding reality exists? Now, I believe that the conscious correlation of our immortal powers to the idea of God, as the Infinite and Perfect, and to that idea alone, is one of the chief grounds of the affirmations of our Intelligence, under consideration, pertaining to God.

4. In all minds, also, there exists a conscious conviction that God *should* be nothing else than the Infinite and Perfect. Morally perfect we know he ought to be. So the Intelligence affirms, that having voluntarily given existence to beings whose nature demands nothing else than Infinity and Perfection in him, he ought to be to those beings what their nature, as he has constituted it, demands. Hence, also, from the depths of our being, there not only comes up a solemn prohibition against attributing finiteness and imperfection to God, but a solemn

admonition to esteem, adore, and worship him as nothing else than the Infinite and Perfect. Every one who properly listens to what is passing in the inner sanctuary of his own mind, will recognize what I mean in these declarations.

5. Worship is recognized by universal Consciousness, as a changeless demand of our nature. Yet every one feels that he does that nature infinite violence, when he worships anything but divinity, and divinity in harmony with any idea opposed to that of God as the Infinite and Perfect. What does such a law of universal Mind indicate? Certainly, that God, the only object of worship, is nothing else than the Infinite and Perfect. In the consciousness of such demands in our nature, the Intelligence perceives at once, as their logical antecedent, the reality of Infinity and Perfection in the Author of that nature.

6. One other ground of conviction under consideration yet remains to be designated, a ground more fundamental, if possible, than any yet pointed out. Mind is everywhere revealed to itself, not only as destined to an immortal existence, but as possessed of powers involving in their own nature the elements of *endless progression*. Every power and susceptibility of our nature possesses this one characteristic, a fixed adaptation to a state of endless growth and expansion. Of this characteristic of his own immortal powers every one is really, though he may not be reflectively, conscious. What do such powers indicate in respect to their Author? Nothing else than Infinity and Perfection. As Mind descends to a contemplation of its own powers and susceptibilities, and perceives in them all the elements not only of Immortality, but of endless growth and expansion in thought, feeling, and action, here it finds those pencilings in which it reads, with the most profound and solemn convictions of its being in the presence of eternal realities, the Infinity and Perfection of the Author of its ex-

istence. Mind knows, that in the endless growth and expansion of its immortal powers, nothing but Infinity and Perfection in God can meet the eternally enlarging demands of those powers. In view of its own powers and destiny, Mind reads, with the most undoubted convictions, the Infinity and Perfection of the eternal Guardian and Disposer of the Immortal interests involved in the possession of such powers.

Such, as I conceive, are the grounds of the affirmations of the universal Intelligence in reference to God, as the unconditioned and absolute cause of all that conditionally exists, and as the Infinite and the Perfect.

RELATION OF THE IDEA OF GOD, ABOVE ELUCIDATED, TO ALL OTHER IDEAS OF HIM.

The two forms of the Divine idea above elucidated, to wit, God, the absolute and unconditioned cause of all that exists conditionally, and God the Infinite and Perfect, are the great foundation principles in the science of Theology. Whatever is correctly affirmed or denied of God, must be done in the light of these two principles. In their light every other truth of God, and all the principles of his eternal government, stand revealed to our minds. Do we, for example, affirm omnipotence, omnipresence, omniscience, justice, goodness, truth, of God; it is because these perfections are involved, as essential elements, in our idea of him as the Infinite and Perfect. Do we legitimately deny anything of God, it is because that, in attributing it to him, we should affirm finiteness or imperfection of him. The same holds true of every *form* in which any particular characteristic is to be attributed to God. That conception of any particular characteristic which most fully harmonizes with the fundamental elements involved in the idea of absolute Infinity and Perfection, is to be affirmed of God;

while every other, and especially every opposite form, is to be denied of him.

THE IDEA OF A SYSTEM OF THEOLOGY.

Theology defined.

Theology is the science of God, systematically evolved in the light of the fundamental ideas of Reason, pertaining to him, above elucidated. This will be admitted by all in whose minds the idea of science is developed at all, as a correct, and the only correct, definition of the subject.

Postulate, Axioms, &c., in Theology.

The great postulate, the foundation principle in the science, as shown above, is the idea of God as the unconditioned and absolute cause, and as the Infinite and Perfect.

The axioms in the science are the two following:

1. Whatever is involved as an essential element of our idea of an unconditioned and absolute cause, and of Infinity and Perfection, is to be affirmed of God.

2. Whatever, if attributed to him, would contradict the idea of an unconditioned and absolute cause, or affirm finiteness or imperfection of God, is to be denied of him.

All particular attributes, *the definitions in the science*, are then to be elucidated in the light of the postulate and principles, or axioms, above presented.

Kind of Proof pertaining to each particular Attribute.

The proof, and the only proof, to be presented, that any particular characteristic is to be affirmed of God, is a demonstration of the fact, that such characteristic is essentially involved in our conception of him as the unconditioned and absolute cause, or as the Infinite and Perfect. This is the kind of proof peculiar to all sciences — proof resting upon the principle of contradiction. While it is shown that such or such an attribute, or any particular form of a given attribute, must be affirmed of God, else we deny of him the prerogative of unconditioned and absolute cause, or the characteristics of Infinity and Perfection, we have presented absolute demonstration of the fact, that such attribute belongs to God.

This Science to be evolved in the light of the Works of God, material and mental, and of the Teachings of Inspiration.

This science also should be evolved with continued reference to the works and Word of God. In developing the attributes involved in the principles under consideration, we should not go to the Bible to *prove* that such a characteristic is to be affirmed of God, but the teachings of Inspiration should be adduced, to show the correspondence between the affirmations of science and the Word of God. Thus the science under consideration would be, as far as it extends, a continued commentary upon the sacred volume. The perceived harmony of the two would give additional force to the influence of each upon the mind. Facts in the external material creation will not be adduced in proof of the reality of particular attributes in God, but creation itself will be thrown before the mind, as the work of God, in the light of all the attributes involved in the ideas of him as the unconditioned and absolute cause, and as the Infinite and Perfect. The great truth to be developed is, What may be accomplished through matter, undér the guidance and control of a being possessed of all the perfections involved in the principles under consideration? Of course, no attempt will be made to determine *particular* developments. But this great thought will be thrown into distinct visibility before the mind, to wit: that all that is possible, through matter, the attributes involved in the ideas of Infinity and Perfection, enable the Most High to discern and accomplish.

In respect to Mind, this science should be evolved in correlation to all the powers and susceptibilities of our nature. The fundamental *object* of the science relating to Mind being mental development, in harmony with the idea of God as the unconditioned and absolute cause, and as the Infinite and Perfect, under the influence of these ideas, it should be so evolved that the natural result upon the Mind, of a knowledge and contemplation of the system, would be endless progression and expansion of the powers of thought, feeling, and action. The demands of the logical department of our nature will be fully met, when each attribute, and each characteristic of every attribute, are seen to follow, as logical consequents of the ideas of God under consideration. The demands of the Sensibility will be met, when the Divine perfections rise before the contemplation in such a manner, as is best adapted to excite all those feelings and sentiments which the finite is bound to cherish towards the Infinite. The demands of the voluntary powers are met when the Divinity stands in distinct contemplation before the Mind, as the proper, and only proper object of the Mind's supreme choice, obedience, love, worship, and delight.

In the development of this science, another great thought would be thrown into distinct visibility before the Mind, to wit: What will be the destiny of Mind, what its future developments, under the teachings, guidance, and control of such a being? Here, also, no attempt would be made to determine particulars. The contemplation, on the other hand, would be turned upon the destiny and developments of Mind, viewed in the general point of light, in the contemplation of the facts under consideration.

THEOLOGY, NATURAL AND REVEALED.

Theology, with truth and propriety, has been separated into two departments, *natural* and *revealed.*

Natural Theology, as a science, is a systematic development of those truths pertaining to the attributes, character, and government of God, involved in the ideas of him, considered as the unconditioned and absolute cause, and as the Infinite and Perfect.

The idea of a Divine revelation, as far as it pertains to God, is, *God the unconditioned and absolute cause, and God the Infinite and Perfect, revealed in fixed and perfect correlation to the necessities of the beings to whom that revelation is made.* Nothing in such revelation would contradict either of the principles under consideration, nor any of the logical consequences of the same. As far as natural theology and revelation pertain to the same things, there will be a perfect harmony between them. Each will elucidate and confirm the teachings of the other. Revelation will extend the sphere of mental vision in relation to divinity and humanity both, far beyond the reach of natural theology. But the natural and revealed will harmoniously blend into one beautiful, all-comprehending unity. Such will be the character of any real revelation from God. Such a revelation the sacred volume claims to be. Its friends have no fear, in meeting the question of its divine origin, in the light of these principles. When the science of theology shall be developed in a form truly scientific, then the harmony between the natural and revealed, and of the teachings of both with the dictates of universal Reason, will become distinctly visible to the world. The accomplishment of this object is a want yet, as it appears to me, to be met with, in the science of theology.

DIFFERENCE BETWEEN A MYSTERY AND ABSURDITY IN THEOLOGY.

The terms *mystery* and *absurdity* are in very common use in theology. Doctrines presented as affirmed by the direct teachings of Inspiration, are often objected to, on the ground of intrinsic absurdities imputed to them. When the element of absurdity is imputed to a given doctrine, the doctrine is often defended, on the ground, that *mystery* is a common element of all religious truth, and that consequently the fact that any doctrine is very mysterious, is no valid objection against it. It belongs to the province of Intellectual Philosophy to discriminate between a real mystery and absurdity.

Absurdity Defined.

When all the elements contained in the subject and predicate of a given proposition are fully and distinctly known to the mind, and when those terms are said to agree, while the Intelligence clearly perceives, from the nature of the elements which they represent, that they cannot agree, or when they are affirmed to disagree, while the Intelligence perceives and affirms absolutely that they do and must agree, here we have a contradiction, or absurdity. If God himself should directly require us to affirm as true, what our Intelligence thus affirms to be false, we could not comply with the requisition. A professed revelation containing any such proposition as the above, we cannot admit to be a *real* revelation from the Infinite and Perfect. The Intelligence, on no authority whatever, can affirm any such proposition of God, while it still affirms his Infinity and Perfection.

Mystery defined.

On the other hand, let us suppose that the subject and predicate of a proposition, each embraces some elements which we know, and some which we do not know, and that in the proposition the subject and predicate, in view of the elements which we know, are affirmed to disagree, and on the ground of the unknown it is affirmed that they agree, or *vice versa,* the admission of the truth of such a proposition involves no contradiction. The grounds of the agreement or disagreement under consideration would be a mystery. As such we might reasonably admit the truth of the proposition, on sufficient testimony.

Mystery and Absurdity defined in another Form.

Further, facts are sometimes presented to us in such a light, that their logical antecedents, or the condition and ground of their existence and explanation, are also given at the same time. On the other hand, facts of the highest moment to us may be revealed as facts merely, while the condition and ground of their existence are wholly unrevealed and unknown to us. In the former instance, if a proposition is presented to us, affirming, as the logical antecedent of the facts referred to, what our Intelligence affirms can never be such antecedent, in other words, when any proposition contradicts the necessary intuitions of our Reason, the Intelligence, on no authority whatever, can admit its truth. The proposition is absurd. On the other hand, when facts are affirmed, as in the second instance above specified, we can admit their reality as facts, while the ground of their existence is unknown, that is, mysterious to us. There is a *mystery* but no *absurdity* in such a case. The proper application of these principles will be found to be of fundamental importance in the science of theology.

FUNDAMENTAL CHARACTERISTICS OF A REAL REVELATION FROM GOD.

We have in our hands a book which claims to be a revelation to man from the Infinite and Perfect. The question arises, In what light shall we regard the book? By what principles shall we test its claims? The following may be laid down as decisive principles to be rigidly applied under such circumstances:

1. As far as the revelation pertains to the same subjects which fall within the legitimate domain of natural theology, as above defined, there will be a perfect harmony between the natural and revealed.

2. In this revelation, the Infinite and Perfect will stand revealed in full and fixed correlation to the condition and fundamental wants of man, circumstanced as he now is, as affirmed by the testimony of human consciousness. The consciousness which every man that truly knows himself and God, has that the truth of what is affirmed is a changeless demand of his nature, in his present and prospective condition, will be to him the highest evidence that the record is and must be true.

3. Such a revelation will present a resolution of the great questions of human duty and destiny, the solution of which is one of the great wants of man.

4. The claims of the record, as a revelation from God, will be urged upon us, by all the external evidence which, in all other cases, distinguishes truth from error.

Such a record the sacred volume professes to be. Its friends, as before remarked, have no fear, in submitting the claims of Christianity to the most rigid test of the principles above elucidated.

Revealed Theology defined.

We are now prepared for a distinct definition of revealed theology. As revealed theology includes the teachings of natural, it may be defined as the *systematic development, in the light of some one great central idea or principle, of the truths of Inspiration pertaining to the character and government of God.* In its most comprehensive signification, it would include the entire system of divine truth, pertaining not only to God exclusively, but to human duty and destiny, in both of which God stands revealed to our minds. Everything pertaining not only to the character and government of God, but to the subjects of that government, so far forth as their revealed duty and destiny would illustrate the principles of the Divine administration, would be comprehended in a system of revealed theology, using the words in their most extensive application. Such, as I suppose, is theology. Its systematic development upon principles purely scientific, still remains as one of the great wants of humanity. This want will remain unmet, till the true conception of such a system shall be distinctly developed in the minds of philosophers and theologians both. If the hints above given shall tend to this result, I shall feel that no small service has been done to the cause of truth.

DEFECTS OF METHOD IN THE COMMON SYSTEMS OF THEOLOGY.

There is no department of human thought where system, scientifically developed, is not a great want of the human mind. In no other department is this want more deeply felt, than in theology. There is no subject of thought which, when developed upon scientific principles, does not become an object of interest. Theology, in itself the most interesting and important of all subjects, will, when as a system it shall be developed upon profoundly scientific principles, possess an interest which shall, as it ought to do, overshadow all other subjects. Every system of truth has some one great central truth or principle about which all the others revolve, and in the light of which they appear as harmonious parts of one great whole. No subject of thought is scientifically developed, until it is evolved in conformity to the conception above given; in other words, till it is systematically evolved in the light of fundamental ideas. To no subject are the above remarks more fully applicable than to that of theology. Theology, like every other department of human research, has its great central truths and principles, about which all other truths and principles pertaining to the same subject revolve, and in the light of which they all appear as parts of one great whole. Unless this is true, to speak of the science, or system of theology, is to use words without meaning, or to "speak of things that are not, as though they were." In the definition given of revealed theology, I have not designated the particular truth or truths, about which, as I suppose, the entire system of revelation revolves, and into which all its diversified parts blend into one sublime and harmonious unity. I leave it to theologians who may condescend to receive a hint from a source so humble, to find, in the light of it, this great central position, and from it to give to the system of theology a truly scientific development. The man is yet to rise, who, by a "wisdom which cometh from above," shall do this great work for humanity. That man, when his work shall come to be appreciated, will be ranked among the greatest benefactors of his species.

But I have wandered much further than I expected, when I commenced this seeming digression from my subject, which is, the defects of *method* in the common systems of theology. On this subject, as a friend of truth as well as philosophy (for philosophy as well as theology is deeply concerned in the subject upon which I am speaking), I may be permitted to speak my thoughts with all freedom. What then are the errors, particularly of *method*, in the common systems of theology? Among these I notice the following:

1. An error frequently noticed in the preceding part of this Chapter, and which I need but hint at here, is the method of *proving the Divine existence.* If in the first step an error of method is committed, the whole subsequent procedure is marred, and the system of theology is developed in a manner not fully satisfactory to the mind. If the question in respect to the Divine existence is not settled to the full satisfaction of the mind, the proof pertaining to each particular attribute will be in a corresponding degree unsatisfactory, and a feeling of uncertainty, in respect to that which the mind really knows with more certainty than almost anything else, a feeling somewhat at least bordering on skepticism, will creep over the mind, in relation to the whole system. Now there are, as it appears to me, three prominent errors of method in the prevailing treatises on theology, in respect to the subject before us.

The first is the fact, as stated above, that the Divine existence is not recognized as a truth already known and affirmed by the human Intelligence, and that the only proper method of demonstration of that truth, is by a method purely psychological, that is, by falling back upon the conviction itself, and finding the real facts on which it truly rests, in the depths of the Intelligence. When the Intelligence has affirmed any truth with profound conviction on any subject, the only real demonstration of that truth which can be presented to the mind, is to throw into distinct visibility, the real facts in view of which the reality of the truth was affirmed. Now theologians, instead of recognizing this fact in respect to theology, have gone beyond the circle of the mind's convictions, to find some facts in the external world from which, as a logical consequent, the truth of the Divine existence would follow. The mind of course returns from its researches more unsatisfied than when, from the center of real illumination, it wandered abroad in search of light.

Another error which I repeat here, is not recognizing the two distinct and prominent forms in which the idea of God is developed in the human Intelligence, to wit: God the unconditioned and absolute cause, and God the Infinite and Perfect. Hence considerations perfectly demonstrative of the validity of the idea in one form, but which are without force in reference to the other, are adduced without discrimination of their real bearing. The Mind perceiving that the argument has no real weight to prove the existence of God in the form in which it expects it to prove it, assumes that it has no real bearing upon the subject, and thus becomes dissatisfied with the whole argument on the subject. This is a natural consequence. Hence many a student in theology has had occasion to confess that he never doubted the reality of the Divine existence, till he turned to the arguments adduced in books and the theological recitation room to prove it.

The other error is in attempting to deduce the evidence of the infinity and perfection of God from the extent and laws of the world of Matter, instead of that of Mind. On this point I have already said so much that I shall not enlarge here.

2. The second, and the great error of method, in the common (so called) systems of theology, is an almost, if not quite, total want of *scientific development.* I know of no professed system of theology, the mode of presentation and development of which accords with any proper conception of a system of truth, much less with a true definition of real science. There is and can be no real system where there are not one or more great central truths or principles which impart unity and harmony to the whole. There is and can be no such thing as a system evolved in such a manner as to realize the idea of science, in which the relations and properties of a given subject are not systematically evolved in the light of fundamental ideas.

Now where is the system of theology that is developed in any degree of conformity to the idea of system or science as above announced, or to any other proper definition of the idea of a system scientifically expressed? I know of no such system. What is the mode of procedure in such systems? The first thing proposed is to prove the *existence* of God. The next step is to take up each particular attribute, and by a separate course of argument, prove that such attribute is to be affirmed of him. Now this can be shown in a moment to be a most unphilosophical procedure.

In the first place, if the proposition first proved, to wit, *God exists,* does not in itself involve a real demonstration of the reality of his particular attributes, the proposition absolutely amounts to nothing; for it is a demonstration of the existence of a God without attributes — that is, the existence of no God at all. For a God without attributes, is, in fact, no God.

If, on the other hand, the demonstration of the proposition, *God exists,* does involve in itself a corresponding proof of his particular attributes, then the only proper subsequent scientific procedure is, to evolve analytically each particular attribute as involved in the proposition already demonstrated. To attempt in any other form, by a separate course of argumentation, a subsequent demonstration of each particular attribute, is a most unphilosophical and unscientific procedure — a procedure which really, as shown above, nullifies all that went before.

Further, when the proposition, God exists, is proposed as a subject of demonstration, the first thing to be done is to define the terms used, especially the term God. Now if this term is not so defined as to involve his particular attributes, the term means nothing, and the demonstration is null and void. If the term is so defined as to involve the particular attributes, then, when the proposition, God exists, has been demonstrated, the reality of each attribute is involved in the demonstration, and the only subsequent procedure really philosophic, scientific, and reasonable, is to evolve each particular attribute as thus involved in what has already been proven. To attempt, by a separate course of argumentation, to demonstrate the reality of any particular attribute, is to confess the futility of the previous demonstration. In fact, if the common procedure is the correct one, we have not proved that God according to any proper definition of the term, exists, till we have presented a formal demonstration of the reality of each particular attribute. For a God destitute of any essential attribute is not God.

In proving the proposition, God exists, according to the two forms above stated, to wit, God the unconditioned and absolute cause, and God, the Infinite and Perfect, we have done what every demonstration should do — that is, demonstrated a proposition which involves every particular attribute, and which has given us a great central position, from which the entire system of theology may receive a purely scientific development. The whole sphere of vision becomes as luminous as heavenly light.

3. The third general defect that I notice in the common systems of theology, is the total unsatisfactoriness of the arguments adduced to prove the reality of particular attributes. Suppose we have fully satisfied our minds of the validity of the two forms of the idea of God presented in this Chapter. Our attention is turned to a particular attribute. We see at once that we must affirm this attribute of God, or deny of him the prerogative of unconditioned and absolute cause, or impute to him finiteness and imperfection. The reality of the attribute as a characteristic of God, thus becomes demonstrably evident. In affirming the attribute of him, every depart-

ment of our nature is satisfied. The demands of the logical department are fully met. The scientific and philosophical ideas also receive a most full and delightful realization.

On the other hand, let us suppose, that having proved the proposition, God exists, we attempt, by a new and separate course of argumentation, to prove the reality of some particular attribute — the Divine omnipotence, for example. What should we naturally expect from such a procedure? Just what, in fact, we shall find — arguments perfectly unsatisfactory and inconclusive. The nature of the argument, as presented in such a system of natural theology, may be thus stated, and these present the strongest arguments that can be met with :

1. The *fact* and the *extent* of creation.

2. The fact that God now sustains and governs the universe, particularly the physical.

Now, here are effects undeniably finite. From them it is argued, that their cause must be infinite, a palpable violation of a fundamental principle of logic, a principle universally admitted, to wit, that no legitimate conclusion is more extensive than the premises from which it is deduced. Hence it is, that the Mind does not and cannot perceive any force in the argument; and as this is the best that can be adduced in the same direction, a feeling of dissatisfaction and doubt arises in respect to all arguments to prove the divine Infinity and Perfection.

When the testimony of Inspiration is adduced in confirmation of such arguments, the feeling of dissatisfaction experienced in the presence of the first attaches to that of the second, and the result very probably is, that feelings more allied to skepticism than joyful confidence and faith, creep over the mind, and it may be, mar its peace and purity.

I mention one other defect. According to the common method of developing truth in theology, we have no proper *tests* which we can apply to determine the question, whether any particular attribute shall be affirmed of God, or the particular *form* in which it shall be affirmed. If we assume the idea of God as the unconditioned and absolute cause, and God the Infinite and Perfect, as the great central idea about which the entire system of truth pertaining to God, his character and government, is to revolve, and in the light of which each particular truth is to be explained, we have a plain and sure test, a standard to which we can apply in all cases in determining what attributes and characteristics we shall affirm or deny of God, and the light in which we shall affirm or deny them. The great question to be asked in each instance is, Must we affirm this particular attribute, and must we affirm it in this or that particular form, or either deny of God his prerogative, as the cause unconditioned and absolute, or assert of him finiteness or imperfection?

But according to the common methods of theologizing, when we take up any particular attribute, we have nothing in what has gone before, or what is to follow, to which we can appeal as a standard or test, to determine what attributes, or what forms of particular attributes, we are to affirm or deny of God. The entire system of theology is thus rendered vague and indefinite, and the truth makes no deep and palpable impression upon the Mind. No other result can follow from such a method of evolving the truths of theology.

USE OF THE COMMON TREATISES ON NATURAL THEOLOGY

The question is often asked, Of what real utility are the common treatises on natural theology — such, for example, as that one so celebrated of Dr. Paley? To me such treatises appear really worse than useless, if presented as grounds of proof of the existence of God, particularly as the Infinite and

Perfect. How many persons have said, "I never doubted the reality of the Divine existence, till I sought for a proof of it in "Paley's Natural Theology." If, on the other hand, such works are referred to, as sources of beautiful and striking illustrations of the "handiwork of God," thus awaking in us a sense of the Divine wisdom and glory, they may be read with great interest and profit. This, as I conceive, is their appropriate, and only appropriate use.

CONCLUSION.

I must here take my leave, for the present, of the inquirer after truth in this field of vast and solemn thought and contemplation. If we were never to return to it again, to renew our researches, I should part with him with the deepest regret. If, however, the inquirer has become imbued with a love of the science which we have investigated, and has understood and appreciated the bearing of its principles, it may be that the time is not far distant when I shall behold him upon elevations, and traversing fields of thought which my own powers never enabled me to reach.

One thing has cheered me on in these interesting and momentous investigations — the thought that they were all legitimately tending in one fixed direction — to God as the Infinite and Perfect.

Here I leave the inquirer, with the fervent hope, that at last, in the unveiled presence of that infinite, all-perfect, and Eternal One, we may again meet; that Eternal One, "in whose presence there is fullness of joy, and at whose right hand there are pleasures for evermore."

NON
CIRCULATING

NATIONAL SERIES OF STANDARD SCHOOL BOOKS.

R. G. PARKER'S SCHOOL READERS.

Parker's First—Second—Third—Fourth, and Rhetorical Reader.

ORTHOGRAPHY AND GRAMMAR.

Wright's Spelling Book.—Wright's Analytical Orthography.—Martin's Orthoepist.—Northend's Dictation Exercises.—Clark's Analysis.—Clark's English Grammar and Etymological Chart.

ELOCUTIONARY WORKS.

1. Northend's Little Speaker.—2. American Speaker.—3. School Dialogues.—4. Zachos' New American Speaker.

WILLARD'S HISTORIES AND CHARTS.

History of the United States (large and small.)—Universal History.—Historic Guide.—Ancient, English, and American Chronographers.—Temple of Time.

DAVIES' SYSTEM OF MATHEMATICS.

Table-Book—First Lessons in Arithmetic.—School Arithmetic.—University Arithmetic.—Elementary Algebra.—Elementary Geometry.—Practical Mathematics.—Bourdon's Algebra.—Legendre's Geometry.—Surveying.—Analytical Geometry.—Calculus.—Descriptive Geometry.—Shades, Shadows, etc.

PARKER'S SCHOOL PHILOSOPHIES.

1. Juvenile Philosophy.—2. First Lessons.—3. School Compendium.

ELEMENTARY SCIENCES.

Chambers' Treasury of Knowledge.—Clark's Drawing.—Reid & Bain istry.—Hamilton's Physiology.—Chambers' Zoology.—Page's Ge tire on the Globes.—Bartlett's Mechanics, Optics, and Astron on Road-making.—Gregory's Chemistry.

PENMANSHIP AND BOOKKEEP

Fulton & Eastman's System, with the Chiro

MUSIC FOR SCHO

Kingsley's Juvenile Choir.—Kingsley's You School Song and Hymn Book.—Sabba

BROOKS'

Latin Lessons.—Greek Less

BOOKS OF RE

Page's Theory and Practice De Tocqueville's Ameri Davies' Logic and U mind.

www.ingramcontent.com/pod-product-compliance
Lightning Source LLC
LaVergne TN
LVHW020915110826
845150LV00004B/676

* 9 7 8 1 4 2 5 5 5 5 4 0 5 *